D-DAY
WITH THE
SCREAMING EAGLES

D-DAY

WITH THE

SCREAMING EAGLES

George E. Koskimaki

With a Foreword by Gerald J. Higgins,
Major General, U.S. Army, Retired

BALLANTINE BOOKS • NEW YORK

2006 Presidio Press Mass Market Edition

Published in the United States by Presidio Press, an imprint of The Random House Publishing Group, a division of Random House, Inc., New York.

PRESIDIO PRESS and colophon are trademarks of Random House, Inc.

Originally published by Vantage Press in 1970. Subsequent editions were self-published by the author. Published in 2002 by Casemate, Havertown, Pa.

ISBN 0-89141-892-X

Cover photograph: Corbis

Printed in the United States of America

This edition published by arrangement with Casemate.

www.ballantinebooks.com

OPM   9   8   7   6   5   4   3   2   1

Dedicated to the memory of the members of the
101st Airborne Division who paid the supreme sacrifice
in the hedgerow country and flooded meadows of
Normandy on D-Day, the 6th of June, 1944.

GENERAL MAXWELL D. TAYLOR: "I congratulate you most sincerely on the quality of the reporting of this dramatic episode. To most of us there, I suspect it was the greatest day of our lives."

GENERAL A. C. MCAULIFFE: "What a tremendous task of research you have accomplished! The quotes from the many participants ring true—no phoney heroics."

GEORGE E. GORMAN, U.S. Military Specialist and consultant: "Your book is outstanding and must become a classic someday. I do hope you may try a sequel on the Holland jump as you surely have the 'charisma' for writing it!"

Former paratrooper JAMES H. MARTIN: "I cannot get over the fact that you could take all this laboriously gathered material and put it into a form that is so accurate, so exciting and which flows so well that it takes people there who were not in the army."

SCHOOL ADM. CHARLES STETTER: "I believe this work will be recognized as a major historical contribution to World War II since it pulls together so many facets of that D-Day operation from a very human and personal standpoint."

Author ROBERT MINICK: "After having completed my 12th year of study on the 101st, it is my opinion that your book ranks by far as the most comprehensive material covering a relatively short period of time to be written to date."

Longtime military career officer TODD WHEATLEY: "I think you are one of the first to use the oral history technique in a publication dealing with our military history. You have one up on Studs Terkel."

General GERALD J. HIGGINS, former chief of staff of the 101st Airborne Division wrote the foreword: "George Koskimaki has compiled a truly amazing compendium of the activities and experiences of hundreds of individual members of the 101st Airborne on the occasion of their D-Day Normandy invasion. The series of events leading up to the loading of the planes, the emotions of the paratroopers en route and the reactions of the individuals during the period shortly after landing are vividly recorded and will certainly bring home moments of nostalgia to all those who participated in the operation . . . . the overall editing is highly commendable—to tell it as it was, and yet avoid a multiplicity of duplicated recitals could only have been accomplished by painstaking attention on the part of a dedicated writer."

Foreword

George Koskimaki has compiled a truly amazing compendium of the activities and experiences of hundreds of individual members of the 101st Airborne Division on the occasion of their D-Day invasion. The series of events leading up to the loading of the planes, the emotions of the paratroopers en route and the reactions of the individuals during the period shortly after landing are vividly recorded and will certainly bring home moments of nostalgia to all those who participated in the operation. Of particular interest is the recording of the actions of the pathfinders and the initial glider assault forces—to my knowledge this is the first comprehensive and authoritative résumé of their vital contribution to the success of the operation. And while it would be manifestly unfair to single out any particular section of this "personal experience" record for special mention, the performance of the medical personnel—those Angels of Mercy—will certainly be eternally remembered for their unselfish devotion to their cause.

The authenticity of the book is self-evident—Mr. Koskimaki has performed an admirable research task in securing, analyzing, and synthesizing the firsthand accounts of more than five hundred individuals representing scores of small assault units in the division. The overall editing is highly commendable—to tell it as it was, and yet avoid a multiplicity of duplicated recitals could only have been accomplished by painstaking attention on the part of a dedicated writer.

This book will without question have a most personal reception by the thousands of American paratroopers who participated in the aerial invasion of Normandy on June 6, 1944, as well as the millions of servicemen who have undergone war experiences similar to those encountered at Normandy. I think it particularly apropos that this book should reach the American public at a time when certain individuals appear to have forgotten, at least temporarily, that just one generation ago thousands of young citizen-soldiers fought and died for their country without asking "What's in it for me?" *D-Day with the Screaming Eagles* could well serve to remind the young man of today that the young man of yesterday was possessed of a courage that he might well emulate.

GERALD J. HIGGINS
Major General, U.S. Army, Retired
1969

Contents

List of Maps

Introduction

This is the story of D-Day as told collectively by former paratroopers and glidermen of the 101st Airborne Division.

The story begins with the marshaling area preparations in England and then proceeds with the flight across the Channel, the approach over the Cherbourg Peninsula, the actual drops and glider landings, and the first day experiences of these men as lost and lonely individuals, gradually assembling in small groups, then into company-sized units, and finally, into the skeleton battalions and regiments, which were assigned the missions. Connecting narrative and summations reveal the success or failure of these missions.

I wrote to over 1,300 former "Screaming Eagles" to get their recollections. Many of them sent me copies of their first letters (while others trusted me with precious originals) written from the battlefield when we were first permitted to describe our initial experiences. A total of 518 former paratroopers and glidermen contributed to this account. Each contribution has been placed in the proper sequence of events.

One chapter is devoted to the work of the pathfinders—those men who served as trailblazers to light the way and guide the main body of the 101st Airborne Division to its drop and landing zones. No one has ever written about them. Information concerning much of their operations was classified for many years after the war. Some of the material was released to me by the former chief pathfinder, Colonel Frank Lillyman, who edited the chapter. It contains the experiences of these "selected" men.

No one has previously related the experiences of these glider troopers. The material on the glider chapter has been edited by former Colonel Mike Murphy who was in charge of the American glider lifts into Normandy. He piloted the lead glider into the "Screaming Eagle" landing area. One of his passengers, Brigadier General Donald F. Pratt, the assistance division commander, became the first Allied general officer to lose his life in the invasion.

An unusual chapter is one which is called "Angels of Mercy," describing the work of the parachuting chaplains and medics. Reports came from three chaplains, one from each of the three parachute infantry regiments. The medics are represented by regimental and battalion surgeons on down to the platoon aidmen. Many of them received Distinguished Service Crosses and other high decorations, though none of them "owned up" to this information. I had to find this out from the fighting men who had such high praise for them and labeled them "Angels of Mercy."

The accounts include those of the two surviving general officers (Generals Maxwell D. Taylor and Anthony C. McAuliffe), former chief of staff Colonel Gerald J. Higgins, now a retired major general who helped with much of the editing of the material, and those of other division staff officers. Reports have come from regimental staff officers, battalion commanders, company commanders, platoon leaders, first sergeants, and other noncommissioned officers on down to the privates who fought in the line companies. They represent 58 of the company or battery-sized units to get a well-rounded picture.

My own experiences are included. I served as radioman for General Maxwell D. Taylor, the division commander, and parachuted from his plane. Throughout the war I kept a daily log of my actions on onionskin paper from the backs of Signal Corps message books. Later, as we returned to the rear areas for rest, I transcribed my notes into the regular diary which had been left behind. My fiancée, now my wife, saved all my letters from the battle areas.

During the summer of 1967 I returned to Europe to revisit the battle sites. I spent five days in Normandy. During that time I tried to locate as many of the battle areas as had been described to me by my contributors. It was amazing how easily I was able to locate the spot where the first group of pathfinders assembled, the spot where I dug my first foxhole, and the hayloft in which I took a nap during the late afternoon of D-Day. I interviewed many Norman farmers and townspeople who still recalled those first contacts with the American soldiers and their stories corroborate the paratroopers' accounts.

The men have been listed with their D-Day rankings in the account. Many of them are still in the service twenty-four years later, some in high military positions. General Maxwell D. Taylor has served his country well in many capacities since he led his young Eagles into combat for the first time as a brigadier general. Colonel Gerald J. Higgins retired from the army not long ago as a major general. Battalion commanders Patrick Cassidy and Julian Ewell are today division commanders in the United States Army. Captain Leo Schweiter serves as a brigade commander in Vietnam. Former company commanders and platoon leaders are now full colonels in the army in both Vietnam and Europe. Enlisted men have risen high in the ranks.

For the most part though, the men are successful bankers, lawyers, doctors, farmers, teachers, professors, and small businessmen. To a man, they are still fiercely proud of the units to which they belonged. Former company commander LeGrand "Legs" Johnson is an executive in a trucking firm in Atlanta, Georgia. He wrote, "I am half blind, having been wounded in Holland. There has *never* previously been assembled a better group of men than those who comprised the 101st Airborne Division, and more particularly the 502nd Parachute Infantry Regiment. Writing this letter to you has made me reflect with awe on the reckless courage and the sheer delight and mayhem that this group exhibited. I am glad they were on our side."

Being involved in the D-Day activities was terribly important for all these men. Elmer Brandenberger was a former platoon leader with Baker Company of the 502nd Regiment. Today, he teaches world history in a high school in Texas that is named in honor of the 101st Division's first Congressional Medal of Honor winner, Lieutenant Colonel Robert G. Cole. Brandenberger's first day of combat was his last in World

War II. He left the fighting with one arm hanging by a few bits of flesh. Many of his former troopers will be surprised to learn that through the work of some wonderful medics and doctors, he still has the use of that arm. He related, "All of us, I believe, down to the least imaginative one, really felt a close affinity with history. Something big was about to happen and we were going to be a part of it. The most terrible thing that could have happened to any one of us would have been to be scratched from the loading manifest."

John Urbank was a mortar sergeant with George Company of the 501st. Today he is an optical lens grinder in Peninsula, Ohio. At the end of his letter he stated, "I feel I'm holding faith with some of the boys who didn't make it. I remember more than once hearing Perry and Mythaler say 'If anyone asks what war is like, we're going to tell them in the best way we know how—none of this crap about War is Hell and we can't talk about it!' So be it. So keep their faith."

Some paused to comment about their former buddies as their accounts ended. Waylan L. "Pete" Lamb went into combat as a medic with the demolitions platoon of the 501st Regiment. Today, he is with the sheriff's department in Columbia, South Carolina. He ended his account with, "I don't remember names too well, but sometimes when I'm alone with my memories I can still see the faces of those wonderful guys, and get a lump in my throat remembering how I was a part of their team."

And so this is their story. They dug out their scrapbooks and looked over those old snapshots taken in basic training, in England, and on the Continent, some perhaps while on furlough, and remembered their old comrades. They dug through letters sent to parents, wives, and sweethearts in which they described first combat experiences. They sent clippings from hometown newspapers which proud parents had sent to editors in the form of first letters from the combat zone. Parachute manifests were sent along with comments about the fate of some of their close buddies. Always the admonition, "Please take care of this material—it is my really great treasure of the war."

The feats of the airborne troopers may soon fade into

legend as the helicopter replaces the parachute and glider, but while the tale can be told, let these exploits of the sky invaders of Hitler's Fortress Europa become part of the annals of history. As Sergeant Urbank put it, "Let's keep their faith."

GEORGE E. KOSKIMAKI
Detroit, Michigan
December 22, 1969

CHAPTER 1

The Marshaling Area

The training period had come to an end for the Screaming Eagles. The rumor mills had been busy for weeks grinding out the endless chain of reports concerning the imminence of departure for the marshaling areas. The experiences were not new for the men in that all units had participated in several dress rehearsals culminating with *Exercise Eagle* during the period of May 11–14. The sky troopers had emplaned from the same airfields to which they were now being sent. During the last week of May, orders were received restricting the men to their unit areas. They packed their personal belongings, were assigned parachutes, refitted with some new equipment, and packed their equipment bundles.

Lieutenant Richard Winters served as executive officer of his unit on D-Day. He wrote:[1] "Leaving Aldbourne was a tough job. A fellow couldn't say a thing to anybody due to security. The English knew we were pushing off. When I went to say good-bye, as if I was off for another maneuver, it got me to see them cry and take it as they did."

Technician 5th Grade Bill Finn, a D-Day communications wireman said, "When we were leaving the company area for the marshaling area, most of the people living in the homes surrounding Donnington Castle were out in the street to wave good-bye to us and wish us luck. They probably didn't know the day we would leave England but they sure knew we wouldn't be back for some time."

An intelligence soldier, PFC Richard M. Ladd wrote, "Regimental Headquarters Company of the 502nd Parachute Infantry Regiment was loaded aboard British buses May 30, 1944, at Chilton-Foliat, Berkshire, England, and driven perhaps 15 miles to Greenham Common Airdrome, where we were quartered until the evening of June 5 in a tent city. The area was enclosed with barbed wire and termed a marshaling area. No one, other than a few high ranking officers, was ever allowed to leave this area until the evening of June 5, when we boarded C-47's for France."

Corroborating that statement, Sergeant Louis Truax said, "Our marshaling area was near Exeter, England, and was surrounded by barbed wire and guarded by army troops not of our division. They had machine guns at the corners of the area and we were forbidden to talk to the guards."

Captain Charles O. Van Gorder was a member of the 3rd Auxiliary Surgical Group and had volunteered for the assignment to go in on D-Day with the 101st Airborne Division. His group had previously participated in the campaigns in North Africa, Sicily, and Italy prior to arriving in England. The detached service with the 101st Division was in the form of an experiment to find out if it would be any advantage to take a surgical team in where the casualties were, rather than to take the casualties back to where the evacuation hospitals were located.

The eight men who volunteered for this mission called themselves the 1st Airborne Surgical Team and they were attached to the 326th Airborne Medical Company. Van Gorder provided his recollections of the marshaling area with these comments: "Several days before D-Day, we were sent with part of the 101st Airborne Division to Aldermaston Air Field for staging and briefing. These were very trying days to remain crowded in a large hangar, going out in only small groups at intervals for chow. Latrines were in or somewhere under the roof of the hangars. Keeping us in the hangar and going out in small groups was to frustrate any enemy aerial reconnaissance."

An enlisted man who was in the same area was PFC George S. Schulist, who was a jeep driver for his platoon leader. His memories of the same staging area include these items: "When we went to eat at the mess hall, we were always taken in groups, such as Battery A or Battery B. When we left the hangar, we had to pass the fence gates. Plainclothesmen were waiting on the other side of the gate to escort us to the mess hall. They were there so we could not talk to anyone outside of our groups at the marshaling area."

The primary reason for placing the men in solitude much like imprisoned men was the briefing for the invasion. With firsthand knowledge of the D-Day targets and objectives, the men were kept isolated to prevent any leaks to the enemy. Some of the men who prepared the briefing aids have good descriptions of these preparations.

PFC Richard M. Ladd of the 502nd intelligence group described, "Regimental S-2 Section was one of the few groups that actually had duties to perform while in the marshaling area. This consisted of building crude tables with wooden sides. Sand was then shoveled into these boxes from some trucks that were driven in. From these crude beginnings, we began our sand tables which were located in each battalion area. On these were developed models from soap and other suitable materials to simulate houses, churches, etc., with paints and some coloring to simulate the general reliefs of the area in Normandy in which we were to jump. Each table was a bit different, in that, it contained different roads and hamlets peculiar to each battalion's S-2 Section. We constructed these sand tables as accurately as we could from the latest aerial serial photographs supplied to us by the Air Force, to coordinate and orient them with wonderfully accurate British defense maps, as well as all the latest information supplied to us by various intelligence agencies, including the latest up-to-date 'poop' from the French underground Maquis."

Ladd added, "After these tables were prepared and the various companies were broken down into platoons, the leaders and sergeants would be briefed in front of the tables as to their objectives, the terrain, directions of the roads, and a general familiarization of their target areas. Each unit would retire to tents and company streets to study maps that had been disseminated to them, and proceed to discuss, argue, and speculate the assigned squads and personnel for specific jobs to be accomplished. Then various trips were made back to the sand tables for restudy by the officers and noncoms."

A former member of the regimental demolitions section,

Corporal Vinnie Utz, had been transferred to the intelligence section of the 506th Regiment for the Normandy operation. He recalled, "The S-2 Section made the sand tables for the invasion and we assisted the officers in going over the objectives, company by company. I was put into a complete German uniform by Colonel Robert Sink and told to visit all the line company tents so they could get a good idea of what a Kraut looked like."

An assistant operations officer for the 377th Parachute Field Artillery Battalion, Captain William E. Brubaker, stated, "I recall my part (and the entire S-3 Section) in preparing for the mission. We had plotted the location for the three firing batteries and spent several days in planning targets and computing the firing data for each target. The balance of our time was spent in briefing the rest of the battalion from sand tables and maps. I remember receiving very fine aerial pictures on a daily basis showing our main targets and objectives, and how delighted I was when we discovered that the Air Force had practically eliminated one of the coastal batteries we were to take."

Recollections of the detailed map reading provides some interesting information. Engineer Lieutenant Harold Young said, "Every officer had maps at a scale of 1:10,000 plus oblique air photos of our landing and target positions. Every G.I. had a map at 1:300,000 of the whole general area. We had our men memorize a section of the map so they could get back if they landed in the wrong place. It was said that every private in a parachute unit knew as much as a colonel in a regular infantry outfit."

After the intelligence personnel had briefed the regimental and battalion staff officers and their men, the briefings continued down through the company commander, the platoon leader, the squad leader, and down to the last private—or almost, as we shall see later.

The commanding officer of the 501st Regiment's Charley Company, Captain Robert H. Phillips, described the painstaking preparation: "Several days were devoted by the unit commanders, of which I was one, studying our assignments and formulating detailed plans for carrying them out. Each individual member was then thoroughly briefed on the detailed plans of his particular unit. Only general information was given as to the missions of the division.

"My company's mission was to seize and secure the road junction south of St. Come-du-Mont, a small village, thus securing a flank of the drop zone (DZ). This position also overlooked the main highway bridge north of Carentan, and later gained the name of 'Dead Man's Corner.' "

A platoon leader with Able Company of the same regiment, Lieutenant Sumpter Blackmon, recalled, "The intensive sand table briefing we received and gave to our sergeants and to the other men lasted for about a week. The mission for my platoon was to take and hold the La Barquette Locks on the Douve River about a mile north of Carentan. The remainder of the 1st Battalion was to blow the bridges over the river to the northwest of Carentan."

Minute details were not forgotten. Sergeant Pat Lindsay, mortarman with the same company, said, "I remember the sand table work in which each man knew definitely which job he was to do, even down to the direction in which the foxholes would be dug."

Part of the briefing included familiarizing the men with the enemy uniforms. Private Robert "Lightnin" Hayes had this recollection to add: "I remember the day we were assembled in a tent for the first time and an officer told us where we were going to jump. He then paused to watch our reactions. There was a sand table near by with a facsimile of the terrain on which we were going to drop. There were two dummies standing near the sand table. One was wearing a German Air Force uniform while the other was dressed in the black uniform of the Armored Corps. I tried on the black beret to see how it would fit me. I didn't realize that a few days later I would meet a German face-to-face wearing one of those caps."

Reconnaissance photography had been so detailed that individual enemy soldiers appeared in recent pictures taken of the objectives. An airborne engineer, PFC John G. Kutz, whose assignment was to be the preparation for destruction of two wooden bridges northeast of Carentan, was briefed with aerial photos of the bridges. He said, "On one photograph you could see a German guard standing against one of the bridges. It seemed he was trying to hide from the low-flying plane." Kutz felt he had already met the enemy!

Two of the men called to mind that they had not received briefings with the rest. Captain Raymond S. "Chappie" Hall, Protestant Chaplain of the 502nd Regiment, said, "I never had time for the briefings and didn't even know the password when it was given nor was I issued a metal clicker."

A communications soldier with the 2nd Battalion of the 501st Regiment, T/5 Harry T. Mole, Jr., walked around the tented area and watched the men of Dog, Easy, and Fox Companies getting their equipment ready. He made this observation: "I watched them as they repeatedly cleaned their rifles over and over again. I watched these men as they sat on boxes and had their hair cut off Indian fashion. I didn't have mine cut. I watched men in circles intently listening to an officer describe their objectives. Their eyes followed every line scratched in the dirt by a stick attached to the officer who was explaining their mission. The invasion was becoming real now. Training could possibly be called over. This was the time they had trained for. Me? Nobody briefed me. I wandered around the area watching the others learn their objectives. How envious I was of the line company men. They knew what it was all about. They belonged.

"My machine gun platoon and our 81mm Mortar Platoon of Headquarters Company belonged. They were assigned to various line companies and were being briefed by them. Each man in my communications platoon had an assignment except me. I was technically a battalion code clerk, a Technician 5th Grade, a rather unimportant role in an invasion of this magnitude. They also gave me an SCR-536, press-to-talk radio probably because they had one left over. As a code clerk, I had a machine to code and decode messages coming to and going from battalion headquarters. Cloak and dagger, eh! One thing was wrong—they never told me what the code was!"

Almost all of the men mentioned honing their trench knives, jump knives, bayonets, and special hunting knives to

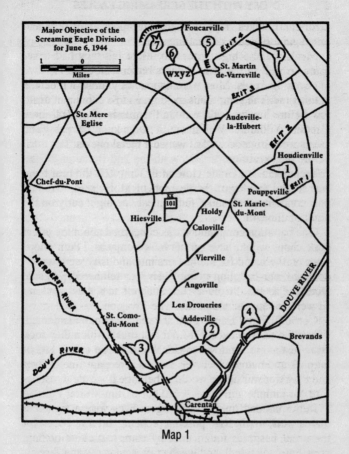

Map 1

No. 1—Capture of the four causeways leading down to Utah Beach (shown as Exits 1–4). No. 2—Capture and hold the locks at La Barquette. No. 3—Destroy the Douve River bridges northwest of Carentan. No. 4—Seize, hold, and establish bridgeheads at wooden bridges northwest of Carentan. No. 5—Silence the coastal battery at St. Martin-de-Varreville. No. 6—Capture artillery barracks complex at WXYZ (Mesières). No. 7—Protect the northern flank of Utah Beach invasion area.

razor-sharp edges. They took their weapons apart time and time again to assure perfect function.

Meals made a big impression. Most felt they had never eaten so well in the army. Others remembered the last two big evening meals. Most were happy not to draw KP details at this time. The sumptuous meal given to a convict in death row before his last walk was on the minds of several men. Captain William J. Waldmann, a surgeon, reflected, "The meals were so good we felt we were receiving our last meal before the execution."

Technician 5th Grade Gordon E. King felt the best meal was served the day of the postponement. He said, "We had our 'condemned person's' fancy meal one night early on the night of June 4th."

One battalion commander was concerned about the effect pork chops would have on nervous stomachs. "Pork chops were on the menu for the last evening and they were turned down by our battalion commander," remembered Sergeant Donald Castona. "Colonel Julian Ewell said they wouldn't sit well on 'queasy' stomachs."

Corporal Virgil Danforth of the same company lamented, "They fed us well except for our last meal, which they took away just as we sat down to eat. We had been eating lots of fat pork and butter which was supposed to improve our eyes and they were afraid we would get airsick if we ate it just before our jump."

Being cooped up in a barbed wire enclosure for more than a week might have posed a problem had it not been for the usual pastimes found in army camps, such as boxing, wrestling, volleyball, and the ever-present cards and dice.

At least one key officer missed out on the invasion because of an injury brought about in horseplay. Staff Sergeant Carwood Lipton recalled, "Lieutenant Schmitz, one of the platoon leaders, hurt his neck while wrestling with one of the other officers in the marshaling area and had to stay back and miss the invasion."

Haircutting pranks developed in several areas. Captain Fred C. Culpepper, an artillery officer, recalled the loss of a prized facial possession. "Just prior to loading out for the

first time (which was postponed at the last minute) my officers caught me and removed my mustache with a dull razor.
I had said that I would not shave the mustache until we were
in France."

Two men who had been members of the same unit on
D-Day related a combination boxing and haircutting incident that was amusing. Corporal Virgil Danforth related,
"We played volleyball and boxed to pass the time. I had
started to let my hair grow long enough to comb, but Lieutenant Marks and the rest of my platoon ganged me and ran
the clippers through the center of my head making one wide
part."

Sergeant John Urbank mentioned, "We gave each other
short haircuts and some Geronimo cuts. We wanted to give
Virgil Danforth one, but he said no, and meant it, so I put on
a pair of 12-ounce boxing gloves with Virg and sparred a
couple of rounds with him. We had his gloves tied on real
good; mine were laced loosely. On a given signal, Hillinger,
Senter, Lewark, and I jumped Virg, held him down and
started to give him a Geronimo cut. While we clipped his one
side, he started cussing and telling us what he was going to
do to us when he got free.

"We grew most cowardly then and decided to let him up. He
had long blond hair and we really scalped one side. When he
was released by us we just lay on the ground and laughed.
He was too much of a gentleman to kick us while we were
lying there laughing, and we had the boxing gloves tied to
him so he couldn't hit us too hard. He then went to the company barber who straightened it out some, but Virg was rather
skinned on one side."

Others resorted to the usual games.

"I particularly recall the gambling—always the gambling,"
said Private Mike Ranney. "I had a Longines watch that I
bought for $150 in the States. Must have lost and won it back
ten times in that period alone. Curley Robbins, then of Sali-
nas, California, was a great crapshooter, while I was a fair
blackjack dealer. Curley occasionally banked my blackjack
dealings while I banked his crapshooting because the action
was fast."

"The most common activity for most was the ever-present game of poker using the invasion money that had been issued to us, the true value of which none of us knew or for that matter really cared about," remembers T/5 Bill Finn.

Music was provided in several forms in the marshaling areas. Regimental bands provided relaxing music. Loudspeakers blared out hit records of the day. Army buglers will always be remembered.

PFC Bob Paczulla recalled, "Our regimental band was there to play for us at mealtimes and I know their music was enjoyed by all and was a significant contribution to the morale of the troops. A popular request was 'Holiday for Strings.' "

But others like Private Warren Ruedy, T/5 Charles D. Chapman, and Corporal Virgil Danforth, recalled that there were too many Spike Jones records like "Old Black Magic" and "Chloe." T/4 Robert "Burr" Smith had memories of "Don't Sit under the Apple Tree" blaring out from loudspeakers.

PFC Clair Mathiason related, "One of the outstanding memories from the marshaling area was the bugler sounding taps. Our battalion bugler and another from the Air Corps got together and did the most beautiful job of echoing taps."

Religion played a very important part in the lives of servicemen and particularly at a time when they were preparing to face the enemy for the first time.

"I was busy with confessions and mass every day in both of our regimental marshaling areas," recalls Captain John S. Maloney, Catholic chaplain of the 506th Regiment.

Captain Raymond S. "Chappie" Hall of Regimental Headquarters of the 502nd "was kept busy going from one area to another for religious services, baptisms, holy communions, etc."

To Private Sigmund F. Zalejski it seemed "everybody went to church and made his peace with God." But Lieutenant Winters has contrasting recollections. "Church services were attended a lot better than usual but not what you'd expect from a group about to start an invasion, which is something I really can't figure out."

Last-minute ailments threatened departures all the way from privates to generals. Chaplain Hall reported, "Doctor Ramey stayed all night before our departure to give attention to a communications soldier who was badly needed for the invasion drop. The treatment worked."

Captain Arthur B. Lunin, the assistant surgeon for the 3rd Battalion of the 501st, reminisced, "I treated General Taylor for an ingrown toenail the day before D-Day. I stuffed some cotton under it and told him if I did more I couldn't be sure if he would be with us, and we wanted him."

Nobody wanted to "goldbrick" at a time like this. Most certainly not Private Jack Schaffer, who related, "I had a high fever but didn't want to report it because I wasn't sure I would get into action because of it."

Communications from loved ones and thoughts of home occupied many minds. Major Allen W. "Pinky" Ginder received a letter from his wife asking if he had changed the beneficiary on his G.I. insurance policy. He said, "My father had lost his life as an officer during World War I and had failed to alter his policy in favor of his young wife. I was remiss in this particular chore just like Dad, and felt certain that history would repeat itself."

A new sense of responsibility descended on Lieutenant Sumpter Blackmon on the eve of departure. "In the marshaling area, mail call arrived with a picture of my wife and newborn son and Colonel Kinnard remarked when I showed it to him, 'Blackie, you've really got something to fight for there.' "

Many of them exchanged home addresses and vowed to visit the families of close buddies if they somehow failed to make it. "I thought we had a serious group as we took each other's home addresses saying we would pay our respects to the folks back home if something should happen to any of us and we didn't make it back," Sergeant Mike "Cat" Miller recalled.

PFC Lawrence E. Davidson and his buddy Corporal Gordon J. Laudick were scheduled to jump from the same plane. Davidson remembered, "We exchanged home addresses and each of us vowed to visit the home of the other if one of us did not survive the war."[2]

PFC James Martin had many nostalgic memories. He wrote, "During the last few days I thought a lot about home, the things we used to do, the places we used to go; those fishing trips to Greenville, those days of mountain climbing at Pike, and all the other excursions we used to take, and I wondered if all of us would ever get together to do those things again."[3]

Because of poor weather conditions, D-Day was postponed for 24 hours. This change was duly noted by three former members. A short notation in the diary of T/5 George Koskimaki stated simply: "We are equipped and packed ready to leave today. Bad weather is said to have postponed the mission until at least tomorrow."

Personal couriers rather than telephone calls were used to transmit such an important change of plans. Major Lawrence L. Legere, an assistant G-3 officer for the 101st Airborne Division Headquarters, recalled, "On Sunday, June 4th around noon, word came that the 'go' was postponed 24 hours; hence we would be jumping in the early morning of June 6th instead of June 5th. Major Paul Danahy and I each took a jeep and drove to the departure airfields—he taking half and I taking half. Our orders were to communicate only with the senior 101st officer at each field, who was the only one officially kept notified of exact times."

According to PFC Stanley "Stub" Shrodo, "Spirits were high, morale was excellent. We wanted to get the show started. After the postponement I got to feeling a bit shaky." Tension did mount and some of the men became extremely touchy. It was not difficult to start an argument and pick a fight. "After postponing for one day a lot of tension seemed to build up in the troops," recalled Platoon Sergeant John Kushner. "I saw a lot of fights among the men." Captain Van Gorder agreed. "We had a time with some of the men confined in the hangars. Some of them were like game roosters when it came to starting fights, especially with everyone under extreme tension and all trained in hand-to-hand combat." Sergeant Russell A. Schwenk recalls a serious flare-up, "One of our privates was beaten severely by several members of the company for showing invasion currency to the cooks."

The rain also brought this memory to mind with one of the men. PFC Richard M. Ladd stated, "For the most part the weather was sunny and pleasant. However, Colonel Bob Cole did keep his 3rd Battalion out in the rain for a few hours trying to find the man who put his map in a trash barrel. British civilians collected the rubbish."

Because of the postponement, some activity had to be quickly substituted to keep the men occupied. Several reported attending movies on the last afternoon in the marshaling area. A large number of men described an incident during a movie shown to the 3rd Battalion of the 506th Parachute Regiment. The account of PFC Clair Mathiason covers the details best: "We were treated to a show that afternoon in the hangar at the airfield. It was a war picture and about the bombing of some enemy city. I don't remember the name of the picture or members of the cast. It was a tense moment in the movie when the incident occurred. The bombs were dropping at the time and then there was a horrible hissing noise in the hangar and something came crashing down at the back of the darkened area. Because of the tenseness of the waiting for the invasion and the situation in the show, it caused a sudden commotion and everyone immediately thought there was a real bombing going on overhead, and in one great movement everyone started for the doors and outside. Chairs were knocked over. By the time everyone was outside and realized that there was no attack, we had suffered the first casualties of the war. There were a couple of boys hurt in the mad rush to get out and as I remember two had broken legs. It turned out that a fire extinguisher hanging at the back of the room had been knocked down and set off, causing all the hissing sound and a toppled chair caused the crashing noise. I can well remember the verbal going-over we got from Colonel Wolverton for being so easily shaken up, and how he wondered what we would be like under fire."

Another movie was in progress in the 377th Parachute Field Artillery Battalion marshaling area. Staff Sergeant Edward "Chief" Benecke recalled, "We were watching a movie called, 'Is Everybody Happy?' with Ted Lewis when we were called out to go to our planes and make ready."

One of the staff officers for that battalion, Captain William E. Brubaker, provided a very coincidental recollection, for it was he who disrupted the movie. "On the evening of June 5th," he remembered, "the battalion personnel were attending a movie when we received the alert. Major Courtney Neilson told me to go to the movie and order the troops to their respective battery areas to prepare for the mission. I recall breaking into the movie to so inform the troops and thinking to myself that this is just the way it would happen in Hollywood."

During the last days, division commander General Maxwell D. Taylor toured the marshaling areas and gave a last fighting pep talk to his men. Captain Thomas J. White served as aide to General Taylor. He reminisced, "I toured all of the areas with General Taylor. He made an impassioned speech at each one. The troops (heads shaved, and faces painted on the last day) were not just ready—they were eager to go."

One of these visits was recalled by Lieutenant Winters: "General Taylor gave the boys a little pep talk and asked for three days of hard fighting and then we would be withdrawn."[4]

The postponements gave various groups an opportunity to make some last-minute changes. Lieutenant LeGrand "Legs" Johnson, commanding officer of Fox Company of the 502nd Regiment, said, "F Company won a regimental competition and was given the 'honor' of being the lead company following the battalion headquarters planes. I was to be the jumpmaster in Plane number 9. Crammed under the aircraft were six bundles of antitank mines and spare flame-throwing equipment. My company mission was to destroy the coastal artillery guns and some other concrete emplacements. The guns were on railroad tracks, and were not completely ready to fire—at least two of them were not."

Johnson continued: "D-Day was postponed and on that day, some Air Force colonel notified me that radar was being installed on my plane and the racks and bundles must come off. This suited me, but I didn't know they would load the bundles on the floor of the plane. Those bundles were five to six feet long, and weighed between 100–200 pounds. I fought this issue, including asking the Air Force colonel to step outside with me, but all to no avail. We were grossly overweight and the poor pilot swore the plane would never get airborne.

"When we reported to the plane on the afternoon of June 5th, faces properly blackened and heads shaved, I met with another miserable circumstance—I had a naval observer assigned to my plane. He was supposed to spot for the navy and direct their fire. He had an SCR-300 radio bundled in a leg bag so padded and large that it took two men to push it in the door. You can imagine my state of mind."

Lieutenant Bill Padrick had an amazing change of plans. He related, "The day before the invasion, General Pratt took my Browning Automatic Rifle for his aide and driver, Lieutenant Lee Mays, and ordered me to fly to Exeter to draw another. I spent the day flying to Exeter in a small plane. Today, I still think how foolish the Army was to turn me loose not knowing what I would do, when I was fully aware of where we were going and what our mission was to be. As I looked down on the many airfields in England, and saw there the many thousands of zebra-striped planes, I was fascinated and awed by the strength and massiveness of the invasion force."

During the last afternoon, the men were also busy with the camouflage work on their faces and bodies. T/4 Bill Maslowski served as a radioman for his battalion commander. He remembered, "We all smeared our faces with burned cork. Most of the fellows had their hair completely cut off."

"We blackened our faces with charcoal to keep the glare of the moon off," explained Private Russell Graham. "I tried to duck putting that black stuff on my face," said Corporal Vinnie Utz, "but being in number 1 plane with Colonel Robert Sink as the jumpmaster, he spotted me and ordered me to the plane exhausts, where I rubbed engine soot on my face."

On that last afternoon in the marshaling areas, General Dwight D. Eisenhower chose to visit the airfields of the 101st Airborne Division. Many of the men have lasting memories of these encounters. Brigadier General Maxwell D. Taylor,[5] the commanding officer of the 101st Airborne Division, recollected, "I toured the airfields with General Eisenhower and answered many of his questions about the plans for the landing the following morning."

"I remember the visit very well," wrote T/4 Tom Walsh. "One of his motorcycle MP escorts wished he was going along with us. We were standing within earshot on the inside of the fence and several of us volunteered to trade places."

Lieutenant "Legs" Johnson probably remembers Ike's visit more vividly than do any of the others. He said, "I was seated on my bottom bunk honing a jump knife. Ike walked into my tent. I jumped up, crashing my poor head against the upper bunk and damn near knocked myself out. The gash required several stitches to close."

Corporal Kermit R. Latta also remembers Ike's memorable visit. The men were resting under the wing of a plane in preparation for the flight. With some stirring down the line of planes, Latta's jumpmaster suddenly called the group to attention. "As we stood in formation waiting to board our planes," recalled Latta, "I was surprised to see General Eisenhower coming down the line of men talking to each one. While he spoke to the man beside me I was struck by the terrific burden of decision and responsibility on his face. He asked the soldier next to me, 'What is your job soldier?'

" 'Ammunition bearer, sir,' was his reply.

" 'Where is your home?'

" 'Pennsylvania, sir.'

" 'Did you get those shoulders working in a coal mine?'

" 'Yes sir!'

" 'Good luck to you tonight, soldier!' "

Just prior to departure for the airfields in some of the areas, the men were stirred once more by memorable speeches delivered by unit commanders. The men of the 501st Regiment were ready to go. They had just come from the last religious services and were gathered about Colonel Howard "Skeets" Johnson, their regimental commander. Many of the men remembered something about that speech. "I remember the bloodthirsty speech by Colonel Johnson when he spoke to us the evening before D-Day and in full battle dress," Sergeant James "Duke" Koller remembered. "He informed us he hoped to plunge the knife he was holding upraised into the heart of some 'Nazi bastard' before the night was done." Private Lyman A. Hurd, Jr., also remembered Johnson's words. "A stirring speech was given by Colonel Johnson a few hours before we climbed into our planes. One line of his speech had a lasting effect—he expected to plunge his knife (he pulled out his long knife and raised it over his head) into the heart of a German before the night was over." Lieutenant Clair L. Hess remembered "the fiery exhibition of Colonel Johnson in stirring up his men, after which he went down the lines of men and shook hands with each soldier."

In sharp contrast, a very different type of "pep talk" occurred at another airfield. PFC Jim "Pee-Wee" Martin reviewed in retrospect, "A lot of the 'Brass' gave the usual line of morale-building talks. Our battalion commander, Lt. Colonel Robert Wolverton, gave the only speech that I think was strictly from the heart. We all got on our knees in full battle equipment and he offered a prayer for victory and asked that those of us who died in battle, die as brave men, and as soldiers should. Right after that we started for the airplanes which were some distance away. S.O.S. and Air Corps personnel lined the roadway quietly and seriously wished us luck. We certainly did need it. As we split into groups or 'sticks' and headed for our planes on the runways, there was a lot of jovial bantering back and forth; last minute 'Good luck!' and 'See you on the ground!' sort of stuff."

Staff Sergeant Jerry McCullough[6] has an even more detailed account of this occasion: "The men were called together and they stood in the orchard on either side of a low earthen mound which fenced the fields. Upon the earth hedgerow stood Lieutenant Colonel Robert L. Wolverton. He said, 'Men, I am not a religious man and I don't know your feelings in this matter, but I am going to ask you to pray with me for the success of the mission before us. And while we pray let us get on our knees and not look down but up with faces raised to the sky.

" 'God All Mighty! In a few short hours we will be in battle with the enemy. We do not join battle afraid. We do not ask favors or indulgence, but ask that if You will, use us as Your instruments for the Right and an aid in returning peace to the world. We do not know or seek what our fate will be. We ask only this, that if die we must, that we die as men would die, without complaining, without pleading and safe in the feeling that we have done our best for what we believed was right. Oh Lord! Protect our loved ones and be near us in the fire ahead and with us now as we each pray to You.'

"All was silent for two minutes, each man with his own thoughts. Then the Colonel ordered, 'Move out!' "7

Lieutenant Richard Winters provided an excellent description of the hustle and bustle of the last afternoon's preparations and departure for the planes in his first letter from the combat area. He wrote, "Tonight is the night! I spent the afternoon getting ready and taking a two-hour nap. After supper things were in a great uproar getting ready. A last-minute leak [urination], faces blackened, and weapons checked, and we were ready to move out.

"At 2030 P.M., we lined up by planeloads and marched off for the hangars. As we passed buddies, friends, and fellow officers, there was usually a stiff smile, nod of the head or pat on the back, but very few showed any emotions at all. It seemed like just another jump—nothing to get excited about. On the way to the hangars we passed some British antiaircraft units stationed at the field. That was the first time I've ever seen any real emotion from a Limey soldier; they actually had tears in their eyes, and you could see they felt like hell standing there watching us go out to battle."

At one of the areas, the men marched off to the music of the band as described by T/5 George Koskimaki. "With the band leading us, each group stepped off smartly. Marches played were favorites of ours from days when we passed in review for various visiting dignitaries during less hectic times. Observing the expressions on the faces of my buddies as we marched along, I noted that all appearances at light-heartedness had disappeared and each soldier seemed to be deeply engrossed with his own thoughts." Koskimaki added: "As we entered the airfield proper, groups peeled off to proceed to their respective planes. Each aircraft had a large number painted just below the pilot's compartment window. Our plane was numbered with a large numeral '1.' Our group halted in the division headquarters area where we were permitted to break ranks and have a last chat with buddies—in many cases we were actually saying good-bye for the last time. I shook hands with my close friends Chuck Chapman and Ed Neils, and moved to the area of my own plane. This aircraft had a special bubble on the underside (it looked like a washtub suspended on the belly side) which contained equipment for picking up the radio beams which would be transmitted by our particular group of pathfinders. They were to drop in our zone about an hour before we were scheduled to jump."

Arriving at the airfields early was part of an old army custom of "hurry up and wait." Private Bob Hayes, in reflecting on this issue, remembered, "After marching out to the fields we had a chance to loaf near our planes. We sat around on the grass while our pilot talked to us. He told us that pilots of C-47's were better all-around flyers than fighter pilots."

PFC Jay Nichols could not be expected to forget the brief speech by his pilot. " 'I will not bring any of you men back on this ship,' he said, and he ended it by patting his .45 in its holster."

Medic Stanley Shrodo expressed confidence in his pilot. "We had a redheaded pilot who was 'A-1'. He told us confidently while waiting, 'I will get you there and when you get the green light, get out fast, or you may have a water landing.' "

Some of the men signed their signatures to French banknotes while waiting. PFC James L. Evans, a wireman attached to Division Artillery, was with artillery commander Brigadier General Anthony C. McAuliffe. According to Evans, "Just before the takeoff General McAuliffe had each man on the plane sign a 100-franc note and pass it on to the others so each would have a souvenir short snorter with all the names of the stick members."

Departure time was fast approaching. Lieutenant Winters added these recollections of those moments at the airfield: "At the hangars each jumpmaster was given two packs of papers, one a message from General Eisenhower, the other from Colonel Sink. Each man synchronized his watch, was assigned a truck, and whisked to his plane. At the plane, the first thing I did was unload all the parachutes and equipment and see that each man had his. Then in a huddle I passed out the poop sheets, gave the men the schedule we would have to follow; 2215 in the plane ready to go; 2310 takeoff; 0120 jump, 'Good luck, God bless you, and see you in the assembly area.' With that done we went to work harnessing up and it's here that a good jumpmaster or officer can do the most for his men. For in getting all that equipment on, tied down, trying to make it comfortable and safe; then a parachute over the top called for a lot of ingenuity and sales talk to satisfy the men that all's well. By 2200 all were ready but myself, for it's no good getting ready yourself and then helping the men. So I whipped into my equipment fast and furious, mounted up and was ready to go.

"One incident at this time is worthy of note; one of the boys, Private 'Jeeter' Leonard, had a terrific load, in fact like others in the stick, I had to push him up the steps into the plane. Well, 'Jeeter' was in the plane and ready to go, and so was everyone else, so I made a final check of all kit bags that held our equipment and in his I found one basic load of M-1 ammunition. Poor 'Jeeter' had everything but ammunition. The sad part about it is that he just didn't have any place to carry it. I told him to see me in the assembly area and I'd give it to him. This was O.K.; for there was to be no shooting on the jump field. At this time I handed out the second motion sickness pill, the first being given at 2200. The idea was to do away with airsickness and the butterflies in your stomach when you're scared.

"All was pretty quiet, a little bitching about all the equipment we had to carry, but outside of that it was pretty quiet. Most of us were just thinking good and hard."

It was time to load up. Parachutes were being buckled on over the heavy equipment. The men at the airfield housing the 3rd Battalion of the 501st Regiment and the Division Headquarters parachutists were being treated to the final visit by General Eisenhower just before departure. T/5 George Koskimaki recorded the last moments in this way: "As the sun was sinking in the west, all eyes seemed to turn in one direction due to excitement further down the line of silent, waiting planes. As the cause of the excitement approached our group, it was noted with pleasure that the supreme commander of the invasion, General Eisenhower, had come to wish the vanguard of the invasion Godspeed and good landings."[8]

Koskimaki added, "He approached with General Taylor, who had accompanied him on visits to the airfields. Major Legere, our jumpmaster, called us to attention. 'At ease, men,' was Eisenhower's reply. He stopped to chat with a number of the men. While the chatting was going on, we suddenly became aware of the fact that the airdrome was coming to life. The sleeping giants had awakened. They seemed almost anxious to be on their way. Above the din could be heard the command of jumpmaster Legere as he directed his men to put on their equipment. Then passing along the column, Legere checked each man to see that he had buckled everything properly. 'Load up!' came the next order. The men mounted into the plane with jumper number 16 moving up the steps first followed by 15 and on down the line. A colonel from Eisenhower's party gave me a helpful boost into the plane. I moved into the darkened interior and took my seat in the fifth jump position near the door. I noted the final handshake between General Eisenhower, the supreme commander, and General Taylor, the leader of his first attack unit which would make the initial contact with the soldiers guarding Hitler's Fortress Europa. General Eisenhower saluted once more and stepped back as the pilot gunned the engines and then taxied slowly down the runway to a position facing into the wind. The other planes fell into single file much like soldiers assembling, and followed the lead craft. As each plane passed his position, General Eisenhower saluted."

Another of the soldiers who noted the General near the planes was Private Walter M. Turk. He recalled, "Ike stuck his head in the door of our plane as we waited to taxi out onto the runway. He wished us luck."

The assembling, the organizing, the waiting were almost over. The time of boarding the planes and the final takeoff had come. PFC James Martins[9] caught that moment when he wrote, "I looked at our plane, a C-47, with newly painted bands of black and white around her fuselage and wings to signify she was an Allied invasion ship. That is when I got a catch in my throat and my heart beat a little faster. To me it was the most beautiful ship there was. It was as graceful in its lines as a Powers model in the line of feminine pulchritude.

"Some of the Air Corps boys shot the bull with us awhile, awe and admiration in the face and voice of each, as they offered us candy, gum, and help. We all pushed and tugged each other into the ship and settled down with the least amount of discomfort possible under the circumstances. Butterflies held a rally in my stomach as I heard the whine of the starter winding up; a few throaty coughs as the engine caught and finally roared into a full crescendo of the most beautiful music there is; engines at the peak of perfection.

"We idled down the taxi strip, tested the engines and started down the runway for a one-way ride."

CHAPTER 2

The Pathfinders Lead the Way

Meanwhile, at North Witham, in the vicinity of Nottingham, a hundred miles to the north of the 101st Airborne Division Headquarters, the special group of pathfinders was already in flight.

Since December 1943, this special force of approximately one hundred and twenty men had been trained by their commander, Captain Frank L. Lillyman. The training was specialized in the art of directing the main body of the 101st Airborne Division to its drop and glider landing zones in Normandy. Their training involved the use of lights, smoke, radar, and luminous panels.

All units had received requests for volunteers to take part in the highly secret mission. Specifically, the request had gone out for men who had previous training in communications work. Top priority was given to men who had background training in sending and receiving Morse code. Many of the volunteers were "busted" former NCO's.

Private Mike Ranney, from Easy Company of the 506th Parachute Regiment, was among those who received pathfinder training. Shortly before the invasion, Mike had requested transfer back to his line company. He desired to go into combat with his close buddies. He remembered, "Pathfinder training was a bit of a lark. Charley Malley was acting first sergeant for the group. I believe that 'Salty' Harris was a platoon sergeant. I served as supply sergeant. Our men were a good group of guys who had 'screwed off' in one way or another."

Acting First Sergeant Charles R. Malley, from Fox Company of the 506th Regiment, had recollections of his protégés. "The pathfinders, of whom most were 'busted down' NCO's, were organized in December of 1943. All of the men had been through the airborne training mill and were 'hot to trot.' Our pathfinder unit was stationed just outside Nottingham, England, home of Robin Hood, and the famous bastille where good ole Robin was incarcerated. Many were the times that I received calls from the good sheriff of Nottingham to come and get our present-day HOODS out of his jail. The good thing about English justice—no fines, no nothing—just get 'em to hell out of here! Lillyman was quite a guy! On returning with these bodies to our unit, he made inquiry as to the seriousness of pending charges from any suffering English civilians. If the situation seemed bad, he gave the guy company punishment at once, thereby forestalling any possible court-martial. He saved me once."

At this point, there is necessity of elaborating on the makeup of this group. Much of the material herein was secret until many years after the war. A total of eleven sticks of jumpers were trained by the 101st Airborne Division for the D-Day Mission. A team of three sticks was assigned to each of the three parachute drop zones, while two sticks were to prepare the way to the glider landing fields. Each stick was composed of from eight to twelve pathfinders. Shortly before D-Day, a security detail was assigned to each stick by the Division. They were to cover the pathfinders on the drop zones while these men concentrated on directing the incoming planes.

Each stick was led by an officer who jumped with his combat load of equipment, and an SCR-536 radio to be used in communicating with other officers of the three sticks who jumped as part of the team, on the same drop zone.

Two men in each stick jumped with Eureka radar sets. These devices sent out continuous signals which were to be received by the leading aircraft in each serial of planes. The reception was through a companion set known as "Rebecca." Immediately upon landing, these sets were made operational. Quickly preparing them for operation was important to the pilots, who could then begin receiving signals that the "trailblazers" had landed.

Four men carried lights of the halifane type in canvas bags

under the reserve parachute. Each of the four men jumped with two lights. Seven of the lights were used in a "T" arrangement. The tail of the "T" pointed in the direction of the jump; the crossbar of the "T" indicated the "go" point. These lights were set into a position where they were easily visible from the air, but almost completely hidden from ground observers. When the motors of the approaching aircraft were heard, the lights were illuminated. The tail light (tail of the "T") was coded to blink out the signal of the drop zone. (Example: On Drop Zone "A" the light blinked out .—, the Morse Code signal for the letter A). These lights were also coded in color per drop zone. (Drop Zone "A" was amber; "C" was green; and "D" was red.) The operator of the lights had a battery with a telegraph key which was on a 25-foot extension cord. The key operator remained at his post throughout the operation, while the remaining men served as security personnel to protect the equipment. The Eureka performed independently when set in operation and was sometimes placed in a tree.

For daytime operations, the men also carried panels and smoke grenades to be used in conjunction with the Eureka sets.

Captain Lillyman had a general briefing concerning the invasion as early as the middle of May. He commented: "I knew the general time and place of deployment of our people. Likewise, I had been briefed on the British plan and realized that each of us were to go in via parallel routes. Of considerable concern to me was the magnitude of the security problem. Until now, briefings had been given to only regimental commanders and key staff officers. I was obliged, in order to assure proper training, to give limited details of the briefings to my officers. After briefing them, I had the constant worry as to whether 'security' would be violated."

Lillyman continued: "This was exemplified by a situation at North Witham when one of my lieutenants, a commander of one of the sticks, visited blacked-out Nottingham. Although our people normally traveled in pairs, he was alone, separated from his partner, and struck by a vehicle. He sustained, along with other injuries, a fractured leg, and was taken to a military hospital. His strong sense of security made him refuse medical attention until I was notified. I was able to send a man to stay with him, to be certain that he did not divulge information while under anesthetic and during recuperation."

The pathfinders didn't move to another area for their staging. When it was time to seal them off, security personnel closed off their area with barbed wire. First Sergeant Malley described it: "I think it was in late May that each of the pathfinders realized that we were nearing the day of invasion. In the last week of May, they threw the 'barbed wire' on us." As PFC John R. Sample remembered it, "We had gone to a briefing session in another area and when we came back to our own barracks they had a fence put up and MP's were already walking guard."

This brought several problems in security. Captain Lillyman recalled one particular situation: "Another unforeseen problem occurred on the 4th of June. We were marshaling at North Witham Air Base which contained, on one side of the field, the Air Force supply depot on which we relied for our administrative support, pay, supplies, etc. Division had increased our mission in having directed us to take in mines and demolitions. I had put in a requisition for the mines to be delivered at the gate of our barbed-wire enclosure on the fourth of June. I was in the orderly room paying my men in French money late on the afternoon of the 4th. Despite our security precautions, a sergeant came in from the opposite side of the air base with these mines and said that he had orders to deliver them to Captain Lillyman. He walked past the sentry and into the orderly room where I was paying my men in invasion currency. I immediately realized that this was a compromise and, although he was their chief non-commissioned officer, I had to lock him up. He stayed in that capacity until the 7th of June. Obviously, his section chief on the other side of the airfield was very concerned by his absence. I could not tell him nor would the Base S-2 give him information or the reason as to why he was locked up. He was concerned by the fact that someone had kidnapped his sergeant, and this created a rather embarrassing situation."

Scheduled to parachute with the pathfinders were other personnel, among them the security forces of the pathfinder group. These men reported into the area around June 1st. Included, also, was a three-man intelligence team which was to find suitable routes to the beach.

A security soldier for the 501st Regiment, Private John D. Mishler from Baker Company, recalled, "For a period of time before D-Day we were under 'live-ammunition' guard. We studied maps, overlays, scale models and information peculiar to the pathfinder mission. Infantry field officers did not receive this extensive preparation."

Lieutenant Robert S. Dickson III, an intelligence officer from the 502nd Regiment, was given a special assignment by his regimental commander. He was to jump with two of his men, with the first planeload of pathfinders. "We were to reconnoiter a route to the regimental objective which was that of the coastal artillery guns, just behind Utah Beach. We spent considerable time studying the road networks to be used in approaching the objective."

Captain Lillyman described the postponement of D-Day: "On the fourth of June, we had our first 'dry run' which was very touchy. The pathfinders, as usual, were the last ones to get the word. After the evening meal, we returned to barracks, drew all of our equipment, camouflaged our men with face coloring, loaded the aircraft, then sat there and waited, and waited, and waited. Finally the cancellation of the mission came through and we again returned to our barracks. We had been scheduled to take off at 2145 in the evening. Meanwhile, many Base administrative individuals had driven by the flight line and had seen us in obvious battle uniforms. Of course, they knew that the pathfinders were about to take off."

First Sergeant Malley described the delay. "On June 4, a plane came wheeling into the Air Base, and a warrant officer was admitted to the compound. A small valise was attached to the officer's right wrist. Captain Lillyman's face became quite pale. Lillyman read General Taylor's message which was inside the container. He turned to me, saying, 'Sergeant, tell the troops to relax—we have one more day.' The letter was burned there on the spot. The valise was returned to the warrant officer who had no realization of its contents. The officer departed."

"I remember the cancellation of the jump on the evening of June 4th," said Private John Zamanakos. "We had waited on the airport apron for more than two hours, 'shooting the breeze' about days at home. One of the boys had received a 'Dear John' letter. The postponement seemed to have taken the starch out of us."

A warrant officer returned the next day. Malley said, "On the following day at approximately 1800 hours—a new plane—a different officer, but the exact procedure was followed. Lillyman went through the same motions. However, this time he turned to me and said, 'Get the troops ready.' The entire company was moved to the flight line, and lo and behold, they had photographers, generals, and all—even Red Cross girls with coffee, to cheer us."

As the Brass watched from the apron, the planes moved off to the runway, tested their engines and took off. Malley said, "They issued our 'puke pills' and vomit bags, then 'fired up' the motors. My remembrance is that the hour was near 2200, English time. Due to the fact that I was jumping a Eureka radar set, attached to my right leg, I was the number one man at the door. Naturally we were loaded to the gills with equipment and were barely able to move. We flew over the English Channel, and low enough that the spray, from the water, came through the doorway. Later, this was said to have contributed to the confusion of the German radar."

PFC Johnny Sample remembered that the planes flew a salute over the people gathered below. "We took off and buzzed the airfield, then we went up to around three thousand feet until we left England," he said.

After that the planes dropped to almost wave-top level. "There are two things that I remember about that trip," said Sample. "One is that somewhere over the Channel I saw a flashing red light and was told that it was a rescue ship, just in case. The other was that at one time we were so low that the prop blast was blowing water in the door."

The men were to be in Normandy from a half hour to an hour before the main body of troops began arriving.

From his position in the first plane where Captain Frank Lillyman was jumpmaster, Lieutenant Dickson recalled that he "looked out and saw the full moon, and the searchlights of the Jersey and Guernsey Islands, blinking the warning of our coming, as we flew by them. I remember the cloud cover over France, and finally, the apparent quiet of everything."

As the planes crossed the coastline and headed inland, from the west side of the peninsula, the unexpected cloud cover caused dispersion, this before the planes were to separate and head for their respective drop zones. Lillyman's three-plane team headed for the northernmost Drop Zone "A," in the area between Ste. Mère Eglise and St. Martin-de-Varreville. This drop zone was assigned to a combat team composed of the 502nd Parachute Infantry Regiment and the 377th Parachute Field Artillery Battalion.

The three planes experienced little or no flak in the trans-peninsula flight. Because of the low clouds and fog at the western side of the Cotentin Peninsula, the plane crews failed to pick out the early identification marks. Because of this, the green light was flashed on the approach to the small town of St. Germain-de-Varreville, which was located one and a half miles north of the spot for which the men had aimed.

As the green light flashed, jumpmaster Lillyman stepped out into the prop blast followed by his 18-man stick. The plane crew noted the time. It was 0015 A.M. on the morning of June 6th.

With an unlighted black cigar clenched between his teeth, Lillyman sought out a clear area, pulled hard on his forward risers, and slipped into a small field near St. Germain-de-Varreville. He said, "After the landing, we met at the church in St. Germain-de-Varreville and traveled through fields to the northwest, where we set up lights as markers, along with installation of other special equipment in trees. Walton and Council shinnied up a tree and set up the Eureka for our sticks of jumpers. Our orders were to do no shooting and we had instructed our men to take evasive action if Germans were sighted.

"A German machine gunner, spotting us through bushes, kept probing with short bursts. This was annoying, and I finally sent two men to convince the Krauts of the 'errors of their ways.' Soon, I heard a grenade go off with a 'whumf,' and then everything was lovely and quiet."

Lillyman continued, "Forty-seven minutes later the planes arrived with the main body of troops. This was the longest forty-seven minutes of my life. Those lights never looked so bright in training, but that night they looked like searchlights. One light went out, and we had to rig an emergency connection. We were silhouetted against it for a few minutes. However, nothing happened.

"Several of my scouts reported a farmhouse, where there were Germans, at the edge of the field. Two others, and myself went to the house where we met a Frenchman smoking a pipe. He was standing in the doorway. He jerked his thumb toward the stairs and said, 'Boche.' We caught the German, in a nice pair of white pajamas, in bed. We disposed of him and expropriated the bottle of champagne beside the bed. We met no more Germans before the main invasion body landed, however, one enemy bicycle patrol approached and then turned back. They seemed to not want any part of us and we wanted no part of them."

The rest of Lillyman's stick was strung out over several hundred yards. "Our flight over enemy territory was a complete surprise to them," Private John Zamanakos observed. "The jump was good, but I landed alone on the far side of a hedgerow. The radar I had hooked under my chest pack interfered with my straps. In freeing myself from my chute, I had to cut my risers. I jumped into a ditch, waited, and listened; then clicking my cricket, crept back along the line of flight. I found other members of my stick—Walton, Jones, and Council. I was a radar operator. We brought a few planes into our area and on our field, but it was a mess. We had no idea where we were. When the planes did come in, they came in from all points of the compass. We had men of the 505th Regiment of the 82nd Airborne Division jump on our lighted

'T.' On occasion, I have wondered about what the Jerries thought: It was so messed up, that no General, of any Army, could have evaluated any part of it. Perhaps that is the reason it was so successful."

Private and medic Raymond "Snuffy" Smith was the first injury with the group. "The jump was smooth," he recalled. "We dropped near a church at St. Germain-de-Varreville. I landed in an apple tree, in the church yard, and injured a foot on striking the ground. Two or three of my group landed within fifty feet of one another. We crawled around the area, snapping our warning bugs. Members of our group assembled, moved off, and set up battery-operated lights and radar as jump identification signals for the main body of troops, provided the fields were clear of enemy and obstacles."

PFC Delbert Jones, jumping from the same plane, remembered, "We had good moonlight and clear weather. The jump itself was very good. I landed in a courtyard surrounded by a stone wall. As I landed, my helmet scraped against the wall, and made a great deal of noise. Because of all the gear I carried, I had difficulty in getting off my equipment. I was very nervous as I lay on my back. I could see a light shining under the door of the house. My thought was, that this was one of those German barracks at the end of our drop zone. On freeing my rifle and signal lights from the harness, I attempted to find my way out of the courtyard. Finally, I climbed over the wall and fell into a cemetery among the tombstones on the other side. I recall meeting Gus Mangoni and two other men, one of whom had a fractured ankle. I carried him with us most of the night."

Jones added, "I was a signal-light man and had to set up the pattern 'T' for the arrival of the 502nd and their drop. We only partially completed that part of the task. Finally, I was with Captain Lillyman and a number of others. We proceeded to the coastal gun emplacement, but found that it had been destroyed by the Air Force."

PFC Fred Wilhelm had a difficult time reaching his straps with all the equipment slung from them. He said, "I found after landing I could not reach my chest straps and had a time getting out of my harness. Once free, I put my M-1 together

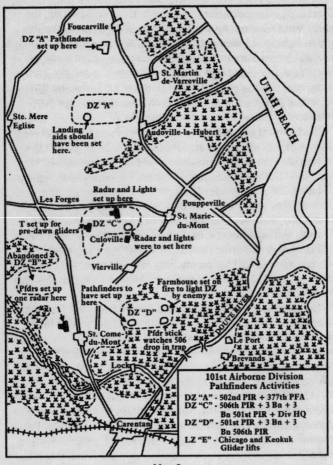

Foucarville

DZ "A" Pathfinders
set up here →

St. Martin
de-Varreville

UTAH BEACH

DZ "A"

Ste. Mere
Eglise

Landing
aids should
have been set
here.

Audoville-la-Hubert

Radar and Lights
set up here

Les Forges

Pouppeville

St. Marie-
du-Mont

T set up for
pre-dawn gliders

DZ "C"

Culoville

Radar and lights
were to set here

Abandoned
DZ "B"

Vierville

Pfdrs set up
one radar here

Pathfinders to
have set up
here

Farmhouse set on
fire to light DZ
by enemy

DZ "D"

St. Come-
du-Mont

Pfdr stick
watches 506
drop in trap

DOUVE RIVER

Le Port

Lock

Brevands

Carentan

**101st Airborne Division
Pathfinders Activities**

DZ "A" - 502nd PIR + 377th PFA
DZ "C" - 506th PIR + 3 Bn + 3
        Bn 501st PIR + Div HQ
DZ "D" - 501st PIR + 3 Bn + 3
        Bn 506th PIR
LZ "E" - Chicago and Keokuk
        Glider lifts

Map 2

and got my landing lights ready. In about ten minutes, I made contact with T/5 Tom Walton. Our mission was to use radar and lights to bring in the rest of the Airborne. We were to form a 'T.' At a given time we were to turn our lights on; the ships were to come up the leg of the 'T' and then give the green light to the men at the crossbar. After getting into position, I by accident turned the switch and my light came on. We heard firing and some shells coming in after my light went on. I thought we had had it. Then as we had some time to wait, Captain Lillyman and I took a walk down to a farmhouse in which we found a German officer."

"This was quite a drop," said Private Francis A. Rocca, who jumped with the same stick of men. "I landed in the enclosed yard of a parsonage. I collected my gear, then attempted an immediate rendezvous with others of the stick. We managed to assemble all of our men."

Another plane carrying a second stick from Lillyman's team dropped a short distance away. PFC William H. "Buzz" Barton, of Dog Battery of the 377th Parachute Field Artillery Battalion, remembered, "The night was beautiful and we had some moonlight—no flak. We came in very low. I believe we jumped at 400 feet. We were seen by no one. I landed 'smack' in the middle of Drop Zone 'A.'[1]

"After getting out of my harness, I contacted the men from our stick. I met Lt. Robert G. Smith and prepared to light the drop zone. I recall that he collected all the men from our stick—we didn't lose a man. My particular assignment was to stand near an amber-colored battery-operated light to make certain that it wasn't shot out near the tail end of the 'T.' Having accomplished my particular task, the 'T' was lit up like a Christmas tree, but the troopers jumped every damned place except on the drop zone. After the drop, we moved to an area nearby where we dug in and waited for daylight."

Another member of that stick was PFC John R. Sample, who was near the front of the stick and had an opportunity to observe some of the action outside the plane. "In our briefings we had been told that the British would be bombing on the coast as we were dropping," Sample recalled. "I was number '3' man in the door and as we were hooked up and standing ready to go for the entire trip across the peninsula, I saw several sticks of bombs go off as they hit."

Sample remembered his landing this way: "Colonel Crouch flew the lead plane and he told us earlier that they would slow down so we would have a good jump regardless of the situation on the ground and, boy, they did just that. It was the best exit I ever had. After my chute opened I saw two objects running across the far end of the field so I frantically climbed my risers and when I got closer to the ground I realized they were two cows. What a relief! There was an anti-aircraft gun near by but with the woods separating us from it we drew no fire—not even small arms. We assembled under a big tree that was on the drop zone and then set up our lights and radar. We waited several minutes before we turned them on. I don't recall all the parachutists who jumped on our signals but I know that not one plane from our battalion did. I do remember that the first wave of planes was off to the right of the 'T' and the lead plane and those with him corrected their line of flight to come right over us. All of our pathfinders were accounted for outside of two or three injuries and they were of a minor nature." (See Sample's pathfinders map on page 32.)

In the 18-man stick, with Lillyman, the last three jumpers were Lieutenant Robert "Buck" Dickson and his two men from the Regimental S-2 Section. Their departure from the aircraft was different from the previous parachutists. According to Dickson, "My two men and myself were last to drop. One heavily burdened trooper fell in the doorway just prior to our jumping. By the time we pushed him out, the pilot was diving and turning homeward. This caused our jump to be at a low altitude and a considerable distance from the others. I had no difficulty getting out of my chute except for the nervousness generated by the situation. I set my 'grease gun' (.45 automatic) in tall grass, then walked away without it. I did some scurrying around to find it again. I located my men in the next field; however, we were unable to completely orient ourselves and joined with other small groups from many units, including the 82nd. During our wandering in the early morning hours, a few of us became separated and were fired on from approximately three hundred yards. My 'grease gun' was so ineffective at that distance, I had to cease firing. Later, I picked up an M-1 from a dead soldier, and later acquired a carbine, which I considered the best compromise among the three. We did not reach our objective on D-Day."

Between 0200 and 0300, after the main body of troopers had landed, Lillyman and a scouting party of twelve men moved out toward the coast. They discovered that the coastal artillery battery had been demolished.

A second team of pathfinders under the leadership of Lieutenant Gordon C. Rothwell headed for Drop Zone "C" near Hiesville. Rothwell's plane was in the lead of the three plane-group. First Sergeant Malley, a member of Rothwell's stick, described their almost fatal D-Day landing: "Suddenly we shot up a couple hundred feet. The damned flak was all over the sky and tracer bullets were a dime a thousand. Bullets were whizzing through the fuselage like bees chasing a 'honey-robbin' bear. All of a sudden the warning bell to clear the airplane rang out. Normally, being airborne, you go without thinking. I was looking out of the door ready to swing. We were all hooked up and I could have grabbed a handful of trees. I hollered to Lieutenant Rothwell, my stick commander, to hold. One motor was on fire and burning fiercely. The crew chief kept hollering, 'Clear the ship! Clear the ship!'

"Clear the ship hell! We were at ground level. The co-pilot came rushing back into the troop section, and shouting, 'Everything overboard We're going down!' We cut and slashed our way out of parachutes, guns, ammo, every damned thing we could," continued Malley. "I pulled the detonator on the radar set and threw it out. Hell, we had nothing on but jump boots and O.D. uniforms. The co-pilot came to the cabin again, and made the overstatement of the century. He hollered, 'Prepare to jump. We are going in!'

"Jump, hell! I can sincerely state that there was no great excitement on the plane. I cut Wheeler through to his rib section trying to loosen him from his harness. He was given the Purple Heart.

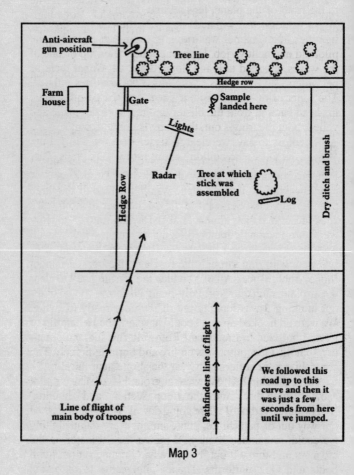

Map 3

This is a sketch of the pathfinder setup as remembered by PFC John Sample of the 377th pathfinder stick which landed in the vicinity of St. Germain-de-Varreville on June 6, 1944, at approximately 12:15 A.M.

"We prepared to ditch as we had been instructed—ass-end to the front of the plane, legs around the man in front. Mae Wests were on and inflated. The pilot fired a red flare for lighting. The Channel was running high that night but the pilot did one helluva job. He brought her in on top of one of the waves, dragged tail, and flopped her in. We sat there as per orders. Rothwell was trying to get the dinghies inflated. The water came up around our knees and the co-pilot stuck his head back in from the blister on the top of the plane and yelled, 'Get the troops out, this baby is going down!'

"Needless to say, we cleared faster than we hooked up. We got the guys who couldn't swim into the dinghies. Pustola, from Brooklyn, had his pockets full of all the pistols we had been passing up the line to throw overboard to lessen the load. Seems like he always wanted some pistols. We swam for about thirty minutes and somebody hollered, 'Ship ahoy!' I couldn't see any ship but it was a British destroyer or submarine patrol boat. We could hear the Limeys hollering, 'Shoot the bastards, they're Krauts!' We kept shouting, 'American paratroopers! American paratroopers!'

"I have a great warm feeling in my heart for the English. They fished us out of the briny depths, gave us grog (we were all frozen), and extended such hospitality as was available on D-Day at very early morning (0100 A.M.)."

With the lead plane down in the Channel, the task of lighting Drop Zone "C" fell to Lieutenant Roy H. Kessler's group and also the 3rd Battalion stick representing the 501st Regiment under the command of Lieutenant Charles M. Faith. Units scheduled to land in this area were the 506th Parachute Regiment minus its 3rd Battalion, which had a key assignment farther to the south, and 3rd Battalion of the 501st Parachute Regiment and the Division Headquarters personnel. Overlapping the DZ "C" was the glider landing area known as LZ "E", on which the two glider lifts were scheduled to drop. (See map on page 32.)

Adversity continued to plague these pathfinders. The plane carrying Lieutenant Faith's group strayed in the approach across the Cotentin Peninsula and dropped the men approximately three miles southwest of the intended landing area. Lieutenant Kessler's crew had, in addition to the Eureka set and several lights, an initially new radar gadget known as the "BUPS" beacon. This had been especially prepared for the pathfinders by the British Branch Radiation Laboratories, and was used as the center point navigational aid for the entire division. All lost planes were to guide on this device and drop their loads of troopers on DZ "C." However, the delicate antenna was broken on landing, and the set was not functional.[2]

Kessler's stick landed in the middle of the intended DZ and was able to set up a radar set and part of the light aids at that point, which was only one-quarter mile from the intended point for signaling. It was fortunate that two Eureka sets were part of the equipment on each drop zone because one of the men assigned to Kessler wasn't able to get his equipment in operation. PFC Terrence "Salty" Harris jumped with one of the ultra-high frequency homing devices. However, he did not get it off his harness to set it in operation. German soldiers spotted him and kept him on the run.[3]

Two other sticks of pathfinders dropped on DZ "C" at approximately the same time. Their assignment was to prepare the landing site for the two glider lifts scheduled for 0400 A.M. and 2100 P.M. One of these groups led by Lieutenant Don S. Driver of the 502nd Parachute Infantry Regiment had difficulty in orienting its position. One of the officers moved toward a farmhouse to find the correct location of his men. Nearby, a dog barked furiously. To prevent enemy troops in the area from determining his location, the officer grabbed the animal and cut his throat with a sharp knife.[4]

According to Lillyman, "This stick proceeded to the field selected for the landing zone, and with their halifane lights, laid out the runway for the gliders. The first glider that landed was piloted by Colonel Mike Murphy and carried Brigadier General Don F. Pratt, the assistant commander of the 101st Airborne Division. The glider landed shortly before 0400 A.M. Unfortunately, one of the early gliders landed directly on top of the lights, destroying each one of the carefully laid out indicators. The remaining gliders had to land in the moonlight without field markings."

Two members of Lieutenant Driver's stick of pathfinders related their experiences. "The pilot must have slowed down to minimum flying speed," observed T/5 Richard Lisk. "My jump was perfect, but I had on so much equipment that I landed off balance, on one foot, fracturing it. I crawled into a ditch beside a hedgerow. The other fellows, passing by later, had to leave me to proceed to the drop zone designated for the gliders. On being left alone, I remained quiet and hidden. I held my breath as German soldiers passed by a short time later. As they passed within arm's reach, they kicked dirt in my face. When daylight came, I destroyed my radar set. Later on, a medic came and gave me a hypo of morphine in my leg to deaden the pain. With the anesthetic action of the drug, I was able to walk. I found several glider pilots, and with them acting as scouts and points, I later found my regimental headquarters, which I joined."

"I had a hard landing among the cows in a pasture just north of Vierville," remembered Private Howard "Hic" Stiles. "I had no difficulty getting out of my chute. The entire stick assembled quickly. T/5 Dick Lisk injured his ankle and was left in a hedgerow. We brought in the first group of gliders, near Vierville, at approximately 0400 hours. I recall seeing General Pratt's glider crash in the hedgerow."

Three planeloads of pathfinders had been scheduled to drop as part of a team commanded by Captain Frank L. Brown of the 501st Regiment. They were to set up their aids before the drops of the main body scheduled to land on DZ "D." The flight encountered sporadic flak several miles from the scheduled drop area. One of the sticks managed to hit right on the button while the other two planes jumped the men short, landing them just to the northwest of St. Come-du-Mont.

Somehow the Germans had sensed that the fields in the Drop Zone "D" area might be used as an airborne landing area and had prepared an ambush with machine guns and mortars zeroed in on it from three sides. Flares were in a ready position for release and a large farm building had been soaked with gasoline and waited only the application of a torch. Meanwhile the well-concealed and dug-in Germans waited in the hedgerows.

The pathfinders had been warned to avoid enemy contact if at all possible and to concentrate on their job of guiding the planes. The trailblazers came floating down to find fire playing on the fields as they landed. Using hand grenades, one group managed to creep forward and silence two of the machine guns without getting hurt themselves. Flares began to pop overhead lighting the entire area so no one dared move for fear of being observed. At the sound of more planes approaching from the west, the Germans applied the torch to the building. The holocaust lighted the entire area with its dancing flames, dwarfing any beacons the men might have lighted for the approaching planes. Because they were pinned down in the corners of the hedgerows, the pathfinders did not get the lights rigged in a "T" and had to rely on the radar set to "home-in" its serials of troop carrier planes.[5]

Almost half of the three-stick team of pathfinders to drop in Drop Zone "D" were killed or captured in the early fighting and yet DZ "D" was to receive the most concentrated drop of troopers for the entire division.

Aboard one of the planes which dropped its pathfinders short was Lieutenant Albert E. Watson from the 1st Battalion of the 501st. He said, "I landed somewhat north of St. Come-du-Mont and collected five or six men from my stick. My group set up one pathfinder radar set." A member of that stick, and also one of the men collected by Lieutenant Watson was Corporal Joe Haller. He had difficulty getting out of his chute because the risers were tangled in the parachute harness. He was one of the men carrying radar sets and had this to say: "I ran to a hedgerow after getting free of my chute and set up the Eureka radar set. It sent out a signal 'D' in Morse Code (—..). This was the signal for our drop zone. Our air transport had difficulty. It dropped our men too far apart for effectiveness."

One member of Lieutenant Charles Faith's misdropped 3rd Battalion stick described his experience. "We were fired on by the Germans, but not in extensive force," explained Private Spencer E. Everly. "We caught them off guard. The jump was all right, but I was really scared. We landed approximately two and a half miles from Carentan, I headed for the hedgerows, and began looking for other members of my stick. I located Alvin Haux, Lester Hunt, Sergeant John O'Shaughnessy, and Lieutenant Charles Faith. Stanley Suwarsky came down in a tree. He was shot without having an opportunity to get out of his chute."

Private Leonard Newcomb, pathfinder from the 501st's 2nd Battalion stick was captured. As he remembered it, "We were just leaving an area of heavy flak; the Germans had sent up a lot of fire several miles west of the DZ, when the sky lit up again as the green light went on for us to jump. Like the popping of corn, the shots were going through the chute. I thought the jump was low, yet, it seemed long in getting down. I landed within fifty yards of an enemy machine gun.

"I got up and ran for the hedgerow, approximately fifteen yards distant from the position of the machine gunner. I met Red Larson and two fellows from the 3rd Battalion stick. We were able to set up radar equipment, but could not assemble together due to the heavy concentration of small-arms fire from a German platoon operating near us. I watched the planes of the regiment pass overhead. The jumpers landed on the opposite side of the road from our position. We were unable to get off the field on which we dropped. Larson had me watch the machine gun crew while he attempted to find a way out of the area, and to locate Captain Brown, our stick leader."[6]

The area around St. Come-du-Mont was ringed with fortifications and therefore had a heavy concentration of enemy troops. Several of the fields bore anti-airborne obstacles. One of the troopers who jumped with the 501st Battalion pathfinder group was Private John D. Mishler, from Baker Company. His assignment was to serve as a security guard. He remembered, "My assignment was to prevent Kraut interference with the pathfinders while they set up their equipment for marking the DZ. I came down through the top of a tree. As 14th man in the stick, I landed near flooded ground in the vicinity of St. Come-du-Mont. With tracers streaming low over the tall grass, I cut myself loose and headed for the hedgerows. The radar equipment was not placed in operation by our stick. Several of our men were captured, but were released by our own men, and reached the company area prior to us."

Summarizing the work of the pathfinders on this drop zone, Captain Lillyman wrote, "The team that dropped on Drop Zone 'D' just north of Carentan, landed between the German outpost line and their main line position. This team consisted of the 501st, and the 3rd Battalion of the 506th Regiment with its attached security personnel. All three, were in a 'helluva mess,' but they did a wonderful job. Credit should be given to the 440th and 441st Groups of the Troop Carrier Command. Using radar only, and no lights because of the tenuous position, forty-seven aircraft delivered their personnel to the intended DZ. This totaled more than the other two drop zones combined."

The various pathfinder teams had accomplished their missions, to the best of their abilities; this, under most trying conditions. They now awaited the main body of parachutists and glider men to become once again a part of their regular units from which they had been "on leave" to serve as vanguard of the invasion.

CHAPTER 3

The Flight Across

As the pathfinders were the vanguard for the main body of paratroopers, so the paratroopers were the vanguard for the giant armada moving across the Channel from the English coast to Normandy. As the pathfinders set up guiding devices for the parachute drops, the paratroopers were to form a front beyond the enemy lines to destroy their communications and gun emplacements, and to harass and distract the enemy as the Allied armada moved in on the beaches.

The preparation period for the paratroopers has already been recorded in a previous chapter. The flight across was now under way.

Technician 5th Grade George Koskimaki, flying with the commanding general, Brigadier General Maxwell D. Taylor of the 101st Airborne Division, remembered, "At 2245 P.M., our plane began moving down the runway, gathered momentum rapidly and gently lifted from the concrete surface. The rest of the planes in our serial followed at seven-second intervals until the entire group was airborne. Our serial numbering 45 aircraft carried the 3rd Battalion of the 501st Parachute Infantry Regiment and six plane loads of division headquarters, signal company, and division artillery parachutists, including Brigadier General Anthony C. McAuliffe, the artillery commander. Three planes were filled with supply bundles which air force personnel would release over the drop zone."

"We took off about 10:00 P.M. on the night of June 5th," recalled Sergeant Louis E. Truax. "As we circled the field gaining altitude and joined other echelons, pyrotechnics were fired at regular intervals. They signaled the number of units airborne to the leaders of the serial."

Corporal Koskimaki described the flight pattern: "The planes continued to circle over the general area until all 45 ships were airborne and in formation. Our plane served as the point for the serial. The planes flew in V's of nine planes. The center plane of the three lead planes of each 9-plane group served as its immediate point. Wing lights were on and it was a beautiful spectacle to behold through the open doorway. (Doors were removed from some of the aircraft prior to takeoff while doors on other aircraft remained closed, since sticks of jumpers elected to keep them on until enemy territory was approached.) What had occurred over our field was also taking place over six other fields in Southern England and the 9th Air Force Troop Carrier Squadron began moving 6,670 parachutists of the Screaming Eagle Division on its missions in France. Other serials from farther north would bring in the 82nd Airborne Division and the British 6th Airborne Division. A total of some 17,000 paratroopers landed during the night.

"Our serial took its place in the line of flight which extended over two hundred miles in length. It took well over two hours to drop their anxious sky troopers before they began their return trip to home bases in England. At 0021, the first of the 101st serials crossed the southern coast of England. The sky train of C-47's flew at an elevation of 500 feet in crossing the Channel to escape radar detection. They climbed to 1500 feet as they crossed the coast of France and slanted down to 700 feet for the drop—at least that was standard operating procedure."

The recollections of the flight across the Channel depended on the position of the man in his stick of jumpers.[1] Those near the end of the stick sat far forward and saw little of what was occurring outside the planes. Blackout curtains had been drawn over the windows. Those who flew in planes which had the doors in place observed far less. These are the recollections of men who were in position to look down or out of open doorways as the aircraft started their cross-Channel runs.

One of the jumpmasters, Lieutenant Harold Young remembered well the flight across the English Channel. "I stood in the open doorway with Libby.[2] There seemed to be thousands of ships below us and the sky was full of C-47's. Somehow we knew that we had fighter cover and high above the big bombers were out on diversionary actions."

Staff Sergeant Elden F. Hermann was the radio communications chief of the 502nd's regimental headquarters. He recalled "looking down at all the ships. I just couldn't visualize that there were that many ships in the world."

PFC James "Pee-Wee" Martin wrote, "The night was beautiful. There were a few stratus clouds drifting about here and there. The moon silhouetted the planes around us so that they seemed to dance on the whitecaps of the Channel below us. The fiery exhaust of our engines reminded me strangely of a blast furnace. The many dark forms scattered in the choppy waters of the Channel were, I realized, part of the world's greatest armada of ships waiting to belch forth thousands of troops into Hitler's 'impregnable' wall, and I suddenly realized that they were waiting and depending on us."[3]

"The moon was shining real bright as we started across the Channel," said Sergeant William Ashbrook. "Sitting beside me was Colonel Gerald Higgins, at that time our division chief-of-staff. I had fallen asleep and he punched me to wake up and look at the sight below. There were so many boats in the Channel that it seemed as if you could step out of the plane and walk to France on top of the boats."

"I was the jumpmaster in my plane," reminisced Captain William Brubaker. "The trip over the Channel was uneventful. My stick was relaxed and they appeared to accept it as just another night jump. I could see the ships on the Channel blinking signal lights and thought to myself that we were on course and this jump would not be like the one in Sicily."[4]

What thoughts ran through men's minds? "While the planes were droning on, I kept wondering how I, a Washington real estate clerk, had wound up in this situation," reflected Sergeant Schuyler Jackson, a demolitions expert. "In all of my years of growing up, my wildest dreams never included flying into France at night to blow up some enemy gun emplacements."[5]

Private Frank Styler, a communications soldier with the 501st wrote: "Strange, but I didn't sleep in the plane as I usually did when we had some time to spend in the air, nor did I talk to any of the boys. I just sat there and smoked an endless chain of cigarettes, and kept thinking of our Dorothy all the time. (One of the other boys in my plane told me later he also had thought about his sister.) When we got over the Channel the order was given that there would be no more smoking, and so we waited anxiously."[6]

"Most of us were thinking of our loved ones at home and wondering what they were doing and how they would take the first news of the invasion when it was broadcast to them tomorrow," wrote T/5 George Koskimaki.[7] Home dominated his thoughts: "For some reason I wondered what they would be doing at the exact moment we were scheduled to jump. I guessed it would be about 8:00 in the evening. This meant Dad would be fast asleep on the couch in the living room with the radio going full blast—he seemed to sleep most soundly in the midst of noise. Mom would be mending socks for my ambitious hard hiking younger brothers, who wore out their socks faster than she could replace or repair them on their numerous fishing trips. Sister Milly would be with her girlfriend Betty listening to the latest records. The boys would be in the backyard tinkering with their version of a World War II hot rod known as the 'Blue Beetle'—that was all they could do with gasoline being rationed. I thought of a particular girlfriend in Detroit who would set her students straight on the importance of this date when she met them in her classroom on the morrow."

Another soldier was already thinking ahead to a reunion with his army buddies after the war. "I thought of the reunion idea of Colonel Wolverton, our battalion commander, to meet in Kansas City, Missouri, on the first D-Day anniversary after the war," recalled T/5 John Gibson.

Some of the men were sitting on so-called "powderkegs"—and they knew it. "I was stewing about the Compound C-2 (a new high explosive) in the equipment bundles slung under the belly of the plane," said PFC Ed Slizewski. "I hoped it wouldn't be hit by enemy fire before it was released."

Occasionally a pilot gave a jumpmaster the impression he wasn't too well versed in his work. Captain Sammie Homan had stewed about what he had observed of his pilot just prior to takeoff. "The plane commander had asked me what those 'funny looking bundles' were slung from the bomb racks under the plane. He had never dropped fully equipped paratroopers before and I lost all confidence in him."

Private William A. "Shep" Howell remembers only that he "worried about dying while sitting there in silence flying across the Channel."

General Eisenhower had missed some of the marshaling areas on his visits during the day and so mimeographed copies of his message were read just prior to and during the flight in some of the planes. PFC Clair Mathiason remembered, "Our Lieutenant Joe Doughty read the message from General Eisenhower and there was very little if any comment." PFC William Druback also remembered the message. "The jumpmaster," he explained, "read a letter to us from General Eisenhower. It was something like a pep talk given by a coach."

And how did the general while away his time? Lieutenant Eugene D. Brierre, who served as assistant jumpmaster in the lead plane of his serial with General Taylor, observed, "This was the fifth jump coming up for General Taylor. He placed a small mattress pad on the floor of the plane, laid himself down, and went to sleep."

Needling provided a pastime in one of the planes. Private Richard E. Frame, a mortarman from the 501st's 1st Battalion Headquarters Company, recalled this episode: "We had a guy named 'Grandma' Wilson in our plane. He had a bugle attached to his harness that was to be used for assembly purposes. The guys were needling him good naturedly and told him the Germans would center their fire on him and the sound of the horn and for that reason they wouldn't go near him when he started blowing it. The poor guy got all shook up. When we hooked up later he left the bugle on the bucket seat. One of the crew members noticed it and called out in a loud voice, 'Who left this horn on the seat?' Poor Wilson had to own up, connect it to his gear and then jumped with it."

Private Frame recalled another episode: "Petrak was playing his mouth organ—the same tune over and over again." Private Chester Brooks was a member of the same stick of jumpers. He related, "I was number '1' in the door and remember seeing the armada below. I also remember Anton Petrak, who later became mess sergeant, playing his harmonica and hitting me on the arm every so often saying, 'We're gonna get 'em, aren't we?' I said, 'Yes,' but was trying to conjure up more pleasant thoughts."

A box of candy made its rounds in one plane. Staff Sergeant Robert E. Kiel said, "I had a full two-pound box of Fanny Farmer chocolates which I passed around several times and of the eighteen men in the stick, the top layer wasn't finished off. I relished the remainder some hours after bailing out."

"I recall the crew chief was giving his passengers cigarettes and candy. Maybe he thought it was our last. He was a pretty good Joe though," reminisced T/4 Nick J. Cortese.

For the most part the men sat in silence. Staff Sergeant Merville Grimes related, "The cigarettes glowed in the darkened plane and the men were quiet."

A description of the flight path is given by T/5 Koskimaki from his position in the Number "1" plane of the 13th Serial. "Our flight flew slightly west of south for fifty-seven miles to a marker boat stationed in the Channel. Here the other aircraft guided on the lead plane in each group as it turned sharply in a 90-degree bank to the left (east) and flew for a distance of fifty-four miles to the west side of the Cotentin (Cherbourg) Peninsula. At this point, it was a distance of about twenty-five miles to the Screaming Eagles drop zones which were nearest the east coast. The trip took slightly less than an hour from the southern coast of England to our DZ's. Looking out through the windows (by raising the blackout curtains) of the unlighted cabins or through the open doorway, one could see the wonderful spectacle of the countless red and green riding lights on the wingtips of the planes. The late rising moon was there waiting for us. Its travels had been predicted with accuracy for hundreds of years."

The planes had to fly past the Jersey and Guernsey Islands off the western coast of Normandy. Both were fortified by the enemy. "We flew near the islands off the Cherbourg Peninsula," Lieutenant Sumpter Blackmon recalled. "The V-formation of those C-47's was really beautiful. I could have pitched a grenade on the one just outside our door." PFC Robert Cahoon added, "The pilot sent back word when we were over the two islands off the coast."

The planes were getting close to the mainland. Tension was building up in the plane crews and the sticks of jumpers. "A plane crewman woke me several times to ask if I wanted a cigarette," said PFC Earle Steele. Another private, Leo Runge, a demolitions expert with 501st Regimental Headquarters, stated, "I was in the lead plane of our serial and Colonel Johnson paced up and down the length of the ship, swearing in his delightful way about what we were going to do to the 'lousy Nazi Bastards.' "

Drowsiness was explained by T/5 Hugh Pritchard: "Before takeoff, we had each been given two anti-motion sickness pills to take. Mine had made me drowsy and I went to sleep in the plane. When I woke up, I managed to dig out a cigarette, then asked the man next to me for a match. His reply—'There will be no more smoking as we are approaching the French coast.' I thought, Oh brother! I'm a long way from home."

"One guy fell asleep and toppled over onto the floor with his full equipment on," said Sergeant Clifton Marshall. "It sounded like two cars meeting head on."

"Usually on these rides everybody goes to sleep and tonight I had to fight the desire," Lieutenant Richard Winters remembered. "I had to stay awake so I'd be able to think and react quickly. But those pills seemed to slow down feelings of emotion. A few of us joined in with Private Hogan. He made an attempt to get a song going. The song was soon lost in the roar of the motors. I fell to making a last prayer. It was a long, hard, and sincere prayer that never really did end for I just continued to think and pray during the rest of the ride.

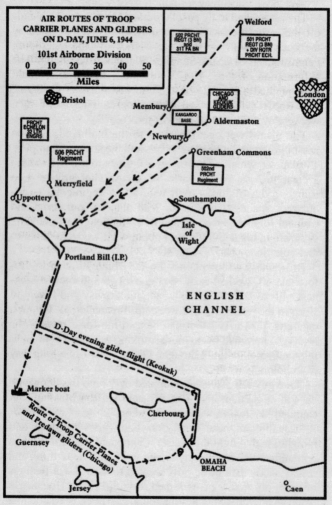

Welford

502 PRCHT REGT (3 BN) and 311 FA BN

501 PRCHT REGT (3 BN) + DIV HQTR PRCHT ECH.

London

Bristol

Membury

CHICAGO AND KEOKUK GLIDERS

KANGAROO BASE

Aldermaston

PRCHT ECHELON 321 LTH ENGRS

Newbury

Greenham Commons

506 PRCHT Regiment

502nd PRCHT Regiment

Merryfield

Uppottery

Southampton

Isle of Wight

Portland Bill (I.P.)

ENGLISH CHANNEL

D-Day evening glider flight (Keokuk)

Marker boat

Cherbourg

Route of Troop Carrier Planes and Predawn gliders (Chicago)

Guernsey

OMAHA BEACH

Jersey

Caen

Map 4

'Twenty minutes out' came back from the pilot and the crew chief took off the door. I stood up and hooked up, went to the door and had a look—all water, nice formation, no fire yet."[8]

The gravity of the situation was sometimes broken by a clown. PFC Walter "Smokey" Gordon remembered, "Some of the men dozed and there was little talk during the flight. I do recall that 'Skinny' Sisk, from West Virginia, asked in a rather loud voice, 'Do any of you bastards want to buy a good wristwatch?' This eased some of the tension that was mounting in our plane. Skinny could always be counted on to get a laugh when it was most desired."

"In our plane everyone was solemn and quiet," said PFC Leopaul C. Sepcich. "Then all of a sudden, one guy, Homer Estes, got up and made believe he was playing a guitar and started to sing. Then everyone was 'OK' and got jolly."

The planes were now nearing the mainland and enemy-held territory. T/5 Koskimaki remembered, "Jumpmaster Legere had been down on one knee peering to the front from the edge of the door. He now called out, 'Here comes France!' This seemed to arouse several troopers who had been sleeping. This included General Taylor, who now arose from his mattress bed in the aisleway."

Corporal Ray Taylor was the jumpmaster in his plane and had a good view from the open door. He said, "I remember coming in low and could see the whitecaps on the water. I do recall seeing something that looked like fencing sticking out of the water as we approached the shoreline."

PFC Guerdon "Mugsie" Walthall wrote, "It really gave you a wonderful feeling when we looked down and saw the coast of France slipping by under us. Our first sergeant was sitting next to me, and I almost had to laugh when he hollered out with his southern drawl, 'By God, we is here!' "[9]

CHAPTER 4

Bill Lee—Geronimo—Let's Go!

After arriving "on the deck" to escape radar detection, the planes were to rise to 1,500 feet to be out of range of small-arms fire. In flight over the Channel, visibility had been perfect. Now as the planes approached the mainland, an unexpected blanket of fog confronted the pilots.

Lieutenant Harold Young of the Engineers had this description of the first part of the flight over enemy-held territory: "About the time we reached the coast of France we entered a huge bank of clouds. This seemed to last for hours (actually seconds or minutes) and when we came out of them we were all alone. I remember my amazement. Where had those hundreds of C-47's gone? Our pilot immediately dropped down close to the ground and the French countryside looked like it did on the air photos."

T/5 George Koskimaki also remembered the clouds. "Shortly after crossing the coast, we began to penetrate cloud cover which appeared like a heavy blanket of fog. This caused the planes in tight formations to increase their interval to prevent collisions. Occasionally the planes burst free of their foggy shrouds and flew in bright moonlight and once more plunged back into the clouds as if we were playing hide-and-seek with the moon."

The men who had positions at the open doorways were able to see the action developing to the front. One of these, Lieutenant Elmer F. Brandenberger related, "After the fog cleared I called Sergeant Singleton to the door and pointed out what looked like thousands of Roman candles going off in the air over the mainland. I told him to 'pucker up' because we were going to be in the middle of it pretty quick."

Sergeant Richard Johnson had been standing directly behind the two pilots for most of the trip. From this vantage point he observed, "As we started across the Peninsula, looking out the front of the plane we could see large fires[1] burning in a straight line, leading the planes to the DZ's."

Lt. Colonel Benjamin Weisberg, commanding officer of tile 377th Parachute Field Artillery Battalion, was in the lead plane of the 502nd Regiment with its commander. His battalion was to give close artillery support in the attacks on the coastal guns. He related, "I stood in the door with Van Horn Moseley, watching the Kraut ack-ack fire coming up at us in long sweeping pastel arcs. We could almost see the gun muzzles in the bright moonlight. The flight patterns broke badly; our pilot put the C-47 into a shallow power dive."

First encounters with enemy anti-aircraft fire (flak) had lasting memories with the men.

According to Corporal John Marohn, "Tracers from the ground fire made a zig-zag pattern in appearance almost thick enough to walk down on." Private Pat Winters wrote, "There was some flak and the tracers from the anti-aircraft batteries seemed peculiar—the way they seemed to be slow moving and arching in their flight upward." PFC Jim "Pee-Wee" Martin added, "The sky was full of golden, orange, and red blossoms of fire, and long serpentine strings of heavy caliber tracers snaked their way up to us and beat a hail-like tattoo as they fingered the tail and ranged the length of the ship."

Describing the action in his first letter, Lieutenant Winters relived the moments: "It's 0110 A.M., the red light is on. Ten minutes out, and all is quiet. Ah, there's some anti-aircraft fire—blue, green, and red tracers coming up to meet us. Gee, it seems to come slowly. They're pretty wild with it. There, it looks like they might have hit one of our planes. Look out! They're after us now. No good—shooting straight up at us, as they start right out for you but seem to make a curve and fall to the rear. Now they're heading us—coming close. You can hear them crack as they go by. There, they hit our tail."

Many of the planes were hit by flak. This was well remembered by the men. T/5 Edward H. Neils said, "We encountered heavy flak over the Peninsula. One piece came up through the floor and came out through the roof. I could see the sky." Sergeant Robert "Rook" Rader was lucky to live long enough to make the jump. "The order to 'Stand up' and 'Hook up' saved my life," he wrote. "After getting up, a shell passed through the metal bucket seat where I had been seated. The jump light was shot off from its position over the door." Lieutenant Harry F. Welsh, from the same company, was probably riding in the same plane with Sergeant Rader. "The flak was heavy. Fire from a machine gun shot the jump signal box off the door of our plane," he related.

During the briefings of the plane crews in England, the pilots of the troop carrier planes had been directed to take no evasive action. They had been told to expect little or no anti-aircraft fire from the ground for it was expected that Allied bombers would have destroyed the anti-aircraft installations by drop time. Fighter planes were to fly cover and protect the troop planes against sneak attacks by enemy planes.

Explaining the unexpected change of events, Private Robert Mawhinney stated, "Our pilot veered off course when he encountered heavy anti-aircraft fire." Sergeant Chester Pentz wryly remarked, "As you may know, quite a few pilots got 'buck fever' when we approached the drop zones." Major Allen Ginder confirmed Pentz's recollection by writing, "We had to be careful because there were planes flying above us and flying crossways beneath us and there were fireworks all about us."

"Our plane was flying low and suddenly went straight up to miss a number of other planes which crossed suddenly in front of us," explained PFC Donald Wilson. "We were all 'stood up' and hooked up and it really caused quite an uproar to get back in position so we could make our jump."

The standard procedure for planes dropping parachutists at night was as follows: jump instructions were relayed backward from the lead plane or point of the serial. The radio operator in the lead plane flashed a red Aldis lamp through the astrodome to the following planes. The point plane in the next Vee would pick up the signal and flash it to his group and to the following point. The jump signal was given in the same fashion using a green Aldis lamp. The planes that followed flashed the green light as they passed over the same area.

Not only was it hazardous flying over the peninsula, but pilots had to swerve and climb rapidly while the men were standing and waiting to jump. Captain William J. Waldmann, surgeon for the 3rd Battalion of the 501st Regiment, remembered, "We were preparing to jump when the plane suddenly speeded up (due to stacking up, as we were told later by the pilot), throwing us to the back of the plane. We jumped at high speed while the pilot was trying to return to the drop zone."

The enemy used searchlights and flares in the vicinity of some of the drop zones to light the area. He had a well-lit "shooting gallery." PFC Frank P. Juliano remembered the searchlights well. "We were caught by searchlights and the anti-aircraft guns opened up on us," he wrote. "Our plane was hit several times. We felt like 'sitting ducks.' "

It was hardly a time to wax poetic but T/4 William House reflected on the strange beauty of the scene below: "What a beautiful sight the spotlights, flares, and tracers made! I remembered how I held my breath when a searchlight seemed to stop right on our door."

To avoid the tracers and ack-ack along with the glare of the searchlights, many of the pilots went "down on the deck" so to speak. PFC Wilbur Ingalls was one who remembered this when he recalled, "I looked out of the window as the plane roared along and yelled to the others that we wouldn't need the chutes as we were so close to the ground."

T/5 Koskimaki offered this description of the approach: "We were suddenly aware of thumping sounds off to either side and above as we began receiving our first taste of enemy fire. Now and then lines of tracers, reminding us of Roman candle spectacles on noisy 4th of July celebrations at home, would appear to be searching for aircraft in the sky. As a radioman, I have been issued a watch having a luminous dial so I might log accurately the times when vital messages were transmitted or received at night before channeling them to the proper recipients. Nearby members of our stick kept glancing at the time as I kept my wrist in a position so all might be able to observe the rapid movement of the minute and second hands as they raced around the dial.

"Flak was still following us but there was some advantage in being in the lead plane. The enemy gunners did not get an opportunity to zero-in on us as well as they did on the following planes. I suddenly noticed the red light appear on the panel over the open doorway and at that moment jumpmaster Lawrence Legere was the most important person in our group as he yelled, 'Get ready!' Heads came up and bodies went rigid as the troopers waited for the next command. 'Stand up!' Soldiers struggled to their feet with their heavy loads. Everybody was anxious to leave the confines of the plane.

"Next came the order to 'Hook up!' The snap of the anchor line fastener clicking into place could be heard the full length of the cabin. Each man made doubly sure he had hooked his static line to the cable running overhead down the center of the ceiling.[2]

"Next came the order to 'Check your equipment!' Each man checked the connections of the man directly in front of him to make sure all items were secure and would remain in place when he was jarred by the opening shock of the chute. The last man in the line was checked by the trooper he had just given assurance to. Above the roar of the engines could be heard the call, 'Sound off for equipment check!' From far forward could be heard, 'Sixteen-OK', 'Fifteen-OK', 'Fourteen-OK', right on down to General Taylor who bellowed, 'Two-OK!'

"Quickly followed the order, 'Stand in the door!' Every man now shuffled forward to a position behind the jumpmaster, who was crouched in the open doorway looking for landmarks. The members of the stick crowded in tightly behind him. Movement was now limited and no one would be able to react as an individual anymore. From now on the sixteen members of the stick reacted in unison."

Equipment out first

Many of the planes had door bundles which had to be man-handled out before the men jumped. Releasing them often caused delays in the drops.

"We had a delayed jump because a parachute-equipped mortar cart became lodged in the doorway and it took valuable time to get it clear," recalled Private Herbert Clark. "Two other planes were guiding on ours and all three dropped their men far south and east of the designated drop area."

Captain Robert H. Phillips, jumpmaster of his stick, recollected, "We had received the red light which was given two minutes prior to jumping. Sergeant Bealls, our operations sergeant, and I had the responsibility of dumping out ammunition and equipment bundles just before jumping ourselves. The lights were directly over the door. As we pushed a bundle close to the door, the cover to the parachute pack at one end was pulled loose. The parachute billowed in and out of the door. We desperately kicked the bundle out of the door, grabbed the next bundle and as it was in position I saw the green light go on—the signal to jump. I yelled the command 'Go!' and with that shoved the bundle out and dived after it."

As described earlier, Lieutenant "Legs" Johnson had been extremely upset because the bundles had been removed from the bomb racks beneath the plane to make room for special radar equipment. The special gear didn't matter, but the fact that the bundles were strung out along the aisle of the plane and had to be moved forward and out of the plane before the men jumped presented a gargantuan problem to Johnson. He explained, "Though lost on our run in, I agreed with the pilot over the intercom that we should go. We started pitching bundles out of the door. Imagine static lines hanging down, trying to retain the proper hold on the anchor cable, and shoving the bundles the length of the plane with your boots in the dark, and under very trying circumstances anyway. This plus being trussed up like Gulliver weighted down with chutes, hand grenades, tommy gun, ammunition, food, clothing, gas mask, binoculars, pistol, raincoat, entrenching tool, maps, and weighty apprehension. I decided the Naval observer should go first, and he had a helluva time getting his leg bundle out of the door. He did manage, however, and I was right behind him, shrieking and hollering like the rest of the idiots."

The emergency bell was ringing

Corporal Harry E. Mole described the action that took place in his plane: "We were standing up waiting to jump. Waiting again; this time the waiting was worse. The air was still rough and it was difficult to stand on our feet. I was being knocked about. Outside I could see shells which seemed to explode at the wingtips. I was really frightened. We were now flying at an altitude of about 700 feet and I could see the railroad tracks which indicated to me that we were close to our drop zone.

"I hoped it wouldn't be long now and if it were much longer I thought we would be shot down before we could jump. The red light flashed on. That was the pilot's signal that we were two minutes from the DZ.

"The emergency bell began to ring; a signal that meant everyone was to jump including the plane's crew. The lieutenant leading the stick shoved the equipment bundle out but it wedged in the door. Frantically I could hear them yelling to get the hell out. 'For God's sake, let's get out of here before it is too late!' Finally the bundle loosened and went out, followed by six troopers. I was the seventh. Incidentally, this was my thirteenth jump. I stepped into the door and was about to go out when the plane lurched and threw me past the opening, back toward the tail. I got to my feet quickly and grabbed the door's edge and pulled with all my might."

Two other men, apparently in the same plane gave descriptions that are similar, and all three men were from the same unit. Lieutenant George W. Sefton was the jumpmaster and the first man in the door. He said, "We had intense ground fire. The ship was hit. An equipment bundle stuck in the doorway. Never did get the green light—I jumped the stick on the red light."

PFC Jim Purifoy was near the tail end of the stick, so his recollections are a bit different because he was not in a position to view the events occurring outside the door. "Our plane was hit in the right engine as we crossed the Peninsula," Purifoy remembered. "The crew chief went to the pilot's compartment. The emergency bell was rung and everybody got out without an equipment check. I was worried about getting out because I was the seventeenth man."[3]

Two other men described aborted departures from a burning aircraft. As in the previous descriptions, both were in the same craft. "As soon as the red light came on, the tail caught fire and we leaped without dispatch," recalled Captain Thomas Mulvey. "The plane and crew were never found to my knowledge." Private Roy "Dutch" Zerbe was near the end of the stick for the jump. "I was the second to the last man out of the plane. Our craft crashed just after we got out. We landed close to Ste. Mère Eglise."

Delays! Delays!

There was a great deal of excitement in every plane, but some had more than their share—and the experiences were varied, often causing delays. Two men, one near the front of the stick, and the other as "pushmaster" and last man in the stick, seem to relate an experience which occurred in the same plane. Both men were from the same unit.

"Before getting the green light, I remarked at all the Roman candles arching up to meet us," recalled Corporal Richard W. Gleason. "I was number '4' in line and as I stood near the door, an Oak shell exploded under the left wing and the old '47 did a handstand on the right wingtip and I was thrown back across the cabin. There was a mad scramble to get out the door, but I was able to get there first, so didn't get tangled in any static lines. The green light came on as we reached the edge of the field. The first three out lit on the edge of that one and I lit on the far end of the same one as the ship leveled out."

Sergeant Louis E. Truax described his harrowing jump from the plane: "The front men were jumping. The first twelve men got out pretty close together. I was running down the aisle. Suddenly the plane was hit in the left wing by flak. The wing went straight tip. My left shoulder crashed into a window. With ammo, a 1903 Springfield rifle, 12 grenade launcher rounds, 2 cans of blood plasma, 2 cans of distilled water, gas mask, helmet, K-rations, sox, and miscellaneous other combat equipment, I must have weighed 225–250 pounds—stripped I weighed 130 pounds. I was surprised the window didn't break.

"The pilot was fighting to right the plane. When he succeeded, I was appalled at the view which greeted me—I was the only one standing. Four men lay in a tangled heap on the floor. I realized it was almost impossible for them to stand up with their equipment loads. Also that an absolute sequence had to be maintained or we'd have a glob of human hamburger dangling outside the door at 150 miles per hour. One man dived out the door head first. I stepped over the top of two men. The closest man to the door crawled out headfirst. I grabbed the ammo belt in the center of the man I thought next and gave him a heave out nose first. The next man made it crawling on his own power. I reached up and pulled the salvo switch, which released the machine gun and mortars attached to the bomb racks under the plane. Then I dived out."[4]

Jump training had not prepared Corporal Virgil Danforth for his delay in departure. "As we stood in the door, ready to jump," he later wrote, "our plane took a close one which threw me down in the door in such a way that my head was outside and my shoulder was inside and I was wedged in this position so I couldn't get up. With the help of the man behind me, I finally managed to dive headfirst out of the door. This seemed like hours but I'm sure it only took a few seconds." Corporal Ray Taylor was one of six men who jumped with heavy equipment in leg bags. "We were lined up in the first positions in the doorway. As first man, I was knocked backward into the plane by the force of a neighboring plane exploding in midair. One of its high-explosive bundles, which were suspended underneath the plane, blew up as a result of a direct hit."[5]

An unusual delay occurred in Corporal Harry Plisevich's plane. In a recording he made over the British BBC Overseas Broadcast in the summer of 1944, Plisevich related, "The first four or five men jumped over the drop zone but the next man had his reserve chute burst from its pack and the red light was turned on. When the situation cleared we were many miles from our field. We had to cut his reserve chute off before we jumped."

Casualties in the planes

Some troopers lay wounded in the planes after being hit by small-arms fire or by shrapnel. Orders were for all men to jump if they were physically capable.

PFC Guerdon Walthall recollected, "We heard what seemed to be gravel rattling against the tail of the plane. The craft rocked heavily and then the noise got louder, like balloons bursting. All of a sudden, one of the boys on the other side of the plane pitched forward on the floor. He had a hole through his helmet."

"They cut loose with the flak. As we approached the DZ, one of the fellows in front of me slumped to the floor," said Private Mike Nassif. "He had been hit. We got him to his feet; then our plane took a direct hit. We got him out of the door."

As Private Waylen "Pete" Lamb described his experience, "As we approached our drop zone I remember talking with Sergeant Stan Butkovich, another demolitions man. A few seconds later he was hit by some 20mm stuff that came through the deck of the plane. He was hit in the legs. Our stick leader, Lieutenant Ted Fuller, unhooked Buck from his place in the stick and we moved him to the first position in the door, sitting in the door with his feet outside. When the green light came on, Lieutenant Fuller gave ole Buck a shove and out he went."

Private Mike Ranney described an injury in his plane: "We had orders to jump unless we had broken limbs or severe body wounds. After we stood up, the fellow in front of me got hit and fell down. The plane was lurching as the pilot was taking evasive action—going damned fast too. I finally decided the fellow in front couldn't jump, so I had to unhook my static line and move it around in front of his snap on the cable and headed for the door. As I went out, I noticed that the jump light was dangling loose on its cable, still lighted, but just dangling. Everyone else had gone, so I came down pretty much alone."

Sometimes the delay was caused by the jumpmaster even though the crew members had given the signal to jump. Staff Sergeant John A. Kushner said, "We got the green light five minutes too soon. I saw nothing but black water below so I didn't jump the stick. The crew chief ran back—seemed panicky—told us to jump. When I saw land I gave the signal and away we went."

No warning light appeared in Captain George L. Lage's plane. The medical officer served with the 2nd Battalion of the 502nd Regiment. He wrote: "I was supposed to get a red light when two minutes away and a green light as a signal to jump. However, the red light never came on. I was just beginning to get worried about it as I knew it was time for it. I had been keeping track of time with my watch. The next signal was 'Go!' by the crew chief. This surprised me as we had not received our previous signals so we weren't quite ready to go. I rechecked with him and he said, 'Get out!'

"Then I saw chutes in the air, so I yelled back, 'Stand up, hook up, and let's get the hell out of here!' I tossed out the door load, tripped the bundles in the rack under the plane, yelled, 'Let's go!' and tumbled out into an inky blackness crisscrossed by tracer bullets."[6]

Take us back over land

Several of the planes didn't get the green light from their crews. The jumpmasters noted the English Channel below and sensed that the pilots were apparently heading back to England.

Captain Leo H. Schweiter was jumpmaster on board one of the Division Headquarters planes. He recollected, "I did not receive the green light. The aircraft was taking violent evasive action. It flew completely over the east coast of Normandy and apparently started to return to England. I told Colonel Tom Sherburne, who was jumping in the number 2 position, to stand fast and not jump under any circumstance as we were over water. Then I unhooked, made my way to the pilot and told him to turn around. After some argument he agreed and we started back. I told him to give us the green light after a certain number of seconds (I've forgotten the number) after he crossed the coastline. I calculated that this would bring us about to our DZ provided we were at the right latitude. Then I returned to my jumpmaster position and after a slight difficulty, Lieutenant Wilson and I pushed the bundles out, perhaps a second or two delay, then jumped on the green light."[7]

A similar incident occurred in Lieutenant Sumpter Blackmon's plane. He said, "I was standing in the door with the equipment bundle and could see the landmarks but felt no kick or tap from the number 2 man, Private Thurman Day, or from Sergeant George Adams. They were watching for the green light. Finally I began to see little whitecaps and all water. I was pulled from the door and told the pilot wanted to see me. The plane commander said, 'Lieutenant, we missed the DZ and are now over the Channel headed back to England. What shall we do?' I replied, 'Take us back over land and we'll get out.' I returned to the door telling the men that we were lost and to assemble on me. The pilot dived into a left turn. We fell around a little bit but stayed in the plane, which was just a little above the waves. As we came to the shoreline the pilot shot almost straight up. As he leveled off, I shoved the machine gun and ammo out and followed the bundle."

A plane carrying George Company personnel from the 501st Regiment also had a similar experience. PFC McIntyre Aiken recalled, "The sky was lit up and the planes split up when they hit the flak. Our plane was hit once. A piece of shrapnel hit Jim Goss in his backpack and knocked him out of his seat. We made a sharp dive down almost to treetop level. You could see the tracers pass right through the rear of the ship. We flew on for a ways and then one of the pilots came back and announced, 'I don't know where I am at.' We had only one radar plane (General Taylor's) with us, and we've lost sight of it. We're over land now. Do you want to jump, or do you want to go back to England?'

"We all answered in a chorus, 'We'll jump!'—and so we were dropped."

We never got the green light

An unusual experience was reported by two men who were members of the same stick of D-Day jumpers. Both asked to remain unidentified because of the nature of the story. The account of one of them is described as the men were preparing to jump. He said, "At last the moment arrived. The red light was on. We were told to stand up, hook up, and check equipment. Many of us said silent prayers. Then we waited. Flak got heavier and our plane lurched as we waited for the signal. There was a long pause but no signal flashed over the door. Then, a member of the flight crew said something to our jumpmaster and he told us we were lost and that we were going back to England. One trooper knew something was wrong. He kicked the door to the pilot's compartment, yelling at him to turn back toward Normandy, but it was too late—the door was locked." This frustrated trooper ended his account on a philosophical note. "We returned to our base, a dejected lot. We were told we would be going in another plane. Then we were told we were going seaborne, but all of us knew we'd miss the big show. Most of us were mad at the pilot for bringing us back. However, we must remember that the pilot could have flashed the green light anytime and we'd have our jump—or a long drink."

The second member who reported on this plane incident described it this way: "When we arrived over the coast of France, the ack-ack was already flying fast and then we went into a fog bank and we were inland a long way but over water. The pilot was hedgehopping much too low for us to bail out. He then turned around and before any of us in the plane could figure why he did not drop us, we were back over the

Channel on the east side of the Cotentin Peninsula and headed back to England."[8]

Bill Lee!

For most of the men the final moments before the jump were tense, anxious ones. T/5 George Koskimaki described the exit from his troop carrier plane into the awesome void below: "As the plane neared the drop zone and began to slow down, the moon broke clear of its shroud and lighted the area below. We seemed to be much lower than on previous jumps. (This impression may have been false because it was my first night jump and perhaps distances are deceiving in darkness.) Time stood still. It seemed like we had been standing there for ages—waiting—waiting—still no signal. Tracers continued to search for the plane. I glanced at my wristwatch which was clearly visible because my arm was overhead with the left hand firmly clutching the lower part of the snap fastener of the static line. The second hand actually seemed to be dragging as it approached 0126. Why doesn't the light change? Did we miss the drop zone? Maybe the pilot was hit. All these things flashed through my mind.

"As we stood waiting and watching over the shoulders of the others, a plane off to our right suddenly burst into flames. Just as we worried about the occupants of that plane, our green light suddenly appeared and the order came, 'Let's go!' We yelled 'Bill Lee!' almost in unison as we followed our jumpmaster out of the door."[9]

CHAPTER 5

Out of the Night Sky

As each man dropped from the night sky, he knew he was now alone to manage, if he could, his own survival. The speed of his plane as he jumped, the barrage of enemy fire, and for the most part, the location of his landing were beyond his control, but how he maneuvered his parachute and how he relaxed for the fall were, hopefully, within his own control. How did the survivors of this new-style invasion make their drop into Hitler's Fortress Europa? Their experiences were many and varied.

"Straight ahead I can see the lights set up on a jump field," wrote Lieutenant Richard Winters.[1] "Jesus Christ, there's the green light! We're down to 150 miles per hour and still eight minutes out. OK—let's go, Bill Lee, God damn—there goes my knee pack, and every bit of my equipment. 'Watch it, boy, watch it! Jesus Christ, they're trying to pick me up with that machine gun. Slip, slip, try to keep close to that leg pack. There—it landed beside that hedge. There's a road, trees—I hope I don't hit them.' Thump—well, that wasn't too bad. Now to get out of this chute."

T/5 George Koskimaki dropped as the 5th man in the 16-man stick in the lead plane of his serial. "I did a somersault between my two sets of risers (parachute straps which extend upward from the harness; two above each shoulder to which the lines extending to the panels of the parachute are connected)," he remembered. "Even though we were in the air floating free, I noticed that my risers were twisted and I had to reach higher to control the direction of my drop. Floating above enemy territory gave me contradictory feelings. I could see no one in the sky—I was all alone. The sound of the roaring engines was gone and suddenly there was the feeling that every gun in that part of Normandy was pointed in my direction."

Koskimaki continued: "I became aware of the colorful tracers reaching toward me like desperate fingers clawing upward. I heard men yelling to each other in a foreign language—and it didn't sound like French. Small-arms fire was snapping about me and the canopy. I looked up hopefully, noting that the chute was still filled with air though there were more openings than had been placed there by the manufacturer.

"I noted the movement of a white cow to my left as it raised its tail and raced to a more secluded part of the field. As the chute continued to drift slowly, the ground came up rapidly. The breeze carried me forward and into a perfect roll over my right shoulder and I found myself facing upward on my back with the chute still tugging at me impatiently. I turned, grabbed the forward risers, and pulled on them. This spilled the air from the canopy and it settled in a puffy heap. It seemed as if I had been in the air such a long time, but most estimates would place it at about 30 to 40 seconds. I lay there perfectly still for a moment—listening—and I thanked God for my safe deliverance."[2]

Intense activity sometimes left no room for fear. This was described by PFC "Pee-Wee" Martin: "The green light flashed on. The lieutenant disappeared. The next man fell down; and I waited until he crawled to the door and dove out. Then I stepped out to meet a ladder of flak and tracers. Thank God, I missed all the rungs on the way down. I can truthfully say that I wasn't afraid. I was so fascinated that there wasn't any room for fear. According to Martin, "The loneliest feeling in the world was when I hit the ground with not another soul near me. I lay on my back, painfully unbuckling my harness. Why it didn't occur to me to cut myself loose, I'll never know. Strings of tracers were knifing the air about 30 inches above the ground, leading one to believe it was safe to that height. The non-tracers were clipping the grass around me and belied that fact, so I proceeded to 'haul out' of there for a place I figured would be a little safer—the nearest hedgerow."

Demolitions officer Lieutenant Harold C. Young had just

flown over his objective, a railroad bridge. He was never to
see it again. As he explained it, "our pilot turned quickly to
avoid the heavy flak which came up to our front. His fear
may well have saved our lives. To minimize the possibility of
being shot down by machine-gun fire in the air, we fortunately were dropped at a very low altitude. My guess is that
we were not much over two hundred feet in the air. As a result the chutes popped open and we were almost immediately on the ground. I recalled my landing vividly. Fence
rows in Normandy are often six to eight feet wide and up to
five to six feet above the surrounding fields with fairly large
trees crowing on the fence row. These fields varied considerably in size. It was obvious that I was going to land in a field
about 100 by 250 yards in length and my eyes almost popped
out as I saw 40 to 50 shapes which I immediately assumed
were men and therefore German soldiers. It was one of the
best and easiest landings I ever made. The shapes turned out
to be about twenty cows which were completely oblivious of
the plane, the parachutes, the ack-ack, and machine guns and
entirely indifferent to me as I landed. They continued to
chew their cuds."

Lost equipment

The average parachutist carried from 125 to 150 pounds of
gear on his person, including the two parachutes. If the plane
slowed down to the normal dropping speed (110–120 mph.),
it was likely he retained his gear. If the plane traveled from
150 to 180 miles per hour—as was the case in a large number of the men reporting—part or all of the vital equipment
got to the ground long before the trooper set foot in France.

Lieutenant Elmer F. Brandenberger had been preoccupied
with fitting one of his men into a new chute when the first
one had been found to be defective. Brandenberger neglected
to break down his M-1 rifle to fit into his Griswold container.
He decided to jump with it cradled in his arms as he had
done on several previous jumps. He said, "On the 'go' signal
over the Drop Zone, I released two equipment bundles from
the para racks, shoved out the door bundle, led the stick out.

When I jumped the aircraft speed must have been at least 150 instead of the normal jumping speed. The opening shock tore the rifle from my grasp. I can still remember the thought flashing through my mind that it would hit some damned Kraut and bash in his head. It seemed as if I hit the ground almost as soon as I lost my rifle. I landed in the middle of an open field and as I lay on my back looking up to ascertain the direction of flight, I could see chutes blossoming out overhead and machine-gun tracers dancing among them like fireflies."

With a heavy pack attached to one leg, PFC Guerdon Walthall was in position near the door. He related, "The green light went on, and I got out of the door surprisingly fast. The plane didn't slow down a bit, and as a result, when my chute popped open, I thought it was torn in half. I felt a wrench on my leg. When I looked down, my leg pack was gone. I looked down and all I could see was tracers racing from every corner of every hedgerow and the boom of mortars and 88's on the field below. This was surprising as we were not supposed to run into enemy opposition on the jump field, but they sure had them covered. I saw a tracer go through the fellow below me and I really started sweating out getting hit before I reached the ground." Walthall was lucky. "I had a soft landing and got out of my chute in a hurry. I reached for my compass and remembered I had everything I owned (except my rifle and my trench knife) in my leg pack. The sky was now clouded over so I didn't know north from south."[3]

PFC Sherwood C. "John Scott" Trotter recalled, "About 0113 A.M., we began to go out of the door. The plane was traveling too fast; its course was erratic, and it was at an altitude too high for jumping—and we were several miles from our drop zone. The clouds were moving by rather rapidly. Part of the time it was dark and at other times bright moonlight. There was some shooting as I came down. My musette bag, with food, clothing, etc., ripped off on the opening shock. I also lost a complete .30 caliber air-cooled machine gun (I was a gunner for 3rd Platoon) which was in one of those bags the English had devised. It had been tied to one leg and the bag also contained a couple belts of machine-gun ammo. I landed on a hard-packed sand road in the town square of a small French village."

Radioman Robert Ryals jumped with his battalion commander, Lieutenant Colonel Julian Ewell. He said, "I jumped with an SCR-300 radio in a leg pack. It broke loose from my harness on the jump because the plane was going too fast."

Staff Sergeant Nick Calabrese from the G-2 Section of Division Headquarters related much the same story. "I lost my musette bag, maps, and SOI along with some drafting stuff on the jump. I think it tore loose after the opening shock of the chute."

Landing with heavy equipment

A trooper who jumped with a leg bag was usually assigned a position near the front of the stick due to the cumbersome weight of the bag and its contents. The trooper lifted his right leg, with its forty- to seventy-pound bag over the threshold. Gravity took care of the rest. He hung on to two straps on the top of the bag. Gloves were worn to prevent the fingernails from being torn off as the chute suddenly jerked the parachutist as it popped open. If he managed to hang on to the bag, it remained with his person. After the chute had opened, the trooper pulled a small rip cord which permitted the bag to drop approximately twenty feet to the end of a rope attached to his harness. Swinging like a pendulum, it preceded the chutist to the ground—but he was free of the cumbersome load. Sometimes the drop was so close to the ground the trooper had no time to concentrate on releasing the bundle, or it became lodged, dangling on the toe of the boat and in this fashion the trooper descended.

Sergeant Ted Vetland was the last man out (number 18) and had to climb to the door which was near the rear of the plane because the craft was diving for safety. He said, "I hit the ground in about five seconds after my chute opened. I had a bag of ten mortar shells strapped to my leg. I never had a chance to release them on a 20-foot rope tether tied to my waist."

With his knees knocking badly, T/5 Gordon King had a

difficult time standing in the plane. He related, "Luckily, I was number '2' man with a full leg bag so I didn't have to worry too much about the plane getting hit but I worried anyway. The jump was fine but too low. I never got the leg bag off until I hit the ground. It was heavy—almost fifty pounds with a padded SCR-300 radio and an extra battery and my ammunition in it. Strangely I had no difficulty getting it off nor was I injured."

Communications men were often loaded down with cumbersome equipment. One of them, Corporal Richard W. Gleason, described the remarkable load he carried on his jump. "I was really loaded down. I had a leg pack—I don't recall everything I carried in it, but I had an SCR-536 radio, seven sets of batteries, three days' K-rations, smoke grenades, hand grenades, shovel, two canteens, first aid kit, bandoleers of ammo, M-1 assembled and loaded, gas mask, musette bag, two identification panels, an Aldis lamp, bayonet, flares, and launcher—I could hardly move. When my chute opened, the jolt flipped my helmet down over my eyes, but I caught it in my hands and slid it back in place. I tried to untie my leg pack, but the knot jammed and my efforts were to no avail. The ground was coming up fast, and as usual I somehow turned around and was coming in backward. It kind of scattered my equipment in the direction I was going, but landing backward kept me from getting hurt. I unbuckled my harness, picked up my gear, hooked everything in place and headed for a hedgerow about thirty yards away."

Landing situations

Normandy offered many types of landing situations for the Screaming Eagles of the 101st Airborne Division. Men landed in pastures, plowed fields, grain fields, orchards, and hedgerows. They landed at the base of anti-glider poles (Rommel's asparagus), in tall trees, and small trees. They landed on rooftops, in cemeteries, town squares, backyards, paved roads, and in roadside ditches. They landed in canals, rivers, bogs, and flooded areas.

The men had been directed to stay away from trees and

anti-glider poles in their drops. This was difficult even when the jumps were from the normal heights of 700 to 800 feet. With most of the D-Day jumps being made from about the four hundred foot level—and from planes which failed to slow to the normal drop speed—and under enemy fire—a soldier didn't often have a chance to choose his landing site with care.

There were many landings into trees. T/4 Nick Cortese related how he untangled himself from the branches of "his" tree: "I landed in the biggest tree in Normandy (so I thought). What a tangled mess! My leg pack containing an SCR-300 radio was in one part of the tree while I was farther down in the branches. About fifty yards away a haystack burned fiercely and some distance from that was an enemy machine-gun nest. The gunner was firing away from me at other planes and paratroopers and apparently didn't see me. After what seemed like hours, I cut myself loose from my harness and climbed down my jump rope."

PFC Paul "Buck" Rogers related the following: "I landed in a tall tree at the edge of Ste. Mère Eglise in the 82nd Airborne Division area. I cut my risers and climbed down about twenty feet but still couldn't reach the ground—just dropped the rest of the way."

Lieutenant "Legs" Johnson was dropped from a high altitude over an enemy ack-ack position. The fire from their weapons seemed to be concentrated on the naval observer who had parachuted just prior to Johnson's departure from the airplane. He said, "I climbed my suspension lines damned near halfway up and collapsed the chute trying to slip away. I managed to slip over a hedgerow, my canopy catching in the trees of the hedgerow. I dangled about ten feet from the ground but with the hedgerow at my backside. German soldiers could be heard approaching my position when I finished cutting my lines with my jump knife and fell into a ditch filled with briars. I scrambled out of there in a hurry and ran to the next hedgerow and hid in a ditch."

Captain Bert Clement tried too hard to avoid a tree line and in the process lit on his rump. He fractured two vertebrae and suffered a slipped disc. He was not able to move for about twenty minutes. He did become aware of other activity nearby. "One of the fellows landed in a tree that was right across the road. Every time he started to come down, a machine gun would fire into the tree. Although he could not be seen (he was very close to the trunk), they would turn their machine gun loose every time he rustled the leaves. I got to where I could move a little bit and crawled up to his hedgerow. I was unable to get up without something to hold on to, so I pulled on the bushes of the hedgerow and crawled through in under the tree where he was located. About that time his helmet fell off and scared me half to death. It hit the ground right behind me."

Landing in a plowed field gave T/4 Thomas Walsh the softest landing of his army career. He shook like jelly as he struggled with his harness. Walsh headed for the nearest tree line when he got free. He said, "When I got among the trees I heard, 'Pssst! Hey, cut me down!' Right beside my shoulder were the feet of a trooper who was hung up in the tree. I used my jump knife to cut him free."

Many troopers landed in canals and flooded fields. The wind played tricks with many of the billowing canopies which served as lifesavers for some and caused terror for others. Sergeant Pat Lindsay had a harrowing landing with his chute serving as a sail: "Instead of the land that I expected, there was only a large body of water below me. I tried to aim for a small finger of land on which stood a large silo. I tried to manipulate my chute toward the projection of land but the wind was not cooperating and kept carrying me out over the water no matter how I tried to slip toward land. I hit the water—went completely under into the soft gummy bottom. I fought my way to the top and flapped my arms to stay afloat with all my equipment trying to pull me under. The billowing chute, acting as a sail, carried me toward land. I had hit the water approximately 150 yards from shore and the "sail-chute" carried me to within 75 feet of the shoreline.

"I recall vividly the trouble I had in getting rid of my parachute harness. I recall standing in the water. I removed my helmet and set it upside down in the water so it would float like a boat near me while I worked on the harness fasteners.

I would take a deep breath and go down to work on the fix-
ings around my thighs and realize that my helmet was sinking. I would dive for it, bring it up, empty the water from it,
stuff it back on my head, start to crouch underneath once
more for the fastenings, come back up, take off my helmet
and set it to floating once more. I must have done this three
or four times before realizing how fruitless it was. After perhaps a half hour, I finally got loose from the harness and
proceeded to work my way slowly toward shore."

Stark terror still haunted T/5 Hugh Pritchard, Jr., as he recollected his drop into the flooded area: "We were scheduled
to drop on DZ "C." I was a radio operator and jumping an
SCR-300 (weight 40 pounds). I had this in a leg bag strapped
to my right leg. I practically fell out of the door, as you cannot do much jumping with 40 pounds tied to your leg. After
the chute opened, I was supposed to release it from my leg
and allow it to dangle on the end of a 20-foot rope fastened
to my harness. This was further provided with a safety release in case I was going into trouble. I could flip the release
and drop the whole mess. Well, all did not go according to
Hoyle. We jumped at no more than 300 feet, and the Air
Force did not bother to slow down. The opening shock was
terrific. This hurt my back and at the same time pushed the
leg bag farther down on my foot. I saw immediately that I
was going into water, and due to my injured back was unable
to pull my leg up. It would have done no good to flip the second release as this would not free it from my leg. Assuming
the parachute took 100 feet to open, that left me with 200
feet, or at 25 feet per second in descent, no more than 8 seconds to prepare for landing. At this time I weighed 140
pounds, and we estimated my total weight at 280 pounds, including both parachutes as I tumbled out of the door. Luckily the water was only chest deep. However, the wind was
blowing and just as I started to unhook my harness, the chute
jerked me down and I was dragged facedown in the water.
Fortunately, when I thought I could hold my breath no longer,
the chute stopped and I scrambled to my feet, and was able to
gulp a few breaths of air before being jerked down again.

This was repeated several times before the canopy collapsed in the water.

"In the marshaling area I had honed my trench knife to a razor-sharp edge just in case I needed it to free myself. I had it strapped to my left leg, and at one time had it out preparing to cut myself free when the parachute jerked me down causing me to drop it. Upon losing my knife I just about abandoned all hope. With an injured back, my helmet double-strapped under my chin, and as much equipment as there was tied to me, I was dragged through the water completely helpless.

"I know I am not the bravest man in the world, nor do I think of myself as a coward, but the stark terror I saw and lived through in the Normandy campaign, and especially that first night, remains so vivid even today, that sometimes I wake up in a cold sweat and nearly jump out of bed."

Private Russell Graham also had a water landing. "I didn't pay much attention to the jump until my chute opened and I saw water below me," Graham recalled. "Thought they had dropped us in the Channel. Then my boots got tangled in the lines and I was in water up to my chest. I had quite a time for a while."

Ridding himself of the parachute harness while under fire and water proved double problems for First Sergeant Paul Vacho, who recollected: "Our plane was not hit until the time I bailed out. I know we were very low because I took one or two swings and landed in water. I figure we were not over 400 feet. The water was chest deep where I landed. Had to cut the webbing of my harness because it was too tight. This I did with my face in the water because the Germans were firing just over the water at a height of about two feet."

The Douve River was not a happy landing site for Corporal Harold Shoutis, who had been the last man in his stick. He had jumped just ahead of the plane crewmen who had been anxious to evacuate the burning plane. "I could see the Douve River and I was drifting across it. Everyone else was landing on the other side. I tried to slip my chute but the wind was too strong and I landed in the center of the river. The wind caught the chute, which probably saved me from drowning and I went across the river like a motorboat. I was dragged about thirty feet on the shore before I could collapse the chute. I ended up on the opposite bank of the river from everyone else and man, was I scared! I crawled to the river and could see lily pads, so I thought I could wade it. What a mistake! The third step and I went over my head. I then scrambled out and went back to where I left my chute and got my Mae West life jacket, inflated it, and swam the river."

Private Louis W. Cione remembered, "Our pilot surely thought he was flying a P-47 fighter plane. We really became scattered because of the speed at which we were dropped. I was the last man out of our plane. When I came out and the chute opened I could see water below. Thought I was headed for the Channel until I drifted past a telephone pole beneath me. I landed about a mile from the DZ to the east of Vierville. Above the water I grabbed for my knife and the chute caught the wind at about the same time. After gliding through the water, I finally cut the chute loose. All I thought about was my cigarettes in my musette bag and my carbine. It wasn't too bad—I could stand up in the water."

Other landings occurred on rooftops, beside burning planes, in telephone wires and on enemy-held fields. Staff Sergeant Mickey Sheridan still recalled that his pilot was named Captain English. He said, "I had a good landing— right on the roof of a French farmhouse. I slid quickly over the side and dropped to the ground without injury. Stayed still until oriented and had trouble finding my cricket."

The German anti-aircraft fire had been deadly accurate. Lieutenant Harry F. Welsh dropped from a plane that had been hit several times in the vicinity of Ste. Mère Eglise. The green light was given long before the plane reached the proper drop zone. Welsh recalled, "I came down over a burning plane that had crashed previously. The heat made my chute go up and away from the flames and tangled in the hedgerow. I fell alongside the hedgerow and this probably saved my life. The field was infested with machine gunners and completely strung with overhead barbed wire on poles."

Telephone wires got in the way of PFC Bill Kopp, who related, "I passed through telephone wires along a roadway and my canopy hung up in the wires. I ended up in a half-standing, half-sitting position. I remember the panic when I heard hobnailed boots running down the road toward me. I couldn't get loose from the harness until, sobbing with fear and frustration, I cut the risers with my trench knife and crawled into the ditch beside the road. None too soon, because the German soldier began jabbing his bayonet around my chute. He was getting closer to me with each probe. Lying there with bated breath, and pounding heart, hesitantly, maybe almost fearfully, I killed him. I still hadn't been impressed with the fact that this was not maneuvers, or mock games, and this was for keeps and a case of kill or be killed."

Corporal Gus Liapes remembered the orders sent down from the Division—"Don't fire your weapons on the drop zone!" The enemy was waiting in the vicinity of his field. As Liapes described it, "I came down in a heap in a field, enemy soldiers came charging across the field with fixed bayonets. I cut and hacked at my harness in a frantic effort to get out of the way. They were almost on top of me when I got my tommy gun and fired into them."

Hazards

Parachute jumping is risky business. There are casualties no matter how ideal the landing conditions. This night offered several hazards to the men. There was a stiff breeze blowing in some open areas. The fields were small and lined with earthen hedgerows which stood five to six feet above the surrounding fields. At their bases they were from six to eight feet wide. These rows offered firm footing to the tall trees which in many cases were spindly in appearance with only tufts of branches near the tops. Others were good solid oaks and other hardwoods. The enemy had planted "Rommel's Asparagus" (anti-glider poles) in many of the larger fields and these offered additional hazards to the men—and then there was the shooting from below. This distracted the men from searching out suitable landing areas. When a parachutist dropped from a height of three to four hundred feet, he didn't have much time to make a decision before he met terra firma rather solidly. Night landings have always been known to exact a high toll among parachutists.

Private James E. Montgomery jumped in an area of intense flak and ground fire. He remembered, "It seemed that some machine gunner on the ground had picked me out as his special target. I could see the tracers which seemed to come directly at me and then curve away. I reached for my front risers and slipped like I never had before. Fortunately, I had enough sense to stop my slip before I hit, but about twenty feet from the ground I realized that I was so tense my legs were absolutely rigid. I relaxed, but even so, I hit the ground quite hard. After getting free of the harness, I crawled off the field to the shadows of the hedgerow. It was there I discovered I could not stand without intense pain. I realized my ankles were either broken or badly sprained."

"I lit like a sack of oats," said PFC Frank Styler. "I cut myself free. Got up and fell right back down. My left ankle wouldn't support my weight. I crawled to another man who was having difficulty getting out of his chute and aided him. The man had a badly sprained ankle. A medical officer came by and while he was tending the other man, I got up and hobbled away. Later I learned I had fractured an ankle."[4]

PFC Lou Sacchetti was a jump casualty before reaching the ground. He remembered, "I was hit over the right eye while in the air. Blood was pouring down my face and it was difficult to see and unhook my chute. I was found by Medic Jack Rudd and he poured sulfa powder over the wound and patched me up."

All but a few of the 6,670 parachuting members of the Screaming Eagle Division were now in France. For some planeloads, the adventure had ended abruptly in loud explosions as planes received direct hits in their equipment bundles which had been packed with a new demolition weapon called 'C-2.' These planes were blown to bits. Others received well-directed hits as the pilots attempted to hedgehop over the area. With an engine burning, or part of a tail or wing shot off, the plane never reached the minimum safe jumping height. Troopers in these planes perished with the plane crews. At least one plane load returned to England as described previously. Another partial stick also had to return after one man slipped in vomit and fell. By the time the remaining men in this plane untangled themselves, it was too late and they went back to England. A few received severe wounds from flak and small-arms fire while within their planes. Because of the seriousness of their wounds, they returned to England with the Air Force crews. For those who survived, this first combat jump was just the beginning of a hectic day.

CHAPTER 6

Into the Midst of the Enemy

The enemy was there. He had been shooting at the men as they floated to earth or passed overhead in the troop carrier planes. He would certainly hunt them out as they struggled to get free of the cumbersome equipment. Almost every man remembered his frantic efforts to free himself and to get to a place of concealment—and in a hurry. Nervousness, darkness, and sharp knives played havoc.

"After I was on the ground, all firing had ceased, and things were strangely quiet," recalled Private Elroy Huve, who landed in a field near a grazing cow. "Not a soul was stirring. The cow just kept on munching grass as if nothing had happened. I felt this was a good time to get out of the harness before some big German found me and decided to stick a bayonet into my stomach. For the love of me, I could not unsnap the harness! It seemed that I had become all thumbs. After trying for a few minutes, I gave up and drew my trench knife and proceeded to cut the straps. In my hurry I succeeded in getting one of my fingers in the way and cut it."

Recalling that he was blinded by a flare as he dropped to the surface of a flooded field, Lieutenant Leo E. Malek said, "I was standing in water up to my chest. My chute was tangled in barbed wire. Trying to cut myself out of the harness, I slashed my finger badly. I kept thinking about booby traps."

Lieutenant George W. Sefton also struggled with his harness. He heard hobnailed boots charging and glimpsed moonlight glinting on bayonets—it turned out to be a herd of cows racing around the field. He said, "I finally slashed free of the harness with my trench knife, slicing several layers of the jumpsuit, O.D.'s, and underwear in the process."

Dry mouth

There was another common experience which might be referred to as the "dry mouth effect." Part of it might have been caused by the anti-motion sickness pills the men had taken earlier, though it is also part of nervousness.

Recalling his frantic efforts to get out of his harness while hanging in a small apple tree, Corporal Vinnie Utz remembered, "My personal reaction was that I could not spit—I had what they called 'cotton balls' in my mouth—no saliva." Private James E. Montgomery also experienced this effect. He crawled hastily from the field in which multicolored tracers zipped over his head. "When I reached a hedgerow, I grabbed for my canteen. My mouth was so dry that I had to remove my chewing gum with my fingers."

Lieutenant Jim Allen described his experience this way: "Before we jumped, I told a trooper named Mars who jumped ahead of me to come over and assist me with my equipment if he got out of his harness first. I'd call to him. We had taken those airsickness pills and when I tried to call him, my mouth was so dry and my tongue so thick that not a sound came out. I couldn't talk!"

Strangely calm

Unusual behavior in unfriendly environments was recalled by troopers who hinted that it might possibly have been the result of the Dramamine pills.

Sergeant Carwood Lipton reacted calmly to the intense action about him. He had landed in a walled-in backyard in Ste. Mère Eglise with heavy machine-gun fire being sent up toward him as he floated down. A building had been burning fiercely down the street, lighting the area with eerie dancing shadows. Yet, Lipton remembered, "I didn't have any trouble getting out of my chute. I was very calm (don't know why). Unbuckled each leg strap, belly band, and chest strap. Checked myself over and saw that the only weapons I had were a trench knife, two fragmentation grenades, and a demolition kit."

Chief Warrant Officer Steve Karabinos had slipped franti-cally to avoid landing in a tall tree and as a result his feet hit the top of a hedgerow bank. His rear end hit the middle of the bank and then he bounced to the middle of the road. The parachute was hanging in the tree and intense enemy fire continued all around him. "I suddenly awoke to the fact that I was unhurt," he recalled. "Instead of getting my knife and cutting myself loose from the parachute, I lay in the road and worked for ten minutes to free myself from the harness. Like a fool I started looking for a glove I had lost. After about three minutes I located it, and then jumped into a hedgerow to try to orient myself."

Lieutenant Harold E. Young landed in a field among a herd of unconcerned cows. The stick had jumped from a low height after the pilot swerved to get out of the line of enemy fire being sent skyward. He related, "I lay still for a few minutes. This was combat? Was this what combat was going to be like? There were no problems in getting out of my chute. When I tell you—you won't believe it. I felt very hungry and relieved because the anxiety of going into combat was tremendous. So I just lay on the ground, out of my chute, I fished a Hershey bar out of my pocket and ate it. It was very good. It was about the last thing I ate for twenty-four hours."

I fell asleep

The same drowsiness that affected the men in the planes and caused many of them to sleep until just before receiving the red warning light returned to some of them a short time after they landed. Some commanders remembered that men fell asleep on their feet—even though soaking wet, and cold.

T/5 Harry Mole landed dry and easy in the middle of a soft pasture. The field in which he landed was crisscrossed with irrigation ditches that were six to seven feet wide, and about four feet deep. Mole arrived at one of these ditches. "Loaded down with equipment, I felt I couldn't jump it," he recalled. "I didn't! I landed right in the middle—my gas-impregnated jumpsuit resisted the water. I was still dry even though I was in the middle of that lousy ditch. The few minutes of struggling up the muddy bank was more than the treated pants could endure. A leak somewhere allowed water to enter my clothing. I stood on the other side of that rotten ditch shaking water from my pants. Crestfallen, I turned and slowly sloshed away. What a terrific war! When I came to a hedgerow only a few yards away, I lay down and went to sleep."

Medic Albert D. Hutto had been pulled from a stream, where he battled his chute until he was dragged to shallow water. Other troopers came to the rescue and helped him out. "[I was] totally exhausted; I found a dry chute and wrapped myself in it. I promptly fell asleep."

PFC George Doxzen had taken two anti-motion sickness pills and slept during the entire trip. The others had to wake him for the jump preparations. After an uneventful drop, he had gotten together with four or five others, including his squad leader. He said, "I met up with Holbrook, Hatch, Zettwich, and a few others. Hatch put me on outpost duty and I immediately fell asleep. The outfit moved out while I slept. It was those damned pills!"

Imagination worked overtime

The eyes and the ears of the green troopers played tricks on them. The men had never been in combat prior to this moment. Their senses were too keenly attuned to the sights and sounds of the night. Lack of experience gave a false sense of perception to the men in their particular predicaments. PFC Leland Baker dropped near the small town of Foucarville. "During the jump, it seemed that fire was coming from all directions," he later wrote. "I landed in weeds about four feet tall. I was lying on my back. I looked over my shoulder and saw something that looked like a big mound of dirt and thought I had landed in front of a machine-gun emplacement and could not understand why the occupants had not fired at me. I looked again and saw the object move and then realized it was the canopy of my own chute."

Major Ginder landed close to Drop Zone "A." He said, "As I landed and got to the edge of the hedgerow, I heard clumpety-clumpety-clump sounds. I thought it must be German cavalry. It turned out to be cows running from one end of the field to the other to escape parachutists as they landed."

"It was like a dream—I lit in a field of cattle and they almost scared me to death," explained Lieutenant Robert Burns. "I thought they were enemy cavalry which we had been told were in the area. All hoofbeats seem to sound alike."

Private Mike Ranney landed in an orchard near Ste. Mère Eglise with a church bell tolling in the distance. While struggling with his harness in the midst of scores of tracers and ack-ack, Mike recalled, "I heard a tremendous noise coming through the orchard, which was covered with fairly tall grass. I left my equipment bag near the base of an apple tree and ducked into some bushes, ready to take them on—if they were just a few in number. The noise got louder and louder, then a whole herd of cows piled through the orchard and straight into the brush where I was hunched. I was in France!"

Frantic and curious farm animals

With so many cattle grazing in the pastures during the night, some were bound to get tangled into the parachute lines. This was the case with PFC Ned Layser. "A cow got tangled in my chute as I hit the ground," he said. "It tried to drag me around a while until I got loose."

Cows were not the only creatures disturbed by the night drop. Private William A. Howell, who came down through some telephone wires at the edge of a field, recalled, "I heard some movement behind me and turned—there was a nanny goat and her little ones."

Private William K. Sturgess had a very low jump but the landing was soft. The knife he had sharpened to a razor edge seemed dull at the moment. He said, "I lay still for a minute, heard a suspicious sound—it was a nosy goat that followed me about until I left that field."

Normandy is also noted for the breeding of fine horses for racing purposes. Each farm had its workhorses as well as those used for riding. These animals were crazed by the excitement all about them. "My landing was in a small horse pasture," said Medic John Gibson. "A scared horse raced back and forth in the enclosure, stamping and snorting."

Crickets and passwords

Never had crickets congregated in France like they did on the night of June 5 and early morning of June 6, 1944. The metal cricket had been selected as a means of communication for the D-Day airborne soldiers because this particular noise-maker was not common in France. Perhaps the French had their own natural species, but the sounds could not be confused with the "click-clack" of this small toy, which was familiar to all of us as prizes in boxes of crackerjacks. The vocal passwords of "FlashThunder-Welcome" were added in case any of the men lost the metal snapper.

In most cases the paratroopers were isolated during the early moments after the drop. T/5 Koskimaki gave his impressions of those first lonely moments in the wheat field in which he landed: "As I lay in the field for a moment counting my blessings, I heard shooting and noticed the tracers being directed at a lone plane which came roaring overhead. The moon was shining brightly. A horse (and rider I am sure) galloped by on a nearby road. We didn't have any airborne cavalry, so I knew it must be the enemy. Like other soldiers in the same situation, I moved near the hedges so I could remain in the shadows. A terribly lonesome feeling came over me, thinking that there were thousands of us who had jumped and yet each was alone.

"I remained in hiding for perhaps fifteen minutes, wondering if all the rest of the people had been shot or captured. Presently I heard stealthy footsteps approaching from the west. I quickly pulled my little metal cricket from my pocket. I waited, crouched in the shallow ditch. I was aware of a quivering over my entire body and my heart pounded loudly and rapidly. The steps came closer—with a pause every so often at which time there was low unintelligible murmuring. I eased the safety catch off my carbine and pointed it in readiness in the direction of the footsteps. Then I squeezed my cricket, 'click-clack.'

"What a feeling of relief welled in me when I got the answering 'click-clack', click-clack'—but I still wasn't sure, so I used the voice challenge of 'Flash' with the answer of 'Thunder' coming swiftly. This was used if some poor soul lost his cricket during the turmoil.

"Out of the darkness stepped Major Lawrence Legere, my jumpmaster and assistant G-3 for the Division, along with his close friend, Captain Thomas J. White, who served as aide to General Maxwell D. Taylor. I was so happy to have located other members of my stick."

A short time earlier, Captain White had dragged a jump-injured division MP soldier[1] to the shelter of a hedgerow and moved on. White said, "I was left alone until I met Major Legere. It was a black night. I was scared. Legere said, 'Flash.' I said 'Thunder.' He recognized my Boston accent and quipped (I couldn't see him), 'Well, Tommy White, imagine meeting you here!'"

PFC Leo Runge landed in a flooded area with forty pounds of TNT strapped to his leg. He managed to cut his risers off while standing in water chin deep. He remembered, "When I looked toward shore I saw men scrambling all over and I didn't know if they were Americans or Germans. I was afraid to use my cricket in fear that if they were enemy soldiers, they would shoot me. I finally decided to use it anyway and thank God, an American soldier threw me a rope and pulled me out."

"I was never so alone or scared in my life," said PFC Charles F. Knight, who remained in hiding after unharnessing his chute. "It didn't last long. There were other people moving about. I was afraid to make contact with them, not knowing if they were friend or foe. It seemed the best thing to do was just lie still and hide and let the darkness conceal me. It couldn't be done—other people were moving. Crickets were sounding all around me. I picked up my gear and answered with my clicker."

A reconnaissance trip in search of others had proved fruitless for Captain Robert H. Phillips, so he settled in the corner of a hedgerow to wait. He related, "I sat with my carbine

across my legs and waited. A short time later I saw some figures floating toward me across the field. I waited until I saw
the luminous disks on the front of the helmets, then snapped
my cricket and got a welcome 'click-clack' in reply."

Sergeant Robert Peterson, an unarmed medic, rolled into a
ditch beside a hedgerow to get out of the line of fire from an
enemy machine gunner. As he later explained it, "I recall
after being in the ditch some time of moving toward St.
Marie-du-Mont. I was moving in the dark cautiously when I
realized someone was moving with me. I would stop, the
other movement would stop. I would snap the cricket, but receive no answer. Move again, and the process was repeated.
Finally, there was a rifle in my face and after a few anxious
seconds, I recognized the faint outline of a G.I. helmet. That
man had a weapon but had lost his cricket."

Sometimes well-rehearsed signs and countersigns were
completely forgotten. Corporal Vinnie Utz met a staff sergeant
from the regimental S-2 Section. "He was a refugee Austrian
Jew. I gave him the 'Flash' of 'Flash-Thunder-Welcome,' but
he froze and yelled 'Kamerad.' I started to tighten up on the
trigger but I recognized his voice, as he had lived with us in
our barracks for the past month. (Later, in a critique, he
could not account for yelling 'Kamerad' for the password except to say that his native tongue came out naturally in fear.)"

Correspondent Robert Reuben, working for the Reuters
News Agency, had parachuted from General Maxwell Taylor's plane. After landing he had twisted over on his side
on the ground and slowly freed himself and crawled to a
hedgerow, which became a temporary haven. He crouched in
the darkness and listened. "From the shadows, an American
challenged me with the password, 'Flash.' I stuttered every
password I could think of, but in my panic I couldn't recall
the proper countersign. I could see the faces of two paratroopers in the shadows concealed somewhat by the darkness. They thought I was a German sniper. I raised my hands
slowly and prayed they wouldn't shoot. Some questions were
directed at me. I told them my name and slowly turned to
face the moonlight. The troopers recognized me as the corre-

spondent who had jumped from their plane. One of them was a military policeman, Private Robert Hamilton, who informed me that he came mighty close to shooting me because I didn't have the countersign."[2]

PFC George D. Doxzen kept a wartime diary of his experiences. He had parachuted from his plane at 0105 A.M. and had landed in a small field meeting no enemy resistance. He commented, "When I landed, I found out that I had lost my cricket. I heard a click of one nearby so I answered by clicking my tongue against the roof of my mouth. On the third click I decided I'd better use the voice password so I said 'Flash,' and was immediately answered with 'Thunder.' It was Harold Holbrook. I often think how fortunate I was that 'Herky' didn't decide to blow my head off."

T/4 Nick Cortese had just dropped from the branches of a tree near an enemy machine-gun position and left his radio snagged in the upper branches. "The first thing I knew, a muzzle of a rifle was an inch from my nose," said Cortese. "The guy behind the gun was telling me to halt. He was a G.I., but I had never seen him before. He asked me what outfit I was from. I told him F Company. He called me a liar—said he was from F Company and he didn't know me. Now, I was with F Company since Toccoa, Georgia, and I didn't know him! It developed that he was from the 82nd Division— F Company of the 505th Regiment."

One challenging cricket brought fireworks. PFC Walter "Smokey" Gordon had joined with two men from his stick. He said, "We heard a noise further down the hedgerow and one of the men went to investigate and challenged with his cricket. A fragmentation grenade was tossed in our direction and we dived for cover. Shortly, we got moving again. We saw another soldier run across an opening and I went to get the fellow and in looking in the bushes for him found myself staring down the barrel of a .45 caliber pistol held by F. M. "Tab" Talbert, our squad leader. I will always remember those white eyes in a blackened face behind that pistol!"

Sights and sounds in the dark

The Normandy hedgerow-lined fields had a strange way of muffling sounds from a distance. However, small sounds were greatly magnified when close at hand. A light displayed in the dark usually brought an undesired response.

Radio operator Nick Cortese moved off from the base of the tree where his radio hung uselessly in the upper branches. With him was the 82nd sky trooper he had met earlier. Enemy soldiers were only a short distance away firing at other troopers floating to the ground in the light of a burning haystack. "We decided to leave the Germans alone until we could find more G.I.'s," explained Cortese. "We walked along a dirt road. Up ahead we could hear voices, and couldn't distinguish whether they were German, French, or Americans. We could see little red lights glowing in the dark. We crept toward them. When we got closer we could hear good old 'G.I.' speech—'God damn it! I knew they'd screw us up on this mission!' One of them was really cussing up a storm. Know what the red lights were? Those guys were smoking—like they were on Tennessee maneuvers!"

Correspondent Bob Reuben was directed by two MP's to post himself near a crossroad. Only a short time before, they had almost shot him because he had forgotten the password. "Before moving to the roadside," Reuben said, "I found a concealed spot in a hedgerow and pulled out my map and compass. I also pulled out a small flashlight to illuminate the map. A shot zinged over my head as a sniper fired at the light. I dived through the bushes and raced across the road and into the shelter of another hedgerow bank. There, I found General A.C. McAuliffe, who was also keeping watch on the same crossroads."[3]

Private Mike Ranney became keenly aware of both lights and loud noises. He had landed in an apple orchard and a few minutes later had located a buddy who was a bazookaman. Ranney said, "As we moved across the fields, our party grew to fifteen members. We came to a road with an intersection and signposts across the way. As we hesitated about heading out on the road, even to look at the road signs for orientation, we heard another bunch coming down the road talking and singing loudly. We thought they must be Germans. One guy walked up to the signpost, turned on a flashlight and yelled, 'Holy shit, we're five kilometers from our drop zone. How far is that, Joe?' We piled out of the weeds along the road and joined them."

An enemy patrol passed along the road as Private Mike Nassif crouched in a roadside ditch. He waited, then proceeded in the dark alone. As he neared a small turn in the road, Nassif could hear whisperings. He related, "I crept to within ten feet of the men. Two of them were up a pole and four were at the base of it. I couldn't make out if they were friends or foes. I wasn't about to change direction, and like most guys I figured the airbornes were the only crickets in Normandy. I was just about to sound off with my little snapper when one of the men up the pole yelled, 'You dumb son-of-a-bitch, this isn't the wire cutter!' I swear they could have heard him clear to England, but it was music to my ears. Someone tried to quiet him but he swore all the louder."

Sergeant Elden C. Hermann of the communications section of the 502nd Regiment had parachuted with two carrier pigeons. The birds were protected in a cardboard container. Hermann related, "I landed just outside a wall which was behind a big house. I had the two pigeons in an 81mm mortar shell box that I jumped attached to my harness. I went for the nearest cover which was in a ditch alongside a hedgerow about twenty yards from where I landed. It was after I had crouched there for a bit that I discovered a German rifleman firing at the passing C-47's from inside the walled enclosure. More parachutists were landing in the area. My pigeons started a loud cooing, and I was worried about the enemy soldier hearing them. I put them in a small puddle of water in the ditch and drowned them."

A concussion had bereft PFC Walter M. Turk of his memory. His jumpmaster had announced 'Five minutes to go' and that was all Turk remembered until 0620 A.M. the next morning. He related, "After we landed, Fred Orlowsky started back down the line, picking up squad members. He came to me and thought I was dead, but he nudged me with his foot and I moaned, so he cut me out of my chute and got me on my feet. He and another trooper led me around all night. I talked loud and long out of my head. We were surrounded by Germans. I guess they fired at the sound of my voice too. I feel I owe my life to Fred and the other trooper."

CHAPTER 7

Early Encounters

As the paratroopers oriented themselves to their environment and began as unobtrusively as possible to determine their locations and to seek out members of their sticks, encounters began with both friend and foe. A directive had been issued by Division Headquarters while the men were still in England that there is to be no rifle, pistol, or machine-gun firing by our troops during the hours of darkness on D-Day morning on the drop zones. The men were to use knives, bayonets, or hand grenades to dispose of the enemy.

Close calls

Some paratroopers had brushes with death in a matter of minutes after dropping safely to the ground. The hidden foe was not always responsible. In several cases, there were incidents in which men almost lost their lives at the hands of green and nervous G.I.'s who seemed to go by the slogan, "Shoot first and ask questions later."

Captain Sammie Homan landed in a field without ammunition for his tommy gun. His equipment bag had torn loose on the opening shock of the chute. He said, "I almost had it when a 'friendly' lobbed a hand grenade in my direction. No harm was done though when it exploded nearby. I did hit the dirt!"

As he dropped beside the trunk of a good-sized tree, PFC Steve Koper wondered why he hadn't any trouble with branches. It seemed he had landed at the base of one of "Rommel's Asparagus"—one of those deadly anti-glider poles set up in the fields. He said, "While lying struggling on the ground with my chute harness, I heard the click of a cricket. Before I could get my snapper out to respond, someone fired a machine gun at me in several bursts. I didn't learn until we returned to England that it was one of my own stick members who had fired in my direction and almost killed me."

Unable to support his weight on a jump-injured leg, Private Elroy Huve used his carbine rifle as a cane. He had landed alone in a field near a small farm building. He described his difficulties: "I skirted around the shack. With my bum leg I wasn't making good time. I would hobble a ways and then pause to rest a bit. After a time I came to a sort of a road. (Back in South Dakota, we called such things cow paths.) There was water in the ditches on both sides of the road. I seemed to be passing through some sort of a swampy area. I decided to follow it and see where it might lead. After some time, a machine gun opened up on me and laid a stream of tracers right at my feet. I was so startled that I froze right in the spot and didn't even hit the dirt. I felt the chills run up my spine. Remaining frozen for a few minutes, I realized that nothing had happened to me. I hobbled on expecting to feel slugs in my legs."

As Captain Robert H. Phillips began his reconnaissance to "roll up the stick," he met with a strange encounter that left him puzzled, yet grateful. "I fully expected someone to run up, or by, but there was no one. I got my carbine and other equipment and started on a lonely reconnaissance. Sometime later I crossed a field and felt an impact at my left hip as though I had been swatted by a big flat board. This was it! I hit the ground, knife out, grenade in hand, and crawled back in the direction from which the disturbance had originated. I never found the source. Later, around daybreak, I reached for my canteen to get a much needed drink—too late! It had been blown wide open and there was a scorched area of about one foot in diameter in my jacket."

PFC Sherwood Trotter's close call came as he landed in the middle of a small town square on a hard dirt road. Unable to unsnap his parachute harness, he got to his feet in an effort to free himself. His suspension lines were draped around him. He recalled, "Just then, someone in the shadows near the corner of a building took a shot at me and knocked me down. I thought, this was it and I certainly was going to die. Sometime later (probably only a few seconds), I realized that my time hadn't come—in fact, I was not wounded. I only had an extremely sore spot in my stomach area. (Later in the day I found out that the bullet had gone through several clips of carbine ammo carried in a canvas pouch attached to my equipment belt and the slug had stopped in the web belt that held my pants up. I still have that belt!) At any moment I expected the Kraut to come out of the shadows and finish me off. All I had access to was a hunting knife strapped to one leg—no pistol, no jump knife. I started cutting the harness with the hunting knife and finally got free of the chute, I crawled to the opposite corner of the building from which the shooting came, found myself on the edge of a garden, crawled through the garden and reached an open field. I stopped to have a drink of water and discovered that someone had shot a hole in my canteen as I came down and there wasn't a drop of water left. Apparently my adversary was just as scared as I was because I never heard or saw him again."

WIA in the first minutes[1]

Lieutenant Clair L. Hess cut his way out of his chute while machine-gun bullets sprayed about him. He became an early casualty. "I got hit in the leg just as I thought I was going to get off the field," he said. "I made it to a hedgerow; met a chaplain and a medic who brought me a chute to hide under because I couldn't walk and they couldn't wait for me. I lay under that chute for a long time. A German patrol came along and one of its members crawled up and looked out over the area. I was under the chute, tommy gun across my chest, and I could hear his steady breathing. After a while he pulled away and I figured I had it made for another mission."

It was dangerous for the point man or forward scout. PFC Guerdon Walthall had just gotten together with five of his stick members. He recalled: "We started moving up a road and were still lost from the outfit. I took over as point man about the time we started to leave the road. I guess we made too much noise in discussing which direction we should follow because as I led out, a German machine gun opened up, and I thought a tank had run over me. I went flat on my back, and it felt like someone had stuck my legs in a pot of hot metal. Two more machine guns opened up on us, and the rest of the boys jumped in the ditch. It was evident that the boys had to pull out, and I was too far forward for any of them to reach me. The numbness began to leave my legs, and when I heard the Germans coming up the road, I decided it was no place for me. I started crawling, and finally got on my feet. I could barely stay on them, but I finally got moving. They kept shooting flares up to try and locate us, but we managed to stay well hidden, and continued to move back. We finally ran into a larger group of troopers and pulled in with them. Medic Bill Kidder was with them and he fixed me up."[2]

Enemy defenses

The enemy troops had been assigned to the numerous small villages and hamlets throughout the Normandy area. Some were at their posts in the foxholes dug into the hedgerow banks or on duty near their anti-aircraft batteries. Others were in billets and rushed off to assigned posts as news of the paratroop drops reached them.

Chief Warrant Officer Steve Karabinos, assistant to Colonel Gerald J. Higgins, described the enemy defenses:[3] "Days before, aerial photography had disclosed that the Germans were building anti-airborne defenses on all possible landing fields. These defenses consisted of poles ten to twelve feet high stuck in the ground at close intervals with barbed wire stretched betwixt these poles. With a setup like that, it was impossible to land a glider safely on those fields, and any parachutist finding it necessary to land there also could be considered a doomed man. However, there were some fields where this defense setup did not exist. But don't think for a moment that they weren't protected. We found that out when some of our boys landed on these fields. The Normandy Peninsula (part of France where the Allies landed) proved to be a terrain not especially suited for offense because of its series of hedgerows (high banks grown over with shrubbery and trees) which served as a boundary between fields. In America we use fences to denote boundary lines; in France the hedgerows served the purpose of fences. So in the end, the battle turned out to be a fight for one hedgerow after another and progress had to be determined in yards and not miles.

"As I stated before, most of the fields had poles as anti-airborne defenses. Those that didn't have the poles, were strong-pointed by means of a series of dugouts built into the hedgerows. It was merely a big hole dug into the side of the hedgerow. The Germans had built bunks in them and had slept in these underground dugouts. Their machine guns and mortars were set up alongside the field with stacks of ammunition to last for weeks. So it can be seen that not one possible landing field was left unprotected. These defenses existed all the way from Cherbourg to Isigny and possibly farther (that's the farthest part of my travels), and as far south as Carentan and St. Sauvier-le-Vicomte. So it can be seen that the Jerries had a hot reception planned for us."

During the early hours, the paratroopers stumbled upon the enemy machine-gun nests, artillery gun positions, and foxholes as they sought shelter in the shadows of the hedgerows. There was intermittent moonlight as fleecy clouds parted occasionally to reveal a full moon which in turn revealed the deadly adversary. It was in these predawn hours that the paratroopers had their early encounters with the enemy, sometimes alone, later in small groups.

Pursued

Private Jay Nichols had a hard landing. The stock of his rifle was shattered on impact with the ground. He headed for a field in which two of his buddies had landed. He said, "I went over to see how my buddies were doing when a squad of German soldiers appeared on the scene. They yelled something like 'Halt!' (We had landed practically on top of an anti-aircraft unit near the small town of Turqueville.) We took off like 'ruptured ducks,' and I had a glimpse of Hawkins tripping, but the Krauts were shooting so I speeded up some. I sailed over the confronting hedgerow, and landed in the middle of a herd of sheep. They became as frightened as myself and so we naturally had a footrace. After clearing several more hedgerows, I ran out of gas, and selected a spot in a ditch running parallel with a hedgerow. I was in the bottom of a ditch and I could hear the Krauts on the other side, when along came a group of Charley Company boys. I didn't know it was C Company until later, but they spoke English, and I took my first breath in several minutes. I snapped the cricket and a bayonet on the end of an M-1 was poked at me."

Another soldier who was the object of a search and pursuit by enemy soldiers was Staff Sergeant John Bacon, who had been dropped eight miles southwest of his drop zone. His chute had draped over a tree, but he had managed to land on the ground. He said, "I ran into a German patrol a few minutes after I got loose from my harness. I killed two of them with a pistol and then made a wide circle and joined the rest of my stick."

Grenades

The grenade was the most effective weapon used in the early hours by the parachutists. When lobbed toward an enemy it did not reveal the position of the thrower as was the case of the report and muzzle flash from a gun. It had devastating effect on the entrenched machine-gun nests in the corners of the hedgerow-lined fields.

Sergeant Tom Bruff of the G-2 Section of Division Headquarters landed in a cow pasture. He relocated a dislocated right shoulder himself, cut himself out of his harness, and hid the chute in the hedgerow. He was not certain of his position, but from the flak bursts which he suspected as coming from Carentan, he felt he was near his proper position. "I set off cautiously in what I thought to be the right direction," explained Bruff. "Moving very slowly, I stayed close to the hedgerows. All of a sudden an extremely low-flying C-47 zoomed overhead and it was immediately fired upon by what I presumed to be a German version of our quad-fifty—not thirty feet from where I was crouching. I didn't have any notions of being a hero—I was supposed to reach the assembly point at all costs, and not pick any individual fights. But I knew I should do something about that enemy gun crew even if it was no more than to say 'Hey stop that!' "

Bruff continued relating his experiences: "I didn't want to expose myself by a muzzle flash from my carbine, so I decided to try one of the four hand grenades I was carrying. I thought I knew exactly where the gun crew was located. So, I pulled the pin, and waiting a moment, threw the grenade. I didn't know that one never throws a grenade where it could bounce right back in one's lap. But, I must have been living right because the grenade went up high, through the trees without touching leaf or limb, and exploded. I didn't investigate to find out what damage had been done, but I noticed that as other low-flying planes came over they were not fired upon by that gun emplacement."

T/5 George Koskimaki had just challenged his jumpmaster, Major Larry Legere and Captain Thomas J. White, who served as aide to General Maxwell Taylor, near a hedgerow corner. They had responded both with crickets and the vocal passwords. Koskimaki describes their first enemy encounter: "I asked the major if he knew where we were, but he didn't know for sure. He said we would move eastward toward the middle of our stick of jumpers. Following the shallow ditches and openings in the corners of the fields, we used the hedgerows for cover and moved in an easterly direction. (We assumed the planes flew directly eastward from our landing points.) What turned out to be one of the first enemy encounters occurred as we advanced on another field corner. From the other side of the thick hedgerow came a gruff command in German—'Halte!'

"Our trio pulled up short and the major quickly responded in French, 'I come from visiting my cousin.' With this he hissed, 'Hit the dirt!' and gave further impetus to the order by giving me a shove downward. All three of us dropped immediately beside the hedge as the unseen enemy cut loose with a burst of machine gun and burp gun (machine pistol) fire. The slugs passed harmlessly over our heads and backs as the bullets cut an opening in the hedgerow foliage."

Major Legere added his recollections of the incident. "When challenged by the Germans, I wanted to stall for time. I figured that, even if the Germans understood no French, they would recognize the language as French and hesitate a little. Of course I can only approximate what I actually said. It did concern my having been out after curfew in order to visit my neighbor-cousin who was sick."

When asked what he remembered of the incident, Captain Tom White replied, "I encountered two men. One was Major Legere, and I don't recall who the other was. We encountered Germans. Legere pretended to be a Frenchman. (He spoke excellent French.) While talking, he tossed a hand grenade and yelled for us to duck. I rolled into a ditch."

Koskimaki continued his account: "The major had been busy with a grenade. This he lofted over the hedge, where it exploded with a loud 'whump.' Immediately we were on our feet running low and retreating in the direction from which we had come. After running to the cover of another hedgerow, we stopped for a breathing spell.

"It was then that the major missed his case of invasion maps. The case had apparently become unslung from his shoulder while we were squirming about on the ground near the hedge. After a short period of discussion I volunteered to go back to the spot to retrieve the maps. This turned out to be hair-raising because we had no knowledge of the effects of the grenade upon the enemy patrol at this time. As I crept stealthily back to the spot, I was afraid the enemy could hear the pounding of my heart—it was so loud. Every time I stepped on a dry twig or a dead grass stem it sounded like a windowpane shattering. Finally I got to the area and groped about in the dark and discovered the case in the shallow ditch. This was hastily retrieved and I retreated in earnest. Apparently the grenade had done its job because no sound had come from the far side of the hedgerow. Panting from my fast return trip, I found the others waiting beside the hedgerow where I had left them. I handed the canvas case to Major Legere."

A member of the G-2 Section from Division Head-quarters, Captain Leo H. Schweiter, was involved in a grenade incident—only he was on the receiving end. He recalled, "While searching for members of my stick, I ran into a Ger-man strongpoint. After a brief firefight I was wounded by a hand grenade."[4]

Ambush

The German soldiers located equipment bundles dropped from the airplanes (possibly by the lighted beacons), and sta-tioned men in places of concealment to await the arrival of Americans on the scene to retrieve the equipment. The troop-ers were usually met with a hail of bullets.

"I took Perry with me and started searching," said Corporal Virgil Danforth in describing his mission to locate equip-ment bundles. "Within a half hour we found three bundles but they weren't ours. We saw two more out in the center of a field. As we reached the equipment, a group of Germans opened fire at us from a ditch at the edge of the field. Perry made a run for the opposite side of the field, but I was caught out in the open and right under their guns. As I hit the ground, my musette bag, which contained Composition C-2 and TNT flew over my head and in front of me. I tried to hide behind it for about two minutes until I got to thinking how stupid it was and got to laughing at myself. I then threw two grenades into the ditch and then ran all over those Germans in getting out of there."

Sergeant Richard "Wick" Goist jumped from the same plane as Brigadier General Anthony C. McAuliffe, the ar-tillery commander of the 101st Airborne Division. Goist lo-cated Corporal Charles Jones and they went out in search of equipment bundles. One of those bundles contained key radio equipment and French currency. Goist said, "We pro-ceeded to retrieve a bundle which was packed with bazookas. While trying to open the bundle, we encountered small-arms fire and a rifle bullet went through the fly of my jump pants.

We left that location in a hurry and headed across the road to retrieve the bundle we had pushed out of the door of our plane."

American paratroopers also set up ambushes for the enemy. Machine gunner Ray Taylor was successful with his strategy. He had floated down into the backyard of one of the homes near Ste. Mère Eglise. He said, "With five or six Frenchmen conversing on the other side of the wall, I damned near shot them because I didn't know German from French, but they went into the house and more planes were coming over. I set up my machine gun to cover a road. I was alone and didn't know where I was, so I thought I would sit tight until someone came along to help me carry some of the ammunition. It was too heavy for one man. I got action sooner than I expected, for along came a motorcycle and a German command car down the road. I just 'laid on' the trigger. There were five in the command car and one on the cycle. I was scared but I felt good. Got my first Lugers and German cigarettes and a few minutes later I heard some one clicking down the road for all he was worth. It was Ed Martin from 3rd Platoon. We both lay in the ditch for some time wondering what we should do."

"I managed to get together with six other troopers along the railroad track," said Mortar Sergeant Pat Lindsay. He had just crawled from the flooded meadowland near Chef-du-Pont onto the railroad causeway. "We waited until shortly before dawn. We closed in on the track which was built several feet above the flooded area and noticed a group of soldiers approaching. We hid in the tall reed grass beside the embankment, perhaps six or seven yards from the roadbed. We were well hidden as the troops approached. They were Russian Georgian troops which we had been told were in our area. There were at least a dozen of them as they marched past. They walked over a bridge, probably with the mission of checking it, and then being satisfied that it was intact, started back in the direction from which they had come. We opened fire on them and got several. The rest fled screaming and in panic down the track. We proceeded to depart from the area as rapidly as possible in the opposite direction. We could hear the sounds of a firefight in the distance and began moving toward it."

To be left behind

Many men who were injured on the jump or wounded a short time later had to fall out as buddies moved anxiously toward their D-Day objectives. To be left behind in a strange land with enemy soldiers searching the area for the lost or "stray" troopers was a lonely and fearful experience.

Private Charles "Swamp-Rat" Maggio had sprained an ankle severely on the drop. So much enemy machine-gun fire had come up to greet them as they descended that Maggio had hit the ground before he was prepared for landing and his lack of proper position and relaxation had caused the injury. He said, "I stayed pretty quiet until I got with a group of about twenty men from several companies. Oscar Saxvik, from my stick, helped me follow this group. I felt I was delaying the men because of my slow hobbling, so I told Saxvik to leave me so he could keep up with the rest of the men. My ankle had become so swollen and painful that I had to stop and watch my group disappear in the darkness."

Private Mike "Nasty" Nassif and his stickmate Pusahanik were to assemble opposite the direction of flight, but the planes were approaching from all points of the compass. Nassif's compass was gone and Pusahanik's was broken. The men had been assigned to go toward the wooden bridges northeast of Carentan. Nassif related, "Pusahanik and I moved about one hundred yards from the point of landing. We paused for a moment to try to get some sort of bearing. A mortar shell exploded between us. I got a flesh cut across my right hip about two inches long, but Pusahanik got it real bad. He kept yelling to me to take off but I couldn't leave him like that. I helped him as best I could and gave him an extra bandage. I took a British commando knife I had in my boot and stuck it in a tree next to him and hung one of my grenades on it. He was as comfortable as could be expected. I left him there with mixed feelings."

Duty required that he move on to find the rest of his company, but PFC Ned "Dutch" Layser paused first to give aid. He said, "I found two men from our stick with broken ankles and helped them dig in after giving them first aid. Then I moved out."

As earlier described, Private Elroy Huve had stood paralyzed to one spot after an enemy machine gun fired at him as he hobbled down a country lane using his .30-caliber carbine rifle for a cane. Realizing the enemy gunner wasn't going to fire more, he continued on down the road. He said, "Probably a half hour later I was challenged. I answered with the countersign. There was a major in front of me with five or six men. I did not know him or any of the men and they were preparing to go after a machine-gun nest which was down a nearby hedgerow. The major told me to come along. I told him I would try, but doubted if I could keep up with them and explained what had happened to me on the landing. He told me to stay right there and wait for aid. After their departure, with a lump in my throat, I looked around for some cover. I found a hole that had probably been caused by a bomb. I crawled in. I felt that I might as well stay right there and see what might develop. I laid my hand grenades within easy reach, stuck the trench knife in the ground beside me, arranged the clips of ammunition for the carbine where they would be real handy, and decided to make my stand there."

CHAPTER 8

Assembly

Out of a total division strength of 14,200 men in the 10lst Airborne, 6,600 had parachuted into France in the early hours of D-Day. About seventy percent of those were dispersed over an area of about eight miles square bounded by Ravenoville, Ste. Mère Eglise, the Carentan-Cherbourg railroad, and the Douve River. The great majority of the remainder who dropped outside this area were killed or captured. Casualties were heavy, too, among the seventy percent who dropped in the eight-mile-square area described above. Those who were able to move, as already indicated in the previous chapters, had begun to get together in twos and threes, and the groups continued to grow in size during the early morning hours.

Ideally, they were to assemble first into squads, then platoons, companies, and battalions in order to coordinate the movement to assigned objectives, but assembly was difficult at night. One thing in their favor, they were not as easily observed by the enemy as they would have been by daylight.

As has been stated, the troopers had been trained to note the "direction of flight of the aircraft and then move accordingly. Those in the front of the stick who had jumped first, were to move in the continuing direction of flight while those at the tail end of the group, who had jumped last, were to move in the direction from which the planes had arrived. The hope was that they would meet in the middle.

Each unit had its own means of signaling the men as to the area toward which they would move for assembly purposes. Some used lights of various colors. Red designated 1st Battalions, white represented 2nd Battalion groups, and blue lights were used by 3rd Battalion forces. Smaller units used a flare pistol to designate the location of a company or battery commander. If the light couldn't be seen, the men listened for the sounds of whistles, bugles or hunting horns and one battalion used a large bell which was tolled to provide the location of the assembly point. One jumpmaster used luminous cords from equipment bundles to whirl over his head to attract men to himself. At least one unit had placed small luminous disks on the helmets to identify members.

Equipment bundles were located through several means. Luminous cord and tape were wrapped around some of them. Others had phosphorescent paint markings on the bundles. On the 501st Parachute Regiment bundles, small beacon lights popped on when the parachutes opened and this provided quick retrieval.

Corporal Vinnie Utz, from the S-2 intelligence section of his regiment, found a few men from S-2, also a trooper from the 82nd who later wandered off in search of his comrades, and finally a machine gunner who was carrying a tripod. Utz related, "The machine gunner didn't stick with us but went off in search of his buddy. We ran into Colonel Bob Sink and a few of his headquarters staff. Simpson, Palys, and myself were sent out to patrol for strays. We directed a few back to the farm but my recollection is that almost all were more interested in linking up with their own sections, squad, company, etc. The reaction was 'Did you hear the bugle?' 'Did you see the yellow flare?' 'Where's D Company?' 'Where's the 2nd Battalion?' "

One of the men found a comrade and promptly lost him. Mortar Sergeant John Urbank had landed in an overpopulated cow pasture far to the north of his DZ. He related, "Three machine guns kept pouring tracers over us as we attempted to get out of our parachutes. One could see the shadowy figures of the Krauts, shoulders above the hedgerows. Those trigger-happy gentlemen shot at anything that looked or sounded suspicious."

Urbank continued: "To my right I noticed what I thought was one of my men and crawled—no, wormed—my way up to him, clicked my cricket but got no reaction. I said our password, 'Flash'—still no reaction. I debated whether to toss a grenade because I could see it was a soldier and he wasn't acting friendly. (Much later I found out it was F. K. Morrison, who had a streamer and he had broken both legs and was in shock.[1])

"I backed away, heard a click behind me. I answered the click with two clicks and called out, 'Is that you, Castona?' I had found a friend, Sergeant Don Castona was our communications sergeant. We discussed our present situation. I said, 'Let's get back behind those trees and find some place where there aren't so many bullets flying. You cover me and I'll cover you.'

"So we wormed our way through the cow pasture to a row of trees behind us. Castona got there first and turned left. I must have turned right because we didn't see each other again for a week until we met at 'Purple Heart Lane.' "[2]

Some of the men were fortunate to land near their unit assembly aids and were able to move toward them for a quick reunion with comrades. Others were mistaken in what they saw or heard.

Staff Sergeant Nick Calabrese landed in the same field as his buddy, Master Sergeant George Galla. He went over to assist Galla as he struggled to get out of his chute in a tree. Calabrese said, "We crawled to a hedgerow. As soon as we got there, two G.I.'s landed on top of the hedgerow. That really made our fannie's quiver! After exchanging passwords, these two troopers lit a lantern they were carrying. We soon realized we had landed on the assembly point for the 3rd Battalion of the 501st Regiment, and Division Headquarters. Soon, others joined us."

PFC Nick Necikowski landed in a fairly large field. Machine-gun and rifle fire could be heard nearby but none was directed at him. Another trooper had landed in a tree which was situated on top of the hedgerow bank and Necikowski helped cut him down. They located three other men and debated the direction in which they should move. "We could hear the whistle blowing from the assembly area," said Necikowski. "Then we began to argue as to where the sound was coming from. I climbed a tree and was able to see the blue light of the assembly point just a few fields away. When we arrived at the rendezvous area, none of the people from the other Division Artillery plane were there yet."

For one small group, which was accompanied by the assembly bugler for the battalion, the use of the horn would probably have resulted in their capture as they landed far south of the drop zone to which they had been assigned. In the nearby hedgerows and fields were men of the German 6th Parachute Regiment, hunting for the dropped American airborne soldiers. Mortarman Dick Frame landed near a hedgerow and a deep ditch. He remembered, "I stayed in the ditch to determine the direction of the flight. I waited for the sound of the assembly bugle. Wilson was to blow the horn so the battalion could rendezvous on a central point. Having determined the direction of flight from a few planes that passed over, I moved along toward the rest of the stick. I met Wilson and we exchanged clickers. I asked him where his bugle was because I hadn't heard the sound of the horn. He replied, 'I threw the son-of-a-bitch away!' Apparently our razzing of him on the plane had left him pretty shaken."[3]

Frame continued: "We found an equipment bundle and waited there for others to arrive. About seven or eight men assembled. Lieutenant Seale and Sergeant Burgess were in charge of our stick but they were not present, so Brooks and Charpentier took over the leadership. We headed south because we felt our mission was in that direction."

Some distance away was a medical officer from the same battalion. Captain Robert Blatherwick never did make contact with his unit. He related, "There was no one in sight when I landed but scattered small-arms fire seemed to be predominantly to the west so I walked in that direction thinking the Battalion was probably there. Some time later I heard what I thought to be the hunting horn upon which we were to assemble in the event we missed our Drop Zone. As I approached this sound, I was challenged by one of our crickets and I joined a group of four or five soldiers who had also heard the horn. Eventually eight of us had assembled on this sound which turned out to be the lowing of a young cow."[4]

Using the luminous cord from around an equipment bundle, Lieutenant Elmer Brandenberger had improvised a method of getting together with the men of his stick. He had landed in a small depression in a field where he felt hidden from the enemy which had been firing on the men and planes. Brandenberger related, "Everything was quiet. I took stock of my situation. Finding myself armed with only some hand grenades and a couple of sharp knives, I decided that the most practical thing to do was to 'roll up the rest of the stick.' I started out in the direction of flight and found one of my bundles packed with some weapons (BAR's[5]) and ammunition. I unfastened the luminous cord from around the bundle, stood up and whirled it about in the air several times. Nothing happened. I selected a BAR and some ammunition and started out again. I came across Sergeant Fuller, squad leader of my mortar group and several other men who had joined him. A short time later, we joined a larger group that had been assembled by Captain Fred Hancock of Charley Company."

Though his battalion relied on a large bronze bell for assembly purposes, PFC John Lacy was having difficulty finding the assembly point. He said, "I tried to get my bearings as to the direction of the assembly area. I recall a bugle blowing every few minutes. I picked up with a man here and another there and finally we had six or seven in our small group."

Expecting to find members of his group who could provide support against a quick enemy attack, Colonel Gerald J. Higgins, chief of staff for the 101st Airborne Division, recalled, "The first parachutist I encountered after landing was a medic. I shall never forget my chagrin when I realized his only weapon was a syrette! I had only a carbine, and had hoped to find not only companionship but firepower."

Private Waylen "Pete" Lamb had been assigned to the medics only because he came in as a replacement with a staff sergeant's rating. The regimental 'T.O.'[6] allowed only one more staff sergeant and so the infantryman was converted into an aidman. Since that time he had lost his rating. Lamb was determined however, to join his buddies on the firing line. He remembered, "The very first thing I did when I fi-

nally got out of my chute was to take the Red Cross armband and stick it in the top of my boot. Then I crawled in the
direction of a voice I recognized as belonging to Sergeant
Frank Freestone. I talked him out of his carbine rifle and
ammo and a couple of hand grenades. He kept his .45-caliber
pistol. He didn't want to part with his carbine. I remember
him telling me, 'Hell no, I need it to fight with!' He finally
consented after I told him all I had was a pack of hypo nee-
dles."

It was fortunate for Sergeant Bill Ashbrook, a member of
the MP Platoon of Division Headquarters, that he quickly
found others. His hearing had been impaired on a practice
jump some time earlier and he felt a need to get with others
quickly. Ashbrook was slammed hard into the ground on the
backswing of an oscillation. "I struggled to keep from
blacking out but couldn't make it," he later recalled. "I was
found by two others from the same stick. They got me up and
out of my harness and waited until I could move. At this time
my head was killing me. My hearing had been impaired due
to an injury on my third qualifying jump, so I told one soldier to walk about ten yards in front of me and that his primary duty was to listen for challengers (the crickets). I knew
I probably couldn't hear them at any kind of distance, but
that I could damned well see. The third man brought up the
rear and we headed in a generally northerly direction to find
the battalion assembly point.

"We hadn't moved more than a hundred to two hundred
yards when we saw our first German soldier. He was moving
very fast, carrying his rifle exactly as we had been taught. He
was on the other side of the hedge and in accordance with
our instructions, we let him go. We had moved about one-half
mile beyond that point when we were challenged. It turned
out to be four of our men, and that made us seven."

One of the men who was with the second group which met
Ashbrook was Chief Warrant Officer Steve Karabinos, an
assistant to the chief of staff. After getting free of his harness in a road, Karabinos proceeded in a northwesterly direction toward what he assumed would be the assembly area. He
related, "At approximately 0200, I met Sergeant Cooper (clerk

from G-4 Section), Sergeant William Ashbrook (Hqtrs. MP), and Private Milbrath (Hqtrs. MP), and a short time later, Sergeant Kundrot (clerk in G-3 Section). We proceeded generally northwest, sticking to the hedgerows until we came to a point where German machine-gun fire was intense. Due to the small size of our squad and the lack of some honest-to-goodness firepower, we decided it best to try to swing around the Germans' field of fire, which was more or less limited due to hedgerows. We traveled due north but were forced to retrace our steps when another machine gun opened up on us. We then proceeded south with the idea of pushing west in a more favorable sector."

Still another man who got in with this group, though he was unknown to the others, was a Division Artillery wireman, Corporal James L. Evans, who had his share of adventures before linking up with the others. He recalled, "I went back in the direction the lanes were coming from as I was 14th man in the 15-man stick. I killed two Germans, found one G. I. from the 501st Headquarters Company with his chin blown off and his tongue hanging below his Adam's apple.[7] I bandaged him up, never heard from him after D-Day. I met a warrant officer, who was an assistant to General Taylor, and a buck sergeant from the MP's (nice guy!). I also met Lieutenant Richardson with a broken foot searching for General McAuliffe. I persuaded him to stay with the group and I went in his place. When I returned, the group had gone on, so I made my way toward Hiesville by myself."

Help from the French

When lost in a strange land, it is logical to seek out the natives to get directions. Some offered it voluntarily. Others were hidden and had to be coaxed into helping.

T/4 John Seney had difficulty getting out of his chute after he had crashed down through a grape arbor. He listened for a few minutes and heard no one. "I clicked my cricket a few times. Nothing happened. I went over to a cottage nearby. An old Frenchman came out, peered at me and then hugged me, shouting something in French. He pointed to an upstairs room, holding up three fingers and saying, 'Boche.' Later we found out they had run off at the sound of the planes. The elderly Frenchman huddled with me over my maps and tried to locate my position. I asked for directions to our objective—I vaguely understood what he was trying to say."

Seney added, "About an hour later, there were approximately six or seven of us gathered in the orchard; I placed the map and compass on the ground and affirmed our position from my conversation with the old Frenchman earlier. We figured we were about six kilometers from our mission area."

PFC Walter Gordon found three members of his group. Nothing was familiar to them in the landscape and they soon realized they were not on the proper drop zone. He related, "We soon found a large farmhouse and carefully approached the door and entered the foyer and in checking the rooms on each side of the hall we flashed a light and saw German uniforms and equipment all along the walls and floor. We knew we were in the wrong spot. Huddled out in a barn were some French civilians and we did our best to question them in our best fashion—three Yankees and me in my best Dixieland draw! I recall someone asked, 'Boche?' and pointed to the house. We left after one of the women counted to twenty on her fingers. She was still counting as we sallied out of the farmyard. We thought it best to head in a generally northeasterly direction and be as close as possible to the troops storming the beaches at dawn."

Sergeant Eugene Amburgey had landed with others in a flooded area near Carquebot. Their plane had crashed just east of the village. As a member of the S-2 Section, and able to speak French fluently, Amburgey was given the job of finding their location. He said, "Lieutenant Myers and I went on a patrol at dawn. We stopped a French girl in a one-horse cart and asked for directions. We were way off the map. We then started traveling east."

Increase in numbers

The men continued to find others and the numbers began to swell to the point they felt they could move on toward objectives. PFC Warren Ruedy had broken a bone in his left foot on the landing but managed to get out of his chute to find other members of his mortar squad. Ruedy related, "I got together with PFC Homer Hughes, our gunner. We heard Corporal George Jordan in the hedgerow where he had come down. His chute was tangled and he was hanging near the ground. He took a beating from the briars and we never did find his rifle. We got him untangled shortly. We moved along the hedgerows looking for more men—we had fifteen or twenty before daylight."

An enemy machine gunner, stationed at the far corner of the field, had continued to fire at planes passing overhead as Lieutenant Richard Winters had been cutting himself loose from his harness. Anxious to find a weapon, Winters had decided to find the equipment bag which contained his tommy gun. He had dropped it in the direction of the enemy gunner as the bag was torn loose from his grasp by the opening shock of the chute. Winters wrote, "Just as I started off, knife in hand, another chutist landed close by. I helped him free of his chute. Got a grenade from him and said, 'Let's go get my equipment.' He was hesitant about taking the lead even though he had a tommy gun, so I said, 'Follow me.'

"It wasn't long before we were away from that machine gun. To find my leg bag would take us near another machine gun we discovered firing at the planes which were still coming over so I said, 'To hell with it!' We started to move away from the strongpoint of Ste. Mère Eglise, the identity of which we discovered a few minutes later. We heard sounds and I cricketed and got a reply from one of my platoon sergeants, Carwood Lipton, who had come upon a signpost. With him were a few other men. We hooked up with them, a total of twelve, and started down a road. In a short while we ran into a group of about fifty men from the 502nd with a colonel in charge. I attached my group to his. With this force we turned east toward the Beach."

An even larger group of men was collecting at the assembly area for the 3rd Battalion of the 501st Regiment and Division Headquarters. The blue light and shrill whistle were in operation and men continued to gravitate toward them quickly.

Corporal Robert Ryals had jumped as a 3rd Battalion radio operator for Lieutenant Colonel Julian Ewell of the 501st. The leg bag with his SCR-300 radio had torn loose from his grip and was lost on the drop. He had landed on the eastern edge of Drop Zone "C." He said, "Since I had lost my equipment, I started to backtrack to see if I could assist T/4 Tom Murphy with an SCR-284, which was a heavier piece of equipment and had been part of a door bundle we had shoved out before we jumped. I rolled up eight or nine men, all from the 3rd Battalion, except for one from the 508th Regiment. I released these men to another NCO so they could proceed to the assembly area which was in the opposite direction in which I was moving. I proceeded across a small sunken road and met General Taylor with a small party. They were traveling in the opposite direction. While attempting to lead General Taylor to our assembly area, we met Colonel Ewell and Tom Murphy who had an SCR-300 radio he had recovered intact at a road junction. We then proceeded to the assembly area."

T/4 Tom Murphy described the same incident: "I landed in a field and found a radio. Pretty soon I ran into Colonel Julian Ewell and General Taylor. While standing on a road, a machine gun opened up at us. This I guess was our first encounter. We assembled in a field and stayed there for a few hours."

Corporal Virgil Danforth had packed his trusty .03 in an equipment bundle and dropped with only a World War I bayonet and a couple of hand grenades as weapons. Having been prevented by the Germans from going to the equipment bundle to retrieve his rifle, he started looking for the men of his squad. He said, "I collected six men of my squad and told them to wait in the corner of the hedgerow while I found the rest of them. I located Dave Mythaler who had come down through a big tree and had been knocked a little silly. I found the remaining members of my squad and returned to where I had left the rest but they were gone. After looking for quite a while for them I headed for the whistle which I could hear in the distance from our assembly area. When I got there I found the rest of my boys. They had assembled with General Taylor."

Having encountered a German patrol shortly after they had joined forces, Major Legere, Captain White, and T/5 Koskimaki continued their search together for the Division Headquarters and 3rd Battalion assembly area. After a fruitless search, the threesome decided to separate and go in different directions. All were to return to the present position in fifteen minutes in the hope that at least one of them would have located the assembly point.

Moving along the edges of the hedgerows so as to remain in the shadows, Koskimaki continued his search in the dark and was the first to reach the assembly area. He related, "An MP on sentry duty challenged me. I asked him if General Taylor was present because I was his radio operator. He directed me to a deeply shadowed area where the general was reclining, using his helmet for a pillow. I saluted and reported in, telling him I had been with Major Legere and Captain White, explaining also that as soon as I found the assembly area, I was to report back to them.

"However, I had no idea as to the direction I had come from—I had been completely lost. The General wanted his radio in working order promptly. I explained that I had only half of my radio—the other half was being carried by a radio operator who had flown in another plane. We were to connect the halves in the assembly area. I left the General to inquire about radio equipment. My company commander, Captain William Breen, and our assistant platoon leader, Staff Sergeant Leo DeGrace, were present and both were handicapped with painful leg injuries. No radios had been located yet. Other members of my platoon were out scouring the fields for communications equipment bundles and some were posted on sentry duty. I was told to stay near the general because the first radio found would be sent to my position.

"A short time later, Major Legere reported in—he had been directed to the proper location by an artillery soldier who was searching for equipment bundles. Captain White was only a few minutes behind. 'Everything seemed to be snafued. I had no means of communication to provide for the general. From the conversation going on about me, it sounded like others were having their problems also. Officers wondered what had happened to members of their groups. Vital equipment was missing. It had already been decided that the jump had been badly scattered."

Conclusion

At 0330, two hours after the jump, eighty-five men had gathered at this particular assembly area. They included forty-five men from the Parachute Echelon of the Division Headquarters and forty men from the 600-man 3rd Battalion of the 501st who had been assigned to Division Headquarters to provide security and to clear the glider landing fields before the arrival of the predawn glider lift.

There were no distinguishing landmarks visible in the dark on which the officers could get a bearing as to location. The main task of these Division Headquarters men was to move into Hiesville to establish the command post from which to direct the overall assault of the Screaming Eagle Division. For the time being, however, it was necessary to wait for daylight in this hedgerow-bordered assembly area which was typical of the other assembly points set up by specific troopers who had been assigned to jump with various aids.

The spire of St. Marie-du-Mont, different in shape from all other church towers in the area, emerged in the early dawn as the first distinguishing landmark. The men picked up their equipment and started out toward their objective.

CHAPTER 9

Johnson's Regiment— the 501st

The 501st Parachute Infantry Regiment, less the 3rd Battalion, which had jumped with Division Headquarters, was given the job of capturing the locks at La Barquette and the destruction of the railroad bridge and four highway bridges northwest of Carentan. Control of the locks was thought to be vital because by means of the locks, the Germans could control the flooding of the surrounding countryside and hamper the movement of the attacking forces. The bridges over the Douve River would be used by the Germans to bring up reinforcements against the troops arriving over Utah Beach. Colonel Howard "Skeets" Johnson was the commander of the regiment, which consisted of 168 officers and 2,175 enlisted men.

A few days before D-Day, a change had been requested on the drop zone by Regimental Commander Johnson. He felt that Drop Zone "B" was too far from his objectives.[1] Invasion planners had also noted the appearance of a large number of anti-airborne obstacles in those fields. The request for the change to drop into Drop Zone "D" had been approved by division headquarters.

The 1st Battalion, under the command of Lt. Colonel Robert C. Carroll, was assigned the mission of capturing the vital locks; Colonel Johnson and his regimental headquarters staff jumped with this battalion. The serial consisted of 45 planes. Of this number, only 18 dropped their sticks on or near the drop zone. The rest were badly scattered with some planes giving the jumpers the green light several miles south of Carentan. (So bad was the situation for this battalion that it

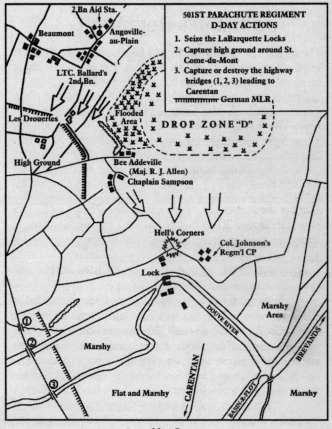

501ST PARACHUTE REGIMENT D-DAY ACTIONS

1. Seize the LaBarquette Locks
2. Capture high ground around St. Come-du-Mont
3. Capture or destroy the highway bridges (1, 2, 3) leading to Carentan

⊤⊤⊤⊤⊤⊤⊤⊤ German MLR

2 Bn Aid Sta.

Beaumont

Angoville-au-Plain

LTC. Ballard's 2nd Bn.

Les Droueries

Flooded Area

DROP ZONE "D"

High Ground

Bec Addeville (Maj. R. J. Allen)

Chaplain Sampson

Hell's Corners

Col. Johnson's Regm'l CP

Lock

Marshy Area

DOUVE RIVER

①

②

③

Marshy

Flat and Marshy

CARENTAN

BASIN-R. FLOT

BREVANDS

Marshy

Map 5

had to be reorganized on D plus 2, or June 8.) Battalion Commander Carroll was killed in the early hours of D-Day. His entire headquarters staff was missing, as were the commanders of Able, Baker, Charley, and Headquarters Companies.

Johnson's makeshift force

The mission to gain the locks was taken over by a makeshift force commanded by Colonel Johnson. The group was made up of paratroopers from several different units.

One of the rarities of the parachute drop occurred when Colonel Johnson's stick managed to land on the proper drop zone. This group was in the lead plane of the serial. The green light was flashed a half-minute prematurely by this lead plane. The other planes had dropped their loads. Because an equipment bundle had jammed in the doorway, no one had been able to jump until it was finally cleared. The delay enabled this stick to land where they had originally planned. The drop zone was close to the flooded areas and Colonel Johnson later reasoned that most of the planes had dropped their sticks over water, which caused the accidental drownings of many of this battalion's members.

Most individuals had narrow escapes before daybreak. Colonel Johnson had been fired upon by a German soldier from a distance of only 25 yards as he struggled with his chute. He returned the fire with his Colt .45. As he roamed the darkness, he encountered fifteen men, some of whom were members of the 506th. As the group moved along the ditches and small streams, its members grew to about 150. Colonel Johnson was able to observe by moonlight that his group was only a few hundred yards from the locks. Near a road junction, later known as Hell's Corners, just north of the locks, he split his group, setting about 100 up in defensive positions along the side of the road. The other 50 were sent on a dash over the open ground to the locks. They reached the objective without suffering any casualties though a few shots were fired in their direction. Members quickly crossed the locks and dug in deeply in the soft ground on the far bank. The area was lightly defended, although the enemy entrenchments led the colonel to believe that the protecting force had been elsewhere when the rush was put on. Downstream from the locks, the river was held in its course by six- to eight-foot high flood banks.

The lock was hand operated and in good working condition. The Germans soon realized that this was an objective of the paratroopers and began shelling the area. However, no enemy counterattack was launched against the position during these early crucial hours.

One of the men who was present in this move was a medic, Private Waylen Lamb, attached to the Demolitions Platoon. As described earlier, Lamb had stuffed his Red Cross armband in the top of his boot and had nagged one of his demolition platoon buddies for a weapon. The reluctant trooper had given Lamb his carbine rifle, keeping the .45 Colt sidearm for his own use. As Lamb remembered it, "I had been briefed along with the rest of the platoon that our mission was to secure the locks and prevent the Germans from blowing them up.

"After the drop, several of us got together and shortly we began hooking up with men from various outfits, none of them I remember knowing before. In a short time we had about forty men in one group. There was a Lieutenant Allen, who got us all organized—did a mighty fine job too considering the confusion. We did not travel far. Most of the time, we couldn't move because of small-arms fire around us. I remember the Krauts switching from ground fire and zeroing in on the glider boys who were coming in. That gave us an opportunity to move each time they did this. When we finally stopped moving and dug in, daylight found us just to the north of Carentan at a place we later called 'Hell's Corners.'

"After daylight I got hooked up with most of the men from our demolitions platoon. One of our platoon officers, Lieutenant Lee J. Bowers, took over. Our men, plus a few from other units, started moving across an open field toward Carentan in the direction of the locks which were located on the Douve River.

"As we were moving out, I was helping Lieutenant Bowers carry one end of an A-5 container equipment bundle filled with anti-tank mines. The lead was flying all around. Some men were hit. I don't recall that anyone was killed yet, but I kept thinking that if a round hits this bundle, somebody is gonna get hurt real bad. I even suggested to Bowers that we leave it behind. He said we might need it. When we got to the stream, we were going to float it across. As we swam it across, things got too hot and we let it sink to the bottom. We finally got to the locks area and dug in on the small dike about ten feet apart and in a straight line. We had one man killed by sniper fire. It was Supply Sergeant Anderson from our regimental headquarters company. I gave him all the first aid I could, but what can anyone do with sulfa powder when a man is hit square in the chest with a rifle slug and you can't move him. I always felt bad about that.

"There was a little trooper who was dug in with me when it got to be daylight. I never knew his name, never had seen him before, nor did I know where he got the second M-1 rifle he gave me. All I remember about that lad is that he had a good shooting eye, and every time he squeezed off a round Hitler lost a soldier. He would holler, 'Sue-eee!' and smile. He taught me more about shooting in five minutes than I learned all the other times on the rifle range.

"I recall Runge, the boy with the German name who was proud as hell that he was an American. That first morning, after daylight, he and two others charged a house occupied by several Germans. Runge, armed with only a .45, accounted for his share during the fight from room to room."

Also engaged in the activity near the locks was Corporal Harry E. Mole. After his drop, Mole had crawled through a narrow canal after he had failed to negotiate it with a leap. In disgust, he had crawled into a hedgerow and gone to sleep. He describes his experience: "At daybreak, when I awoke after three or four hours of sleep, it was very quiet. I peered through the bushes that grew atop every hedgerow and saw a house with a few G.I.'s milling about. They were gathering wood for a fire and were looking for water with which to bathe. I joined them. Not much was said; nobody had anything to say. I believe each one of us thought we all should be out fighting someplace. The feeling we were shirking our duty seemed prevalent. I think each one wanted to say to the others, 'Why aren't you where the fighting is?' The soft rumble of distant firing along the beaches some miles away could be heard. Why look for trouble when none existed? This made it easy to eat a K-ration breakfast of eggs and bacon, Nescafe (hot if you were lucky enough to get a fire going and had your canteen cup full of water), four hard biscuits, and something sweet, malted milk tablets or a fruit bar.

"After a while an officer poked his head in the doorway and told us to get ready to move on. A bunch of officers were organizing a patrol consisting of the men they found in and around the farmhouse.

"As always, halfway through my K-ration breakfast the words, 'Let's go!' rang through my ears. Some 2nd lieutenant was standing in the doorway of the house rounding up us G.I.'s standing around a hot stove drying out our wet clothes. Gulping down half a tin of scrambled eggs and bacon, grabbing my carbine and my SCR-536 radio, I was off. We were only to go down the road a ways to scout around and would return later in the day. We were to travel light. Traveling light always sounded good to me. I removed my musette bag, gas mask, code machine; stuffed a K-ration or two in one of the many pockets of my jumpsuit and fell in line with the others. We never did get back to that farmhouse.

"The officers were in front; the rest of us trailed behind. As we tramped down the road, rifles slung, not a sound could be heard except the muffled sound of marching feet and that distant thunderlike noise over on the beaches. A 2nd lieutenant would turn around, walk backwards, survey his squad and being satisfied they were following in a soldierly manner, would turn back and resume his conversation with the fellow officers. At times we would hear one of them shout, 'Hey, you two guys! Spread out! Suppose a shell should land nearby, we would have two casualties instead of one!' Those officers were still on training problems in England!

"About a mile or so beyond our starting point, we came to one of those terrible irrigation ditches. Fortunately it was bridged. The leaders, feeling it would be safer to go through the water than expose ourselves by going over the slightly domed bridge, waded across the ditch. I went over the bridge. There wasn't a German around for miles. I guessed they were all fighting the men on the beaches. Anyway, I was severely reprimanded and told I would be dealt with later when we got to where we were going. We were overtrained.

"Finally we came to another farmhouse located near some locks. Fortunately there were more troopers in that area. Now there were more leaders. One was Colonel Johnson, our regimental commander. Wow! My heart skipped a beat. This guy will lead us on some suicidal mission and we'll all be killed! We now became a part of the force defending the locks."

The ease with which the first objective, the locks, had been gained encouraged Johnson to try for the next goal—the highway bridges less than a mile upstream. Patrols were sent out from several points and they came under heavy fire quickly. They found the bridges well guarded by the enemy.

A member of such a patrol was PFC Laverne Carlson (another demo man who had been assigned to 2nd Battalion for this mission). A mortar shell lit near him after he located one other soldier, Private Boland. In a short time they had ten men in a group and quickly it swelled to about forty. Carlson reminisced, "The only officer I remember in our group was Lieutenant Peterson from regimental headquarters. We started out toward St. Come-du-Mont and the bridges and I can remember wading through a swamp with the water coming up to my neck at times. When we contacted the enemy, Lt. Peterson sent me and PFC Harden back to get more help. We took a dirt road back to avoid the swamp and we stayed about fifty yards apart because the road was under machine-gun and rifle fire and we had a lot of running and crawling to get to a covered area. At this point we found Captain Brown (D Company). He had several men but somehow we ended up at the La Barquette Locks. I found out later that Lieutenant Peterson was killed and several men who were with him were killed or wounded when they were caught in an artillery barrage."

Addeville

Meanwhile, Major R. J. Allen was assembling forces at Addeville, less than a mile northwest of the locks. Corporal Harold Shoutis was among these men. "After crossing a river," he recalled, "I ran into more and more men. An officer took charge and we went into the small town of Addeville. We set up a defense line and an aid station."

Major Allen had been organizing this group well. They had searched the nearby area for equipment bundles that had been dropped by parachutists and had returned with well-stocked farm carts. A good supply of arms and ammunition had been recovered. Corporal Harold Shoutis, PFC Robert W. Smith, and PFC Frank Carpenter were among those who were engaged in this task.

According to Shoutis, "My machine gunner (Hopper) and I hooked up a horse and buggy and retrieved some equipment bundles."

"After we arrived in Addeville, we were sent out to get equipment bundles," said PFC Robert Smith. "Others in this group were led by a Lieutenant Murray." PFC Frank Carpenter described his actions: "After the drop, I ran into Del Santo. The canals in the area kept us apart from other men. I remember getting into a small town. I helped Sergeant Huttner, our supply sergeant, bring in supplies from the chutes to the town we were near. The Germans had us pinned down several times but 'Hut' and I fought our way out and always got back to town."

Word soon reached Colonel Johnson about Allen's force in Addeville. Johnson felt he needed them to reinforce his own troops in the task of holding La Barquette and in attacking the highway bridges less than a mile west of the locks. The bridges were to be destroyed as quickly as possible to prevent the movement of enemy armored forces toward Utah Beach.

Therefore, Colonel Johnson left a force of fifty men defending the locks while he proceeded north with the remainder of his men to make contact with Major Allen. Addeville was reached at 0900. The hundred men Allen had on hand were already engaged with the enemy. One-fourth of the group was suffering from sprains and broken bones resulting from the night drop. Allen had planned to attack toward St. Come-du-Mont when he had gathered more men.

Leaving Allen with a rear guard force of about thirty men, Johnson was preparing to return to the locks. It was then that he received a report that Lieutenant Colonel Robert Ballard had a force heavily engaged with the enemy at Les Droueries, about a half mile west of Addeville.

Using a small SCR-536 radio, Johnson called for Ballard to break off contact with the enemy and proceed to Base Addeville as quickly as possible. From there he should pick up the remainder of Allen's forces and continue to the La Barquette area. Ballard notified him that such a move was impossible at that time with the enemy entrenched in strong numbers between his and Allen's forces. Johnson ordered Ballard to make his break as soon as possible and reinforce him at the locks so they could proceed with the important bridge mission. (The actions of Ballard's 2nd Battalion are found later in this chapter.)

After leaving Addeville, Johnson proceeded with his reinforced unit back toward the locks. They were observed by German forces who waited until they arrived at Hell's Corners, just above the locks. There, the Americans came under heavy artillery and mortar fire and were pinned down in an exposed area.

Involved in this action was Captain Sammie Homan who remembered, "We moved with Colonel Johnson to the locks. Most of the firing on us en route was from positions on high ground and relatively inaccurate. There was no cover or concealment so we felt like we were walking in front of targets on a known distance range."

One of the troopers moving down into the locks area with Colonel Johnson was PFC Frank Carpenter. He and his company supply sergeant had been collecting supplies from the fields under fire from German soldiers. A short time before they moved south, they had orders to destroy these supplies. Carpenter described the move to the locks: "The mortar fire at the locks from the bridge upstream gave us trouble. They got Campos there. He was running across the lock when a round hit right next to him. Foxholes we saw in pictures back in England were ready made for us by the Germans. I'm glad we didn't have to pry them out."

Jim Purifoy went down to Hell's Corners and the locks with Johnson. "I was in on the fighting with Colonel Johnson at Hell's Corners," he recalled. "Bart Tantello and I were great quid chewers and we were both chawing away while lying in wait on a manure pile for some Germans to come into range. Bart turned and asked me, 'What do you want me to tell your parents in Arkansas when I get back to see them after the war?' A few minutes later he was dead with a bullet between the eyes."

PFC Alex Philip also joined Johnson. He had been in and out of several canals before he finally reached Addeville. He stated, "I remember seeing the spire of the church in Carentan in the early morning light. There were dive-bombers over the town. We were in Addeville with Father Sampson for a while and then headed toward the locks to reinforce Colonel Johnson. As the men approached the farmhouse Johnson was using for a command post, he would send the men out about 150 to 200 yards in advance for perimeter defense."

During the evening of D-Day, Major Allen left Addeville with a 30-man rear guard force. Father Sampson had arrived on the scene during the late afternoon and had learned of Johnson's decision to move all the troops to La Barquette. Only the wounded who were unable to walk were left behind.[2]

At 2200 in the evening of D-Day, Major Allen arrived at the locks with his men from Addeville. One of these men, PFC William A. Druback stated, "I remember moving toward the locks. Father Sampson stayed behind at Addeville. I and others were assigned to rear guard duty to cover the rest as they moved out toward the locks."

Johnson had sent out a patrol earlier to seek out division headquarters. It failed to return. Contact had been made with a small group of 506th Regiment men who were at the small wooden bridges downstream from the locks. No help was available from them—in fact they needed assistance. Their commander, Captain Charles Shettle, arrived during the day to request help for his position. Johnson turned him down explaining he was hard-pressed hanging on to his own position at the locks as well as preparing for the destruction of the road bridges upstream.

As night came, Johnson sent another patrol up the river toward the highway bridges. Heavy small-arms fire met them several hundred yards from the nearest bridge. Flare shells lighted the area to daylight brilliance. Shortly after midnight, the patrol reported back to Johnson. It would take a force much larger than was on hand at La Barquette to accomplish this mission.

Pete Lamb described the nighttime activity that took place at the locks. "We had a Sergeant Buddy Biles who would crawl out to our front at night and fill our canteens with wine at a farmhouse and then take his chances getting shot by his own men when crawling back," Lamb later remembered. "Sergeant Bruce Cook devised another type of communications, using instead of signal, voice, wire, or radio, what he called 'suspension line commo.' He took the lines off discarded chutes and tied them between the foxholes and had the men occupying the holes attach it to themselves. We could alert the whole line dug in on the dike in a matter of seconds."

As the day came to a close, the men had orders to dig in deep and establish strong outposts several hundred yards north and south of the locks. No food or water was available. The men were down to a basic supply of ammunition. The bridges continued to remain in enemy hands and probably carried considerable reinforcements, both mechanized and foot soldiers during the night.

Why the 1st Battalion didn't make it to the locks

What happened to the men of the 1st Battalion who had the original assignment of capturing the locks? Why were so few of them available for duty on the first day at La Barquette? The battalion commander, Lieutenant Colonel Robert O. Carroll, and two of his staff officers, Captain Thomas Chastant and Lieutenant John W. Atkinson, Jr., had run into a German ambush at a crossroads before daylight. PFC Leo Runge remembered, "I was near Colonel Carroll when he was killed before daybreak."[3]

Other 1st Battalion planes had dropped their sticks of jumpers several miles southeast and southwest of Carentan. Several sticks of men landed in the marshy area near St. Georges-du-Bohon, seven kilometers south of Carentan. Some of their action follows.

T/4 William W. House had jumped from the same plane as his company commander, Captain Robert H. Phillips of Charley Company. From the shelter of a hedgerow he had watched in awe as several C-47's crashed in flames. He found two other members of his stick. House remembered, "After the three of us got together, we assembled on a light and joined a group from 1st Battalion Headquarters Company. We were pinned down all night in a ditch that was surrounded by a small thicket. About noon on June 6, we tried to escape our trap by crawling out through the ditch. We were surrounded by Germans from a parachute outfit and Captain Simmons (CO of 1st Battalion Headquarters Company) surrendered the group. We were taken to a French church where our two battalion doctors had set up an aid station under the direction of the enemy. Our battalion exec was there badly wounded."[4]

T/5 John R. Armstrong was a platoon radio operator and had jumped with Captain Phillips and House. "I found another member of my stick, Bill House, and we tried unsuccessfully to orient ourselves," Armstrong recalled. "Finally turned on my SCR-536 radio to contact other members. No luck! I did very little fighting. We gathered up a hodgepodge group headed by the company commander, Captain Simmons, of 1st Battalion Headquarters Company. Most of this group was finally captured and most of our efforts during the day were devoted to trying to locate ourselves and avoiding capture."

Sergeant Alex Haag, who served as a radio sergeant for Headquarters of the 1st Battalion, had found three bundles of equipment, which included radios, rations, and bazookas along with their ammunition. He located his first man about three-quarters of an hour later. Haag remembered, "I had six men at daylight. We headed toward an area where a good skirmish was going on. Upon approaching a chapel on a rise nearby, I saw what looked like half of the German army. I decided we would go a different way. A Kraut patrol got on our trail and pushed us in the opposite direction. We went round and round but couldn't break through so finally I tried the easy way which was back in the direction from which we had come. Later I ran into Captain William Paty of A Company who had about six or seven men with him. We were run into a dead-end hedgerow and trapped. Captain Paty gave us orders to dig in and try to hold out until dark. After the group under Captain Simmons (CO of 1st Battalion Headquarters Company) was put out of action, the Krauts moved in on us. By this time we were no match as our ammo was low and quite a few of us were wounded and I think there were three dead.

"Sergeant Beall was the other man killed.[5] I knew him personally. I can still see one lad just as if it had happened yesterday. I had sent him to the edge of the hedgerow to protect that end of our front."

Haag was from a German-speaking family in Wisconsin and his knowledge of the language gave him an inkling of what the enemy was planning. "My knowledge of German came back in a hurry when I heard the Krauts issuing orders. We were surrounded by men of the German 6th Parachute Regiment and they used all oral means of communication. I had a pretty good idea of what was going on although when their company commander gave the order to close in and finish us off, I wished I had never heard or understood a word of German. They closed in on us and set up two machine guns, one on each end of the hedgerow. After a few minutes of tremendous small-arms and machine-gun fire, a lieutenant hollered, 'Give up!'

"We just fired back. So they gave us another 'chorus.' Then this Kraut lieutenant ran out in front of our position with his burp gun blazing away and once again hollered, 'Give up!' Captain Paty, badly wounded by now, somehow managed to stand up and put his hands up. How that German managed not to get shot—I am still wondering today. He certainly had guts.

"We were rounded up and taken to the same chapel we had passed earlier.[6] There were a number of our battalion officers besides Captains Simmons and Paty. Major Gage was there and badly wounded. Our surgeons, Captain Robert Blatherwick and Lieutenant Tom Johnson, were in the group being held.[7]

"Just before we had been captured, I had told Schwartz (our pigeoneer) to release the two birds he had so they would not fall into enemy hands. Dale Courtney tried to destroy his SCR-300 radio. I don't know if he managed to do so. The set was not in working order."

The destruction of useful information was important to T/5 John Armstrong of the same captured group. While held under the guns of the enemy paratroopers, he recalled, "I ate my SOI (Signal Operating Instruction) under the eyes of the enemy soldiers in that church."

Headed for Paris

Privates Chester Brooks and Dick Frame landed two miles south of Carentan. Brooks said, "After assembling part of the stick, the men asked me to take charge. I promptly led the group south, reasoning that all our objectives were south of the drop zone and on the Douve River. I figured whatever units we ran into we'd then know whether to go right or left. The logic was good but we were already many miles south of the river so I led them toward Paris and away from the objectives all night. We found out where we were in the morning. We got in with the French underground and we picked up a stick from 3rd Battalion that afternoon and hid out that night. We had a rather easy war of it that first day."[8]

Dick Frame had found an equipment bundle and waited in a ditch nearby for other members to arrive. He said, "About seven or eight guys assembled. Lieutenant Seale and Sergeant Burgess were in charge but they were not present so Brooks and Medic Leo Charpentier, who spoke French fluently, took over the leadership. We headed south because we felt our mission was in that direction."[9]

Able Company

Able Company, one of the line companies of the 1st Battalion, was under the command of Captain William Paty. This company had received the specific assignment of capturing the locks on D-Day, but didn't make it. The men had been well briefed to the point that they knew the directions in which to dig their foxholes once they gained a foothold at La Barquette. Paty's stick was dropped south of Carentan and most of them were killed or captured when they encountered an enemy paratroop unit.

Three other sticks dropped in the vicinity of Chef-du-Pont, in a flooded area about a mile and a half southwest of Ste. Mère Eglise. Staff Sergeant John Kushner, who had served as jumpmaster in one of these planes landed in chest deep water, unhooked himself, and waded toward shore. He related, "I met Roscoe Giles from my company, but from another stick in the same area. We later ran into Lieutenants Wagner and Puhalski and about 14 men from our company.

"We had a holding action outside of Chef-du-Pont that lasted a few hours. We ran a flank guard for a column moving toward Ste. Mère Eglise. Got pinned down in an orchard outside of town. Several hours later we regrouped with our A Company men and officers and headed for Division Headquarters where we joined the bulk of A Company being commanded by Lieutenant Craighill. Our medic, Francis Harbaugh, was awarded the DSC for action at Chef-du-Pont."

Sergeant Pat Lindsay, from the mortar section of his platoon of Able Company, had been part of a seven-man group that had ambushed a squad of Germans in the early morning hours. They heard sounds of a firefight to the east and moved toward it. He describes, "Enroute, we met an assorted group. We checked our maps and learned that we had dropped approximately eight miles from our Drop Zone which was located just east of St. Come-du-Mont.

"We moved on to Ste. Mère Eglise and at approximately

1300 hours, we started walking down the asphalt road toward St. Marie-du-Mont. We crossed a dirt road when we noticed a column of enemy soldiers go rushing past (15 to 20) on the double and going north. We could hear a brisk firefight going on in the vicinity of St. Marie-du-Mont which was to the east. We crawled through the hedgerows to observe where the Germans had gone in such a hurry. There they were, lined up in close formation of perhaps a platoon in strength with an officer in front of them and addressing them. We opened fire in a group and dropped many of them. The rest fled in panic.

"At 1500 P.M., we joined forces with a mixed group of troopers under the command of an 82nd Division lieutenant. He assumed command of the entire group and set up a road block about one mile east of Ste. Mère Eglise. We dug in. At about 1600–1700 hours, we saw a long column of [Allied] tanks and jeeps approaching from the east and the Beach. The lead elements came up to the road block and halted. The lieutenant went over and conferred with the commanding officer. They were the forward elements of Colonel Van Fleet's 8th Infantry Regiment of the 4th Division.

"The decision was then made to have the troopers ride the tanks into Ste. Mère Eglise. The mile of road between our position and Ste. Mère Eglise dropped into a valley and then sloped up to the edge of the town. The troopers thought this was great fun riding the tanks initially. We had gone perhaps a couple hundred yards before the column was raked by machine-gun fire. The tanks took direct hits but were not disabled. The miracle of the whole incident was that not a single trooper was hit. One soldier who was wearing an overseas cap in place of a helmet had a bullet hole through the front point. We bailed off in record time and dove for the ditches on either side of the road.

"We spent the rest of the day with the 5th Infantry digging in to protect the roadblock and facing Ste. Mère Eglise. I stayed awake all night—in fact I didn't get any sleep for the first 90 hours." Lindsay ended his D-Day about eight miles from his D-Day mission at the locks.

Lieutenant Sumpter Blackmon of Able Company and his stick had landed near Foucarville about eight miles north of their objective, the locks. Private Thurman Day and his platoon leader, Lieutenant Blackmon, took a machine gun and two boxes of ammunition from the equipment bundle and headed south by compass. Their loads got so heavy that they hid them in a hedgerow and covered them with leaves.

While standing near a roadside, Blackmon and Day observed troops moving toward them in the moonlight. A major from the 82nd Division came by with 34 men (five of whom were from Blackmon's stick). The entire group was lost and headed north. Blackmon convinced them that heading south was proper. He then added to his account: "Shortly we arrived at Foucarville where I had a chance to try out my French. We surrounded a house. I knocked on the door. A lady came. Another lady was sitting at a table with three empty chairs, two bottles of wine and some bread. No matter how hard I tried, I could not get her to understand that I wanted the direction to St. Come-du-Mont. I did, with the aid of the flag on my sleeve, make her understand that I was an American paratrooper. This scared the devil out of her. She yelled something and started for the door. I put my rifle to her stomach and had her sit down. I closed the door and backed out to the road with nothing accomplished.

"Just around the bend in the road we ran into our first enemy fire. A burst from a German machine gun got the arm of a sergeant from the 82nd. He was leading us about ten yards in front of me. We moved off the road to the left trying to avoid the enemy. I remember crawling through a grain field and hearing that 'tearing paper sound' of the German machine gun. I started to run and jump a ditch and just as I got to the ditch, a Kraut stood up in the ditch with his hands up. He was yelling something, and Nick Denovchik, my operations sergeant, who had jumped with me but had gotten in the 82nd major, understood him. (Now for some reason the Germans had stopped firing. We were not visible when we left the road. They had previously been firing.)

"This enemy soldier and Denovchik began talking. One of his buddies came out from hiding about fifty yards away. They led us to an underground place which contained a ton of ammo—potato masher grenades, antitank bazookas, burp gun and rifle ammo, a big radio set, and an airplane detector device. (The four large earphones of this device were so well camouflaged in the trees above us that we hadn't even noticed them.)

"Our two captives helped us blow the place up, oriented us, and with day breaking, we began to feel at home. We were able to move without incident to the causeway (Exit 4) near St. Martin-de-Varreville. We hoped that someone was taking care of our mission and that we could help the 4th Division come in OK. I'll never forget those beautiful (they seemed so then) G.I.'s just marching up that causeway on either side of the road. They seemed to be discarding something with every step.

"My six men got bikes confiscated from a German headquarters group at St. Martin and headed for the Locks on the Douve River. With no fanfare, we arrived at the statue in the middle of St. Marie-du-Mont. While behaving as tourists and resting there, some unfriendly soul ricocheted two bullets off the statue. We moved on toward Vierville. Some 500 to 600 yards from Vierville a Frenchman ran out of the hedge beside the road and stopped us and told us, 'many, many Boche everywhere.' We were tired and decided to head back and join the 4th Division for the night.

"On the outskirts of St. Marie-du-Mont, we came within a hundred yards of a German tank getting into position with a lot of Krauts running around. We coolly did an about-face on those bikes and were never fired upon. We took a side road which we thought would lead us over to the St. Come-du-Mont road. At this time, an evening glider serial started coming in. We left our bikes and decided to orient the glider men. We helped some and saw many we couldn't help—those poles were rough, but the hedgerows brought those gliders to a halt too quickly! As night came on somehow (I don't know what road we were on), we ended up at 4th Division Headquarters. I talked to General Barton. He contacted 101st HQ and talked with Lieutenant Colonel Kinnard (EXO of the 501st at that time) and with Lieutenant Colonel Ewell, the CO of 3rd Battalion. We pinpointed them on the map but decided to try to get some sleep. After about 30 minutes of good sleep we were awakened by the patter of rain. There seemed to be no rest for the weary so off we went. Down the road we came to a barn that looked rather safe and dry. Went in and rolled a couple dead Krauts out and fell asleep."

Sergeant Nick Denovchik from Blackmon's stick, related, "I met up with Jack Bleffer and a medic. Everything was mixed up. We met up with 82nd guys at about 0200 or 0300 in the morning. As we moved forward, we stumbled upon either a mortar position or a machine gun position. We threw some grenades and ran. Next I remember cutting a lot of wires strung on poles. We met Lieutenant Blackmon and a few more men in the early morning. I talked to some Russian-speaking enemy troops and they surrendered to us."

PFC Bruce E. Fess was a member of that same stick. He recalled, "I wandered about for several hours before meeting friendly troops. As morning broke, I lined up with a mixed outfit working its way south. Fought small skirmishes with them that day and night until I ran into some of my own outfit on the second day."

T/5 Martin J. Knafl was a platoon radio operator who also jumped with Lieutenant Blackmon. He related, "Dawn of D-Day found Sergeant Adams and myself joining up with officers and men of the 2nd Battalion Headquarters Company of the 502nd. We ran into an enemy roadblock. This was about two miles up the road which ran alongside the pasture into which I had dropped. Later while trying to find the 501st, we tied in with a group of 506th men and after a few skirmishes, Adams and I left to seek our unit after things got quiet. There for some reason, we split up. I was to sit tight while Adams scouted around. If he was not back in 45 minutes I was to strike out on my own.

"This I did, going in the general direction I figured my plane came from. I walked all afternoon through hedgerow after hedgerow and although there was firing going on, I didn't see a single person. About 1800 hours, I found an 82nd officer, a medic, who had fifteen wounded lying in concealment, most of them hurt in the jump itself. He informed me that the 501st was just ahead of his position, but there was an enemy group on the move in between which he estimated at battalion size. I was put out on the flank. All the wounded had tommy guns. At 1900 hours, the enemy attacked our position. My gun was practically useless as the troopers put out a wall of fire. I felt helpless on the flank. My machine gun had been partially disabled when it broke from my grasp on the jump. I had to fire it as a single-shot weapon.

"Hearing some noise, I found the enemy setting up a machine gun five feet in front of my foxhole. After dropping two grenades on it, I started running toward the troopers in the ditch. I had 300 rounds of .45 caliber ammo. I figured to give it to the men in the ditch. As I jumped the hedge, I collided with a German soldier. We both fell backwards, but his buddy was behind him with a burp gun. That was it for me. Looking past them I could see the troopers being herded on the road and I was forced to join them. Another 101ster was among them."

Baker Company

Company B was also having its problems. Captain Loyal Bogart and his headquarters platoon was dropped over the marshes near Graignes, six miles southeast of Carentan.

PFC Frank Juliano jumped with Captain Bogart, his commanding officer. He stated, "After getting loose from my harness, I listened for Germans and our men. I didn't see anyone that night. I kept hearing our cricket signal, but they were probably real crickets in the swamp."[10]

Juliano continued, "Captain Bogart collected 16 men from our stick. One man was missing and I believe he drowned in the river because the men on either side of him straddled the stream on the landing. I spent the night in the swamp, joining up with my stick in the morning. Captain Bogart injured his leg when hit by flak in the plane, but he insisted on jumping with us. He was injured again during the day and wanted to be left behind but the men refused his request. We joined a larger group of 82nd Division men in the town of Graignes. Our first prisoner was a French policeman. We dug in to hold the town. I don't know why."[11]

PFC Donald W. Wilson jumped with his platoon leader,

Lieutenant John Sallin. As a member of this stick, Wilson was several miles north of his proper drop zone. He said, "Lieutenant Sallin was able to collect 15 to 20 men. We moved through a small town and went out to Division Headquarters. We had a few skirmishes along the way. We put out one machine-gun nest."

Corporal Tony D'Angiolini, also of B Company, found an injured member from his stick. He said, "The trooper had been hurt as the result of the opening shock and couldn't walk. I stayed with him all night. In the morning I saw and got together with several members of my outfit. The next thing I knew, we were battling through the hedgerows."

Charley Company

Captain Robert H. Phillips of Charley Company had dropped several miles south of Carentan. His command grew to eighteen men. They went to a nearby farmhouse to get information but the French people were too frightened and excited to be of any assistance. With dogs barking furiously and cowbells ringing, the men retreated into the darkness and struck out across the fields. At daybreak they settled down in the corner of a field where they rested against a hedgerow. Phillips heard activity on the other side of the hedge. He said, "I raised my head over the hedgerow and saw a group of eighteen or twenty German soldiers on the double with their rifles at the ready go rushing past. I faded down and motioned the rest to be quiet. This was our first look at the enemy.

"Later in the morning, and just before joining Sergeant Barney and Lieutenant Edwin Hutchinson, our small group encountered a small enemy patrol among the group of four or five houses surrounding a courtyard, including a barn. I passed through an archway between several outbuildings and came face-to-face with a German. We were both completely surprised! I ducked back, pulled out a grenade, and peeked around the corner of the building. The Kraut was no more than ten or fifteen yards away. He was preparing his 'potato masher.' I heaved my grenade and started running back toward the houses. His grenade came into the archway and that was all there was to that. Moments later several of us were trying to pick off Germans who were crawling and those whose heads were bobbing up and down in the field. I never could manage to zero in on one of those heads and they were clad with only cloth overseas caps. We disengaged just as silently and mysteriously as we came together.

"I had come to the conclusion that my primary mission was to get back to my unit alive with my men. I didn't know what skills that would require or what problems we would encounter, but one thing was clear—we were in the midst of the enemy and could count on no help but that of God and our own resources. In order to join our own forces we were going to have to deal with each situation as we encountered it. I can truthfully say it never entered my mind that we could be forced to surrender. This did happen to others. Perhaps the circumstances were such that we never had to consider such a proposition, but we did engage the enemy on numerous occasions at close quarters. We were stealthy, cautious, and bold at proper times."[12]

From the original stick that jumped with Captain Phillips, all were not as fortunate as those who joined with Phillips himself. T/4 Bill House and T/5 John Armstrong had spotted the assembly light for their battalion headquarters and were surrounded by Germans and captured as they assembled with other Americans. Sergeant Henry Beall joined Captain Paty of Able Company near St. Georges-du-Bohon and lost his life fighting in the hedgerows.

2nd Battalion

The 2nd Battalion of the 501st Parachute Infantry Regiment was under the very capable leadership of Lieutenant Colonel Robert Ballard. Along with 1st Battalion and Regimental Headquarters, his group had been scheduled to land on Drop Zone "D."

The 2nd Battalion had always prided itself on excellent and rapid assemblies on practice night jumps. This had been accomplished with a large green lantern and a heavy bronze bell. Paratroopers had moved toward the sound of the bell and had spotted the green lantern which was usually placed in a prominent spot. Fate didn't smile upon the two parachutists who carried the bell and the lantern. Neither one appeared after the jump nor were the two items ever recovered. It is believed the troopers were drowned in the flooded area.

Of all the battalion commanders within the division, Ballard was the only leader to know instantly his exact position upon landing. He had dropped only a short distance from his first target, the town of St. Come-du-Mont. His jump had been greeted with the usual fireworks and his planeloads were badly scattered. Releasing himself from his parachute, he remained perfectly still for ten minutes waiting to see if the enemy would seek him out individually. After this, he sought the shelter of the hedgerows. Here he unstrapped the small SCR-536 (walkie-talkie) from his leg. Repeated calls to his commanding officers of Dog, Easy, Fox, and Headquarters Companies met with silence.

A sergeant from Dog Company crawled up to Ballard through the hedgerows and described how he had struggled in from the swamp. Most of his stick had landed in the water which was less than one hundred yards southeast of where the two men now stood huddled.

The battalion executive officer, Major Raymond V. Bottomly, was found by another sergeant in the corner of a nearby hedgerow. He had been sitting there nursing a broken ankle. Ballard and the two noncoms moved to his location. Asked if he could walk, Bottomly had gallantly reminded the others he would keep up with them at a fast crawl. The group moved to an area of higher ground where the major was directed to remain. The other three set off in different directions to gather paratroopers. These were sent to Bottomly's position.

Sergeant James B. Koller, a noncom with Dog Company, landed in a swamp. He stated, "My commanding officer was Captain Jones. He broke his leg on the jump. I got together with five members of my stick. We located equipment and assembled men. I went out on a field at least six times with no cover to bring in 60mm mortar ammunition and bazookas."

PFC Albert J. Jacobs had too much equipment when he dropped. There were eight rounds of mortar ammo, a rifle in a bag across his chest, and his backpack was filled with rifle bandoliers and two hand grenades. Jacobs later recalled, "I was in and out of numerous canals and streams. I found four members of my stick. My company commander, Captain Jones, broke his leg on the jump. I carried him to the aid station. Lieutenant Richard Snodgrass was in charge of my platoon and he became Dog Company commander two days later. He collected thirty men."

Lieutenant George W. Sefton, intelligence officer for the 2nd Battalion, became a man of many jobs. He said, "My original assignment for D-Day was to disperse the 2nd Battalion scout section to key points, predetermined, and secure intelligence on enemy positions or movements at those locations. I jumped with a rifle squad from Dog Company and started assembling men and leading them in the direction of the assembly area—had about sixty collected, including two other lieutenants. We fixed bayonets and started to attack higher ground near St. Come-du-Mont. We ran into our battalion commander, Colonel Ballard. I was sidetracked into locating the 1st Battalion on a dawn patrol. Was trapped under water by machine-gun fire. I spent an interesting half hour in a pond that had at least eight feet of water under the sights of a Kraut machine gunner. I breathed by surfacing beneath a patch of scum. I was finally pulled out by PFC Joe Newman with a jump rope. We found Colonel Johnson with a small force at Addeville. We took and held a neighboring château where Newman was shot through the shoulder. I carried Newman over my shoulder while the medic alongside held a plasma bottle. I left him in Addeville with Father Sampson, who won the DSC for remaining there with fourteen wounded, including Newman. I followed Johnson's group to La Barquette by the trail of abandoned equipment."

By 0330, the last of the group in the vicinity had trickled in. Colonel Ballard found that Major Bottomly, despite his injury, had inventoried all of the arms that had been brought in. Much of it had been recovered from bundles located in the fields. These arms came in handy because many of the troopers managed to crawl from the waters with nothing more than what they had worn. All arms and other equipment had been ditched in the fight for survival with the mud and water, or had been lost when they were torn loose on the jump.

Bottomly had also organized the paratroopers into their various company units. Three line companies (Dog, Easy and Fox) had assembled with about thirty men each (normal strength about 136 men per company). A sprinkling of men from Battalion Headquarters Company was also on hand. Only two of the sixteen medics (PFC's Kenneth Moore and Robert Wright) assigned to the battalion showed up. Upon landing, these two medics immediately began to collect and care for the jump-injured soldiers.[13] A few of the engineer specialists were also on hand. They were demolitions experts and had been assigned to destroy the highway and rail bridges with a special explosive.

One of those bridges, the one spanning the Douve River on the rail line from Paris to Cherbourg, had been the assignment of Lieutenant Harold Young from Charley Company of the 326th Airborne Engineers. Young related, "I had the explosives in my platoon and special wire so that we could do this using flashlight batteries. I was in charge of the mission and never got enough men that night nor got anywhere near the objective. Our specific task was never accomplished."[14]

It was noted that those men who had landed in the swamps and were soaked tried to move about to keep warm. Many of the others had difficulty in remaining awake. Occasionally a standing soldier would drop to the ground with a thud. No shot had sounded. These men had fallen asleep on their feet and toppled over. It had been a long sleepless night.

Les Droueries

A soldier from an incoming group of paratroopers, who had scouted the nearby village of Les Droueries, reported seeing enemy soldiers enter a building. This small hamlet was about six hundred yards southeast of the assembly point. It was also about halfway to Ballard's first objective at St. Come-du-Mont. It had to be cleared of enemy troops before the paratroopers could continue on to St. Come-du-Mont. Ballard could not risk them attacking from his rear as he moved beyond the town.

At 0430, the order to clear Les Droueries was given to the companies. Easy Company was to move down the main road leading into the town using the inside of the hedgerow for cover. Advancing down the far side of another hedgerow along a second road two hundred yards farther east, was Fox Company. The two "platoon-sized" companies began their advance at 0530 in two parallel columns. Dog Company followed at a distance to serve as the reserve unit. (See Map 6 on page 144.)

One of the platoon leaders involved in this action was Lieutenant Leo Malek, from Fox Company. His Company's D-Day assignment was to assist in the taking of St. Come-du-Mont. Malek stated, "We participated in the attack toward Les Droueries. By daybreak, most of the 2nd Platoon had assembled behind a hedgerow. In front of us was an open pasture and a farmstead, from which we were receiving enemy fire. We set up a mortar and scored several hits on the buildings. Enemy fire persisted. We tried to advance along a lane running perpendicular to our hedgerow. More enemy fire. We contacted the battalion commander for artillery fire. This proved effective."

A point man for the Fox Company attack on Les Droueries was Private Jack Schaffer. Earlier he had assembled with a group of twelve Fox Company men under the leadership of Sergeant McClosky. Schaffer describes the lonely and dangerous position of a point man: "While crossing a field, we were fired on by a machine gun. I proceeded to the forward end of the field as the point man and took refuge in a hedgerow as it started to brighten into day. When I could see, I realized that I was left alone except for those who did not survive the night. The others had gone back. I proceeded again toward the town and a few hundred yards later I was fired upon so I started back to find the others. I was pinned down for about a half hour before I started my return trip. I continued on back and met a patrol of Americans and got directions to where the others were located. Sergeant Haley

(F Company) and gang were busily engaged in dislodging a Kraut from his haven in a barn. We remained in that area with Colonel Ballard."

Corporal John "Wyck" Marohn was an Easy Company radioman who had assembled with Ballard's group. Colonel Ballard needed additional communications equipment and explosives for the attack. Marohn stated, "After dawn, we were engaged in the attack on Les Droueries. I was sent back to the drop zone to secure extra radio and communications equipment as well as all the Composition C-2 (explosive) we could find."

Private Woodie McKinney of E Company crawled away from the area in which he had dropped because the fields were being lighted by enemy flares. He managed to make his move during periods when the flares would go out. He and one member of his stick, Bob Ogle, managed to group with Lieutenant George Schmidt from Easy Company. McKinney explained what occurred as they got to the jump-off point for the attack: "Lieutenant Schmidt had us pile all of our equipment in a neat stack except for our weapons and ammo. We went in on an attack on some farmhouses near St. Come-du-Mont. The Germans made a counterattack and we lost all of our equipment (cigarettes, candy, and rations). It was here that Lieutenant Schmidt was killed by machine-gun fire. We had several casualties and we were getting sniper fire from almost every direction. As time went by, more men kept coming in and we grew stronger."

Both lead companies, Easy and Fox, were soon pinned down by mortar fire. Each unit had suffered seven or eight casualties by 0700. The men rushed forward several times but were thrown back on each occasion.

Colonel Ballard soon realized that the enemy force blocking his moves was too strong for his company-sized battalion. He could not attack toward St. Come-du-Mont, which was his first D-Day objective. The area to his front, including Les Droueries and St. Come-du-Mont, was on higher ground than the surrounding marsh and meadowland where his own men were positioned.

From this well entrenched high ground, the enemy had excellent observation of both the bridge and lock positions. Ballard would be unable to move either to the locks area or on to St. Come-du-Mont until the enemy position could be cleared.

As if he didn't have enough problems to his front, the sounds coming from Angoville indicated that his aid station was in the midst of a battle.

Angoville

Before his attacking force set out for Les Droueries, Ballard sent his adjutant, Lieutenant Edward Allworth, into Angoville-au-Plain to set up an aid station in the church. The two medics, Moore and Wright, had located farm carts and were busy shuttling the jump-injured to the aid station, which was about three hundred yards northwest of the assembly area.

During the morning, a seesaw battle for Angoville developed between a platoon-sized enemy force and some of the 326th Airborne Engineers of the 101st, who had dropped with the infantrymen. Lieutenant Harold E. Young, from the 326th Engineers, had dropped near Hiesville and had to proceed southwest of the Angoville area where his stick had been scheduled to drop. Along the way, they ran into an enemy outpost on a hilltop just to the northwest of Angoville. Two of the men on the outpost were wounded and the third fled. The engineers provided first aid for the wounded enemy soldiers and continued on into the village.

Young said, "By mid-morning there were between 40 and 50 men from my own company proceeding toward the village. Libby[15] took command, and we started to form as an infantry unit with outposts, etc. Things were in a state of flux. The Germans were approaching the village in some force. In mid-afternoon, I went to one side of the village to check a four-man outpost. A German platoon approached and the four men picked off over twenty of the enemy. The Germans kept approaching and were so close that when they threw a hand grenade, my men threw it back. That's when I forced our small outpost to retreat. When I got to the village, it was deserted except for the wounded and the attending medics."

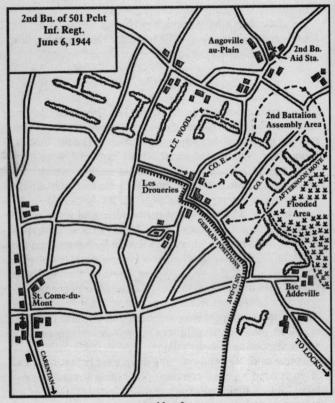

2nd Bn. of 501 Pcht Inf. Regt. June 6, 1944

Angoville au-Plain

2nd Bn. Aid Sta.

2nd Battalion Assembly Area

LT. WOOD

CO. E

CO. F

AFTERNOON MOVE

Les Droueries

Flooded Area

GERMAN POSITION ON D-DAY

Bse Addeville

St. Come-du-Mont

CARENTAN

TO LOCKS

Map 6

The movements of Lieutenant Colonel Robert Ballard and his 2nd Battalion of the 501st Parachute Infantry Regiment near Les Droueries.

A 326th machine gunner, PFC C. E. "Stub" Storeby and his buddy, Duke Conway, had been walking across a field in the Angoville area when Duke was hit in the thigh. "I put him in some brush to wait for the medics and left him a couple of grenades and sulfa powder," recalled Storeby. "I reported this to a medic station in a church. Got into some action when I found a machine gun in an equipment bundle. I tried to knock out Krauts in a farmhouse. The gun mount was bent. I killed two cows before I hit the house."

First Sergeant Jim Cox of the engineers was part of Harold Young's group. After his stick had been rolled up, he had headed southwest with his men toward their objective, the railroad bridge. Cox stated, "When we finally made our way to the town of Angoville-au-Plain, we had assembled 52 men.

"There was fierce fighting going on in Angoville and the Germans were shelling the town with 88's and mortar fire. The men of Charley Company (326th Engineers) were fighting as infantry at this time and decided to evacuate the area and move out to the CP of the 506th Regiment which was located to the northeast at Culoville. There were men from all units on this move back through an inundated area in our roundabout way to Culoville. This took place about 1900 hours on D-Day."

Meanwhile, Lieutenant Young had gone out to an outpost and when he discovered the enemy was moving into Angoville again with a large force, he ordered his men to retreat with him. They found the town deserted except for the aid post and the medics. Young recalled, "We met one of our men who was wounded so we told him to get in a ditch and hide as we could not take him with us. It was approaching dusk. I had Sergeant Cloutier, Botko, and Cowie with me. We went out into the middle of a flat area with many irrigation ditches that we crossed and spent the night of D-Day shivering, cold, miserable, in a clump of trees that was almost like an island. We had no idea how the war was going."

A number of individual soldiers of various units participated in the action at Angoville. Several men from the 3rd Battalion of the 506th Regiment had gravitated to Angoville because they were unable to break through the German positions to move on to their assignment of the wooden bridges two miles to the southeast. Private Mike Nassif was one of them. He had crept up to a group of men "whispering" rather loudly beside the road in the early morning darkness. He was relieved to hear some genuine G.I. cussing during the cutting of telephone wires. Nassif quickly joined the men. They were communications men from the 501st. He said, "They directed me to a place about fifty yards off the road where some of the men had assembled. One of the men in my company, Guerdon Walthall from California, was lying there with a machine-gun bullet through each leg. I got a patch on my rear and told the medic about my buddy Pusahanik. Jim Foster, Scoof, myself, and several others decided to make a break for the Douve River. We joined others in the capture of a small town. Then the Germans came back strong and ran us out. We picked up some more men and drove them back out. We had a line outside the town but couldn't keep the Krauts off our flanks. When we were exchanging fire, a bullet hit the helmet of one of our men, piercing the shell, struck the rivet on that side of the liner, and came out the back of the helmet. He was running up and down the hedgerow showing his helmet to everyone and telling them what a close shave he'd had. All of this was going on while we were receiving intense fire from the enemy and we lost the town again."

A trooper from the 501st who became involved in the Angoville action was Private Ralph R. Smith. He had found some of his buddies from Fox Company and others from 2nd Battalion. They had found their way to a larger group headed by Colonel Ballard shortly thereafter. As he described it, "Under Colonel Ballard's command, we engaged Germans near a small village. Midday, some officer detailed four to six of us to guard the aid station. It was attacked by Germans. I was on the second floor of a barn firing through shell holes in the roof. We then proceeded to retreat. After wandering through the woods, we found a regimental headquarters after dark."

While the battle went on, the medics and the adjutant, Lieutenant Allworth, worked tirelessly. Each time the sound of German fire neared the church, Allworth would leave the church and return when the firing faded in the distance. Since he was not a medic and was not wearing the Red Cross armband, he knew that his presence could endanger the others.

Possession of the church had changed hands three times. On one occasion, German soldiers entered the church. They noted the Red Cross flag in the doorway. The unarmed medics worked feverishly without looking up as they walked among the wounded. Noting among the wounded the presence of some German soldiers with American-applied bandages, the enemy soldiers had nodded approvingly and walked out. During the ensuing exchanges, they left the aid station alone.

In the meantime, Ballard's forces were pinned down in the fields and beside the hedgerows. Lieutenant Walter Wood of the 1st Battalion of the 501st came up to Ballard's position with a group of twenty 506th Regiment paratroopers who had failed to locate their own units. They were itching for a fight. Ballard decided to send them on a wide end run to flank the German position. (See Map 6 on page 144.) Wood ran into opposition but managed to skirt it by using the cover of hedgerows. Attacking along the hedges across the road from Easy Company, Wood's group forced the enemy from the first house at the crossroads with a blast from the one bazooka available to them. The enemy fled into the larger building south of the one evacuated. Company E now moved into the third building which was just northeast of the large building. This was accomplished by a volley of grenades through the windows. The surviving enemy soldiers fled through the front door as the Americans smashed through the back entrance.

Using the heavy stone walls for cover, the two groups now concentrated on the large enemy-held building. With fire coming at them from two directions, the enemy soldiers retreated across the intersection into well prepared positions. An enemy force of thirty men attempted a counterattack to regain the three buildings. They were driven back by well-placed small-arms fire from Wood's force.

"Nasty" Nassif was a member of Wood's force. He had

also been in on the earlier defense of Angoville. He recalled, "We continued to engage the enemy all morning long and our little group grew to about twenty men of the 506th. We were unable to break through to our mission at the wooden bridges. A 501st officer by the name of Lieutenant Wood joined our group. He was an all-right guy with plenty of guts. We fought all day long and into late evening. I don't know how many Germans we put out of action. We lost over half of our little group. One of our men, Private Martinez, was killed in this action. (He received a posthumous award of the DSC medal.) Also, I recall that Lieutenant Wood asked if we would lead an attack in this particular direction again. We were unable to gain any more ground than when we had twenty of us. The Germans counterattacked and we had to fall back. Then we were asked to try again. Lieutenant Wood said that a naval officer was along and if we got stopped this time he would call for naval fire. We got back about the same amount of ground and the Germans stopped us cold. The naval officer radioed to the battlewagon in the Channel. He gave our position and they fired three rounds of smoke. They hit perfectly. The ensign then asked for a three-minute barrage. Well, something happened: the rounds fell 150 to 200 yards behind us. The officer radioed frantically to stop the barrage but they told him it was already on the way. I don't recall which battalion we were leading but it was awful. The naval fire cut them to pieces. The Germans made a quick attack after the barrage, but this time we stopped them. We lost another man in this counterattack (Milton Anthony). I could not believe he was dead. Another guy and myself ran back to make sure as we didn't see any visible signs of injury. There was a medic present. They were moving the dead and wounded. He showed us where a piece of shrapnel entered Anthony's mouth and lodged in his head. We spent the night there. We still had no word on our outfit."

As described earlier, Colonel Johnson had radioed Ballard from Addeville to bring his force to Addeville and then on to La Barquette. He felt that with a larger force his regiment could accomplish its vital task of destroying the highway bridges. In the heat of battle, Ballard explained, "I'm in no position to move right now. I've got my hands full with a good-sized enemy force right in front of me." T/4 Richard C. Rowles was company radioman for Easy Company and had assembled quickly with his SCR-300 with Ballard's group. He stated, "I worked the radio for Ballard and contacted Colonel Johnson and Major R. J. Allen. We were slowed down. We had orders to join Colonel Johnson. Lieutenant Schmidt was killed while we were trying to move out."

Having heard the crackle of small-arms fire, the ripping sound of burp guns, and the thumping of exploding mortar shells, Johnson decided it was more prudent to delay Ballard's move. He said, "Break off when the pressure eases. We have friendlies here at Addeville. I am leaving Allen here to hold and wait for you. They'll come down with you—but get those guys moving as quickly as possible. We've got to get those bridges."

"Yes sir! Roger! Wilco! As soon as possible!" said the harassed 2nd Battalion commander.

One officer from the reserve unit, Company D, was sent with fifteen men toward Angoville to reconnoiter a less exposed route to Addeville. It would take a lot of doing to move from Les Droueries to Addeville and La Barquette by the direct roadways. There were just not enough men to force a path through the enemy positions.

Half of each of the attacking units of Ballard's groups remained in place as a covering force while the others pulled back taking the wounded with them. As the firing became sporadic, the withdrawal operation began. With the Dog Company patrol preceding them by half an hour, Ballard's force moved northeastward following the cover of the same hedgerows which had provided protection for the attack. In their circuitous northward movement, they skirted to the south of Angoville and moved on through the assembly area and headed down a narrow belt of dry land between the hedgerows and the flooded ground (see Map 6 on page 144).

A heavy mortar barrage and automatic weapons fire began to search them out as they began to move toward the southeast. The patrol waded into the swamp where its members slogged along in the chest-deep water. A little cover was provided by the tall reed grass growing in the marsh water. Tracers from the machine guns continued to follow the wading soldiers until they reached a low hedgerow bordering the marshy area. This low earthen bank ran toward the southeast in the direction of Addeville. Rifle fire was being placed on the column from enemy positions 300 to 400 yards southwest of the extended American column. Progress was slow as Ballard's soldiers crawled on their bellies to provide as little target for the enemy gunners as possible.

Reaching the low hedgerow which held the marsh in its confines, Ballard decided to storm the enemy strongpoints. Sending out the remainder of Easy and Fox Companies, the rush was put on in a two-pronged attack with Easy on the left. Rushing over the open field, the soldiers had to travel about 250 yards before they could expect to find shelter in the next hedgerow. Upon signal, the troopers broke through the hedge and headed for the enemy positions. A dozen men went down during the mad rush, but a small number succeeded in reaching the cover of the tree-lined embankment. The enemy was now in fixed positions across the roadway and beyond the far side hedgerow. Grenades were flung by both sides but most fell short. However, the Americans were close enough to the Germans to receive respite from the mortars. A short round by the enemy would have landed upon their own German troops, so the enemy mortarmen had to search elsewhere for targets.

As night fell, a radio message from Major Allen was received stating he had pulled out of Addeville and was now at La Barquette. Addeville would be in enemy hands shortly and Ballard had no friendly forces near enough to aid his movement.

The enemy continued to fire flares throughout the night to prevent any movement over the open ground between the adversaries. Members near the rear of the column were directed to go back to the area of the drop zone and search out more equipment bundles because the ammunition supply had reached the critical stage. They were back shortly after midnight with enough ammunition to give them some firepower for another day. The rest stayed in place, dug in as best they could. A patrol had gone northeast to find another passage around the far side of the swampy ground. They had met heavy opposition and returned to report that route blocked for any movement in that direction.[16] The night was cold, particularly for those soldiers who had waded through the swamp. Thus ended D-Day for the 2nd Battalion of the 501st Parachute Infantry Regiment.

Summary

When the first day of combat ended for the 501st, Colonel Johnson's regiment, it was well dug in around the locks in perimeter defense, but the highway bridges and railroad bridge stood unscathed, still in use by the enemy.

The battalions were scattered over the countryside. It would take many days to get the survivors back to their units. By D plus 2, less than half of the 2,300-man force was able to assemble.

For 1st Battalion, the situation was critical. The battalion had to be reorganized. Its command personnel were gone. Lieutenant Colonel Carrol and two of his staff members, Lieutenant John W. Atkinson, S-1, and Captain Thomas Chastant, S-3, were ambushed shortly after getting together near a crossroad and all three lost their lives. S-2 officer Captain Charles Seale, and S-4 leader Lieutenant Newt Holt, worked their respective ways back to the battalion a week or so later. Major Phillip Gage, Jr., the executive officer, had been badly wounded while attacking a machine-gun nest and was captured. Captain Simmons, Headquarters Company commander, and the two medical officers, Captain Robert Blatherwick and Lieutenant Tom Johnson, had been captured. The three line company commanders were missing from their units on D-Day—Captain William Paty of Able Company was badly wounded and captured; Baker Company commander, Captain Loyal Bogart, was far south of his drop zone and lost his life at Graignes; Captain Robert H. Phillips of Charley Company was to return a week later with the 17 survivors of his misdropped group.

In the interim, the skeleton battalion was commanded by Lieutenant Harry Howard of the 81mm mortar platoon. On

D plus 3, Colonel Johnson would assign his regimental executive officer, Lieutenant Colonel Harry Kinnard, to fill the post of the 1st Battalion commander.

Colonel Johnson's makeshift force had succeeded in taking the locks. Because so few men had assembled, no full-scale assault was made on the bridges. The high ground near Les Droueries and St. Come-du-Mont was not occupied and the enemy continued to have good observation of Johnson's force. Second Battalion, under Lieutenant Colonel Robert Ballard, had not gained ground in this area but it had harassed the enemy and held him in his positions preventing him from movement toward the beaches where the Allied invasion landings were occurring.

To the north, their fellow troopers of the Reserve Battalion, the 3rd, ended the day on a bright note for Johnson's men. As will be related, they captured Pouppeville on a causeway route from Utah Beach.

CHAPTER 10

So Few Led by So Many

The 3rd Battalion of the 501st, commanded by Lieutenant Colonel Julian J. Ewell, was a reserve battalion that did not jump with its sister battalions, the 1st and the 2nd, whose actions were described in the previous chapter. Instead, the 3rd Battalion was assigned to drop as protective cover with the 101st Airborne Division's Headquarters personnel on Drop Zone "C" near Hiesville. It also was to clear the enemy soldiers and airborne obstacles from the glider landing fields. From its centrally located position with Headquarters, the 3rd Battalion could be moved to bolster any sagging defenses if the situation arose.

Headquarters personnel included the commander of the 101st Airborne Division, Brigadier General Maxwell D. Taylor, with his staff, which consisted of Brigadier General Anthony C. McAuliffe, Colonel Thomas Sherburne, Colonel Gerald J. Higgins, and a dozen other officers, along with radiomen, code clerks, and wiremen from Signal Company, clerks and draftsmen from the G-2, and G-3 Sections, numerous enlisted men from the Division Artillery, military policemen, and war correspondent Robert Reuben.

Despite the assumption of protection for members of the staff, each man from general on down was on his own on his lonely jump and landing, taking equal chances on injury, capture, and death. And so it was that General Taylor, upon his drop, found himself safe among Normandy cows, elated, upon unharnessing, to find a 501st rifleman in the hedgerows to accompany him. Later, he was to join with Brigadier General McAuliffe and Correspondent Robert Reuben.

The commanding officer of the 3rd Battalion, Lieutenant

Colonel Julian Ewell, had an uneventful landing. He stated, "The first thing I did was hide my miscellaneous gear and I started looking for company."

But for many in the 45-plane serial, there had been a scattered drop and three of the planes, two with George Company personnel and one with members of How Company, were shot from the sky. The drop had occurred at approximately 0120 and initial assembly for those in the vicinity of the assembly aids was good. The troopers who carried the assembly aids, a shrill whistle and a blue light, dropped directly in the midst of division headquarters troopers as was described by Sergeant Nick Calabrese in an earlier chapter. Upon landing, there was the immediate search for vital bundles dropped from the planes.

Sergeant Richard "Wick" Goist had jumped from the plane carrying the artillery commander, Brigadier General Anthony C. McAuliffe. Goist had kicked out the door bundle which contained a vital SCR-610 radio set and a large amount of French currency. He found a buddy, Corporal Charles Jones, a boy from Louisiana and they proceeded to retrieve a bundle packed with bazookas. A bullet went through the fly of Goist's jump pants and the two men left that location in a hurry and headed across the road to retrieve the bundle they had pushed from their plane. Goist added, "As we approached the highway, we met ten to fifteen German soldiers and were forced to take to a ditch. After the enemy troops went by, we moved across the road, but were unable to reach the bundle due to small-arms fire. We then returned to the drop zone and picked up Ken Duncan and one other man and went on to assemble at the rendezvous which was designated by a shrill whistle."

PFC Julian Necikowski found three other men from his Divarty group.[1] They had heard the assembly whistle blowing and began to argue as to the direction the sound was coming from. Necikowski climbed a tree and was able to see the blue assembly light just a few fields away. They headed across the fields. Necikowski stated, "When we arrived at the rendezvous, none of the people from our plane were there yet, so I decided to go out and try to find the bundle I was to help bring in. This container had a white chute with the large letters 'J.M.' painted on it, and fluorescent cord wrapped around it. While traveling about looking for it I saw a lone plane come over the DZ and release its bundles and stick of jumpers. I did not know it at the time, but this was the plane that carried the bundle I was to help recover. The plane also carried three members of our Divarty in it. A few minutes later, I spotted the bundle in a field that had all the above markings on it. I heard the sound of people approaching. I challenged and got the countersign. These people were Colonel Tom Sherburne, Lieutenant Cecil Wilson, and John Miller who had jumped with the division headquarters stick and had been in the plane that had swung back part way across the Channel and returned.[2] Miller and I split the equipment load and I led them to the assembly area."

Corporal Ray Lappegaard got together with a 3rd Battalion medic and four infantrymen from H Company. They saw the assembly light and heard men getting together in an area two or three fields away and so they dashed across the open areas without drawing enemy fire. He said, "It is my recollection that we assembled rather quickly and found that there were few line company men in our particular area. Our CO, Colonel Ewell, was placed in charge of the group as was appropriate, but we found we had an unusually large number of division headquarters personnel with us, including General Maxwell D. Taylor, the division commander."

In the assembly area General Taylor called his officers together. It was decided to wait in the field until there was light enough to find a landmark such as a church spire on which the group could get its bearings. The first light of day would be on them shortly. It was already turning gray in the east. Members of the group returned to the rest areas and waited. During the wait period Major Legere accompanied by Corporal Virgil Danforth went to seek help from local farmers who could pinpoint the position of the men on a map.

"As it started to get light, Captain Vernon Kraeger told me to go out with Major Legere to try to pick up information as to our position," remembered Corporal Danforth. "We went up to a large farmhouse where we found an old couple who were sure we were going to kill them so they wouldn't go with us. The major finally found out from them where we were and so with the information and a bottle of wine we returned to the assembly area."

Major Lawrence Legere described the same incident. "In regard to Danforth and myself; although I was convinced that I knew exactly where we were, Colonel Higgins and General Taylor obviously could have used some reassurance. Hence Danforth and I set out. As I remember, everyone in the assembly area saw the top of a steeple several hundred yards away and Danforth and I simply headed for it.

"In any event, a U.S. soldier was in a farmyard with his rifle or carbine trained on a French farmer and his wife. He spoke no French and they no English, so they were at a total impasse. I went inside with the couple; don't remember whether Danforth came in or not. The old man and I pored over my map. He confirmed our location as I had believed it to be. Meanwhile his wife had sliced a little French bread and poured a little rouge ordinaire, so before heading back to the assembly area I shared both with them. Danforth and I went back. With our exact location having been confirmed, General Taylor ordered the move-out not much later."

Asked when he became certain of his position, General Taylor recalled, "So far as I was concerned, I became sure of our location by seeing the church spire of St. Marie-du-Mont (it was distinctive from all others in nearby towns), just at first light. About the same time, we surrounded a French farmer's house and got additional information from him." The church spire at St. Marie-du-Mont became very familiar to the men during the next few days as a landmark for orienting their positions.

As Koskimaki remembered it, "We had studied air photographs of the area for several days and this particular church steeple had been stressed. The officers hurried to General Taylor where they huddled over compasses and maps. Sighting their compasses on the steeple which was easy to recognize because of the structure of the bell tower, the general determined that our group was assembled near two of the vital exits leading from Utah Beach. These were Causeways 1 and 2."

Two battalions of the 506th Parachute Regiment had been assigned to capture these causeways. Since not a single man from these infantry units had assembled with the group or had been seen in the vicinity, General Taylor reasoned that they must have been dropped on the wrong DZ.

As was discussed earlier, the 3rd Battalion of the 501st had been dropped with the general to serve as the division reserve unit and to provide protection to division headquarters. Of the entire battalion (normal strength about 600 men) the commander, Lieutenant Colonel Julian Ewell, had assembled about forty men by daybreak. Forty-five members of the Division Headquarters had also arrived. Many of these were officers. The group included two generals, three colonels (one was Chief of Staff, Gerald J. Higgins), a major, several captains, and a sprinkling of lieutenants.

General Taylor decided that this vastly understrength group would have to move for the causeways. A force of 85 men was available to do the job that had been assigned to two battalions. Because of the limited personnel, it was decided to go only for the lower causeway (Exit 1). Colonel Ewell was given command of this force. As the group moved off, General Taylor was heard to comment, "Never have so few been led by so many!"

Daylight found the skeleton force advancing along a dirt road until it came to the main road leading to Pouppeville, which was located on the landward end of Causeway 1. Sergeant "Wick" Goist described this force: "We assembled with members of the 501st, our artillery, and division headquarters men. At that time we discovered our Lieutenant Marvin Richardson had a broken foot as the result of the drop. Everyone was concerned about what we could do with him, so we decided to leave him behind with a medic. We moved out from our rendezvous about daybreak, and headed for the little town of Pouppeville on the coast."

PFC Bill Kopp stated, "There were so many officers and so few enlisted men in the group outside Pouppeville that even lieutenants were assigned as riflemen."

"I remember the attack on the town of Pouppeville," said PFC Fred Orlowsky. "We were going down a dirt road. We had flanker guards out. It was very early in the morning but the day was breaking. Then there was shooting up ahead. Corporal Virgil Danforth and Captain Vernon Kraeger (my CO), two very brave men, were shooting some Germans in a ditch at the side of the road."

According to Corporal Danforth, "We took off for Pouppeville. It was only two miles away. Captain Kraeger insisted on walking down the center of the road toward the town carrying his carbine, which was almost as big as he was. Sergeant Lionel Cole was on his right trying to kill all the Germans in the ditch and the hedges on that side while I was on the left side doing the same thing. We kept telling the captain to get back where he belonged, but he kept telling us to mind our own business. He had almost lost his whole company (two planeloads crashed) and he was just plain mad. I had an M-1 rifle with .03 clips and I was having a rough time feeding the bullets into the gun one at a time and at the same time out ran the captain and killed a number of Germans on my side of the road. I shot eleven in one group in the ditch—all in the head. That was the only part I could see sticking out above the ground so it wasn't much of a trick."

Scouts were out on the flanks ahead of the main body. As they moved along, the group picked up additional men near St. Marie-du-Mont. Many of these troopers had landed on the rooftops in town and in the walled-in backyards. Several of them had been captured and been badly beaten. Two paratroopers had been lined up before a wall to be shot, only to be saved in the nick of time by the arrival of other chutists.

General Taylor, adept in French, inquired of a peasant the nearest town and was notified it was Pouppeville. Correspondent Robert Reuben described this meeting: "Along the route of march, General Taylor was uncertain of our location. The general, who spoke fluent French, and Legere and I approached a farmhouse to make inquiries. A farmer and his wife came to the door, and I was amazed to find them not at all surprised to see us. 'Bonjour, monsieur,' said General

Taylor. 'We are American invasion soldiers. Can you tell us the nearest town?'

"The elderly couple acted as if they had an invasion every day. They told us that the next town was Pouppeville and gave us directions in a matter-of-fact manner. Many of our boys were later disappointed to find many of the coastal peasants similarly unemotional. I think they had been waiting so long for the invasion that when it came, it was almost anticlimactic. Later, as the significance of it became apparent, I found the vast majority of French jubilant over our arrival. And before we left this farmhouse the Frenchman gave us a bullet which he asked us to use on the Germans. He wished us good luck."[3]

By the time the group had reached the outskirts of Pouppeville, its members had swelled to 150 men. Koskimaki described the approach to the town: "Our group drew fire from the outlying buildings. Members dived into the shallow ditches. Shelling of the beach areas began almost simultaneously. The armada's guns were opening up on the shore defenses with all they had. The crashing roar of bombs exploding and the steady drone of high-flying bombers to the east and south of us could be heard. P-47's could be seen diving on bombing and strafing runs. I watched one particular plane which had been hit by antiaircraft fire as it climbed back into the sky trailing a red flame. As the plane continued its climb, the glow grew brighter and brighter until it engulfed the entire plane. Finally it turned over ever so slowly and began to plummet toward the earth. I wondered if the pilot got out safely."

Koskimaki continued, "With light coming on, my company commander, Captain Bill Breen, observed me in the ditch across from his position. He had managed to keep up with the group using a tree branch as a cane. Wondering what Signal Company people may have straggled in since the last check, he called to me to move down the road toward the rear of the column and count our people. Encumbered with my radio equipment and other gear, my movement was rather sluggish as I got up and started toward the rear. Apparently I was observed by a concealed German because he opened fire at me. With bullets whanging off the road surface, I dived back into the ditch. The shooting stopped. After waiting a bit, the Captain suggested I go back to do the checking. As I returned to the road, the firing resumed. I dived into the ditch with the bullets zipping by my head again. I wasn't asked to try again.

"Before I realized it, someone behind me was nudging and shaking my foot to urge me forward. I had dozed off from exhaustion. Men were moving up the ditch on the other side of the road but the person in front of me was still lying there. I reached forward to shake his leg, assuming he had dozed like I did, and found he was wearing hobnailed boots. It was a very dead German—the first dead person I had seen though it was now several hours since the drop. I took a quick look at him, grabbed a few bullets from his belt, and continued up the ditch at a crouch.

"Major Larry Legere, assistant operations officer for General Taylor, had been given a squad to command in the attack on Pouppeville. He moved past me and up the center of the road about twenty yards to my front. A shot rang out and he was down writhing in the road, brought down by a sniper's bullet. The call 'Medic!' immediately went down the column. From the ditch some distance behind me arose a young trooper with a Red Cross armband on either sleeve to identify him. He raced to the major's aid. As he knelt beside the victim, the unseen sniper fired again. Technician 5th Grade Edwin Hohl was killed instantly with a bullet in the chest."[4]

Ray Lappegaard corroborated this story: "We headed for the beach from our drop area and shortly after daybreak engaged in our first firefight for the village of Pouppeville. In this engagement, a good friend, Luther Gulick, was killed and also in this action one of our medics was killed when he went out to attend a wounded soldier."

Bill Kopp related, "Colonel Ewell stationed me with a .30-caliber machine gun, not mine, but one we found in an equipment bundle, to draw fire from an intersection corner while he led the physical attack himself. From this intersection I saw Major Legere lying on the road and someone was calling 'Medic!' I knew the medic who answered his call. I can still picture his face, because he was attached to the company shortly before D-Day. I saw him topple on top of the major after being shot."

Staff Sergeant Nick Calabrese, from Division Intelligence, recalled "seeing Major Legere in the corner of a crossroads just outside of Pouppeville with a badly wounded leg and a dead medic near him. We followed the 501st into Pouppeville—and that is all we did was follow them."

The scouts on the flanks discovered where the firing was coming from and stilled it with several bursts. The column began to move once more. The major was pulled into the roadside ditch. Another medic took care of his most urgent needs.

Koskimaki continued, "As I came up, I paused to look at the unlucky medic. He was just a kid. Major Legere's wound was a huge gaping one. Later in the day I examined one of the shells I had taken from the dead German and discovered the unusual type of pink-colored slug. It was a hollow wooden projectile. It worked on the same principle as a dum-dum bullet—barred from warfare by the Geneva Convention."[5]

The infantrymen of the 3rd Battalion went through the hamlet of Pouppeville using tactics for which they had been trained. The headquarters personnel felt rather useless having been trained for communications work, both on the company, battalion, regiment, and division level, or as draftsmen and G-2 staff work. Koskimaki explained, "I felt very useless because I had trained for a year and a half as a radio operator on the division level. Because of the weight of the general's radio I had been assigned to jump with half of it. The operator with the other half had lost it in the jump. Captain Breen had sent other radiomen into the neighboring fields in search of communications equipment bundles. They had not returned yet."

Infantrymen from 3rd Battalion continued the attack on the town. Fred Orlowsky describes the entry into town: "We got fired at from Pouppeville. They sent some of us in one direction and some in still another to try and surround a large house where most of the firing was coming from. Kraeger was wounded in the arm but refused to leave.

"I saw Lieutenant Nathan Marks get shot in the forehead while peering around the corner of a small building towards the larger house where the Germans were holed up. Sergeant Tom Criswell and PFC Bob Richards were shot within a few yards of me as they were running towards the big house in the height of the attack. It was a short fight. We gathered some prisoners, most of whom were Russian Georgian troops fighting for the Germans."

"I almost got General Taylor with a grenade when we were fighting for the houses," said Private Richard Evans. "I tried to heave a grenade through the window of a house from which snipers had been firing at us. It hit the cross-frame of the window and bounced back out near our position where it exploded."

Corporal Virgil Danforth said, "As we came into the town, the Germans began to withdraw into their headquarters, which was on the edge of the town nearest the beach. Until that time, my squad hadn't lost a man. Their defense in the town wasn't very well organized so we cleaned them out pretty quickly, but when we hit the headquarters building it was a different story. They had two snipers in a tree that we couldn't see, and they killed Lieutenant Nathan Marks, PFC Bob Richards, and one other from my squad. A sergeant from our headquarters platoon was hit in the open and every time the medic, T/5 Harold Nolicy, tried to get to him, the Germans would drive him back. I got over at the side and tried to draw their fire so he could get to the downed men, but they put a bullet in me too. It hit the ring of my helmet and split in two and half of it went into my skull and I still have the headaches to prove it. Captain Kraeger then got hit in the arm with a wooden bullet. About all this did to him was make him madder.[6] We brought up a bazooka and fired a few rounds into the headquarters building and they decided to surrender.[7]

Colonel Ewell thrust his head around the corner of a house as his group attacked each house with rifle and grenades. A

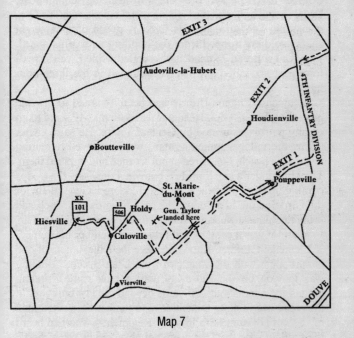

Map 7

D-Day movements of the 501st Parachute Infantry Regiment's 3rd Battalion and the 101st Airborne Division Headquarter's parachute echelon.

sniper glanced a slug off his helmet leaving him with a large dent for a souvenir. Fire had come from the outlying houses. The enemy retreated slowly toward the schoolhouse which seemed to serve as the German headquarters.

A German officer rushed out of the building just as Colonel Ewell peeked over the wall near the schoolhouse. Ewell shot at him with his Colt .45 pistol but missed. The German wanted to surrender his force. A group of thirty-eight enemy soldiers trooped from the building with arms raised. They had suffered 25 dead and wounded while Ewell's small force lost six killed and twelve wounded in the three-hour fight.

Lieutenant Eugene Brierre had been assigned to provide protection for Division Headquarters with his MP's and to go on any patrols requested by General Taylor. He said, "After taking the village, some Germans were observed retreating toward the beach. I gathered about six men and pursued them. They hid under a small bridge, but when they saw the troops coming up from the beach, they surrendered. General Taylor then ordered me to go down the road towards the beach and bring the highest-ranking American officer back to him. This I did and it was a captain, but I do not remember his name."

Lieutenant Luther Knowlton described the union of the paratroopers with the vanguard from Utah Beach: "Nothing was moving on the causeway until a tank came grinding around the bend about 250 yards beyond the last building. In the reeds overlooking the entrance to the hamlet waited men of the 4th Division's 8th Infantry Regiment—who had heard the firefight ping on. They were not observed by the airborne soldiers. The tank approached slowly up the narrow road. Its identity was unknown. One of our men fired his machine gun from the shelter of the stone wall. The bullets ricocheted off the heavy armor plating. He was not taking any chances. It might have been an enemy tank retreating from the beach area."

The tank stopped. An orange identification panel was displayed quickly from behind the protecting hatch cover. Orange flags, flares, and smoke were used to identify Allied forces. Lieutenant Knowlton added, "I tossed an orange smoke grenade into the road from my place of cover beside the sergeant."

Almost immediately the two paratroopers became aware of small orange flags waving from the previously empty-appearing reed beds on either side of the causeway embankment. Both groups stepped out onto the roadway and advanced toward each other from a distance of two hundred yards. More tanks appeared.

Captain George Mabrey of the 8th Infantry Regiment of the 4th Division stepped forward to shake hands with and embrace Lieutenant Knowlton. More soldiers joined in the festivities as Mabrey was brought forward to meet General Taylor.

The tanks moved to the landward side of the village where they halted. Koskimaki recalled, "I remember how elated I felt when the first tanks poked their way through the streets. One paratrooper rushed forth and planted a kiss on the first tank."

The shooting died down completely. The local populace soon were peering from the windows and moments later were in the streets offering refreshments to the soldiers.

PFC Norwood W. Thomas, Jr., a Divarty radioman reflected, "Earl Rinehart and I had our first encounter with the local cognac. The Frenchmen would ask if the Americans were in such and such town and we would answer, 'Oui!' and they would pour one. As I recall we had the Americans in every town from LeHavre to Cherbourg. I remember that Earl and I got pretty happy when the 4th Division came into town, we shared our bottled wealth with them."

With no radio communication with any of his combat forces, other than the small group at Pouppeville, General Taylor asked to be briefed on the events as the seaborne troops had observed them. One of the tank officers offered the use of his radio so the division commander could communicate with the invasion leaders out in the Channel.

Colonel Gerald J. Higgins stated, "We did have communications with the command ship—General Omar Bradley—early on D-Day but indirectly. It came about when we linked up with elements of the 4th Infantry Division at Pouppeville.

They had a direct link and General Taylor talked to someone on General Bradley's staff over the 4th Division command channels."

Meanwhile, war correspondent Robert Reuben of the British Reuters News Service had prepared his first dispatch to the world. The simple terse message was attached to the leg of one of the pigeons. The bird was given a little pat and told to "git on home." It arrived at its loft in Dover, England, early in the afternoon with the first eyewitness account of the fighting in France. The message read, "Paratroopers take Pouppeville."[8]

While this action had been taking place, Captain Bill Breen sent T/5 Charles Chapman and PFC Hank Rogers into the fields nearby in search of communications equipment bundles. A container beside a collapsed green chute was the fruit of their search. It contained an SCR-300 radio in good condition. This was rushed to Breen. Koskimaki added, "Captain Breen sent it forward to my position near the staff officers. I experimented with both the long and short antennae as I called each regiment in turn, but no amount of calling brought any response from the other forces of the 101st Division."[9]

After briefing General Taylor and his staff on the events as they had witnessed them, the tankers and their accompanying infantrymen moved inland up the road in the direction from which the paratroopers had advanced. They had taken care of the wounded who were now sent on their way to the beach for early evacuation.

As the last tank passed through the small force of paratroopers, the 101st men turned to follow on their way to Hiesville. Major pockets of enemy resistance were bypassed as the paratroopers now numbering well over two hundred proceeded west along the deep, rutted, rocky farm lanes. The hot sun beat unmercifully down on the men. Heavy equipment began to bite into the shoulders. Koskimaki had memories of this. "Strapped on my back, the radio with its short antenna felt more like a millstone as the hours passed. Shots rang out from time to time and the column dropped into the ditches on either side of the road. Noncoms, moving along the column, designated fields of fire for each soldier. As a radio operator I did my only shooting that day firing into another hedgerow. My area was between two trees, perhaps twenty yards apart. This was my field of fire. I don't know whether I hit an enemy soldier or not. It was a good feeling just to be able to fire back."

Farm carts were put into use as the column moved along. As PFC Norwood Thomas remembered, "Someone acquired a two-horse wagon and when we moved out, it was carrying cripples and equipment. Captain Breen (Signal) was a passenger and our Lieutenant Richardson was chief mule skinner. Both had foot or leg injuries. We ran into a hard spot and unloaded some communications equipment to get out a mortar and ammo. We moved on without reloading the commo equipment. Why, I never knew."

Koskimaki said, "As the group neared Culoville, we halted once more. Colonel Robert Sink of the 506th Parachute Infantry Regiment had situated his command post at that location. He met with the generals and other staff members for a short while. The rest of us lay in the ditches. The officers made plans for the continuing fight on D plus 1. After that stop we continued on to Hiesville, which was already occupied by battalion paratroopers as well as the first-echelon glider riders who had landed in the early morning darkness."

Discovering that communications equipment was scarce for their group at Division Headquarters, Divarty officers remembered that communication equipment had been dropped off the cart during the ride up from Pouppeville. Three men were ordered to return to the spot to retrieve it. One of these men was Norwood Thomas. He related, "After we got to Hiesville it was decided that the equipment was needed so Miller, Rinehart, and I were elected. On the way we were moving quietly down a roadside ditch when we heard steps on the other side of the hedgerow. We very cautiously stalked the sound to the gate. We were ready to blast that Kraut into destiny when slowly out of the gate came a cow.

"We picked up the equipment and were starting back when a most welcome patrol came along heading our way.

We tagged along for a while when the group became involved in a firefight. This ended after a short while when some officer came charging up the road, waving an orange rag, and gently (?) questioning our people's intelligence, ability, sight, and hearing. It seems that a small group of Germans became engaged on two sides, then moved out from between and left two U.S. groups firing at each other.

"After this encounter, we moved off again toward Hiesville. It was by now late afternoon and somehow we became separated. Miller and I made it back but Rinehart lost us or we lost him and radios being what they are, needing all the parts, we were a useless group until the next day when we got together again."

The men now moved in about the Lecaudey Farm at Hiesville and began to dig in. Koskimaki offered, "Hiesville now became our division headquarters. My cumbersome radio was placed beside a deep foxhole that Chuck Chapman and I excavated shortly after arriving in an orchard beside the farm buildings. We camouflaged the immediate area with a tent of mottled parachute cloth which blended with the surroundings. The fresh mound of earth beside the excavated shelter would be undetected if an enemy reconnaissance plane chanced to pass overhead. We were not in communication with any of the regiments with our radio, but two other operators had managed to straggle in with our group on the march from Pouppeville with an SCR-300. They had heard the calls from a radio with Kickoff Blue (3rd Battalion of the 502nd Regiment) before they moved out of range of that set."

General Taylor had learned something about his forces. A good item of news had been passed on to him by Captain Frank Lillyman of the pathfinders, who reported that the German coastal artillery battery at St. Martin-de-Varreville had been completely destroyed. He had also reported that the 502nd was busy holding up its part of the D-Day action.

Where were the others from 3rd Battalion and Division Headquarters who had not straggled into the command post during the day? A large number of the planes had veered off during a period of intense flak and dropped their sticks of jumpers in the vicinity of Baupte and Appeville, about eight miles from the intended drop zone near Hiesville. Others had landed west of Ste. Mère Eglise. Others were battling in the hedgerows only a few miles from Hiesville unaware that they were near their destination.

PFC Tom Fabac, a 3rd Battalion machine gunner, reported, "I followed the back pattern of the planes. Only seven of us got together. We landed in the 82nd territory near Ste. Mère Eglise and fought beside them for the first four days."

"We missed our DZ by 12 miles," said PFC Edward Gryzinski. "We fought with the 82nd for seven days."

The executive officer for the 3rd Battalion Headquarters Company, Lieutenant Jack F. Thornton, had dropped from a plane that was out of formation and the stick was dropped at high speed while in the midst of heavy antiaircraft fire. He related, "Our point of landing was just east of Baupte. The stick was strung out across the flooded lowland with water about waist deep. The antiaircraft guns over on the railroad track kept firing at my chute until I got it deflated.

"I was apparently on the edge of the flooded area because as I walked west I found our bundle on dry ground. I waited but no one else showed. Finally in desperation I walked 'down-stick' across the flooded lowland and found Wiltsie and Blau.

"About this time it was starting to get light and we could see that the antiaircraft gun on the railroad had an excellent view of the area and that we should get into the woods to the north before daylight. This we did. We had no idea where we were—the only reason we went north was because of the enemy to the south.

"A small French girl at a farmhouse pointed out the Appeville church steeple when I showed her my map. With this we moved north hitting the mile or so wide Douve River. We spotted a flat bottom boat at a farmhouse. Before dark we read a compass bearing on the church steeple in Liesville and after dark we stole the boat and poled across without incident.

"We got a few hours sleep just south of Liesville and then

started back moving east toward Houesville. The back-flooded river made the land between Liesville and Houesville in effect a narrow peninsula. We spent a night hidden in a hedgerow just behind the enemy position."

Radioman Vincent F. Blau reported, "Our planeload was dropped far from the drop zone. We landed near Appeville west and south of the Douve River. Sergeant Paul Wiltsie and Lieutenant Jack Thornton and myself proceeded to try, to locate other men and to find our location. By daylight we were fired on and forced to move out. By talking to a French girl, we got our bearings and proceeded northeast. At sunset we crossed the Douve by taking a farmer's boat and taking advantage of nightfall. We made it across undetected. We picked up another trooper and saw several groups of Germans, but remained undetected."[10]

Into that same general area around Baupte and Appeville had dropped one of the sticks of men from the Division Headquarters Parachute Echelon, which was jumpmastered by Major Paul Danahy, the assistant G-2 officer for the 101st Division. For one member of his group, Lieutenant Colonel Raymond Millener, the plans and operations officer (G-3), it was his first parachute jump. The plane carried other headquarters personnel, including some military police and eight Signal Company radiomen.

Private Robert "Lightnin" Hayes was one of these eight radiomen with Lieutenant Colonel Millener and Major Danahy. Hayes, a tall, lanky, unexcitable Texan, was moved to reconstruct the D-Day activities of himself and his fellow Texan, PFC Johnny Hickman. Dispensing with the initial activities of the jump and the early assembling of the group, Hayes' account is resumed with the discovery by Major Danahy that they had landed some eight miles west of their intended Drop Zone "C." Bewildered, sometimes forgetful, amazingly lucky, Hayes somehow blundered through the day without losing his life or his sense of humor. He related, "A trooper was sent down the road to look at a sign. The major then looked at his map and found we were many miles from our drop zone. We started down the paved road and met some other paratroopers who joined our group. Farther on

down was a farmhouse, with a girl standing on the front step
wearing a pretty dress. There was a red rosebush growing
beside the barn. I kept smelling the roses and looking at the
girl. Major Danahy was standing next to me talking to a
Frenchman. One of the boys was acting as interpreter. We
were told that an enemy machine gun was located on this
side of the road and to the rear of the house. The major ordered Johnny, and Sergeant Shank and myself to attack it;
and they would go around and get behind it to attack it from
the rear. We walked across a field and passed a woman milk-
ing a cow. We got behind a hedgerow and I could see a German running and putting something in a foxhole. I said, 'I
see one, I see one.'

"Johnny said, 'Well shoot him then.'

"I could see his head sticking up and I took a good slow
bead on him and fired. I missed. He opened up and sprayed
the hedgerow where we were hiding. Sergeant Bill Shank
turned around and asked, 'Am I hit?' Johnny looked over at
him and started to shake his head. Finally he noticed Shank's
helmet and said in his southern drawl, 'By golly, Shank, they
almost got you.' There was a hole clean through the helmet.
The bullet had passed right over his scalp.

"An armored car dropped off a mortar crew on the other
side of the machine-gun nest while Johnny and Shank were
down in the corner of the field. They were under attack from
it. I left the field and started walking down the road where
the machine-gun nest was located, just off to the right. All of
a sudden the armored car came around the corner. I stopped
and stared at it. A man's head and shoulders were sticking
out of the turret and his machine gun was pointed at me. (He
was wearing a black beret with the German insignia on it. It
was the same kind of uniform I had seen on the dummy back
in England.) We must have stared at each other for a few seconds, when I realized what he was. I turned around and
started running as fast as I could, all the time expecting bullets to start ripping through my back. I ran straight into the
field the machine gun had been covering all the time and
headed for the hedgerow I had just left. I hit the hedgerow

with full force and got only halfway through, backed up, and with more determination got through the second time.

"Both the crew of the armored car and the men in the machine-gun nest were watching me but they never opened fire. They may have been laughing so hard they couldn't pull the triggers. When I got on the other side, I lay on the ground facing the road. I took all the clips of ammo and laid them on the ground in front of me. I was going to make my stand right there. I had taken my pack off some time before and left it close to Johnny, but with all the excitement I had forgotten all about it. I never saw it again. I heard someone to the rear and left of me yell. I turned around and a trooper called, 'Come back here, I'll cover you.'

"I raced back, crouching low, and dove into the ditch beside him. He told me everyone was waiting back behind us. We went back down there and waited a little while for a few stragglers, then moved out.

"We next came to an area where some troopers had dug some foxholes and left a few packs and things lying around. I found some chocolate bars in one of the packs. They came in handy during the next few days, as I had left my K-rations in my pack when I left it behind. This area was rolling hills with hedgerows everywhere. Before long, we were on top of one of those hills sitting on the ground, resting against a hedge. My friend in the armored car spotted us. This time he didn't hesitate. He raked the whole line with machine-gun fire. You could hear the slugs hitting the hedgerow just above our heads. We all hit the ground and started crawling towards a low area. Some would get up and run a little bit while others just kept crawling. We came out on a dirt road. The major told me and two other troopers to act as scouts and we started moving away from that area. We crossed over the same road we had walked down early that morning.

"As the day wore on I was talking with Johnny Hickman. He was carrying the SCR-300 radio and I was carrying the antenna case for him.[11] By this time we were strung out in a loose column. A message came down the line that there were two enemy tanks in the woods and men were working on them. We all hit the dirt and word was passed down the line to a man at the end of the column who had a grenade launcher on his rifle. He was told to move up to the head of the column.

"I was lying next to a blond-headed fellow who had lost his helmet that morning. He told me in a comical way about the Germans taking potshots at him because they could see his hair so easily. I was laughing so hard when the word came to move out that I forgot the antenna there. We bypassed the patch of woods to get away from there."

Hayes ended his account by adding, "We came to a field located next to a farmhouse, where we spent the night and all of the next day."[12]

Other strays were only a short distance away from the assembly area near Hiesville, but their initial moves in the darkness carried them out of the sights and sounds of the assembled group. Sergeant Bill Ashbrook of the MP Platoon said, "I collected two men. We moved about one-half mile beyond that point when we were challenged. It turned out to be four of our own men and that made us seven. One of the seven was a warrant officer named Steve.

"We moved to the northwest. At times we thought we could hear the whistle signaling the location of the assembly point but we never got there. About a thousand yards on our left was a huge woods and occasionally we would hear screams which sounded like someone was being tortured.[13] We crossed a road which appeared to go through the woods, but I did not think it wise for us to travel along it. We continued in the same direction for a while and turned east toward the sea. As we crossed the road, we came under enemy fire. Not knowing exactly where we were, I told the men to hide themselves in a ditch along a hedgerow and wait for daylight.

"It soon became light and we could see the balloons protecting the boats off Utah Beach. Shortly thereafter, a group of men came by and told us where their regimental command post was located, and also pointed out the direction to the Division CP. We started back in the opposite direction and encountered quite a scrap on our right. We had found a .30-caliber machine gun and plenty of ammunition, so we set up shop about five hundred yards from the woods where a battle was going on.

"I told the warrant officer and another soldier to get into the ditch on the other side of the hedgerow. I also told them that one man could sleep, but the other must stay awake. I positioned myself next to the machine gunner and told him and the other three men that I would stay awake. It so happened that we had positioned ourselves on the escape route which the enemy decided to use to retreat from the woods. I opened fire and one enemy soldier jumped into the ditch within three feet of me. I could count the hobnails on his boots. One of my sentries on the other side sat up and yelled, 'Don't shoot, they're friends!' I guess this was because the one behind the first one I shot yelled, 'Hans' or 'Franz' before he jumped into the ditch at my feet. My machine gunner woke up and wondered what in hell I was doing. When I told him I was shooting Germans he thought I had lost my marbles. Then he saw for himself.

"The ensuing activity brought enemy fire from the woods, and I decided to move. We moved about one thousand yards to a crook in a hedgerow situated on a rise overlooking a road. We placed the machine gun so that it was at point-blank range down the ditch along the one side of the road. Here again, we had inadvertently placed ourselves on another escape route of the Krauts from the woods.

"We had no more than set up shop than we had the enemy starting up this ditch. While this was going on, my problem was to make my machine gunner wait for the proper time to open up. When this came, he opened up. The enemy was caught in a position where they couldn't move. We methodically covered the ditch from about fifty yards in front of us to a maximum of about four hundred yards. When all movement ceased within the confines of the ditch, we moved on. (By this time it was about 1200 hours.) We had several other experiences before we reached Division Headquarters at about 2200 on D-Day night."

In an official report on the same incidents that Ashbrook described, but one that sheds some light on adventures later in the day, Chief Warrant Officer Steve Karabinos[14] stated:

"We proceeded generally northwest sticking to hedgerows until we came to a point where German machine-gun fire was intense. Due to the size of our squad and the lack of some honest-to-goodness firepower, we decided it best to swing around the Germans' field of fire, which was more or less limited due to hedgerows. We traveled due north, but were forced to retrace our steps when another machine gun opened up on us. We then proceeded south with the idea of pushing west in a more favorable sector.

"Within the next two hours, we met and attached to us some twenty enlisted men from the 501st and 506th Parachute Infantry Regiments. Shortly after daybreak, we met a patrol from the 506th which was proceeding toward Causeway 2. Not having been able to accomplish anything up to this time, it was decided that the patrol could use all the men from the regiments, but that I should proceed toward Division CP with the clerks and the two M.P.'s. At this time we were at a point south of St. Marie-du-Mont.

"We proceeded toward Hiesville. Sometime later, we picked up Private Nolan (3rd Bn. of the 501st), and two signalmen from Division Artillery.[15] Intermittent firing was going on all around us. We observed that stray German soldiers seemed to be making their way from St. Marie-du-Mont and proceeding toward Vierville. It was assumed that the 506th was fighting in St. Marie-du-Mont and slowly driving the Germans out. We were at a vantage point, so we hid in a hedgerow and fired on all Germans coming in our way and driving them back.

"Some equipment bundles lay in the field next to us. Two men were detailed to look for a machine gun and ammunition. For a while nothing came our way, so two men were placed as lookouts while the other six had a bite to eat. We were 'caught with our pants down.' Five Germans suddenly appeared on top of the bank of the ditch we were sitting in (about four feet deep). Two shots whizzed past us, followed by more and then a hand grenade. Somehow, none of us were hit, except that I got nicked on the hand by a couple of fragments from the grenade. Private Nolan picked up the machine gun and fired it from the hip (he was not a trained machine gunner), while the rest of us fired our carbines. The result was that all five Germans were killed.

"We then changed our position to the next hedgerow closer to the road. The machine gun was dug in, zeroed in on a clearing on the road, and the riflemen dispersed along the line posted so that we had observation in all directions. Shortly thereafter, Private Milbrath reported a patrol of six men coming down the road proceeding from Vierville toward St. Marie-du-Mont. Apparently our machine gunner, Private Nolan, was a wee bit anxious and opened up on them too soon. Then followed an exchange of shooting whereupon we drove the patrol in the direction of St. Marie-du-Mont. We only got one out of that patrol, but believe the rest didn't get very far if the shooting in the general direction of the 506th meant anything.

"At about 1700 hours, and after no activity for a little spell, we decided to again start out for Hiesville. We met a patrol from the 506th and joined forces with them proceeding through Vierville and then toward Hiesville. We entered an orchard where it was presumed a German CP was established. However, we were too late as the 3rd Battalion of the 506th had cleaned out the place and were in the process of establishing their own CP there. Two wagonloads of captured German documents were being transported to the 506th Regimental CP, and upon request of the drivers, the division headquarters patrol of eight men acted as guard for this mission, although only sniper action was expected. None occurred."

Karabinos concluded his account with, "We stopped off at the 506th for a short rest and then proceeded to the Division CP, arriving there approximately at 2100. Our score was: No men lost. Germans—six known dead and seen by myself, 11 claimed but not verified with the possibility that there were many others. Although most of the men were technicians of one sort or another, they proved their capabilities in that they roamed for twenty hours within the German lines, shot well, were aggressive to the point of overeagerness, and did a pretty good job."

It wasn't always antiaircraft fire that caused the planes to swerve off course and drop their troopers miles from the proper area. In the case of jumpmaster Staff Sergeant Chester

Wetsig, communications sergeant for the 3rd Battalion, it was another plane crossing and dropping its paratroopers in the path of Wetsig's plane that caused the pilot to shoot straight up, and tumble the men to the rear of the plane in one mad confusion. By the time the pilot got the plane in level flight once more, the men were far from the drop zone. One radio operator near the end of the stick had difficulties because his leg bundle containing a vital radio had become loose. Wetsig shoved him aside and told him to remain with the plane.

Wetsig described his experiences on the ground: "I picked up a private from the 506th who was wounded and as I was trying to assemble, I ran into a large number of officers from a glider which had landed early. They were high-ranking officers of the 82nd Airborne. They were going to follow me to our headquarters, but en route to one glider, we were under heavy mortar fire and only one Lieutenant Colonel and a private were with me when we reached the glider. We continued west reaching the Division Command Post in the afternoon."

The bulk of the fighting at Pouppeville had been done by men of the 3rd Battalion's George Company. However, one of its planes was lost and the officer jumpmaster had gone forward to order the pilot to turn his craft so the men could jump over land. Aboard that plane had been mortar sergeant John Urbank. After landing, he got together with Sergeant Donald Castona only to lose him quickly when Castona turned in one direction and Urbank turned in another. They didn't meet again for a week. Urbank was able to determine that he was seven miles north of Pouppeville. Urbank described how it was to be left alone again: "I strolled around in the darkness for an hour or so and couldn't find anybody. By then I was dog tired and so being the country boy that I am, I found a stand of wheat, walked so I wouldn't beat a path into it, curled up under my innocence and slept until dawn.

"At first light a group of light bombers churned up a gun emplacement some two or three miles away. I then proceeded to a road and saw Hillinger scoot across about thirty yards in front of me on the other side of the hedgerow. I yelled, 'Hey Paul!' and we met real quick like. He had been lying in the ditch most of the night while Krauts walked up and down the road—companies of them!

"Paul and I were kind of easing along from one field to another when we met four fellows from the 82nd. They were lost and led by a corporal, so they joined us. We went a few more fields and found Howard Lewark, so there were now seven of us. Three were equipped with M-1 rifles and four with carbines. We needed more firepower, so we went looking for a machine gun.

"We noticed a number of equipment bundles. All of them contained rations, radio batteries, wire, ammunition, but no machine guns and no mortar, so we decided to find out where we were and headed to where we were supposed to go. We finally hit a road junction and got ourselves oriented. We were seven miles from Pouppeville, so we headed in that direction.

"We had covered about three miles staying off the roads, moving cautiously, being shot at, shooting back and getting away, until we came to a farmhouse and the boys were pretty well played out, because those three miles on the map had some pretty wide detours around places that had too many unfriendly faces.

"Whenever we hit a road in our detour, one of the fellows had a pair of wire cutters and he'd crawl up those concrete telephone poles and cut wires. I went to the door of a farmhouse, knocked most politely, and a French housekeeper in uniform answered the door. She took one look at my unsanitary likeness and very inhospitably slammed the door in my face.[16]

"I knocked a little more firmly with my gun butt and the gentleman farmer, white mustache, smoking jacket and all, answered the door. He asked, 'Anglais?'

" 'No, American, Etats Unis!'

" 'Oui!'

"This was about 1500 army time. All we had to eat was some D-ration chocolate and we hadn't bothered to take any K-rations from the equipment bundles in our search for a machine gun. Poor leadership and poorer logistics. He invited us in. We told him where we were heading. He said, 'Don't go that way—too many Germans. Go this way—longer, but no

Germans.' We headed about a half mile across fields and some Kraut in a church steeple cut loose at us with a machine gun and we dove for cover and decided to go back to the French farm and 'hole up' in a cider mill to rest up, and wait for dark and see if we could travel a little safer that way."

In summary, the day had proved only partially successful in the fulfillment of the objectives set for headquarters and 3rd Battalion. Seventeen aircraft of the 45-plane 3rd Battalion serial had dropped west of the Carentan-Cherbourg highway, too far west for ready action; three of the planes had been shot from the sky with the loss of 36 paratroopers. Sixteen sticks had landed within one mile of St. Marie-du-Mont, but only 85 men had assembled with General Taylor. These were the men involved in the attack on Pouppeville. The others were still in the hedgerows of the small fields, which became isolated battle areas for individuals and small groups.

Besides providing protection for the Division Headquarters, the 3rd Battalion troops had been assigned to remove airborne obstacles from the glider landing areas and were then to protect these reinforcements from being ambushed by enemy troops. Preliminary plans had called for an entire company from 3rd Battalion under the leadership of Colonel Thomas Sherburne of Division Artillery to provide this protection. Sherburne had waited until definite verification of their assembly position before he set out with Lieutenant Cecil Wilson, PFC Julian Necikowski, and ten infantry paratroopers. That was all General Taylor had been able to spare for that mission. Along the way they picked up reinforcements. However, the predawn glider lift had already landed before Sherburne reached the fields.[17]

Men continued to trickle into Division Headquarters at Hiesville throughout the long day. It wasn't until shortly after 1700 hours that the command post began to function with some semblance of organization, as staff officers arrived to operate with a skeleton workforce. However, many key officers were missing—G-3 leader Lieutenant Colonel Raymond Millener, and assistant G-2 Major Paul Danahy, were moving eastward from eight miles away and would not reach the scene for several days. Millener's assistant, Major Larry

Legere, had been wounded and evacuated from Pouppeville, and Captain Leo Schweiter, another assistant in the G-2 department, had been knocked unconscious by a German grenade. Schweiter was in enemy hands for approximately 24 hours before the retreating Germans left the prisoners and fled.

Before midnight, over 200 of 3rd Battalion's 600-man force had assembled in perimeter defense about headquarters.

The highlights of the day had been the capture of Pouppeville (an emergency operation), and the juncture with 4th Division on Causeway 1. The division commander, General Taylor, was already busy preparing for tomorrow's attack with his available forces.

CHAPTER 11

The Five-O-Deuce

The original parachute regiment of the 101st Airborne Division was the 502nd or "Five–O–Deuce." It had been commanded since its organization by Colonel George Van Horn "Ole Moe" Moseley. The four D-Day assignments for the 502nd were the destruction of the four-gun coastal battery at St. Martin-de-Varreville, the capture of "WXYZ"—the artillery personnel's barrack complex of the Germans at Mesières, the setting up of strong roadblocks to the north near Foucarville to prevent German reinforcements from moving to the beach area, and the seizure of the upper two causeways (Exits 3 and 4) to enable the 4th Infantry Division to move inland toward Cherbourg.

Colonel Moseley jumped with the 2nd Battalion of the 502nd. The 2nd Battalion had been given the specific assignment of destroying the coastal battery. With Moseley was Lieutenant Colonel Benjamin Weisberg, commanding officer of the 377th Parachute Field Artillery Battalion, which was assigned the task of providing artillery support for the 502nd in storming the coastal battery. Weisberg was to coordinate his artillery fire with the 502nd's infantry attack.

The headquarters men gather

The 502nd was to have parachuted on Drop Zone "A" near its objectives, but a large number of planes dropped their sticks in the vicinity of Hiesville and Drop Zone "C" about three miles south of Drop Zone "A." This, of course, immediately complicated the task of assembly and the realization of objectives.

There had been the usual flak and antiaircraft fire sustained by the men as they dropped. Landings produced injuries among many. One of them was Colonel Moseley himself, who broke his leg on the jump. He lay for a short time in the field where he landed.

Private John Zaika, of the 2nd Battalion, a young farmer from White Pigeon, Michigan, dropped nearby. He remembered, "Eight or ten men assembled near the spot where I landed. We were in the middle of a field where our regimental commander, Colonel Moseley, lay with a broken leg. I left to scout the area for a horse but they were scared and I couldn't catch one, so I came back to the same spot and only Colonel Moseley lay there. I told him I wasn't able to get a horse for him and that he shouldn't lie there in the open, so I decided to carry him on my back to a ditch where we hid until he told me to scout around and find members of his regimental command group. This I did. I found three or four of them, but when I went up to one of these men and asked if he was from Regimental Headquarters, he threw a hand grenade at me and we both ran off in different directions. I spent the entire night trying to find someone friendly to whom I might attach myself."

As the night wore on, and more and more men of Regimental Headquarters congregated, Colonel Moseley was able to receive medical attention. T/4 Tom Walsh of Regimental Headquarters described the scene: "We moved out on a road near a field where a large group of men were congregated, including Colonel Moseley and Major Doug Davidson (regimental surgeon). I remember providing a perimeter defense for the regimental commander in the field where General Pratt's glider crashed."

Sergeant Schuyler Jackson of Moseley's headquarters staff was a demolition man who had been assigned to assist in blowing up the artillery positions at St. Martin-de-Varreville. He, too, had dropped in the wrong drop zone, as had Moseley. With the dawn came the thunder of the great naval and air bombardment signaling the landings on Utah Beach several miles away. Jackson felt a sense of helplessness over a mission unaccomplished. He said, "I'll confess I said a prayer for the men who would be coming in over the beach and storming the heavy German fortifications along the coast. It was a short prayer because the dawn also brought the German snipers out after us."[1]

T/4 Tom Walsh, who was with Jackson, spotted the first sniper. "I noticed a German helmet in the hedgerow," remembered Walsh. "I called 'Sky' Jackson and Corporal Vic Nelson (from S-3) to follow. We saw an enemy platoon advancing toward us on the road. We opened fire and moved down the road calling 'Kommo heraus hande hoch!' Germans still able, came out on the road with their hands up calling 'Kameraden!' Help came to round up the prisoners. I helped an old German toward the medical aid station at Hiesville. He died on the way."

Sergeant "Sky" Jackson described the same incident: "There seemed to be snipers everywhere. There were four of us now and we chased two snipers behind a hedgerow. Feeling sure of the odds being with us, we rushed up and sprayed the hedge with bullets. Imagine our consternation when we found there were twenty-eight Germans behind that hedge. Those who survived surrendered to the four most startled American soldiers in France."

After marshaling the prisoners to the regimental CP, "Sky" Jackson came upon the wreckage of a glider. "There was an incident concerning a burly paratrooper I found at dawn," Jackson remembered. "He was badly wounded and lay propped against the wreckage of a glider. He was puffing on a stubby cigar as he waited patiently to be moved to the overcrowded aid station. We talked about many things, but the conversation always returned to his farm in the Midwest. He told me about the new tractor he wanted to buy, how the barn needed paint and about a new strain of hog he was going to raise that would be the best in the world. We talked for about fifteen minutes. Then he took the cigar butt from his mouth, carefully laid it on the ground, closed his eyes and said, 'Come visit us.' Then he died in that French pasture."[2]

Other Regimental Headquarters personnel were scattered over a wide area. T/4 Tom Pastorius was a communications man. He landed in a field miles from the proper drop zone. He got together with Captain Ivan Phillips (communications officer), who had collected an assorted dozen men. Pastorius described the scene: "He started marching us up the road. He told us to rest and then he lit a flashlight trying to read a map. All hell broke loose from a machine gun. The officer told us to retreat. I shook the fellow in front of me (Jim Santini), and thought, 'My God, he's dead!' No, he was asleep. We found a Frenchman named Pierre. The captain called me up (I had some college French). I told Pierre to take us to St. Martin-de-Varreville. Pierre and I walked along ahead of the motley crew. We ran into one machine-gun nest, but no casualties and we cleaned them out. Pierre got us there where we were to set up communications."

Captain Ivan Phillips, communications officer for Regimental Headquarters, described the same incident: "We had three encounters with the Germans. Earlier in the morning I routed a Frenchman out of bed and used him for a guide. He guided us to three German positions, which we wiped out. On the fourth engagement, our group walked through a defile (old overgrown canal) in the middle of a fight. We later learned this scrap had taken place between Captain James Hatch's group and the enemy.

"After several reorganizations, we arrived at our CP location[3] and successfully cleared the village prior to the arrival of Colonel Michaelis to take over command of the regiment. Up to that time it was only fighting in scattered groups."

As the day progressed, Colonel Moseley was brought to the aid station at Hiesville.[4] Sergeant "Sky" Jackson related, "I saw Colonel Moseley in a wheelbarrow. He was in great pain. (I saw the bone sticking out of his leg.) He was still the same aggressive leader, barking out orders as he had when I knew him in training before D-Day. He had refused to be evacuated, but I heard General Taylor, who had also arrived there, give a direct order that he was to be evacuated and Colonel John Michaelis was to take over."

Another plane carrying Regimental Headquarters personnel dropped its men approximately 500 yards almost due south of St. Germain-de-Varreville. Two members of the Intelligence Section (S-2), PFC Matthew H. Foley and PFC

Bob Paczulla, were members of that group. Foley had a good landing and contacted two of his buddies, Sergeant Mike Sefakis and Bob Paczulla. Foley related, "On D-Day we raised hell, but nothing like we were assigned to do. We were off the DZ and didn't link up with our company until much later. We found two guys with a machine gun and set up. We waited until morning and then took off toward the DZ. We met up with seven or eight men from the 501st. Found some Germans in a farmhouse—fired on them and then proceeded to look for our own outfit."

Bob Paczulla, Foley's buddy, described the actions in more detail. He found two men from his stick and then remembered he had left his communication equipment near his chute. "When I returned," he said, "others had assembled and Sergeant Mike Sefakis took note of who was there from S-2 and we moved out to try to find a landmark. If we could establish our position, we could move toward our objective. Our specific mission was to establish an OP (Observation Post) at Turqueville, and to communicate enemy movements to regimental headquarters. That mission was not accomplished for various and sundry reasons.

"We set off in single file through the hedgerows. It was difficult to maintain contact because the hedges were so thick and you caught your webbing or gear in the branches. By the time you had disengaged yourself, the person in front of you let a small bush or sapling snap back at you as he went through and you soon became wary of following too closely.

"It didn't seem too long before the entire composition of our original group had changed. Sefakis, Foley, and I were the only S-2 men and we had picked up two machine gunners and three riflemen from a line company. We had come to an embankment that ran the length of the hedgerow, so we took up positions with the two machine guns on our flanks, while Foley and I assembled the SCR-300 radio and tried to contact headquarters. Our call signals received no reply. We checked our frequency settings and tried again to no avail. I do not recall what time it was, but we knew it wasn't much longer until dawn, so we decided to stay put until we could see where we were.

"We moved out that morning and came to a roadway. Coming down the road was an officer with about two squads of men. We approached them and Sefakis talked to the officer, who then told us to fall in with the rest of the group. Farther on down the road we came to a French village. The officer banged on the first house to arouse the occupants. A Frenchman appeared at the door and was interrogated by one of the GI's who spoke French. Through the interrogation we learned that the Germans were occupying a farmhouse not too distant from where we were and that they were using it as an ammo dump. The officer called for the S-2 men for scouts, gave us a briefing from his map and selected me as lead scout with Matt Foley as second scout."

Paczulla continued, "I led the column with Foley about fifty feet behind and the officer brought up the rest of the group. We hadn't gone far when ahead on my right I saw an opening in the hedgerow. I signaled for Foley to come forward since I could see a farmhouse behind the hedge and I figured we could observe from the opening. As I approached the hedgerow a rifle shot split the silence and a slug whizzed by, grazing my cheek. Foley had come alongside and we both began to fire into a tree near the farmhouse. There was a sniper in that tree and we laid down our fire from the top to the base of the trunk. This stirred activity in the farmhouse and they returned fire with rifle and automatic weapon fire. In the meantime, the officer had deployed his group and they were laying down a barrage of fire on the farmhouse. Suddenly a fire started inside the barn, and as it grew in intensity, ammunition began to explode. We withdrew when the explosions were such that to remain would have been dangerous.

"The only thing that happened in this immediate area was that after the above incident, we were able to locate Regimental Headquarters CP. Captain Phillips requested our SCR-300 (which we were glad to part with) because he had lost most of his sets and was in need of them. I was then assigned to contact the 4th Infantry Division because no communication had been received as to their progress. I proceeded toward the line of approach of the 4th Division and contacted a battalion commander who was leading his men up from the beaches. I told him my mission. He reported light resistance upon landing. One enemy machine gun had given them a little trouble but they had knocked it out. He also commended the airborne for doing a good job."

Captain Ivan Phillips may have participated in the same action as the two intelligence men. He added this recollection: "One of the interesting details of the Normandy operation that has never been told was how two units had passed through a small village where, unbeknown to them, the German gun crews had hidden. The Regimental Headquarters Company had its first real baptism by fire as a unit at this village. I believe we encountered 65 Germans. Five were saved as prisoners. This was where I picked up a camouflaged 1941 Ford car marked, 'Assembled in England.' This car had been booby-trapped. This was no difficulty to our trained demolitions experts to debug. One man was killed in this fight because he either failed to hear my order to stay out of the dugout entrenchment or disregarded it and entered one end of the fortification. He was killed by a booby trap."

After they had made contact with the 4th Infantry Division men coming from the beach, Phillips added, "We were able to obtain support from the 4th Division Artillery. While with them, I arranged to pick up signal equipment and used the captured Ford sedan (later turned over to Colonel John Michaelis) to haul equipment to our position."

Colonel Moseley and his regimental headquarters personnel were to have combined forces with the 2nd Battalion on the assault of the coastal battery, but as has been noted, their scattered jump prevented a complete linkup on D-Day. Depending upon their drops, headquarters personnel fought in actions involving small groups from all three battalions of the 502nd. Their stories are incorporated into the descriptions of these actions.

The story of 2nd Battalion of the 502nd will follow the account of Lieutenant Colonel Cassidy and his 1st Battalion.

Cassidy's Battalion

The 1st Battalion of the 502nd was assigned the task of capturing "WXYZ" at Mesières. This was a barracks complex of buildings that housed the personnel of the German coastal artillery battery at St. Martin-de-Varreville. The 1st Battalion also was to set up strong roadblocks at Foucarville and Beuzeville.

Lieutenant Colonel Patrick Cassidy, the commanding officer of the 1st Battalion had parachuted only two hundred yards east of the St. German-de-Varreville church where Captain Frank Lillyman's pathfinders had assembled about an hour earlier. Shortly after the drop, Cassidy was joined by three paratroopers, one of whom was a radioman, T/5 Leo Bogus, who had jumped with a heavy radio set attached just below his reserve parachute. It had been responsible for a bad opening shock. Bogus said, "It was my first night jump with a piece of heavy equipment. I thought I had broken my back when I hit the ground, but found later it was only a bad sprain. The first person I ran into was Colonel Cassidy's runner, Talmage New. Then we joined with Colonel Cassidy and some of the other men from communications. From there we started on our way to the beach."

Cassidy moved with these men along the hedgerow into the next field, where Lieutenant Colonel Robert Strayer of the 506th Regiment had assembled a group. Despite a jump injury, Colonel Strayer limped along the hedgerows with Colonel Cassidy, rounding up men and looking for some signpost to locate their position. Lieutenant Jack Williams, Captain Fred Hancock, and Lieutenant Samuel B. Nichols had joined the two colonels, each bringing along a sizable group of strays. Hancock had come upon a road sign pointing to Foucarville, two kilometers to the north.

The two colonels now decided to separate their men and go their ways. Most of the two hundred men assembled were Colonel Strayer's men from the 506th. After gathering more men, Strayer would head for Causeways 1 and 2.

Cassidy's objectives were nearby. He and his men set out toward WXYZ. En route they met pathfinder Captain Frank

Lillyman with a detail of men just returning from a scouting mission to the coastal artillery battery position, which had been bombed out by Allied planes. Cassidy sent Lillyman to the north to set up a roadblock near Foucarville.

Colonel Cassidy's column rushed the first house in the WXYZ complex but found no enemy. The house was put to use as Cassidy's first command post. Later in the day it was found that the landlady had concealed two Germans in the building.

The rest of the WXYZ complex lay to the southwest of the newly acquired command post. The German battery position was just a few hundred yards to the east of the command post. Cassidy walked to the battery position and found Lieutenant Steve A. Chappuis, commander of the 2nd Battalion of the 502nd, sitting atop the rubble of one of the gun positions holding an orange flag in his hand. This had been his objective, and he and a dozen of his men had gone there after their drops nearby.

Radioman Bogus, saddled with his heavy radio, remembered the hike with Cassidy to meet Colonel Chappuis at the battery position. He said, "I recall trying to contact other units as well as the 4th Infantry Division several times. At about 0730, I managed to contact someone from the 4th Division. I sent them a message stating that two of the coastal guns had been completely destroyed. The other two were not in operation."

Returning to his command post, Colonel Cassidy sent troopers of his command to set up roadblocks to the north and south of his positions and sent others to set up a perimeter defense to protect the CP. Another group of men was assigned to clear out the artillery barracks situated in the small village of Mesières, just a few hundred yards southwest of the command post on the Reuville Road.

WXYZ

With only a limited number of men to send on the WXYZ mission, Colonel Cassidy chose Staff Sergeant Harrison Summers to lead a patrol made up almost entirely of misdropped troopers from other units. Only a few of the men were known to Summers. He didn't know anything of their fighting capabilities. Summers led the fifteen-man group along the hedgerow-lined fields. The country was open for several hundred yards to the west with little cover other than what was provided by the hedgerow-lined roadsides. Summers arrived at the first building at 0900. He turned as if to give directions and noted that his men hung back, unsure of his leadership. The sergeant decided to lead by setting an example, hoping the others would follow. The barracks buildings had thick walls of stone with fire slots or ports through which the enemy within could fire upon exposed paratroopers without offering themselves as targets—much in the same fashion that fire slots were used in the walls of forts during the days of Indian fighting. The clusters of buildings stretched on both sides of the road for approximately seven hundred yards to the west.[5]

The men dashed for cover in the roadside ditches as ineffective fire came through the low hedge in their direction from within the first building. Summers crawled through the hedgerow, got on his feet, and calmly walked to the back door of the small farmhouse. He braced a shoulder and crashed the door open. Bringing his tommy gun to waist height, he sprayed the defenders who were lined up and firing through the slots. Four enemy soldiers dropped and the rest fled through another door.

Summers came back through the hedge. He glanced at the men. He said nothing. The survivors of the first building had fled across the road, so he decided to move in that direction. Summers wiggled through the hedge on the south side of the road and approached the second building. He broke through the door, but the enemy had already fled.

A lone soldier arose from the ditch. Private William Burt had been inspired by the bravery of one man. Armed with a light machine gun, he crawled along the ditch beside the hedgerow until he could see a third barrack beyond the second. Burt commenced firing at the ports through which enemy fire was spewing. This forced the enemy to fire blindly through the ports, as they had to keep their heads down. Summers was able to approach the third building unseen.

Someone else had begun action in the WXYZ area. Lieutenant Elmer F. Brandenberger, an officer from Harrison Summer's own Baker Company, recalled, "I believe I was the first one to attack the barracks at WXYZ. My attempt failed. I believe that Summers came along sometime after my try and successfully carried out the attack. Somewhere along the line that morning I had exchanged my BAR for a tommy gun and found myself among some members of my own company, including Staff Sergeant Harrison Summers and Private William Burt. I remember going through a couple of houses in the village that I now know to have been WXYZ. In one house, I was just about to let go a burst of fire at some movement I saw at the top of a flight of stairs. For some reason I hesitated. On taking a second look, I saw a tousle-headed, pale-faced boy who couldn't have been more than twelve years old peering at me from under a pile of bedding. Moments later, a Frenchman darted into the house and pointed toward the boy and cried over and over, 'Malade! Malade! Malade!' Even yet when I think about it, I feel a little twinge of horror at the mistake I almost made, even though it had been in the heat of battle. I searched out the house but found only evidence of hasty German departure."

Brandenberger added, "As I left the house, I heard someone shouting that there was a machine gun firing from a stone building at the far end of the village. I called to a couple of men to follow me and started out in the direction of the enemy position. I still remember Burt with his machine gun alongside the road covering for us. I made my way across the road with machine-gun fire clipping off the leaves on the trees over my head. I clambered over the hedgerow on the far side of the road. Over to my left I could see what appeared to be a burning vehicle beside a shed. I crept forward along the hedgerow in the direction of the building. From this point, I yelled for someone to bring up a bazooka for me. I didn't get any response and couldn't see the two men that I had instructed to follow me. After I had shouted for the bazooka, a couple of potato masher grenades landed nearly

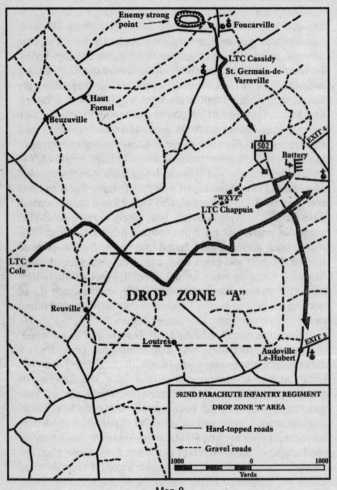

Enemy strong point →

Foucarville

LTC Cassidy

St. Germain-de-Varreville

Haut Fornel

Beuzuville

EXIT 4

502

Battery

"WXYZ"

LTC Chappuis

LTC Cole

DROP ZONE "A"

Reuville

Loutres

Audoville Le-Hubert

EXIT 3

502ND PARACHUTE INFANTRY REGIMENT

DROP ZONE "A" AREA

→ Hard-topped roads

--→ Gravel roads

1000   0   1000

Yards

Map 8

beside me. They didn't go off. I can remember my feeling of fright when I saw them hit the ground so close to me that I could have spit on them if I had any spit left. My mouth was real dry. I didn't know why they stopped coming in and I couldn't determine where they were coming from. I figured, however, that I had better get out of this spot, so I moved off to the left. After I had traveled a short distance I ran into a sergeant from the 4th Infantry Division. (He had the patch on his shoulder.) I suppose he was as surprised as I was. I asked him where the hell he came from, and he told me that his unit was moving up from the beach. By this time I had worked my way into such a position that I could see through a little archway into the courtyard of the stone building and thought I could see where the machine-gun fire was coming from. I told the sergeant to cover me and ran toward the building with the intention of getting that machine gun. I had just made the archway when the next thing I knew I was staring stupidly at my tommy gun which was lying on the ground at my feet. I tried to pick it up, but my left arm swung out in a crazy wide arc as I leaned over. I couldn't control it. I didn't realize until I tried to pick up the gun that I had been hit. I must have panicked right then, for I let the gun lay without making any more attempts to recover it and backed out of the courtyard, retracing my steps. I didn't see anyone. The 4th Division sergeant was gone and not a soul was in sight."

Brandenberger continued, "I came back along the side of the hedgerow that I had followed earlier toward the building. I was getting tired, my arm was beginning to hurt, and the blood was streaming off my fingertips. Holding my left arm against my body with my right, I finally managed to get back over the hedgerow I had crossed previously. I don't know how I managed to get back over but I fell off it into the ditch on the roadside and lay there for a while before I made a feeble dash back across the road, which was still under machine-gun fire. That is where Lieutenant Homer Combs found me. He was, I understand, killed sometime later. He was a fine soldier and a good friend. He gave me a shot of morphine and tried to stop the bleeding. Private Jack Rudd, our medic, came to me, did what he could and got me back to a small stone farmhouse where Lieutenant Colonel Pat Cassidy had set up a temporary CP. I finally lost consciousness, but before passing out, I can recall noting the look of concern on Cassidy's face and seeing several people, including my company commander, Captain Cleveland Fitzgerald, lying wounded on the stone floor of the little house."[6]

Sergeant Summers and Bill Burt continued their action. Summers moved toward the entrance of the third building, kicked open the door, and dropped all six Germans with one sweep of his tommy gun. In the meantime, Summers' patrol moved up and was strung along the ditch on either side of Private Burt. They were now firing at the fourth building. This smaller structure was a short distance west of the third. Summers came out of the far end of Building 3 and sprinted quickly to the fourth building. He heaved his weight against the door, and found it slightly ajar. His momentum sent him sprawling. Summers was in no position to take care of the Germans. Fortunately, the enemy had sought cover elsewhere. As he lay there panting, he noted an occasional slug ricochet off the inner walls as a lucky shot found its way through an open port. It was safer outside, so he crawled out and plunked himself down beside the building to rest.

From the orchard to the south arrived a tall lean captain from the 82nd Airborne Division. He had been misdropped into the 502nd area. The captain had observed only one man raising a ruckus about the three buildings. Those in the roadside ditch were hidden from his view.

After Summers had managed to catch his breath, the two decided to go for a larger building on the north side of the road. Enemy soldiers had been seen rushing toward the building which served as an officer quarters. A large open area had to be traversed without the protection of natural cover. The men in the ditches were directed to fire at the windows and nearby buildings to keep the Germans from observing the movements of the attackers.

With a nod to the captain, Summers started through the hedge. Both sprinted over the open area. Before they had gone twenty yards the captain fell, shot through the heart. He died without the sergeant ever learning his name. Sergeant

Summers continued on alone. Another door was kicked in and another six German defenders fell before the spewing lead of his chattering tommy gun. Others fled from the building, circled it, and came around to the front with their arms raised. They surrendered to the men lying in the ditches.

Private John Camien arose from the ditch as the captain fell. Camien went to Summers' aid. Like Summers, he seemed to lead a charmed life. As a team, they entered four buildings using the carbine of Private Camien as a cover weapon while they took turns breaking into the buildings and blasting the interiors with a tommy gun. Private Burt moved his light machine gun up along the ditch facing each building as the fight slowly progressed to the west. The enemy soldiers were unable to observe the movements of the attacking team because they were forced to keep their heads down at the ports. The fire from the buildings was rapid and noisy, but very ineffective. Summers and Camien moved through Buildings 6, 7, and 8. Fifteen enemy soldiers fell to their combined efforts.[7]

The two soldiers now crawled through a hedgerow which formed a boundary for a field. They moved westward hugging the inside edge of a low embankment which ran parallel to the Rueville Road. The next building, which was a mess hall that served the enlisted men of the German artillery group, was 150 yards in front of them. Private Burt followed along the roadside ditch with his machine gun. The remainder of the roadside force also came forward. It had been considerably reinforced as the fighting progressed. As men had been directed toward WXYZ, they had fallen in at the rear of the roadside column not really knowing what was occurring at the head of the procession.

The mess hall was a long low building. With all of this action and noise taking place in the vicinity, one would think this building would have had all its occupants in defensive positions. Not so, for the fifteen hungry Germans were bound and determined to eat at this time; they were oblivious of the fighting until the door burst open with Summers spraying the interior with his machine gun. They sprang for nearby weapons but too late.

One more breathing spell and then on to the last building—
the main barracks. It had the usual two-and-a-half-feet-thick
stone walls, but unlike the others, it was two stories high and
was situated on a gentle rise with an open area more than
fifty yards from the hedgerow behind which the two soldiers
studied the situation. Enemy machine gunners had fairly
good observation to the east along the Reuville Road, which
was now being used by the troops coming along the ditches.
There was no cover for attack from any direction. Any dash
across the open area would have left a soldier exposed to rifle
and machine-gun fire from the ports in the walls.

Colonel Cassidy had become concerned with the continued firing as the day progressed. As newcomers reported into
the CP, he had sent them forward as reinforcements to WXYZ.
Such a group was now attempting to approach through an orchard at the left of Summers' force. Somewhere behind them
a sniper observed their movements and quickly picked off
three of the Americans. The rest plunged through the hedge
they had been using as cover and came into the line of fire
of the enemy soldiers stationed at the gun ports. Four Americans were killed and a like number took wounds. The rest
bolted up the Reuville Road. Again, Summers' patrol had
followed along to provide covering fire, but their firing was
ineffective as their bullets did little more than chip away at
the hard stone walls.

Looking for an easier way to do the job, Private Bill Burt
crawled forward to a position near the drive. He noted a
haystack beside a large wooden shed, which was a short distance from the barracks. Using tracer ammunition, he quickly
fired the stack. The flames spread rapidly to the shed, which
contained ammunition. Shells began to explode as flames
consumed the structure. A platoon-sized group of enemy soldiers had been caught inside and they dashed out and tried to
flee across the open ground. They were fired upon by the entire attacking force. About thirty of them were killed by the
volley. The action did not disturb the force inside the larger
building. They continued to keep the Americans pinned
down behind the hedge.

On the scene arrived another reinforcement—Staff Sergeant

Roy Nickrent came along carrying a bazooka. He had approached through the orchard located on the south side of the road. Nickrent described his action: "I had managed to cross the road without being hit and moved up along the hedgerow behind the mess hall to a position just north of Sergeant Summers and his group. Finding a good spot for my type of work in the hedgerow, I fired two rounds to adjust my range. The first one fell short while the second hit the stone wall of the building near its base. I continued to adjust my aim until the seventh round went through the roof. Black smoke began to pour through the hole."

Unknown to Summers and his group, two large friendly forces were advancing. A spearhead of the 4th Infantry Division that had come up from the beach was moving westward through the orchards just north of Summers' position. The other group was made up of 502nd Regimental Headquarters Company personnel led by Lieutenant Colonel John Michaelis. They were moving eastward along the Reuville Road.

As flames began to consume the interior of the building, the Germans broke out of it and began to flee northward across an open field, where they were caught in the crossfire of Summers' force, the 4th Division, and Michaelis' men. About fifty of the enemy were killed and thirty-one came out with their hands raised. The capture of WXYZ at Mesières was now complete. A battalion's objective had been accomplished by a fearless sergeant and a handful of helpers.[8]

Action at Foucarville

Several hours before Colonel Cassidy set up his command post near WXYZ, members of his battalion had been engaged in action at Foucarville, a little more than a mile northwest of the CP. This was one of the first engagements with the enemy in the invasion. Captain Cleveland Fitzgerald and Lieutenant Harold Hoggard, with a group of nine men, were fired on at 0200 A.M. by a German sentry posted in the courtyard of a German headquarters. Fitzgerald received a shot in his chest and ordered the others to let him lie there for he thought he was dying.[9]

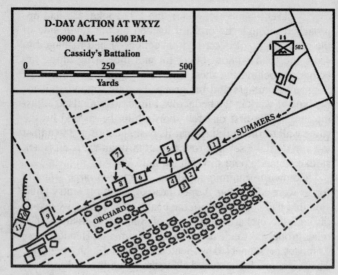

Map 9

1. Operation began at 0900 with move by S/Sgt Summers and his patrol from the 1st Battalion CP. Solo charge by Summers on Building 1 netted four. Others escaped to building across the road.
2. Building 2 was empty of enemy troops when entered, they having flown the coop. Lt. Brandenberger joined Summers. He entered Building 2 and discovered a sick child at the head of the stairs.
3. Pvt. Burt covered Summers with his machine-gun fire as the sergeant entered Building 3 alone and downed six more enemy soldiers.
4. Summers burst into empty building.
5. Summers was joined by unidentified captain who is slain before they reached Building 5. Summers entered alone and gunned down six more.
6. Camien joined Summers in the attack on Building 6 (home of Madame Louis Caillemer). The two men continued on through Buildings 6, 7, and 8. Fifteen enemy soldiers were downed by their combined assault. (While their action was progressing, Brandenberger moved west along the road toward Buildings 9, 10, and 11.)
9. Mess hall where fifteen unconcerned enemy soldiers were downed as they scrambled for weapons. This was the area in which Brandenberger believed he was felled by enemy fire but managed to find his way back to the orchard on the south side of the road. This occurred before the arrival of Camien and Summers.
10. Wooden shed set afire by Burt as he fired tracers into the haystack. Thirty enemy soldiers were killed as they fled the flames.
11. Large, well-fortified two-storied barrack which was finally fired by bazooka rocket aimed by S/Sgt Roy Nickrent.

(*Map and action reconstructed with assistance of Summers, Brandenburger, and Nickrent.*)

This action occurred at the base of a heavily fortified rise of ground just to the northwest of Foucarville. This enemy stronghold became the focal point of much activity on D-Day because several planeloads of 1st Battalion paratroopers had dropped into and about this area.

One of the soldiers involved in this early fighting at the Foucarville fortified area was Able Company Sergeant Charles Asay. Part of his stick had jumped as his plane passed directly over the fortified position. As the last man of the 18-man stick, Asay had dropped safely outside the barbed wire confines of the hilltop. After landing, he hid everything he couldn't put in his pockets and found one other man from his stick. They were fired upon by a hidden sniper and Asay felt the heat of the passing bullet. Unable to find his platoon leader, Lieutenant Joseph Smith, the two men moved off. Asay said, "We circled around and came into Foucarville from the south. The other soldier dispatched three or four Germans outside of Foucarville not far from where we landed. I surmised from the oscillations that we had jumped from a very low altitude. My machine-gun crew was captured.[10] One man, Private Philip Stands, was killed. We found Captain Fitzgerald shot up in Foucarville. He was Baker Company CO. We made him comfortable and set about cleaning up the little town. Our CO, Captain Davidson, and part of his stick were dropped in the Channel and drowned."

At least three of the 1st Battalion planes passed over the same enemy strongpoint at Foucarville while they were dropping their men. Some men from both Able and Baker Companies were taken prisoner before they had an opportunity to get out of their chute harnesses. Several described their experiences. Corporal Mike Gromack said, "My drop was soft. I landed in an enemy strongpoint. Had difficulty getting out of my chute as there was a Kraut bayonet tickling my ribs. I was taken prisoner and marched downstairs into a large dugout. There were others there from my stick, including Lieutenant Joseph Smith, Hewitt Tippins, and Sergeant Charley Ryan. Our assignment had been to blow up a shack with communications equipment in it. Needless to say, we didn't accomplish it. Lieutenant Smith was in charge of our group and he was shot and captured after a helluva battle he gave the Krauts."

PFC Donald DeSalvadore was one of the Baker Company men who also was captured in the same fortified area. He remembered, "We came in very low and I just remember my chute opened and I bumped the ground right in front of a German machine gun. Instead of shooting me, they held me and took my harness off and dragged me into a trench. There were four of them and hampered with all the equipment I was carrying, I couldn't move. I tried to get my knife out, but they took it away and threw it aside. I'll admit I was damned scared. The first words I remember being spoken were, 'Are you vounded?' I said, 'No,' so they herded me into a trench where I was ordered to lie facedown for most of the night. Then, after what seemed like an eternity, I was taken into a dugout—some kind of underground cave or bunker. There I found about six other 502nd boys. One was Ralph Gentile. Another was Tippins from A Company. The rest I didn't know."

PFC John Steinfeld who had carefully packed a box of chocolates in his gear to "use for bartering purposes with the girls in France," related his experiences in the Foucarville area: "I landed in a fortified position. I got in a ditch trying to figure a way out. I knew there were machine guns on three sides of the position. John Suski, Dutch Slaysman, Wendall Eldridge, Neidhammer, Mike Gentile, and myself, plus some A Company boys were there. Our group was supposed to provide security for six artillery men from the 377th while they laid three miles of wire from Division Artillery Center to Hiesville.[11]

"It was partly cloudy that night. A trooper came toward me using his cricket. I clicked my cricket. He asked the score. I told him about the machine guns around the lot. He said he was going to reconnoiter the area. A few minutes later I heard a grenade go off, then a German machine gun replied. I believe that man was Hewitt Tippins of A Company. After I heard the Krauts coming, I waited till the moon was covered and crawled toward the wire, repeating the same procedure back to the spot that I left. The same thing hap-

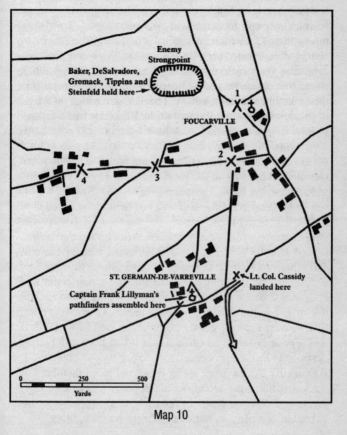

Map 10

Action at Foucarville and St. Germain-de-Varreville. Able Company roadblocks 1, 2, 3, and 4 set up near Foucarville.

pened again. The third time back in the original place in the ditch I heard a voice in German say 'Kaput!' I looked up—there were ten or twelve Krauts. I came out of the ditch with my hands on top of my helmet. The sergeant in charge searched me and took my knife out of my boot. They took me to their CP, which was in a barn. There, the officer in charge dumped my musette bag on the table and took the cigarettes (two cartons) and my box of candy. I motioned toward the cigarettes and he handed me a couple packs. I was then taken to a dugout, which seemed to have logs on top of it. Inside was my best buddy, Johnny Suski. He had a kidney to lose from a malfunction as he hit the ground very hard. There was Dutch Slaysman. He had a bayonet stab behind his knees when he tried to play possum with a German. Mike Gentile had been hit in the hand and chest."

Farther to the south, Lieutenant Wallace A. "Swede" Swanson had landed in the flooded area just behind the beach near Exit 4. His assignment was to take the town of Foucarville with members of his Able Company. After noting that he had landed at 0105 A.M., he said, "I collected men of the unit and others and moved to higher ground. About three or four o'clock in the morning we were moving along trails and hedgerows, backyards, and fence lines. We were shooting at the enemy in the distance as dawn came. After discovering that we were near the coastal battery site, we checked it as it was a priority target and found that it had been completely destroyed. We then proceeded toward our second objective at Foucarville. As we went along more and more members of our company came along, as did soldiers from other regiments and division units. In the early morning we were involved in company action and house-to-house fighting."

Roadblocks

When a messenger brought word to Colonel Cassidy at his CP near Mesières that Lieutenant Swanson was at Foucarville with approximately fifty men, Cassidy sent orders to Swanson to set up roadblocks around Foucarville in line with

1st Battalion's mission to prevent the Germans from moving in and out of the beach area.

Four roadblocks with bazookas, machine guns, and mines were set up. Snipers from the church steeple and other buildings in town maintained a continuous fire on the east roadblock. This firing continued to increase as the day progressed, due to the addition of soldiers who were being pushed back from the beach areas. The Germans had platforms in large trees upon which machine-gun nests were rigged and from these they continued to fire at the second roadblock through most of the day.

Sergeant Asay was on duty at one of the roadblocks. He and a friend sat on a low stone fence relaxing. He said, "Sergeant Olin Howard and I were sitting on a stone wall—this may sound like something out of a movie—near a crossroads in Foucarville. Suddenly a German Schmizzer opened up. We watched the slugs stitch the road coming toward us and one hit Olin in the right hand."

In the meantime, the enemy from the beach area and the houses in Foucarville gravitated toward the hilltop stronghold. A few more Americans were brought in as prisoners. Mike Gromack, John Steinfeld, and Don DeSalvadore described some of the action that took place in the bunker during the day.

Gromack said, "I gave a shot of morphine to one man with a bad chest wound. Our troops were shelling the dugouts with mortars. They didn't even dent it."

Steinfeld added, "Mike Gentile had a grenade in his pocket. The dugout was L-shaped. He told us to get around the corner and he would pull the pin and drop it on the floor. Gentile was lying on what looked like a table, but we would not let him drop the grenade as he would have been killed—also some of the other men had been hit and couldn't move.

"We asked the Germans to get a doctor for Mike. We had a hard time making them understand, but they said their position was surrounded."

DeSalvadore was also called on to administer first aid. He said, "A German sergeant told me to treat Gentile. He had a bullet in his leg. The Krauts didn't have any medical supplies, but we were allowed to keep what we had. The enemy sergeant said, 'We have milk, bread, and butter in the cupboard. Eat—get comfortable.' He didn't know what they were going to do with us at the time. We didn't seem to be in any immediate danger. They brought in another of our wounded, but didn't bring in any of their own. I don't know how long we had been there. There was plenty of action going on outside. We could hear American shells hitting the position quite often. The Germans came in, cleaned their guns and reloaded, and went back out. However, this one German noncom kept talking to us real decently. I couldn't understand him too well, but I caught some of the conversation. He was from the Russian front and had been sent to Normandy for rest. They didn't want to fight, but their officers threatened them if they didn't."

As the day progressed, the captive paratroopers began to think of ways of getting free. The enemy wasn't watching them that closely. The English-speaking sergeant was in and out of the dugout on numerous occasions. One of the captives had a brainstorm and decided to bluff the Germans. The position had been scheduled for assault at H-hour plus fifteen (2130 P.M.) by the 1st Battalion. The captured group had expected to hear heavy fire from the approaching paratroopers. This had not occurred. Word was passed along to the rest of the prisoners to act increasingly nervous and agitated as the day progressed. The prisoners checked their watches, whispered to each other, and shook their heads in hopelessness.

Finally curiosity got the better of the Germans, who, upon interrogation of the prisoners, learned they were anxious because the 377th Parachute Field Artillery Battalion was scheduled to begin bombardment of this fortified position at 2230. The position was to be blown off the map. The uneasiness began to spread to the German garrison.

As the time approached 2200, the American group that had been laying down a sporadic mortar and machine-gun barrage on the position was amazed to see the white flag raised over the position. PFC Hewitt Tippins had been taken to the entrance of the fortification as the prisoner for this purpose.

Mike Gromack described the incident this way: "The Krauts finally decided to surrender. They selected Tippins to go up and do the honors. This was sort of humorous. Tippins was from Georgia and always argued with us Northerners. It was the kind of friendly needling we always had between the guys from the South and the North. This Kraut sergeant took Tippins above. We could hear 'Tip' shouting, 'Don't shoot—I'm a Yank! Don't shoot—I'm a Yank!' Tippins got the needle a lot after that."

With arms raised over their heads, 87 enemy soldiers along with the French widow of one of the defenders, rose from the earthen bunkers. They were quickly seized by the former prisoners. A die-hard group of Germans refused to surrender and bolted toward the rear of the position where they were caught in the cross fire of the advancing paratroopers, the former prisoners, and the advance units of the 4th Infantry Division, which were just moving into position beside the paratroopers. About fifty Germans were killed.

Steinfeld described the surrender: "We finally heard rifle and automatic weapons fire not too far off. It kept coming closer. Finally, the German sergeant told Tippins to go out with a German soldier. A lieutenant and some dogfaces from the 4th Infantry Division came up. The officer wanted to know if there were Krauts in the dugout. I told him, yes. He told one of the men to throw a couple grenades in. I told him no—some of our men were in there, and the Krauts wanted to give up. So I went there and brought them out. They sent a doctor in to take care of our men. That was roughly 20 hours after we were captured. I found a company from the 502nd where I spent the night."

DeSalvadore ended his account this way: "As the Americans came closer, the English-speaking sergeant gave up to us and we turned the prisoners over to the CO of the 4th Infantry Division unit and we proceeded to look for our own regiment. It was evening by then. We found some unopened equipment bundles and rearmed ourselves with American weapons."

"When we all came out of the bunkers," Gromack explained, "we figured we'd attach ourselves to the 4th Division. The captain in charge of that group told us to join the troopers just across the road. They turned out to be members of my own platoon manning a roadblock position."

Off the beach

Several planes dropped their troopers in the flat and flooded areas just behind Utah Beach. Able Company men were among them. Almost to a man, these men dropped in water ranging from boot-top level to chest deep.

The green light had flashed in the plane of Captain Richard L. Davidson, Able Company Commander, near the flat inundated area northeast of Drop Zone "A" and east of St. Marcouf. Half of the eighteen-man stick went quickly out of the door. An explosion of an antiaircraft shell near the plane caused it to lurch, and the next man may have fallen in the doorway blocking the exit of the remaining members. The stricken craft lost altitude rapidly thereafter and plunged into the cold waters of the Channel off Utah Beach. Captain Davidson went down with the remaining men and the crew of the plane.

One of the fortunate members of this group of troopers was Corporal Louis Merlano. As the men had loaded into the plane in England, communications sergeant T/4 Louis Perko saw Merlano struggling on board with his cumbersome radio bundle. Perko offered to switch places in the jump order so Merlano would be closer to the exit. As a result of the switch, Merlano was saved and Perko lost his life. Merlano had a hard landing in a dummy minefield close to Utah Beach. He related, "I met Bob Barnes of 2nd Platoon with a complement of twelve men and we went about hunting Jerries. At early dawn, Private Howard Stiles, myself, and one other man held a crossroads leading down to the beach until about noon. We were under heavy machine-gun fire and mortar shelling. We had a headquarters in a house near the road until we were blasted out. We held out in a hedgerow until we met troops of the 4th Division moving up from the beachhead. I ended up joining a moving tank column that was headed toward Ste. Mère Eglise.

Two other men from Able Company recalled how they dropped in the flooded area behind the beach.[12] PFC Matthew C. Jemiolo landed off his drop zone in this marsh, where he struggled to get free in chest-deep water. He got out of his chute and headed for a spot of high ground, where he found about a dozen men. One of his friends, Private Morris Lansdale, was killed a few minutes later. Jemiolo recalled his experiences: "After getting about twelve men together, we proceeded toward the beach going by a German machine-gun post. We didn't even know it was there at the time. Going up the road, we were interrupted by B-26 bombers, which were bombing a coastal artillery position. I never knew people could bounce off the ground during a bombing attack. After finding nothing at the farmhouse toward which we were headed, we started back. We were fired on by mortars from the German post. The 4th Division finished the rest of that skirmish."

PFC Robert F. Barnes, who served as first scout of the same platoon, stated that their assignment was to clear some buildings that housed enemy troops, and set up some roadblocks to help secure the causeways. He described in more detail: "Our squad (1st Squad of 2nd Platoon), was the last to leave the plane. About halfway through the squad someone had trouble leaving the plane. The delay caused the rest of the squad to be separated. I got together with Fred Terwilliger, squad leader George Barner, Morris Lansdale, Matt Jemiolo, and Elmer Charles. After the above men assembled, we searched for high ground and at last we came to a causeway. It was a road and of course it meant danger for us, but we felt it was necessary to get oriented—as the area around us was under water. We decided to move on the causeway until we made contact with either friend or foe. We had proceeded about one hundred yards when we were fired on.

"We hit the ground and rolled off the causeway and back into the water. One of the fellows didn't make it. Private Morris Lansdale had been hit. Someone crawled to him and dragged him off the road but he had been stitched from hip to shoulder. There were a few minutes of bewilderment that followed, but we soon decided that our next course of action was to draw their fire again. We moved the grenadier into position to fire in their general direction. The blank rounds that launch the grenades wouldn't fire. After a few attempts we gave it up.

"It was obvious we couldn't go in the direction we were supposed to, so we went back down the causeway in the direction of the beach. We thought maybe we could find another exit through the flooded area. We traveled in that direction for some time. Along the way we picked up some men from the 82nd Airborne Division. We also found some equipment bundles. They contained mortar shells, grenades, etc. We loaded up on grenades.

"Shortly after daybreak we could see the beach and in the distance were German bunkers. As we looked we could see figures running back and forth. Out to sea, boats were coming in and out and of course this was the 4th Infantry Division. At about the same time, we noticed American planes overhead. They were bombers and headed in our direction. As they were passing overhead, the bomb bay doors opened and they released their sticks of bombs. The bombs landed around us and between us. We were right in the middle. Fortunately, they were small, but the ground shook and heaved. I believe they were intended for minefields that were in the area.

"I received a small wound in the arm and Fred Terwilliger had a piece lodge between his head and helmet. I shall never forget those bombs.

"After the noise and confusion abated, we decided to hit the inundated area and travel across water to try to join up with the rest of the outfit. We were pretty sure of our position now as we could tell from the beach and the invasion force just about where we were and the general direction we should travel. We plowed through water all that day. I almost drowned once as we were in water above our waists. I had six or seven grenades on my belt and I guess their weight pulled me down before I could react. I lost my rifle and tried to reach the other side of the bank. Someone grabbed me and pulled

T/4 Joseph Gorenc (HQ3/506) climbs on board the C/47 just prior to departure for the D-Day jump in Normandy. His unit, which went in with over 700 men, returned to England with only 180 on July 13, 1944.

General Maxwell D. Taylor, commander of the 101st Airborne Division, salutes as his plane moves out to its take-off position. Author (Koskimaki) served as his radioman on all combat missions.

General Dwight D. Eisenhower paid visits to the airfields from which the 101st was emplaning for Normandy. Here he is speaking to Lieutenant Wallace Strobel (E/502 PIR) of Saginaw, Michigan.

Colonel Howard Johnson, commander of the 501st Parachute Infantry Regiment poses with his pilot, Colonel Kershaw, moments before boarding for the flight to Normandy.

Stick No. 1: 502nd Parachute Infantry Pathfinder Team. Back row, from left to right: 1Lt. Samuel McCarter, 1Lt. Robert S. Dickson, Pvt. Charles S. Mcfarlen, Pvt. August M. Mangoni, Pvt. Bluford R. Williams, Pvt. John Zamanakis, T/5 Owen R. Council, Pvt. John Funk, T/5 Thomas C. Walton, Pfc. Delbert A. Jones. Front row, from left to right: Pvt. Paul O. Davis, Pvt. Francis A. Rocca, Pvt. Raymond Smith, Pfc. Fred A. Wilhelm, Pvt. John G. Ott, Pvt. Jarris C. Clark, 2Lt. Reed Pelfrey. (Capt. Frank Lillyman not in picture.)

Half-hour to take-off on June 5, 1944. Left to right: Major Howard W. Cannon; co-pilot: Lieutenant Colonel Robert Wolverton, commander of 3rd Battalion 506th Parachute Infantry (KIA on drop); Lieutenant Colonel Frank X. Krebs, pilot and commander of 440th TCC.

Demolition specialist Pvt. Clarence Ware puts on the finishing touches to the facial camouflage of his buddy Pvt. Charles Plaudo. Both were members of the "Filthy 13" of the 506th Parachute Regiment.

Buddies from "Fox" Company of the 506th Parachute Infantry Regiment check equipment to make sure it is secured before they board the plane for the flight to Normandy. (Photo provided by Colonel Charles H. Young, 439th Troop Carrier Group commander.)

Glider troopers of the 327th Glider Infantry Regiment shown in the cramped quarters of a Waco CG-4A. This glider carried thirteen troops and a crew of two. On occasion the troopers substituted as a co-pilot. These troopers were not equipped with parachutes. (Keystone photo)

Captain Frank Lillyman served as chief pathfinder for the 101st Airborne Division in Normandy. He is credited with being the first Allied soldier to set foot on French soil at 0015A on D-Day.

The church spire at St. Marie-du-Mont was used as a major landmark for disoriented paratroopers of the 101st. The spire was very different from the typical Normandy church.

Lieutenant Colonel Mike Murphy's CG-4A "Fighting Falcon" glider smashed into the hedgerow and trees at 0454 on D-Day morning. Brigade General Don F. Pratt and co-pilot 2nd Lieutenant John M. Butler were killed. Only 1st Lieutenant Lee John Mays, the general's aide, escaped unscathed. (Picture was taken by Dr. Charles Hubner during the afternoon of D-Day.)

A Horsa glider carrying men and motorcycles of the 101st Airborne Signal Company on the evening flight crashed into trees in a hedgerow killing several troopers, with others being badly injured.

The only battery of artillery pieces which had not been plotted by Allied planners was near Holdy. The remains of several of our troopers hung from the branches of the trees overhead. The above action and capture of these guns appears in the account. (Photo provided by Dr. George Lage.)

The glider in the foreground hit the posts (Rommel's Asparagus) placed in fields to prevent landings of airborne troops. In the background, other gliders which floated safely to landings are parked in a field. (U.S. Signal Corps photo)

A 33-passenger British Horsa glider made of plywood with no metal framework smashed through a stone wall near Ste. Mere Eglise on D-Day morning. Note the dead trooper lying left of center in the wreckage. These aircraft carried double the load of the smaller CG-4A Waco glider but splintered badly when colliding with immovable objects, such as trees and stone walls.

The remains of the 101st Airborne Division hospital at the Chateau Columbieres in Normandy. It was the first time a field hospital had been set up behind enemy lines. German bombers dropped delayed-action "block busters" on this complex on the night of June 9, 1944. Fortunately the four hundred casualties had been transferred to Utah Beach for evacuation back to England earlier in the day. The 326th Airborne Medical Company lost several of its members due to the terrific explosions. (Photo provided by Dr. Charles Hubner.)

101st medics minister to survivors of a Horsa glider crash that occurred on the evening of D-Day near Holdy. The glider hit tree tops on descent. A total of 17 troopers of 33 on board lost their lives. (Photo provided by Captain George Lage, surgeon for 2nd Battalion of the 502nd Parachute Regiment.)

Lieutenant Colonel Robert G. Cole, commander of the 3rd Battalion of the 502nd Parachute Infantry Regiment (left) proudly displays a Nazi flag his troops captured on D-Day. At the other end is Major John P. Stopka. Others in the picture are battalion officers. Both Cole and Stopka died in combat. Cole was awarded the Congressional Medal of Honor posthumously.

me to shallower water. Elmer Charles later retrieved my rifle for me.

"As we moved along throughout the day we were fired upon several times, and on each occasion we returned their fire. After some time on each of these occasions the firing would subside and we would push on.

"Toward evening we reached high ground and saw a farm-house. We reconnoitered the buildings but found no German troops around—only an elderly French couple. As far as I can tell, we were around Exit 4."

Mort Smit's Patrol

During the morning, Battalion Commander, Lieutenant Colonel Pat Cassidy, had directed Captain Fred Hancock of Charley Company to set up a perimeter defense of the command post. These men had been posted for several hours. In the afternoon, 200 troops under the command of the 502nd Regiment's executive officer, Lieutenant Colonel John Michaelis, proceeded east after the termination of the fighting in Mesières at WXYZ. Michaelis took over the command post. The new arrivals relieved some of the 1st Battalion troops. Cassidy then directed Captain Hancock with his company to move west of Mesières and Foucarville to set up additional roadblocks both to the east and west of Beuzeville. The lead element of this force was assigned to platoon leader Lieutenant Morton Smit.

Moving westward along a dry streambed toward Beuzeville, Smit and his platoon had to pass through the small hamlet of Haut-Fornel. Smit had an opportunity to reenact a portion of a movie he had once seen. He recalled, "Inasmuch as the enemy was in continuous movement and we were trying to locate them, my platoon was given the mission of proceeding toward Haut-Fornel. We encountered some resistance at this group of dwellings on the road to Haut-Fornel. I moved my men in to mop up the pocket and as the platoon moved through the small community, Private Harold Boone and I entered the main building looking for action.

"We came upon a large room. Some cots were there, and a couple of field desks. In looking over the correspondence and taking what looked important for G-2, we noticed some backpacks made of fur. Later we discovered that this information proved the existence of Russian troops in this sector.[13]

"While in the midst of this, Boone and I heard several German trucks arrive. We went into the little courtyard in the back of the main house and by looking out of the gate opening (a large wall, seven to eight feet surrounded this courtyard) I saw three or four German trucks unloading troops. I had an M-3 'Squirt' gun and used it to advantage (blazed two of the trucks and must have knocked out 25 to 30 troops). We lobbed several grenades as well. Then they started moving in on the two of us.

"By this time we had realized that we were definitely alone, so we looked for an avenue of strategic withdrawal. The Germans were entering the house, so the only way was to go over the wall. I boosted Boone over and followed immediately. Once on the other side, we found a small mud pond and a copse of trees. The Germans were all around the area. (A company if not more.) So, into the ooze we went. I remembered an old flicker where the actor used a reed to breathe through to escape detection, and so I took the barrel off the M-3 and proceeded to enjoy the luxury of solitude.

"Some time later, we heard some mortar shells land in the area. We came out of the slime (what a mess we were!) and as we were getting our bearings, some of my boys came back. They came charging out of the copse of woods with drawn bayonets. If I hadn't yelled out and identified myself to Sergeant Charles Tinsley, I am certain he would have gone right into me with his bayonet.

"The squad passed through our position quickly and out of sight. Then, like a comic opera, the Germans came back and we went back into the mud. Shortly thereafter, we pulled out of the pond, cleaned our weapons, and the three of us proceeded on. We finally rejoined our outfit a day later after another series of incidents."[14]

Strays

1st Battalion soldiers of the 502nd were involved in other actions which were not under the direct control of their commander. A large number of the men were dropped short of the DZ and ended up fighting for the town of Ste. Mère Eglise with men of the 82nd Airborne Division. One of them was Private Nichols from Baker Company. Nichols met two of his close buddies, Bob Mawhinney and "Sadie" Hawkins. They ran into an ambush near an equipment bundle and the men took off running. In the dash to get away from the enemy, the men were separated, and Nichols finally met up with some men from Charley Company. They moved from hedgerow to hedgerow until the force numbered about a dozen men. Two hours had elapsed since the jump and they hadn't found an officer to take charge of the group.

As Nichols recalled it, "As dawn approached, we were able to make out the outline of an equipment bundle in a small field. Another man and myself crawled out to see what it contained, and found a machine gun plus several boxes of ammo. The ammo boxes were bent but we found a couple in fair condition, so I now had a weapon. I had been without a weapon except for hand grenades, and even though the .30-caliber light machine gun was a little heavy, I was glad to have it.

"It was now daylight—the Krauts were still around. We didn't know it but we were on the outskirts of Ste. Mère Eglise and the fighting was hotter than somewhat, from the sounds of things. We moved on into town and started having a little problem with snipers. You just couldn't find a place that bullets didn't seem to be nicking your ears, and a few were finding their way into men's bodies. Some of us went one way; others another until we hooked up with different parts of the 82nd."

Nichols felt terribly lonely fighting beside total strangers. He added, "I was like an orphan boy at a picnic. I had been with the same men for over two years. In the evening I went over to a well to get a canteen of water, when who should come along but my two buddies, Mawhinney and Hawkins.

They both had been captured along with our platoon sergeant, Pinson, and he had been badly wounded. The Krauts took all of the first aid equipment these men had on them. Pinson died—"Maw" told me he and some of the others carried the sergeant until they were released by some of the infantry that reached them. The funny part about this operation was that the troops we were fighting were Russian, led by German noncoms and officers.

"Sadie, Maw, and I were a machine-gun team to start with, so now we were back together and we had a machine gun. We were attached to a mortar squad of the 505th Regiment of the 82nd Division and we were used for first one thing then another. Whatever our particular mission was, we had accomplished nothing, except to confuse the Krauts."

Farther to the east Private Douglas Garrett had been knocked out of breath by an enemy bullet which struck his reserve parachute pack. He managed to get out a .45-caliber pistol his cousin had scrounged for him from the Air Force. The weapon saved his life when an enemy soldier rushed up to him during his struggles with the harness. As Garrett tells it, "I shot that German before he could kill me. When my breath was normal again, I got out of my chute harness, fixed my rifle, and started away from that spot. I walked right into a machine-gun nest and after firing a few shots, beat a hasty retreat. About a hundred yards from there I met a good friend, Bob Chance. Our company clerk came up about then with two other men from B Company. He was a corporal and told us to come with him. When I saw he was headed straight for the German machine gun, I told him so and that I would not follow him. Chance and a man from C Company decided to stay with me, but the two men with our clerk went with him. A few minutes later, we heard the machine-gun fire. I did not know until the next day that the corporal was killed. He had been hit in the legs by the bullets and as he lay in the ditch moaning, the Germans cut his throat from ear to ear. The two with him managed to escape being hit and ducked into a hole barely large enough for one.

"After leaving the clerk and his two buddies, Chance, the man from C Company, and I went the other way. We came

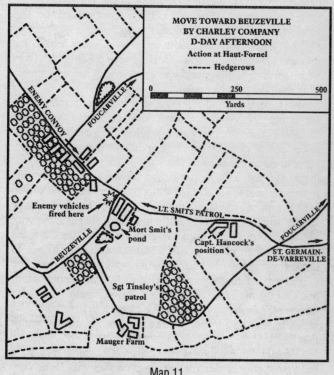

MOVE TOWARD BEUZEVILLE
BY CHARLEY COMPANY
D-DAY AFTERNOON

Action at Haut-Fornel

- - - - Hedgerows

0   250   500
Yards

FOUCARVILLE

ENEMY CONVOY

Enemy vehicles
fired here

LT. SMITS PATROL

FOUCARVILLE

Mort Smit's
pond

Capt. Hancock's
position

BEUZEVILLE

ST. GERMAIN-
DE-VARREVILLE

Sgt Tinsley's
patrol

Mauger Farm

Map 11

(*Assistance in preparation of map and action provided by Morton Smit and M. Robert Mauger.*)

upon one paratrooper who had landed on the roof of a house. His parachute collapsed and he slid off the roof, broke his leg, and was apparently knocked out by the fall. He had made no attempt to unbuckle his harness. He had been shot between the eyes. We kept on going and found another man with a broken leg. It had been put in a splint by a medic. The aidman was over helping another wounded man at the time. I do not know who this medic was, but he had a broken leg himself. He had splinted his own leg, cut a crude crutch from a tree limb or sapling, and was going about helping others. That man deserved a medal.

"We kept going and came out on a small peninsula jutting out into a flooded area. A staff sergeant from C Company was there with two of his men. While we were deciding what to do, one of our officers came upon us and took command. He told us to dig in while he went to find the 502nd Regiment. He started to leave but as he walked around some bushes he came face-to-face with three Germans. He leveled his Thompson submachine gun at them and ordered 'Hande Hoch!' Instead, they reached for grenades. He cut loose with his tommy gun and fired the entire clip as the Germans calmly set their potato mashers and threw them at him. I do not know if it was just poor shooting or trying to get back out of the way of those grenades that caused the lieutenant to miss all twenty shots. We had a small skirmish with those Germans, but they pulled out. We chose a better spot to dig in while waiting for the officer to return. He did not return that day."

Sergeant Dick Johnson of Charley Company may have been a member of the trio that made contact with Doug Garrett's small group. He stated, "I met Staff Sergeant Jay B. Shenk, who had dropped with another stick nearby. We got together with one other C Company man and tried to figure out where we were. Our company mission on D-Day was to provide security for a battery of four 75mm howitzers from the parachute artillery. We did not accomplish our mission as we were so scattered. The first officer I met after the drop was Lieutenant Rogers from Baker Company."

In point of effective dropping, the men of 1st Battalion

had a better situation than any other battalion of the 101st. All but five planes carrying 1st Battalion personnel dropped their men within a three-mile radius of Drop Zone "A."

Mesières was in 1st Battalion hands by 1600 hours. Roadblocks had been set in Foucarville shortly after daybreak and the enemy strongpoint northwest of Foucarville fell at approximately 2200. Additional roadblocks had been set to the west near Beuzeville and Haut-Fornel.[15] Cassidy's men had performed their tasks well.

Chappuis' 2nd Battalion

Second Battalion's objective was the coastal battery position at St. Martin-de-Varreville. These were 122mm guns which the Germans had captured from the Russians and had moved to Normandy. They were mounted on railroad tracks that ran in and out of formidable fortifications with concrete walls six feet thick. The Allies were fearful that these guns would do great damage to the invasion fleet, and Allied planes had been pounding the area in hope of destroying them. There was no certainty before D-Day that this bombing had been effective. It was the job of 2nd Battalion to accomplish this task if the bombers had not succeeded.

The C-47's were to drop 2nd Battalion personnel near the battery in Drop Zone "A," but only the plane of Lieutenant Colonel Chappuis, commanding officer of the 2nd Battalion, dropped its stick near this designated area. Thirty-four planes dropped their loads more than three miles south in the Drop Zone "C" area.

Colonel Chappuis suffered a painful leg injury on the jump, but after collecting a dozen men, had managed to arrive at the gun emplacement. There he found a welcome sight—the almost total destruction of the entire Battery positions. Sitting atop the rubble of one of them, he waited as his battalion trickled in to join him. Another mission for his battalion at this time would have been impossible. Time-consuming engagements with the enemy throughout the day, as well as the misplaced drops, kept his men from joining Chappuis in any great numbers. The nearly 200 who assembled with him by 0700 A.M. represented every regiment of the 101st Division as well as the 82nd.

Fox Company had won a regimental competition and was given special assault training to spearhead the attack on the battery. Its company commander, Lieutenant LeGrand K. "Legs" Johnson, was in the lead plane. Johnson recalled, "In my plane was one squad (twelve men) plus Sergeant Welsh (our operations sergeant who could speak French), a radio operator named Clay, and a company clerk named Senger on board. He was killed later in the war."

"Legs" Johnson had landed in a tree and struggled to drop free as an enemy patrol came in search of his group of men. While hiding in a hedgerow ditch, waiting with bated breath, he heard the enemy soldiers talking excitedly. They moved off in another direction in search of others. According to Johnson, "The silence was deathly. I waited a few minutes and headed east, away from their antiaircraft gun position, which I assumed the Germans had deserted. I kept walking through the hedgerow gaps until I came to a paved road. I hid in the ditch, and watched several good-sized German patrols go by. Finally I heard someone coming from behind me; gave the cricket recognition signal and was immediately answered. It was Lieutenant Nick Schiltz, one of my platoon leaders. Nick had most of his squad with him—a squad anyway. Also with him were several men from my plane. We left, not using the road, in the general direction of the coast. In the next hour we must have accumulated over a hundred men from all outfits. We came to a town about 0300 A.M. which I believe to have been Ravenoville, but I am not sure. Anyway, we were six miles from St. Martin-de-Varreville, which was our destination. I figure we had been dropped about nine miles from our DZ (so I later testified in a hearing after returning to England). We had to try three houses before anyone would answer, but Welsh, with his knowledge of the language, got the directions and the distance pretty quick. We (Welsh, Schiltz, Sergeant Simmons, and two or three others) had gone ahead, leaving the main group behind, until we could find out something. We were in a courtyard, surrounded by high stone walls. We learned we were next to a

German barracks (a block away), which was pointed out to us. About this time the 'Allemands' started dropping grenades on us from the adjacent courtyards—they had us cold. We planned to all throw return grenades on signal, then take off—this we did, running away from the larger group. Welsh and I, the only two with automatic weapons, ran down the street a ways, then stopped and sprayed the pursuing Germans. We did this two or three times, running between bursts. The Germans chased us through the town, and through a couple of hedgerows, but then left off the pursuit. We notified the larger group, orienting them, and giving directions to their various assembly areas. A warrant officer was in our group. He was hit in the courtyard and two or three others were wounded.

"The journey to St. Martin-de-Varreville was hectic—but involved little enemy action. Mostly, we ran at a fast trot, picking up men as we went along. We arrived at a heavily mined area near a paved road, adjacent to St. Martin-de-Varreville a little before 0600 A.M. I had about 30 men, which, as far as I know, comprised the force that was to destroy the guns and the enemy headquarters, which was supposed to be about 300 men. We determined that the mines were not armed and took off in approved infantry school fashion, swarming over the area with no opposition. Colonel Steve Chappuis was there with several men—by 0700 we had less than two hundred men assembled. We set about putting up a perimeter defense, and I was to destroy the guns. We found the British heavies and American B-25's had all but accomplished our mission for us—great holes 150 feet in diameter were everywhere, especially where the guns had been. Only two were near operative, and we put Bangalore torpedoes down the muzzles, in the breeches, and under the railroad tracks. The Germans made two minor attacks that morning but they amounted to nothing. Colonel Chappuis and Captain Hank Plitt were 'accepting' surrenders of the German troops in the underground area, which was a huge affair, like subway tunnels with ammunition and food, etc. The Heinies were sure chagrined when they came out with their hands up and learned that they outnumbered the hell out of us.

"We spent the rest of the day getting the men in—some of them didn't come in for two weeks. The Germans attacked from the north at about 1600 hours with about a battalion of men, but it only lasted an hour or so. They went off licking their wounds and hotly pursued by some 'crackers' from another battalion."

Several of the 2nd Battalion men were involved in small skirmishes as the men fought their way toward the coastal battery. Sergeant Mike "Cat" Miller stated, "We had small battles with groups of the enemy on the way to the beach. One battle in particular was almost a one-man job by PFC Ben Shaub. He challenged the enemy with walking fire while two of us gave him support."

"We retrieved some guns from equipment bundles. It didn't take us long to realize that we were not on the right DZ," said Private Jim Plemons from Dog Company of the 2nd Battalion. "We were held up at St. Martin-de-Varreville in a firefight. We lost Rurrs, Ramirez, Morris, and Sergeant Long that I know of. German planes strafed later in the day after we had cleaned out that village."

PFC Lemuel L. Nicholas had experienced machine-gun fire while landing in waist deep water. His group had waded in water for about two hours. He related, "Shortly after daybreak, we encountered small-arms fire and engaged the enemy. The Germans kept falling back but put up a fight just before entering a village. I was hit in this fight as were several others. Lieutenant George Eberle, a West Pointer, a good officer and soldier, and well liked by his men, was killed along with his platoon sergeant, Bill Monroe, by a German who rode up on a bicycle and pretended to surrender. The Kraut had a burp gun under his coat and took them by surprise. The German was killed too."

One of the men who didn't reach the 2nd Battalion area until the next day was Staff Sergeant Robert E. Kiel, who was with a composite group that he said "caused me many a silent chuckle over the years. During training it was always stressed that 'an officer would be near the point.' A lieutenant whose name I don't recall detailed me as the lead scout and his little ole tail was as far back in our group as was possible.

We didn't get back to our outfit until the 7th (D + 1). The individual who came up with the crickets: God bless him! And never shall I forget the most welcome sight of the 4th Infantry Division troops coming ashore."

A large percentage of the 2nd Battalion men landed in the Drop Zone "C" area and were involved in firefights with enemy soldiers quartered in that particular location. T/4 John Seney found six or seven men in an orchard within an hour after the jump. They placed a map and compass on the ground trying to locate their position as Seney had understood it from talking earlier with an elderly Frenchman. They figured the group was six kilometers from the mission area. Seney said, "Shortly thereafter, a 2nd lieutenant, a staff sergeant, and one other man joined our group. We moved out until two machine guns pinned us down. One of the weapons was in a house and firing high while the other was in a culvert firing low. Some of the men were hit each time we tried to go around the guns as we were fired on from a different area. Finally it got light enough to see the individual soldiers firing at us. We then returned the fire and someone finally knocked out both guns; the enemy soldiers were shot or left the area. We heard a man moaning for hours prior to daylight and when it was light enough, observed him across the road in another drainage ditch. We took a large multicolored quilt from a nearby house and carried him back to the house. By now there was a medic inside treating the wounded. (I don't know where he came from.) Just then, a tall German infantryman rounded the corner of the house and proceeded to uncap a stick grenade. One or two of us shot him from approximately twenty feet with our folding stock carbines. He grunted but kept on readying the grenade. The carbines were not heavy enough to put the man down. Someone, I believe it was the medic, picked up an M-1, held it at waist height and fired one shot. This put the Kraut down before he could pull the string. He had a large hole in the side and we could see that he was dying.

"Then large shells started to fall in the field across the road making large craters close enough so we had to get on our hands and knees due to the explosions. (We later found the shells were from battlewagons off the coast.) Father Andrejewski, our Catholic chaplain, came by and gave the German last rites."

T/5 Dave Jackendoff was a member of this small group. His recollections are as follows: "Nine of us started out for our objective by following the flight of incoming planes. We were stopped by two German machine guns at a road crossing. I split the group with Lou Zotti and we crawled up the ditch on both sides of the road. On my signal, we threw our grenades and knocked out both guns, apparently killing the Germans."

One of the platoon leaders of the 2nd Battalion who was involved in fighting enemy soldiers on Drop Zone "C" was Lieutenant Bernard McKearney.[16] In describing the first actions, he wrote, "We collected a force of about sixty men. All this time we had no idea where we were. We had become hopelessly separated from the rest of the battalion. As it was getting light, I was looking for some place to hole up. There was spasmodic firing going on all around us. Finally we came to a little village. As it was surrounded by a stone wall, I decided to move in. As we approached we were challenged in English. Inside was a medic captain from our own battalion—Captain George Lage, from Portland, Oregon, and three aidmen.[17] I might say here that these are the unsung heroes of the paratroopers.

"We set up a perimeter defense around the village and remained tight until dawn. And what a dawn! With typical Irish luck, I had stopped just short of a battery of eight German fieldpieces. They were just as amazed to see us as we were to see them. We were so close that they could not deflect their fixed field positions to hit us. They tried to dislodge us in a halfhearted manner. The morning wore on. The wounded were staggering in. At one time, 'Doc' Lage had forty or more wounded men. The dirty bedroom he had as an operating room was sticky with blood. The wounded were laid in the town court. It seemed fantastic. It was like a scene from a film. You would crouch, tense, and waiting, then make a mad dash across the open court. The poor shooting of the Jerries was the surprising feature of the morning. At the time, we attributed it to the fact that they were artillery men.

"About ten that morning a considerable force of paratroopers passed through us, and the Jerries retired. We were assigned the mission of destroying the fieldpieces. I took a squad of demolition men over to the gun position to carry out the detail. What a scene of carnage! This was my first initial association with violent death. A man at one hundred yards seemed so impersonal. About ten paratroopers had landed in the gun emplacements. We had expected sudden death or capture, but most of these men were slashed about the face and body. Our men said nothing. Words are so useless at a time like this. We removed them from the trees, and wrapped them in their chutes. Your mind functions oddly under stress. I tried to think of a suitable prayer. All I could think of was my Mass prayers in Latin. So very slowly I said, 'Requiesce in Pace.' One of my Italian boys standing near me answered, 'Deo Gratias.' This broke the tension. I spoke to him and we moved on to complete our mission. Then we returned to our village.[18]

"All during the day we were harassed by snipers. One was especially dangerous. He had already wounded three men during the morning. We could pick out his approximate location by the sound of his rifle and the thud of the bullet as it hit. Finally Sergeant Wilburn, a tall lanky Texan, decided to go out after him. He spotted the Jerry up a tree wrapped in one of our camouflaged chutes. His first shot tumbled the sniper from his perch. Before Wilburn could reach him, he had disappeared. A little French boy, who could not have been more than seven years old, took Wilburn by the arm and pulled him into a barn. Inside was the sniper, cowering and trembling. This Nazi superman presented a sorry picture. D-Day night passed uneventfully."

Sergeant Carl H. Robare of Dog Company had a problem in linguistics as he attempted to gather equipment from the fields. The officer in charge of Robare's group directed the sergeant to go to a farmhouse to get a horse and conveyance. The platoon leader knew his sergeant had some knowledge of French. Robare recalled, "We needed transportation to carry ammunition and other equipment from gliders that were wrecked in the fields and hedgerows, so in using my high school French I couldn't remember the exact word for horse. I said, 'Chapeaux' instead of 'Chevaux,' and this Frenchman and his wife scratched their heads, looked at each other, turned and went upstairs. A short time later they brought me a whole trunk full of hats. Finally I drew a picture of a horse to get my thoughts across to them."

The mopping up of the coastal artillery battery position had been left to Colonel Chappuis' men. Lieutenant LeGrand Johnson's men had put the finishing touches to the guns and the remnants of the enemy force were evicted from the underground bunkers.

Second Battalion men kept small enemy forces occupied and thereby prevented additional harassment of the 4th Infantry Division troops moving inland over the four causeways.

Cole's Battalion

The 3rd Battalion of the 502nd Regiment, under the command of Lieutenant Colonel Robert G. Cole, had two D-Day assignments. The first and most important was to be the backup force for 2nd Battalion in the destruction of the coastal artillery near St. Martin-de-Varreville. The securing of Causeways 3 and 4 was the second assignment to prevent the movement of German forces to and from the beach, and to clear the way for Allied invasion forces from the beach. Causeway 4 ran through the battery area and the WXYZ barrack complex, and was particularly vital to the Germans.

As with other parachute units, the job of orientation after the drop caused delays in arrival at the objectives. Several sticks of the 3rd Battalion landed about a mile east of Ste. Mère Eglise.

Colonel Cole was as lost as the rest of the division members after his landing. Within a short time, two regimental staff officers, Major Alan "Pinky" Ginder, the operations officer, and Major J. W. Vaughn, the S-4 supply officer, joined him and the party started off, gathering men from the 506th Regimental and the 82nd Airborne Division.

Major Ginder felt that the originator of the idea to use the metal cricket for assembly deserves a medal. He described getting together with Colonel Cole and the move along the road. He said, "As we finally got a few men behind us, Major Vaughn and I followed Colonel Bob Cole who, with flashlight on, read a map as we marched up the road with quite a few troops behind us."

As they neared a town, the colonel pounded on a door until it was answered from within by a very frightened woman. She refused to open the door, but a French-speaking private was able to find out that they were near Ste. Mère Eglise, which was the main objective of the 82nd Airborne Division. Colonel Cole now knew that he was about three miles west of the causeways. Time had been wasted in going west instead of east. The colonel muttered as they began to follow a road running slightly northeastward. Gradually they picked up officers and enlisted men until the task force numbered about eighty men.

One officer who met Colonel Cole near Ste. Mère Eglise was Lieutenant Richard Winters of a sister regiment, the 506th. He had about a dozen men with him. Finding a road sign at a crossroads, they pinpointed their position and discovered they had dropped several miles from their objective. Winters said, "We started moving along the road toward the coast. In a short while we ran into a group of about fifty men from the 502nd with a colonel in charge, so I attached my group to his. With this task force we turned east toward the beach. The rest of the night was spent in walking down the road, while the colonel and majors tried to find their way to their objectives. My intentions were to stay with them until we reached the beach, then cut loose and go south to my own objective. To do that with twelve to fifteen men though, would have been foolish when I could stay with fifty more. The only real excitement we had all night was when we ran into four wagonloads of Germans with harnesses and saddles. Most likely the saddles were for the reported Russian cavalry in the area. We knocked off two wagonloads and the others escaped."

For operations officer Major "Pinky" Ginder war became a shocking reality during this wagon episode for he lost his close friend. "We came to an intersection where we ran into a horse-drawn supply train," recalled Ginder. "For some reason Major Vaughn went to the left at the intersection while I went to the right. A few minutes later Vaughn was killed by a German machine gunner in a ditch. We immediately knew of his death and we now were really in a war. It was quite a shock."

Another soldier from the 506th Regiment, Private Art "Jumbo" DiMarzio of Dog Company got together with about fifteen or twenty men from another regiment. He remembered: "It was still dark. About ten or fifteen minutes later, we heard horses coming up the road. We all jumped into a nearby ditch. As the noise got louder, we knew they were German by their conversation. We killed over a dozen and destroyed the train of equipment. Come daylight, we broke away from this other group and headed for our own designated drop zone area."

Sergeant Chester Pentz and PFC Redmon Wells from Baker Company of the 502nd's 1st Battalion also joined Colonel Cole's force. Wells was about to face the horror of killing for the first time. Pentz remembered, "We came to a house but it was empty. We went along a hedgerow and found a road where we decided to wait until we could get our bearings. Not long afterwards we heard troops coming. It was Colonel Cole and his army. So Redmon Wells and I were elected flanker scouts. All went well till we hit a crossroads. Then we ran into a German unit coming up the road from our left. After the fighting stopped, Wells and I got together again and he told me, 'Pentz, I just impaled a man!' He said, 'It went in so easily but didn't come out that way.' He was white as a sheet. We took off again in the same direction the retreating Germans had taken."

It is possible that some of the Germans leaped from the wagons into the cover of the ditches while the horses raced on without guidance. One soldier, PFC Joseph A. Blain, from 3rd Battalion recalled, "Three men from my plane met at an equipment bundle which landed in a hedgerow near us. No one else appeared. Starting from the drop zone everything was quiet, when all of a sudden, a wagon drawn by two horses was running wild and making loud noises. We did not see anyone on it."

Intelligence officer Lieutenant Robert G. Pick apparently came in contact with the same enemy forces.[19] He said, "I flushed Lieutenant Leroy Bone from a hedgerow and the two of us gradually collected a dozen men as we moved along a road. Suddenly machine guns opened up on our small group. Posting a pivot of fire, I led a group around to the right in an enveloping movement. We ran into a group of enemy riflemen and I lost my first soldier. The firing ceased. Lieutenant Bone had worked his way toward the enemy positions. A German soldier raised up and shot him dead. My first shot killed that Kraut."[20]

The fight was brief. Several Germans were killed and ten captured. The wagons were emptied and commandeered. The mixed force continued its move eastward.

As Cole and his force marched along, they were notified that the coastal battery position was no longer a threat to the landings. He could now concentrate on the two causeways to which his troops had been assigned. He divided his group into four parties. The 506th men went south to make contact with their own regiment; the 1st Battalion men went toward Mesières; and the last two headed for Causeways 3 and 4. Colonel Cole went along with the party moving to Causeway 3. At 0730 they were in position on the landward end of the causeway. German troops began retreating from the beach area at 0930, and about 75 were picked off like sitting ducks by the well concealed paratroopers.

Chester Pentz ended his part of this action this way: "At last daylight came and soon we hit the 3rd Battalion objectives. Then Wells and I got together with about 12 to 15 men of the 1st Battalion and Company B and went to our objectives. We helped Sergeant Summers wipe out the last of the enemy in that immediate sector."

Major Stopka's Group

Another small force of paratroopers was moving toward the beach along a nearby east-west road. Major John P. Stopka, 3rd Battalion executive officer, was leading a mixed group from several regiments and at least one man from the 377th

Parachute Field Artillery Battalion. Three of those men were from the 502nd Regiment's Charley Company. The men got together after the jump and started looking for others. Private Robert Cahoon described the actions in which he was involved with his buddies, PFC Layton Black and Sergeant Junior Nutter. Cahoon said, "We had only traveled a few yards when we came under machine-gun fire. Not recognizing any landmarks and not sure where we were, we decided to wait until daylight. When the sun came up, we went to a farmhouse and the Frenchman showed us where we were on our maps. While looking for the rest of our group, we met Major John Stopka from 3rd Battalion with four or five men he had collected. He told us he wanted to knock out a machine-gun position. We attacked but the fire was too heavy. Coming back to our starting point, we met a group of paratroopers who were marching a large group of prisoners down the road. Joining them, we arrived at a road junction where there was a barn and several German barracks. We set up roadblocks and a defensive position, which we held against several attacks until contacted by men of the 4th Infantry Division on the morning of D plus 1. The group of 30 to 35 men was made up of men from all battalions and regiments of the 101st plus a few from the 82nd Division."

An enemy machine gunner had fired at troopers floating down east of Ste. Mère Eglise. Corporal Dalton Gregory of the regimental intelligence section heaved a grenade from his place of concealment in the shadows—no more firing was seen or heard from the gun. Gregory found one trooper and together they wandered aimlessly for an hour before they met others. He said, "We joined a group of about thirty men. Major Stopka was the only officer I recall with the group. We started walking in the ditches on both sides of the road. We came to a strongpoint and a fight started. In a few minutes we captured the enemy position. It was about a thousand yards from the Channel. We killed about fifteen Germans and then we sent a team to knock out a Kraut 88 about 300 yards away with no casualties to our group. We set up a defense and a sniper killed a young trooper with one shot between the eyes. We sent out a patrol and got three snipers in trees. That first night we were attacked by Germans with grenades. They were trying to free the twenty or thirty prisoners we had captured."[21]

An artillery paratrooper, Corporal Eugene Haupt, jumped with the 502nd Regiment on D-Day. His function was to serve as a liaison between his unit and the infantry regiment whose assignment it was to wrest the coastal artillery position from the enemy. Haupt remembered, "I was with a small group of men from several outfits who stuck together under Major Stopka. We attacked and took a small command post for German bicycle troops. We were surrounded but held the area until relieved by regular ground troops several days later. Can't remember the town but the place was later called the 'Stopka Strong-point' on the map."

"Our group was led by a very colorful major," remembered PFC Walter Gordon, who had found three other members of his company and had gravitated toward a larger group. He added, "About dawn of D-Day, we joined 25 to 30 other paratroopers from various regiments and wrested a large quadrangle farmhouse from the Germans. It had been used as a billet and there was equipment and food and uniforms all over the place. I recall the huge beef hanging in the kitchen. We defended the billet all of D-Day and were relieved by members of the 4th Division on D plus 1—or later." Gordon didn't know the name of the officer because he himself was a member of the 506th Regiment and wasn't familiar with the faces and names of the men of other regiments, but it is safe to assume that he was also a member of the "Stopka Task Force."[22]

On target!

Long before Colonel Cole reached the vicinity of his causeway, objectives near St. Martin-de-Varreville and Audoville-la-Hubert, men of his battalion had reached the area—in fact they had landed on target. Ten planes flashed the green light for the paratroopers over the assigned objectives. Three plane-loads landed close to St. Martin-de-Varreville. PFC Harold

Revord and Private Robert C. Darcy were members of two of these sticks.

"I landed on a hard road outside of St. Martin-de-Varreville," said Revord. "I injured my back on the landing. I loaded my gun before discarding my chute and after getting out of the harness I rolled off the road into the ditch. A German came riding down the road on a motorcycle. I assembled with about five others. We worked our way towards the beach. We met many Germans. Finally returned to St. Martin-de-Varreville, where more men were assembled. Heavy sniper fire occurred in the area. We were set up on roadblocks throughout that area."

Private Robert C. Darcy, from H Company, was also dropped on a blacktop road near St. Martin-de-Varreville. His chute draped over the telephone wires. He crawled off the road and into the shelter of a hedgerow as a motorcycle with an attached sidecar came down the road. A machine gunner in the sidecar sprayed the ditches with his weapon. Darcy said, "We were not allowed to shoot until daylight. There wasn't too much action. I got together with about fifty to sixty men from different outfits and Colonel Pat Cassidy took command and moved us into a big barnyard. The first day or two was spent in regrouping and getting organized and back to our own outfits."

Captain Cecil L. Simmons, commander of H Company, had also landed near his objective. He dropped into a triangular patch of farmland and was being fired upon by a machine gun. He said, "I put out that gun with one of my grenades. I gathered about 36 men of various organizations and rendezvoused at one of the guns we were to knock out only to find the Air Corps had done our job prior to our landing. We, of course, had numerous brushes with the Germans in small groups. I recall the first gliders coming in just at first gray light of morning, but was so busy fighting at the time that I paid little attention to them."

Eight of the planes dropped the men between Causeways 3 and 4 just behind Utah Beach. Two of the men from Item Company described their experiences. Sergeant John R. "Whitey" Brandt went to the aid of a fellow trooper who was having difficulty in the four-foot-deep water. He said, "We started through the flooded area toward the road in back of St. Martin-de-Varreville. We had four men from our company along with about twenty others. It was too dark to determine who they were. Lieutenant Painschab was in charge of our group, but we didn't meet him till dawn. We fought small groups of Germans until late afternoon. We had little communications as all of our equipment was lost in the flooded area. We had to rely on runners until we were resupplied that afternoon."

Tracers followed the men from PFC Robert Hartzell's stick all the way down until they lit in a flooded area. He pulled his buddy Paul McKenna from water deeper than he was in. He got in with his platoon leader, Lieutenant Jack Dulaney and about eight men. Hartzell remembered, "While looking for the coastal guns at night, we walked up to a German machine gun. It fired at us from close range of about 25 yards. We were pinned down there for about a half hour. Verle G. Kerr was shot through the jaw. He was unable to keep up with us so we hid him and came back after him later in daylight."

Many 3rd Battalion troopers landed far from their own objectives and ended up fighting alongside other units or other strays.

Four miles to the west of his assigned objective, Private Frank P. Garofano had dropped into the town of Ste. Mère Eglise, which was the objective of the 82nd Airborne Division. He said, "I landed between two buildings in an alley in Ste. Mère Eglise. We went to work on the ack-ack gun that was set up in the center of town. We spent the day fighting in town beside men of the 82nd."

Sergeant Eldon C. Dobbyn had landed in a tree near a German position on the Ste. Mère Eglise–Carentan highway. His movement had been slow so as not to call attention to himself in the branches. He said, "I joined up with about twenty other boys from different companies. My group landed several miles west of our drop zone. I took over a group of twenty men that had come from different units and they stayed with me until we rejoined our own outfits. We set up roadblocks and held a main road leading down to Carentan.

A captain from our 502nd Regiment gave me this assignment, but he was killed in the fighting. We did have one convoy try to come through, but we stopped it and killed several with bazooka and machine-gun fire."[23]

Private Donely Johnsonte had helped another out of his chute in waist-deep water. He had landed three or four miles north of Carentan. He said, "We were pinned down by Germans. Sergeant Cummings was killed. We stayed in that position the rest of the night; then in the afternoon we advanced. I was picked as a point man with Private Davis. We drew no fire and went to a German barrack and found no one. We stayed there for two or three days."

The 3rd Battalion's jump had been spotty. The sticks dropped within the same three-mile arc circumscribed for 1st Battalion. Almost half of the planes had dropped their men along a two-mile stretch of countryside from the outskirts of Ste. Mère Eglise northeastward toward Ravenoville and Foucarville. Eight of the planes had given the green light to the men over the flooded area between the two causeways which had been their D-Day target.

Causeways 3 and 4 were in the hands of the 3rd Battalion and mixed groups early on D-Day morning. However, Exit 4 was not safe for travel as it was under continuous enemy artillery fire from the northwest. To gain their footholds on the northern flank, soldiers of the 4th Division had to slog through the waist-deep water on either side of the raised roadway, much as the paratroopers had done during the predawn hours.

Five-O-Deuce in Summary

Though Colonel George Van Horn Moseley had been disabled at the instant he touched enemy-held soil in Normandy and was not in position to command his beloved regiment any longer, reports did come through before the D-Day fighting had ended that his troopers had gained all their objectives at WXYZ, Foucarville, St. Martin-de-Varreville, and Causeways 3 and 4. His men were in good defensive positions along the northern flank preventing enemy movement toward the beach. The 4th Infantry Division had moved through his positions toward Cherbourg as well as toward Ste. Mère Eglise to provide relief for the 82nd Airborne Division. The Air Force had come to the rescue in completing the most important mission of destroying the coastal battery position. It might have been a far different story if the bombers had not succeeded in destroying the gun emplacements because Moseley's artillery support from the 377th Parachute Field Artillery Battalion did not materialize, as will be described in the next chapter.

Command of the 502nd Parachute Infantry Regiment had gone over to Lieutenant Colonel John Michaelis, the regiment's executive officer.

CHAPTER 12

The Scattered Artillerymen

The 377th Parachute Field Artillery Battalion was assigned the task of supporting the 502nd Regiment in its assaults on the coastal artillery battery at St. Martin-de-Varreville and the fortified hill position at Foucarville. Able, Baker, and Charley Batteries of the 377th each carried four 75mm pack howitzers. Each howitzer was disassembled and packed into six bundles, daisy-chained together, and slung under the belly of a C-47 troop carrier aircraft. Dog Battery had made last-minute preparations to drop six 37mm antitank guns along with its regular paratroop equipment instead of bringing them in with the glider lift. The antitank guns were to be used against the armored vehicles, which Allied intelligence reported the enemy had moved into the 502nd combat area. Dog Battery's 94-man unit had not had the opportunity to test the feasibility of such a drop prior to entering combat.

It will be remembered that Lieutenant Colonel Benjamin Weisberg, commander of the 377th, had flown into combat with Colonel George Moseley, commander of the 502nd, to provide quick coordination between their units. The senior officer with the actual artillery flight was Major Louis Cotton, the battalion's executive officer. In addition to the four batteries already mentioned, there was a fifth, the Headquarters and Service Battery, which provided the communications, command, survey, and fire directions.

The plans were in good order but their execution was not to be realized, for as the 54-plane artillery serial roared over the western shore of the Cotentin Peninsula (also referred to as the Cherbourg Peninsula) in its deceptive roundabout approach to the drop zone, the plans went astray. Suddenly, the majority of the planes veered to the left, heading northward towards Valognes, Montebourg, Morsaline, and almost to Cherbourg itself. A few veered to the right to drop their troops and cargoes west and east of Ste. Mère Eglise but not one dropped its load directly on the designated area, Drop Zone "A," near St. Martin-de-Varreville.

The planes veered to avoid an unusually heavy concentration of antiaircraft and small-arms fire. In the desperate maneuvering to get beyond range of the flak and tracers, the pilots lost contact with the radar-equipped planes leading the serial.

The men of this battalion had the most scattered drops in the entire division. As previously related, only one of its 54 planes dropped its men near Drop Zone "A." Four planes gave the green light to the men west of Ste. Mère Eglise with the flight paths straddling the Chef-du-Pont to Ste. Mère Eglise highway. Nine planes carrying Able Battery dropped the men east of St. Marcouf between four and five miles from the correct designation, and the remaining three planes dropped near Le Ham. Most of Baker Battery landed two miles south of Montebourg and six to seven miles northwest of the drop zone. The bulk of the men composing battalion headquarters Personnel and Charley and Dog Batteries landed in the St. Martin de Varreville and St. Vaast-la-Hougue area, which was eight to eleven miles north of the Drop Zone "A" area. A few of the headquarters planes flashed the "jump signal" in the Montebourg-Valognes area over heavy concentrations of enemy troops.[1]

Such was the experience of Captain Felix Adams, battalion surgeon for the 377th, who described his unusual drop in this way: "I was number '13' in a stick of 14. The jumpmaster was Major Courtney Neilson, our operations officers. The night was as pretty a moonlit night as I have ever seen. However, I didn't enjoy it very long as a piece of flak clipped across the front of my helmet (good old helmet!) and I very suddenly lost all interest in the battle.

"I landed on the roof of a one-story shack of a German command post several miles east of Valognes. When I came out of the fog about half an hour later, about fifteen Germans were standing around me, doubtless debating what to do with the 'body.' A German soldier cut my chute off. When I tried to get up they were very cooperative, but I couldn't use my right leg and was scared to death I had broken it at the knee. I was immediately taken inside a barbed-wire enclosure about ten yards from where I landed. 'Dapper' Neilson was killed a short distance from the same barbed-wire enclosure."

One soldier from Charley Battery, Private Tom Mulligan, also landed in the vicinity of Valognes. He didn't last long as a combat soldier. "A load of bazooka ammo exploded," he later remembered. "Our plane was tossed around quite a bit. I do know for a fact that after we jumped our plane did go down. This was somewhere around 0100 A.M. Four of us got together around 0300. Shortly after that, one member went forward to do some scouting and never came back. Around daybreak, two of us under Lieutenant James Pearson ran into a squad of Germans. During the short fight we had, Lieutenant Pearson took several hits in the head. I received gunshot wounds in the face and abdomen. We were immediately taken prisoner. Lieutenant Pearson and I spent much of the day lying in the field under the guns of the Germans.[2] Later we were evacuated to an aid station. The other soldier was marched to a PW cage."

Still another Headquarters plane flashed its green light for its stick of jumpers in the Montebourg-Valognes area. Captain Bill Brubaker, the assistant operations officer who jumpmastered the plane, came down in a field by himself. He was unable to find others from his stick. Brubaker said, "I landed a couple yards from a large hedgerow and almost on a cow. I didn't see anyone in my stick. They were killed or captured except for the number '1' man and myself.

"I didn't contact any men during the predawn hours and made my first contact with German troops at about 0700 A.M. in the morning. They were medics and they were armed. I worked my way to a tree carefully getting on the right side as the field manual prescribed, and I remember thinking what a peculiar position to be in as I was left-handed. I found three American soldiers about 0800 and stopped a Frenchman at about 0830 to find out where we were. Being told the Boche were in all directions, I finally found myself three maps away from where I should have landed."

Operations Sergeant Franklin K. Van Duzer also landed near Montebourg. He said, "I found a trooper from another plane and we started walking to the west. At daylight, a Frenchman saw us and warned us that the Germans were near. He hid us until it grew dark. Starting out after darkness set in, we walked unexpectedly into a German command post. The other trooper was captured and I was slightly wounded. When I was captured the next day, I was sent to a German prison camp hospital to be cared for by a captured American doctor, Captain Felix Adams, of Vinita, Oklahoma."[3]

Three miles to the east of Montebourg, at the little town of Octeville, a collective group of 101st and 82nd paratroopers rallied around Lieutenant William E. Shrader, one of the battalion S-2 officers. Recalling his part in the action, T/5 John Kolesar, a radio operator, wrote: "We spent considerable time collecting men and trying to determine our position from maps. There were eleven men from our Headquarters Battery along with a bunch of strays including a 1st sergeant from the 82nd Division. All told we collected 33 men. Our particular mission was to establish communications with the 502nd Infantry Regiment and control the firing of our pack howitzers. Being so far from the drop zone, we were all confused. Through one of our French-speaking boys we were able to find out from a farm woman just about where we were. Lieutenant Shrader lost twelve men the first day because we kept running into German roadblocks."[4]

Other planes carrying headquarters personnel were even farther north and east. Corporal Kermit Latta's plane had passed completely over the Peninsula and returned before the jumpmaster sent his men out. Latta's D-Day assignment was to lay field telephone wire from the 377th Battalion command post to the Division Artillery Headquarters at Hiesville. With him on the mission were two buddies who were to accompany him on the cross-country trek. On Drop Zone "A" they were to pick up three 502nd Infantry Regiment paratroopers who were assigned to provide security for the wire team.[5] Latta did not get to that assignment. He was instead to experience a lonely adventure.

"I landed in a field in very bright moonlight," Latta remembered, "but soon hid in the shadows of the tall Normandy hedgerows. I couldn't find Americans but there seemed to be plenty of enemy soldiers. Deep German voices and the sound of small-arms fire came from every direction. I wandered around in shadows for about an hour, took a drink from a pond of stagnant water in violation of G.I. training, found a deep ditch covered with bushes, and went to sleep. And so I slept while the battle for the Normandy beaches built up.

"After daylight, I ate a 'D' bar from a K-ration, and headed north. Because the plane had circled toward the south before we jumped, I figured I was south of our division objective. Actually I was far north and getting farther all the time. As I traveled through woods, I ran when I was shot at and fired back when I could see something to shoot at. This was like the game of Cowboys and Indians we used to play as kids, except too much like the real thing for comfort. Only those who were in like circumstances will ever know how lonesome I was that day. When I saw our fighter planes overhead I thought, 'There's an American up there; Oh, to be with him!' As I crawled through a field of wheat and wild poppies, I thought of the World War I poem, 'Flanders Field,' which we committed to memory as kids in a country school in Kansas. I asked God to help me and although I had no right to expect His mercy, I've thanked Him many times that I did.

"In the afternoon I climbed a hill and could see a lighthouse on a point of land out to sea. When I had oriented myself with my map, I realized I had traveled the wrong way all day. Soon after I turned back, I encountered a group of German soldiers and was wounded and taken prisoner. I'll never forget the compassion of a German medic who applied a tourniquet to my arm, gave me a shot of morphine, fed me eight sulfa pills, and gave me a drink of ersatz coffee from his canteen. Just before I lost consciousness, I saw an American soldier, also a prisoner, who carried my 185-pound body on his back, I don't know how far. I remember gaining consciousness once as a French girl gave me a drink of wine from a bottle. Maybe it was a dream."[6]

Another small group of Headquarters artillerymen was even farther to the north in the vicinity of St. Vaast-la-Hougue (ten miles north of St. Martin-de-Varreville and Drop Zone "A" as the crow flies). They got a "warm" reception. "We landed in a field covered by machine-gun fire, crawled out of the line of fire, and gradually got together," recalled Sergeant Robert Passanisi. "We figured out our approximate whereabouts and started to head in the direction of our troops far to the south, but every time we made an attempt to cross a main road we seemed to run into machine-gun fire, and several of our men were hit."

Another member of the same group, Sergeant William Crowell, related, "My group spent the first few hours of darkness after landing cutting every telephone wire we could get our hands on. After daylight we were lying in a ditch when a column of enemy troops passed. Some of them saw us and threw hand grenades. We opened fire and killed about twenty of them, wrecking four horse-drawn ammo carts, and then took off across the fields."

Some time later the group was standing at a crossroads of a small town trying to get directions from a farmer with the aid of a phrase book. Hidden by a tall hedgerow so typical of Normandy, the soldiers failed to note the approach of a long column of marching men that rounded the corner. A large group of Frenchmen was being marched to neighboring fields to continue their work of setting up anti-airborne obstacles for the "coming invasion." The group stopped near the huddled soldiers and the helpful farmer. One paratrooper nudged his lieutenant with his elbow. The soldier turned and found himself face-to-face with a German officer who raised his right arm in the Nazi salute, gave good morning greetings, and said, "Heil Hitler!"

The American officer, who spoke German asked, "Don't you know that we are Americans?"

Dumbfounded, the German stood still with shock while

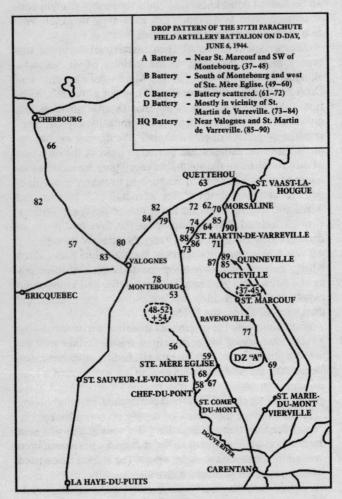

**DROP PATTERN OF THE 377TH PARACHUTE
FIELD ARTILLERY BATTALION ON D-DAY,
JUNE 6, 1944.**

A Battery — Near St. Marcouf and SW of
Montebourg. (37–48)
B Battery — South of Montebourg and west
of Ste. Mère Eglise. (49–60)
C Battery — Battery scattered. (61–72)
D Battery — Mostly in vicinity of St.
Martin de Varreville. (73–84)
HQ Battery — Near Valognes and St. Martin
de Varreville. (85–90)

CHERBOURG

66

82

QUETTEHOU
63
ST. VAAST-LA-
HOUGUE
82   72 62 70 MORSALINE
84 79   74   85
57   79 64   90
88   ST. MARTIN-DE-VARREVILLE
57   80   86 71
83   73
VALOGNES   87 89 QUINNEVILLE
            85
78   OCTEVILLE
MONTEBOURG
53   37-45
BRICQUEBEC   ST. MARCOUF

48-52
+ 54   RAVENOVILLE
                77
56
        59   DZ "A"
STE. MÈRE EGLISE   69
        68
ST. SAUVEUR-LE-VICOMTE 58 67
CHEF-DU-PONT
        ST. COME   ST. MARIE-
        DU-MONT   DU-MONT
                VIERVILLE

            DOUVE RIVER

            CARENTAN

LA HAYE-DU-PUITS

Map 12

eight riflemen detailed to guard the impressed labor force started to run and were cut down by the paratroopers' guns.[7]

One of the men who was involved in this action was Staff Sergeant Clyde Tinley, battalion radio chief for Headquarters, who described his meeting with the men. "After wandering around by myself for two or three hours, I found a group of men from my battery led by Captain Charles Knight.[8] Was I glad to see them! But the feeling didn't last. There were about twenty of us. We were going somewhere in single file. I didn't know who was leading us, but I tagged along. After it got light, we stopped for a rest. Captain Knight ordered me to guard the entrance to a ravine a short distance away from the group. It was perhaps an hour later and, not hearing any voices, I walked to where the men were, only to find they were all gone! This burned me up plenty. I had no idea which way they had gone, so I just stomped off in a rage. I came to a little town and walked the streets not seeing a soul, but feeling eyes upon me.

"Later I met some young Frenchmen who led me to where Captain Knight and the others were resting. When I asked the Captain what was the idea of deserting me, he said, 'I'm sorry.' That was that.[8]

"Several hours later, when we were all sitting in a ditch, we were surprised by a group of Krauts. Somehow we got split up and I ended up in a group of eight men. The next day we had a fight with some Germans. Garrity was killed and the seven of us left were captured."[9]

Aldrich's A Battery

Nine planes carrying Able Battery did a fine job of dropping men into a small area just to the east of St. Marcouf. There was only one problem—they were three to four miles north of the drop zone in a swampy area.

"I never saw the drop zone," said 1st Sergeant Howard K. Bloor. "My plane was too near the beach when we jumped. I was jumpmaster. My plane was filled with communications personnel. Captain Charles Aldrich, the battery commander, was also on board. We all landed in a minefield in waist-deep water in a swamp a few miles north of Ravenoville. I was the last one out and nearest the water. Our task was to destroy four pillboxes with concrete a yard thick. We had a 75mm howitzer as our weapon, and the shells would have bounced off the pillbox anyway. All twelve battalion guns got lost in the swamps, so our mission failed. The pillboxes were knocked out by someone else. I never saw them. By daylight there were fifteen of us who got together. We moved into Ravenoville. Troops came through the town on their way from the beach."[10]

Another soldier who landed in a mined field near Utah Beach, PFC Leopaul Sepcich, remembered, "I jumped into an area of barbed wire and on a mined field. I was tangled in barbed wire and had to cut my harness and gas mask off to get free. I started in the direction of the objective. Louis Labrack, one of our men, was no more than fifteen feet from me when he stepped on a mine and was blown up.

"Shortly after daylight, I met Boge Tackett and he said Homer Estes was pinned down by machine-gun fire in a minefield. Tackett and I crawled into the field and got Estes out, because I had remembered the way I had gotten safely through in the darkness.

"We were involved in fighting and taking a pillbox on the beach with no artillery support—just rifles and hand grenades. Later, we ran into the 4th Infantry Division. They had tanks to support us. We were under the command of Lieutenant Thomas Swirczynski from our battery, until we met up with the 4th and joined them for several days before we were called back to our own outfit. We numbered about twenty men then, and lost five of them before joining the 4th Division."

Sergeant Fred Surbaugh was somewhat handicapped in his movements because he jumped with a bandaged right hand and splinted forearm—the result of a bicycle accident a fortnight earlier. After some difficulty, he got loose and met his buddy Joe Wasirick. He said, "We joined Lieutenant Tom Swirczynski, who eventually got a group of seventeen men together by noon. We approached a fortification on the coast in an attempt to signal some ships standing offshore. We needed supplies, as most of our bundles were lost on the jump."[11]

Having been delayed in his jump because one equipment bundle failed to jettison when he flipped the salvo switches, Staff Sergeant Ed Benecke came down far from the rest of his stick of jumpers. He said, "I landed at 0106 A.M. I located three men, a lieutenant and two men from the 502nd Regiment. We wandered around all night long. We moved toward Ravenoville to the southwest. Along the way we encountered a group of French people in a ditch. They were dodging bombs. We gave medical supplies and cigarettes to the wounded. Early in the morning, I ran into 1st Sergeant Howard Bloor coming across a field. We united with his small group and later more of these small groups came together. One of our gun crews under Sergeant Emerick found a complete gun to assemble, but could not haul it out of the marshy area. We finally made contact with Captain Fred Culpepper from Dog Battery and other officers from some infantry units. We took up positions around the perimeter of Ravenoville and received enemy fire all day. Many were wounded. We located German soldiers in many of the houses and other buildings. We set up a prisoner of war cage. The enemy attacked us strongly the first night. We finally united with the battalion two days later."

One Able Battery soldier who remembers D-Day for aimless wandering is Corporal Robert "Zimmy" Zimmerman, who related, "My group kept getting bigger as the day wore on; kept on the move more or less aimlessly on D-Day. Every now and then we'd run into German small-arms fire, which we'd return generally without seeing the enemy. We captured two Germans, however, and one was a boy of 15 or 16."

The last three planes of "A" Battery's echelon landed near Le Ham, two miles southwest of Montebourg. For Lieutenant Robert A. Matthews there was no recollection of the landing. "We were carrying binoculars slung just under the chin," he recalled. "When I got that tremendous opening shock, my chin snapped down on the binocular case and out I went. Came to just off the ground, and was knocked out again when I hit the ground. I don't know how long I was out.

"I met one of our gun section chiefs, Sergeant Emerick. We found one member of my stick, Private Fred A. Hersch, dead on the road past Le Ham. I had landed in a field south of Le Ham, which is two miles southwest of Montebourg.

"Our group eventually consisted of a mixture of A and B Battery men. One officer from the 82nd was with us. Sergeant Richard Jones of B Battery had his men and pack howitzer. We sent them to a crossroads to wait till other men and equipment could be located. He got into a fight with some enemy cavalry and couldn't stay. He rejoined us. Heard noise around Le Ham of explosions and a firefight. We moved on to a mill to see if we could find out what was going on. Got fired on and returned it for a while, then moved out. We were joined by Captain Grover Robinson, from Baker Battery, with others later. Captain Robinson moved out to locate our battalion. I moved the group into an area to wait for his return. Near nightfall, I moved the group to join H Company of the 507th Regiment of the 82nd Airborne Division, where we took a piece of the perimeter and remained that night and the next day.

"The action around Le Ham on the part of my group was of little consequence. We didn't know what was going on, just returned fire when shot at. Several men on our flanks did cause some casualties among the Germans in Le Ham. It was Captain Robinson and his group (a mixed group from the batteries) that took aggressive action and initiated the firefight there. This group deserves a great deal of credit.

"Two of the gun sections A Battery did assemble in the vicinity of Le Ham, in addition to Sergeant Jones and his section. Late in the day, when it became obvious we could not take the guns with us, we disabled them and left them. Sergeants Emerick and Faust were the Able Battery gun chiefs in our vicinity. Sergeant Jones told me he had fired his howitzer, 'direct laying,' on the enemy troops at the crossroads."

Baker Battery

Flak split the twelve-plane echelon of Baker Battery as it crossed the Cotentin Peninsula. Serving as jumpmaster on board the eleventh plane was Sergeant Bill Gammon, in charge of battery communications. The eight-man stick had the job of establishing wire and radio communications from the battery to the fire direction center and to the forward observer, who was to be with the 502nd Regiment. The men had map overlays with coordinates of fixed targets, gun emplacements, crossroads and other suitable targets.

"I landed in a tree along a road about a mile southwest of Ste. Mère Eglise," remembered Gammon. "I had trouble getting free of my chute. I cut the risers frantically, then crashed through the branches to the ground. There was an officer in another tree a short distance away. He was struggling with his harness and the Germans were shooting at him—I thought they were firing directly at me. (I saw his body in the same tree later in daylight.)"

Gammon added, "I got on the road, and heard troops moving toward me. I jumped headlong into a ditch. They were Germans. I was facedown daring not to breathe. I could hear them, talking, not knowing what about, as they went by hurriedly. It was a long 'brief' period. I didn't find anyone else from my stick until two days later."

To the south and east, many 82nd Airborne Division soldiers landed in the 101st drop zones and spent the early days assisting the men of the Screaming Eagle Division. To the north and west, many 101st men were busy lending a helping hand to the 82nd. Gammon was one of those contributing to the 82nd cause. He added, "I got with the 505th Parachute Infantry regiment of the 82nd Division and the only other 101st man encountered was Lieutenant Ed Mitchell (later KIA) from Baker Battery. He had been assigned to the 502nd as a liaison officer. We went into Ste. Mère Eglise about dawn. I was acting as Scout and Lieutenant Mitchell was Scout 2—by that time there was about a platoon of 505th men with us. We hit some light action in town. We thought we had it secured. About that time, two Mark V tanks started into town. They fired a few rounds point-blank down the streets. There were three or four bazooka rounds that hit one tank and set it afire on the road near a hedge. They got the other one farther on in town. It also caught fire. Both 101st men who fired the bazookas were killed by machine-gun fire. One trooper burned as he was so close to the tank he had destroyed.

"We then moved about two miles out of Ste. Mère Eglise, where we encountered heavy resistance. We were pinned down for about twelve hours in a circular German-dug trench. We suffered heavy casualties at that position."[12]

The bulk of Baker Battery dropped in the vicinity of the railroad station, a mile or so south of Montebourg. Corporal Arley Goodenkauf related, "My planeload was one of those far off target. We dropped to the northwest of our DZ, somewhere south of Montebourg. The crew chief of my plane had been 'extra' helpful in securing my equipment to my harness. Consequently I spent an agonizing five minutes trying to cut myself free. A Frenchman just across the road from my position was shouting his fool head off. I got together with Gerald Jones, Verline Smith, Ambrose, Coen, and Winhoven, of whom all were killed on D-Day except Smith.

"On D-Day morning, I was part of a group of 25 to 30 troopers whom our battery commander, Captain Grover C. Robinson, had picked up after a very confusing night. A part of this group had ambushed three or four German ammo trucks in the village and burned them.[13] We pulled out of town and were resting about a half mile away when the Jerries counterattacked us. I was on one flank with Pat Rodgers and can still remember the leaves floating down over my eyes as the machine-gun bullets cut them off the branches overhead. The enemy was moving up under cover of the hedgerows and pasting us in the process. Anyway, our main group moved back (unknown to me), and my first inkling of it came when Captain Robinson came back across an open field to call me back. Of course, I didn't need a second invitation and promptly sprinted past him. Halfway across the field, my training finally asserted itself and I dropped down and started giving him some covering fire. He was walking back across that clearing, bullets kicking up dust all around him, but deliberately sizing up the situation and making sure the stragglers were rounded up. But for him, my D-Day morning would have been very brief, and I'm sure he is held in high regard by all those who served with him.

"After a short fight, we had very little more action on D-Day itself as we moved south and east toward the beaches. We spent the night at the edge of an inundated area at the base of a hill from which antiaircraft fire was being directed at our C-47 coming over with reinforcements."

Another of the Baker Battery troopers who landed in the area near Montebourg was Private Bob Kane, who did not make contact with Goodenkauf or Captain Robinson. Kane related, "We landed a few miles south of Montebourg. The first man I met was Sergeant Nick Pickard, then Cole, Koper, Shuman, and Sauvageau. After we grouped with others, we searched through the night for our 75mm pack howitzer. We lost two men from our stick, Reeves and Kalinowski. We never did see them again. At daylight, we found our equipment. Sauvageau, who was of French-Canadian origin, could speak French fluently so he went to question a farmer. When shown on our map where we were located, we decided to render our equipment useless."

While part of the group was conversing with the Frenchman, others were busy locating all the bundles dropped from the plane. The artillery piece had been dropped in sections that could be quickly assembled on the field. Kane added, "The Germans had spotted our chutes and had placed a guard on them. We exchanged a few shots with them and then decided to move on. We buried the firing mechanism for the howitzer and tried to make contact with other troops. During that long day we were hiding and dodging German searchers."

Another Baker trooper, PFC Steve Koper, who served as the barber for his unit, remembered his early adventures in France: "Sauvageau, Cole, and myself went up to a farmhouse to see if we could learn our position and the direction toward the beach. The farmer was extremely nervous and frightened as eight or nine youngsters peered curiously at us from the adjoining rooms. The farmer was evasive in his answers because he was afraid the Germans would punish his family severely if he gave aid and comfort to the paratroopers. He would give no information about the Germans, but we learned that our position was southwest of Montebourg.

"After leaving the Frenchman, we went back toward the fields into which we had dropped. Near one of our equipment bundles which contained medical supplies (they were identified by the color of the chute), we observed a German soldier bending over the bundle. Ralph Cole raised his rifle and fired. The soldier straightened up with a jerk and tumbled over the para-crate.

"Other enemy soldiers must have heard the shot because a few minutes later an armored car came down the road. We dove through the hedgerow as machine gun bullets kicked dirt up around our heels. We ran through several fields until we came to a rather large wooded area and stayed hidden there for several days, as we noted constant movement on the part of the enemy."[14]

Parrott's Charley Battery

Captain Charles Parrott's Battery headquarters plane was catching the first bursts of flak as it came over the Peninsula. From his position at the door as the number "1" man, Private Dave Begault had trouble remaining on his feet as the plane swerved and rocked. The pilot maneuvered to remain clear of the streams of multicolored tracer shells. This plane jumped its troopers far from the proper drop zone. As Begault recalled it, "I landed in water that was neck-deep. Thought I was in the English Channel; cut myself out of the chute frantically only to find I was in a flooded field. After getting out of the harness, I crawled around using my clicker and in response I received machine-gun fire. (I knew this was not from our guns because our orders were for hand grenades and knives until daylight.) Thinking the damned thing (clicker) could get me killed, I threw it away. Thereafter I relied on the voice passwords only. I got together with Tolaski, Gomez, and Chapman. Captain Parrott was at the end of our stick and he was captured. We had a medic named Hanna with us. I heard he was killed while giving first aid."

In the same plane but near the end of the stick was Corporal Francis Chapman, who had a different perspective on the action. The pilot finally flashed the green light when the plane had almost run out of peninsula below them. "I landed in water about five feet deep," Chapman later explained. "Managed to stand up after a bit of swimming. Reached down, got my jump knife from the boot top and slashed my harness, cutting right through my jump jacket in the process. I managed to wade toward shallow water."

Chapman was anxious to get on dry land quickly. He carried a special flare pistol with which he was to assemble the battery on the commander's position. Somehow, the pistol was forgotten in the following excitement. Chapman added, "As I sloshed through shallow water some of the others from my stick heard me. The troopers turned out to be two of my own stick members, Gomez and Tolaski. They were on a piece of dry land about the size of a small house. We stayed there until daylight. Out of nowhere came another soldier who looked familiar. He was following a telephone line through a field. He didn't have a helmet on his head and deciding it must be an enemy, I borrowed a rifle from one of the other two and sighted it. Just as he bent down I fired. The bullet passed over his head. He hit the dirt and then I realized what I had almost done. We were only a few hundred yards from the ack-ack tower and to the east a short distance away, we could see the Channel. Had Begault hit one hundred yards further inland on his jump, he'd have landed right on top of the flak tower. We spent most of the daylight hours hiding and did our traveling at night. We got back to our battery five days later."

Another of the Charley Battery men took even longer to get back to his outfit. As a member of a group in a second plane, PFC Walter "Putt" Murphy landed on dry ground. He said, "My jump was all right but I landed against a glider pole and almost broke my back. I got quickly out of my chute, crawled into the shadows and began clicking my cricket. The entire stick managed to assemble nearby. First

Sergeant Garland Fitzgerald was a member of our group. We looked around for our equipment until daylight, at which time Fitzgerald concealed the group. Then 'Fitz' and I went out to scout around. We were cut off by a Kraut patrol and tried for seventeen days to find our way back, flirting with enemy patrols all the time. We learned later that the rest of our stick had been taken captive."

Aboard a third plane were three men who were listed as having eventually gotten together as part of a group with Captain William Brubaker from Headquarters Battery. Among them was PFC Daniel Krinsky. "It was an uneventful and smooth flight until a burst of flak hit our plane," explained Krinsky. "Our plane was an ammunition plane, carrying six bomb rack loads of 75mm ammunition and a tremendous doorload with a cart that became uncontrollable at the door as soon as the flak hit. Two of the men from that stick were McKay and Harry Hoots.

"We received a lot of machine-gun fire when we got the red and green lights simultaneously. I was standing at the door, trying to hold the bundles in position. After a struggle with them, we pushed them out and followed close behind. It was very quiet; I saw no one else in the sky on that moonlit night. Accounted for McKay as he landed near me. It was difficult to determine our position. I heard a lot of church bells and small-arms fire in the distance. Not knowing where we were, we gathered our chutes and hid in a hedgerow waiting for further developments. My assignment was to serve as an ammunition carrier and as messenger for the battery commander.

"After a few hours we located the rest of our stick along with a few men from the 82nd Division. Towards morning, still not knowing where we had landed, a young French boy made contact with our group. As no one in our group spoke French, we had to communicate by sign language and were led to understand there were pockets of our men in the whole area. We found more men later in the morning. I also remember that Harry Hoots blew off his hands with his own grenade. We tried to do as much as possible by applying tourniquets to both hands and thought it best if we left him with the German medics. All in all, we must have numbered one hundred men, mostly from the 82nd as I think we dropped in their area. I recall being with a group led by Lieutenant Schaefer, who was at one time in our battery, but in Dog Battery on the jump. We were attacked and scattered. Schaefer was surrounded and finally overwhelmed by a large number of enemy soldiers and was killed."

Another man on board the same plane was Private Al McKay. McKay corroborated Krinsky's account: "There was lots of ground fire directed at our plane. The jump light went on and the doorload hung up in the doorway. The few seconds it took to correct this probably saved us from landing in German troop areas. The fields in the area were full of glider poles.[15] We were near the town of Montebourg.

"One of the first incidents I remember was Harry Hoots having his hands blown off by his own grenade. Krinsky and I got Hoots to a Frenchman who turned him over to the Germans. The Frenchman returned a few hours later and told us Hoots was getting medical attention. The same man also got us together with Staff Sergeant Werner Angress, from the 82nd. With assistance from another Frenchman, our helper led us to contact a battalion officer and his group.[16] I do remember a 'gun-toting' medic who was the only one in our group who had an M-1 rifle. Most of us had folding stock carbines. I recall he was the first to detect and fire at a group of Germans who finally surrounded us and forced us to surrender. In this engagement, Angress and our own Sergeant Bob Clifford were wounded. Not all of our group was captured at this time. We had some prisoners with us but they escaped during this skirmish."

Captain William Brubaker commented about this wandering group: "My action was mostly trying to find our soldiers. Avoiding Germans, I eventually found about 20 troopers, mostly from 82nd, and did contact the local French underground official. He was no help at all. Two escaped Frenchmen (one a sailor and one a former soldier) joined me. Both were very bloodthirsty but most helpful in keeping me advised of where the Germans were located. We cut numerous communications lines and captured several messengers and about eight soldiers. There was also a staff sergeant named Werner T. Angress from the 82nd who spoke German.

"There was one medical NCO with my rounded-up group. He insisted on fighting and I finally made him remove his Red Cross armband. One man from our group went to a small nearby creek to fill his canteen with water. As he was doing so, a couple Germans were doing the same thing on the opposite bank. He ran back to tell me what happened and just about that time, the medical NCO was standing straight up and began firing. Immediately thereafter we were hit from three sides by mortars, automatic weapons, and small arms. Part of the group was able to disengage and move back through the open side. The prisoners, of course, got away. We had kept them in a small blackberry patch. We had removed their shoes and socks so they couldn't move around on us, but we had been using only one man to guard them."

Charley Battery suffered the greatest number of casualties among the five batteries of the 377th Battalion. Only one officer, Lieutenant James Denning, and twenty-seven enlisted men were on hand when the battalion returned to England to refit for another operation.

Culpepper's Dog Battery

Captain Fred Culpepper, jumpmaster aboard his plane, searched the sky in vain for other planes. They had vanished completely after the flight had broken clear of the fog and clouds and had begun to attract enemy artillery fire. The pilot streaked on toward the east, dodging the tracers as well as might be expected with the slow C-47 troop carrier plane.

Some time later the green light flashed on. The jumpmaster slapped the leg of the first man and sent him out, followed quickly by the second, and third. As the last man tumbled from the plane, Culpepper observed, "We were quite low, couldn't have been much over 300 feet when I jumped as last man. I landed near a crossroads, opposite the Isle of St. Marcouf. There was a group of buildings near the crossroads that had obviously been taken over by the Germans as a command post and it was well fortified with observation posts overlooking the coastal area. Actually, it turned out to be a part of Utah Beach. I was captured before I got out of the harness. They marched me to the group of buildings described above and placed me in a locked room. At that time there was a great deal of bombing activity in the vicinity. Prior to locking me up, an attempt was made to interrogate me; however, no one spoke English and little progress was made along this line. They actually had me stand against a wall, and I thought they were going to shoot me; but for some reason, they changed their minds and locked me up. Surprisingly, when they searched me they took my weapon, but did not find any of the articles in the parachute escape kit sewed into my jumpsuit. They also failed to find my jump knife. At dawn, there was a firefight in the area, and during the confusion I escaped. I used the hacksaw blade from the escape kit to cut the lock from the door."

Culpepper joined a mixed group of Able Battery men, some troopers from the 502nd Regiment, and a few men from the 82nd Division in holding the small town of Ravenoville.[17]

The plane carrying Dog Battery Commander Culpepper was the only one carrying his personnel to drop in the area. The rest were scattered over a huge area with most of them far to the north in the areas of Valognes, St. Martin de Varreville, and St. Vaast-la-Hougue.[18]

Ten miles to the north of Captain Culpepper's position, two of his men experienced good jumps. Unfortunately they were in areas of enemy troop concentrations. Lieutenant Herbert L. Garris remembered that his assignment was to provide perimeter defense for the artillery battalion. He recalled, "I had no difficulty assembling my stick of men. We jumped about five miles northeast of Valognes. Lieutenant Dick Soliday's stick joined a short time later. It was only an assembly and we waited until we found assistance to lead us south toward the main body."[19]

The original assignment for T/5 Loren S. Culp's gun section was to have been the cutting off of supply and troop movements to Ste. Mère Eglise. He landed far north of this.

He said, "Our plane was hit and we jumped about 18 miles from our drop zone. I had a good jump—landed in the middle of a battery of coastal guns. I wandered around looking for others in the stick. I was taken prisoner about dawn on D-Day. That's where I found the rest of the stick. Was questioned by the Gestapo at Bricquebec—then sent to Cherbourg and joined a larger prisoner camp."[20]

Liaison personnel

Lt. Colonel Benjamin Weisberg and others from his Headquarters Battery had preceded these men in the lead planes of the 502nd Regiment. Weisberg said, "I had a low fast jump over the Hiesville area on Drop Zone 'C.' After getting free of my equipment, I crawled near a hedgerow where I lobbed a grenade at a machine gunner who was firing at our planes. I found others from the 502nd Regiment. I spent the day collecting my men and equipment which were badly scattered over a forty-by-twenty-five-mile area."

Captain St. Julian Rosemond and his radio operator had been in a plane carrying lead elements of the 2nd Battalion of the 502nd. He said, "I jumped with Colonel Steve Chappuis, whose battalion was to make the initial assault on the coastal gun position.

"After getting free of the harness, I ran, hit the dirt and rolled one way and continued the process, but rolling the opposite way until I snaked over a hedgerow onto a field where there was no firing. My parachute tray was still on my back, but I got loose of it in the field and spotted a machine-gun nest in the corner and like a damn fool, sneaked up to it ready to throw a grenade. However, upon inspection, I found it was unoccupied.

"We finally got a group together which I'd estimate to be the size of a platoon. We proceeded to move northeast toward our objective. We ran into resistance in a small town (could have been Reuville), and we wiped them out. It wasn't much. I got my first chance to kill one when I saw him sneaking around to our rear. However, I found my gun sight was filled with mud and after cleaning it out he was gone, so I just sprayed the area.

"We came upon Colonel Chappuis later in daylight. The mission was actually accomplished by the Air Corps, which had bombed the emplacement. The area and barracks were taken by remnants of the 502nd without artillery support. Our guns were lost save one that was later located."

By evening of D-Day there had assembled in the Foucarville area to the north about eighty-five artillerymen of the 377th Parachute Field Artillery Battalion who had jumped with the 502nd Regiment. They had only one 75mm howitzer with them. Five other howitzers had been recovered by artillerymen, but at such a distance that they could not be used and had to be abandoned.

In summary, the 377th Parachute Field Artillery Battalion suffered the worst misdrop of any parachute unit on D-Day. Consequently, its personnel and artillery were scattered from as far south as Ste. Mère Eglise to almost as far north as Cherbourg. Wounding, capture, death, or loneliness became the lot of a large percentage of these beleaguered artillerymen. Their assignment to assist in the capture of the coastal battery at St. Martin-de-Varreville fortunately was canceled by the Allied bombing of the battery. Their mission to aid the 502nd in the capture of the Foucarville fortification was supplanted in part by a quick enemy surrender. However, they had aided in the general harassment of the enemy behind the lines.

Of the 450 men of the 377th dropped on D-Day, 218 were assembled for return to England to recoup for a new assignment. (This included two officers and thirty enlisted men who arrived with trucks and other vehicles over Utah Beach with seaborne units during the evening of D-Day.) The artillerymen were not intended to be expendable, but their contribution was well nigh sacrificial.

CHAPTER 13

The 506th Regiment

The 506th Parachute Infantry Regiment was commanded by the legendary Colonel Robert F. Sink, who popularized the term "hostiles" when speaking of the enemy. The assignments of the 506th included the capture of Causeways 1 and 2 (the lower exits from Utah Beach), the blocking of enemy routes to these exits at St. Marie-du-Mont and Vierville, and the capture of two wooden bridges over the Douve River, two miles northeast of Carentan. Bridgeheads were to be established to the east of the bridges.

The U.S. 7th Corps, of which the 101st Division was a part, was to link up with the 5th Corps moving from Omaha Beach. The bridges would be a vital meeting point.

Second Battalion, under the command of Lieutenant Colonel Robert Strayer, was to do the actual work of seizing the causeways, while 1st Battalion under Lieutenant Colonel William Turner was to protect 2nd Battalion from rear attack by the enemy. First Battalion would also serve as regimental reserve in covering its headquarters in the CP at Culoville. Third Battalion, commanded by Lieutenant Colonel Robert Wolverton, was to capture the wooden bridges and the high ground east of them at Brevands for the establishment of bridgeheads.

First and 2nd Battalions had been scheduled to land on Drop Zone "C" between Hiesville and St. Marie-du-Mont. Only ten of the 81 planes gave the green light over the correct area to their sticks of jumpers. Regimental headquarters jumped with them, and they occupied most of the ten correctly oriented aircraft.

As was the case in the other regiments, communication

with other division units was nil. Every radio operator belonging to regimental headquarters was missing, as was almost the entire communications platoon, whose drop had occurred 22 miles to the north near Cherbourg. Many were not located until their marked graves were found weeks later. Some were found as German prisoners in the hospitals of Cherbourg when that city was finally captured. It was small wonder that Colonel Sink was left in the dark for much of D-Day as to the whereabouts of his fighting forces.

Parts of 1st Battalion landed just north of Hiesville, near the position of Colonel Sink, the regimental commander. After he had spent considerable time fighting his way out of a too-tightly buckled parachute harness, Sink prowled the hedgerows until he came upon a member of his regimental group, Lieutenant Sam Burns, who was incapacitated with a broken leg. Looking for a place of concealment for the handicapped officer, Sink spotted a hole dug in an orchard into which farmers placed apples for storage over winter. The now empty hole provided an ideal hiding place. He assisted the officer into the hole and covered him with leaves and twigs. He would send medical aid later.

As almost everyone was doing, Sink followed the hedgerows. However, after about four hundred yards, he realized a blacktop road ran beside the hedgerow embankment. Moving onto the road he came to an intersection where he met four members of his group trying to determine their position.

A dog attracted by the sound of their voices began barking loudly near a small farmhouse. Colonel Sink went to the door and banged on it while yelling "Fermez la porte!" several times. One of his junior officers reminded him his pidgin French was rusty because he was actually shouting, "Shut the door!"

A Frenchman appeared at a window. Using some of the phrases the men had practiced, Sink announced in French that the Allies had come. After excitedly slamming the window, the Frenchman quickly appeared at the door. The colonel unfolded a map of the area and asked about the enemy. With wild arm gestures, the farmer related that the Germans were all around, particularly at St. Come-du-Mont to the south-west.

Noting their position on the map, the group realized they were only a few hundred yards from the site chosen for the regimental CP. They started in that direction and picked up four more jumpers. Arriving at the spot, they noted that no one had preceded them. The junior members of the party were sent off in different directions to bring in any nearby paratroopers. In the area where most of the 2,000-man regiment was to have dropped, only 41 men were located in a two-hour period.

One of the enlisted men who had jumped with Colonel Sink and had been a member of the early arrivals was Corporal "Vinnie" Utz, of 506th Regimental Headquarters. He related, "We ran into Colonel Sink and a few unidentifiables and on his order, 'Skip' Simpson and myself, and Frank Palys were sent out to patrol for strays. I also saw two darkly bereted men whom I took to be French, but I never spoke to or bothered them. After returning from our patrol, I was posted from the farm by Sergeant Schroeder in a ditch, where I simply heard noises, watched the fireworks in the sky, sneaked a smoke, and returned to the farmyard in the morning.

"Later in the day, my company commander, Captain Edward Peters, spotted me in a French house. He told me to get moving, and was killed within a half hour when he attacked an enemy machine-gun nest by charging right into it.

"We 'ran' for Colonel Sink, brought in prisoners with the help of Captain Samuel 'Shifty' Feiler who spoke 'Yiddish' German. We manned outposts, gathered cargo equipment chutes. My task was accomplished, I am sure, only because I was one of the few to hit the drop zone, joined with Sergeant Schroeder and Colonel Sink and performed what they asked of me.

"By late on D-Day we had about 80 men in the area of the farm and came to realize we had little or no communications men and no demolitionists—some of course being attached to 3rd Battalion."

"We came down near the village of Hiesville," remembered PFC Frank Kough. "I was a member of our demolition platoon which was split up to work in three sections with each section of 15 men assigned to each battalion. The second section of which I was a member was assigned to Easy Company of the 2nd Battalion. We were to jump with 2nd Battalion; however, they forgot to assign a plane to us, so we were split up into twos and threes, and put on different planes of our own Regimental Headquarters Company. We were scattered pretty well over Normandy, so could not carry out our mission. I spent my time doing patrol work and protecting the command post. We lost our captain (Peters) on the first day on our third or fourth patrol. He was struck in the temple by a German wooden bullet and died instantly. One of my buddies landed way up near Cherbourg and didn't get to us for nine days after we had taken Carentan."

The demolition man mentioned above by Frank Kough was PFC Steve Kovacs, whose D-Day assignment had been to prevent German troops from flooding the roads leading up from Utah Beach. Members of his group were to blow up the obstructions so the land would drain. He said, "Unfortunately our stick was way north of the area to which we had been assigned. Most of my squad was captured by Germans up around Montebourg. About all we accomplished was to confuse a company of Germans east of Montebourg by mining the road from Dangueville to the sea at Bas de Fontenay; they were pulling back toward Montebourg. We were only five men, lost and confused. I lost my first friend, Art Demaio from New Jersey, there. The enemy was satisfied and did not follow us after seeing Art fall."

A member of the S-2 (Intelligence) section for the regiment, T/5 Frank A. Palys, spent the early hours and days on patrol assignments around Culoville and recalled that they were hampered by the lack of radio communications and even lost the special radio and fire control people the Navy had sent with them. He said, "A Naval fire control officer and his radioman jumped with us. We never saw them after that. We came upon a disabled pathfinder with a back injury. We hid him in a hedgerow and destroyed his equipment. We saw a few of the enemy; had some small skirmishes, but always had to back off so we could proceed on our patrol mission. Only two of the enemy were examined after shooting them. They were Ukrainians in the German army."

In the predawn hours, Lieutenant Colonel William Turner, commander of 1st Battalion, appeared at the regimental command post. With approximately 50 men on hand, Turner was directed by Sink to go for Causeway '1' though this was the job of Strayer and his 2nd Battalion. Both causeways were to be taken, but with 50 men it would be wiser to go for just one of them. (This was the same reasoning General Taylor had used with his group for the same task.[1])

Having sent Colonel Turner and his group on the mission to capture the lower causeway, Colonel Sink continued to fume and fuss throughout the morning due to the lack of communications with any of his units, particularly the 3rd Battalion, which had been scheduled to capture the wooden bridges at Brevands, and the 2nd Battalion, which should have landed on his drop zone. He knew next to nothing about the progress of the fighting due to the complete absence of his headquarters communications personnel.

As a few stragglers filtered into the command post, Sink sent them out as patrols to look for "hostiles" in the vicinity as well as to locate his lost battalions. The patrols returned to the command post to report no encounters with men of either battalion.

Brooding over the lack of knowledge of his fighting units was frustrating for Sink. He craved action. He noted the presence of a jeep in the CP. It was a vehicle from a glider that had landed nearby during the predawn hours. Its driver, Private George Rhoden of A Battery of the 81st Antitank Battalion, had found himself in the 506th Command Post. Here he had been waiting since early morning for other members of his unit.

A plan for a "look-see" trip had been developing in Sink's mind. He turned to his S-3 officer, Major H. W. "Hank" Hannah, who was standing nearby.[2] "There's a jeep and driver parked over there doing nothing," he said. "Let's go out and see if we can't locate Bob Wolverton. We've got to find out if those bridges have been taken. If they haven't we'll have to get some people to do the job."

"Good idea, sir," replied Hannah, who unfolded a map he was carrying. A trip like this needed some planning.

The two officers moved over to the jeep where the map was spread over the hood. The logical route was along the main road between St. Marie-du-Mont and St. Come-du-Mont. They could pick up that highway at Vierville. Approximately a mile south of Vierville was a road leading off to the southeast toward Angoville, Les Droueries, and Addeville. All were on the most accessible route to the bridges near Brevands.

"Get a couple more men," said Sink, who had now brightened considerably in anticipation of adventure.

Hannah went over to a small group which had recently collected. "I need two volunteers." He eyed the group and quickly pointed to a pair. "You guys will do. Follow me. We're going for a ride." He had collected Privates Amory S. Roper and Salvadore Ceniceros because both were armed with submachine guns. Hannah reasoned that it would be wise to bring along as much firepower as possible.

In the meantime, Sink had notified the driver that he and the jeep were being commandeered. The two submachine gun-toting paratroopers climbed on the hood where they were in good position to cover the jeep and its occupants. Hannah climbed into the backseat with a good supply of hand grenades and his revolver grasped in his hand. Sink had his service revolver at the ready. The driver had his carbine across his lap.

"OK, driver—let's roll," said Sink as he climbed in. "We'll go that way," he said, pointing left, as the vehicle pulled out of the farmyard. As he drove, Rhoden had to peer around the two troopers sitting on the hood, who hung on with the free hands clutching the folded windshield.

At Vierville, the road joined the wider blacktop highway leading to the southwest. On the left was a small field surrounded by low hedges and an occasional tree. Grazing peacefully in the pasture were a large number of horses. As they turned to admire the animals, Hannah, sitting in the backseat, spotted a German soldier on sentry duty raising his rifle to the firing position. Hannah shouted a warning as he fired his frontier-style Colt .38 revolver. Others in the party also fired. The soldier, who had been standing at the gate of a horse park, crumbled beside his post.

The shooting, which occurred at a slight bend in the road, caused enemy soldiers who had fallen out into the ditches on either side of the highway to stand up and look around. Seeing the jeep bearing down on them, they dived back into the ditches for cover. It looked like a line of dominoes falling down from the force of the first one falling. The paratroopers on the hood blazed away at the ditches with their automatic weapons. The two officers were firing their revolvers.

The driver stepped on the gas and the jeep raced along between the long lines of enemy troops in the ditches. These were part of a German battalion moving northeast toward Vierville and St. Marie-du-Mont. They were apparently headed toward the Utah Beach area.

The jeep had gone along for about five hundred yards in this fashion when Colonel Sink spotted a group of about twenty enemy officers standing in the road. They were studying maps, making plans for the disposition of the troops presently in the roadside ditches. The group scattered like quail as the jeep bore down on them. As the enemy officers dispersed, several unattended artillery pieces could now be seen blocking the road. The gun crews were in the roadside ditches resting. Spotting a widened area in the road at the intersection, Sink yelled at the driver to get the jeep turned around and to go back the way they had come. Sink had no idea how many enemy troops were still in front of him or down the side road. He wasn't anxious to press his luck further. He did know that the road had been peaceful and quiet earlier near Vierville. It was best to retreat from whence they had come.

Rhoden came to a screeching halt as the two privates on the hood hung on for dear life. They were in no position now to fire at the enemy soldiers, but the Germans were content to keep their heads down as the driver deftly whipped his vehicle about and raced back up the road.

The enemy column was sprayed once more as both officers fired into the ditches and the tommy guns chattered noisily. The firing wasn't too accurate because each of the hood-riding soldiers was hanging on with one hand and firing without support with the other. An enemy machine gun near the artillery pieces fired a burst at them and missed just as they reached the slight bend near the horse park. Rhoden didn't slow down until he reached the Culoville turn at the south end of Vierville. The jeep continued up the road into Culoville and back into the farmyard.

Hannah casually concluded, "I had a flock of grenades which I didn't think to toss out along the ditches and neither did anybody else. We laughed about it afterwards. The action was too fast."

While they had been away on their "reconnaissance," Sink found his forces had been augmented by 75 additional 1st Battalion men. They were already on duty protecting the regimental command post. Word arrived at Sink's headquarters that a mixed group of 502nd and 506th paratroopers was battling an enemy artillery force in the small hamlet of Holdy, a half mile to the northeast.[3] The 75 men were sent to reinforce the Holdy group. Assigned to lead the support elements were C Company commander, Captain Knut Raudstein, and 1st Battalion Headquarters Company commander, Captain Lloyd Patch. This enemy battery had been the only artillery position not pinpointed on the pre-D-Day intelligence reports. With the arrival of the 1st Battalion reinforcements, the enemy battery was quickly overrun.

Thereafter, Captain Patch and his group were directed to move toward St. Marie-du-Mont. As he moved toward the buildings, slightly more than half mile northeast of the artillery position, Patch became aware that mortar fire was following the moves of his men much too closely to be of a sporadic nature. Taking note of the high spire on the church, he reasoned that his movements were being observed and transmitted to the mortar gunners by a well-placed observer. Returning to the enemy artillery guns in Holdy, Patch contacted regimental headquarters and received permission to fire on the church steeple. One of the guns was bore-sighted

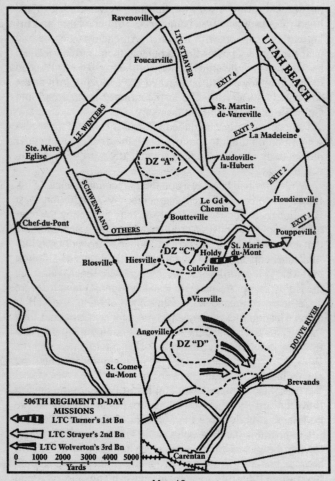

Map 13

by the infantrymen, then loaded and fired. The first round missed, hitting a nearby building. The second round hit the steeple and caused the quick departure of several U.S. paratroopers who were observing enemy soldiers from its vantage point.

Though he had flushed out troopers of his own regiment, Patch noted that the mortar fire on his men had abated. The troopers moved into the village, where they were held up on the western approaches by enemy fire coming from machine guns placed south of the churchyard wall. Neither the paratroopers or the enemy defenders gained an advantage in several hours of fighting until the arrival of the 4th Division tanks from the Pouppeville causeway during early afternoon. A short time after the armored reinforcements arrived on the scene, the enemy soldiers fled toward Vierville.

Back at the 506th CP in Culoville, Sink was now facing attack from the "hostiles." Apparently the Germans had observed the activity in the farmyard command post and began creeping forward into nearby hedgerows to do some sniping. The scattered firing built up and waned several times during the afternoon. Sink expected a heavy attack that night.

However, as evening approached, General Maxwell Taylor and his entourage arrived en route to Hiesville. There was a pause with Taylor's group dropping into the ditches to wait the outcome of the discussion. General Taylor made plans with Colonel Sink for D plus 1 and brought news about the capture of Pouppeville and the linkup with the 4th Division at Causeway 1, which his group had reached before Colonel Turner's force. Sink remained in the dark concerning his 3rd Battalion and the fight for the wooden bridges, but he reported his wild ride south of Vierville to his commander.

Corporal Vinnie Utz described the encounter: "Later in the day I saw and heard General Taylor 'chew out' Colonel Sink for personally reconnoitering a way to the bridges while many of us were just loitering around the barn."

The 1st Battalion mission

The paratroopers of Lieutenant Colonel Billy Turner's 1st Battalion were to provide protection to the 2nd Battalion men who were to seize the two lower causeways. Turner's 1st Battalion troops were to block the roads in the vicinity of St. Marie-du-Mont and Vierville a mile and a half to the south, thus preventing the Germans from moving in with counterattacking forces to hinder the beach landings.

Colonel Turner's assignment was changed by Colonel Sink when not a single 2nd Battalion soldier was seen on Drop Zone "C." Sink sent Turner toward Pouppeville with a group of fifty men to accomplish 2nd Battalion's assignment of clearing the lower causeway for the seaborne troops scheduled to land in a few hours.

One of the officers to whom Colonel Turner issued the order to alter the planned moves was Lieutenant Heber L. Minton, 3rd Platoon Leader from Baker Company. Minton related, "By daylight I had 50 men, but what a conglomeration—those fifty men represented just about every outfit in the 101st Division. We realized at daylight that we had dropped within 500 yards of our designated drop zone, which wasn't too far from St. Marie-du-Mont. By noon I recall that I had assembled 21 of my 35 man platoon including my assistant, G. I. Davis.

"Our 3rd Platoon was to secure the small town of Vierville, located on the road between St. Marie-du-Mont and St. Come-du-Mont. We were directed away from this mission by Lieutenant Colonel Billy Turner."

Minton continued, "B Company remained pretty well scattered that first day and like many other units were involved in small group firefights. The 3rd Platoon joined a larger group under the command of Lieutenant Colonel Billy Turner (our battalion CO). Colonel Turner ordered me to go to Pouppeville. I was fired at by a German sniper about one mile from Pouppeville and due to a previous injury I had received on the last practice night jump in England, I was unable to crouch or crawl because of a bad knee. We were spread out and walked directly into a Kraut position. His

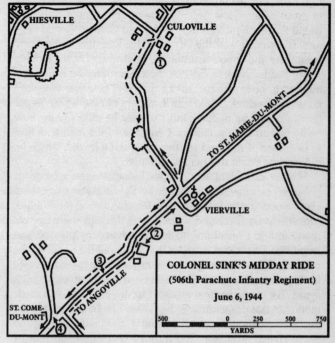

Map 14

1. Regimental command post of the 506th from which the famous ride by Colonel Sink and his group originated.
2. The enemy horse park where Sink's patrol admired the horses before noting sentry raising his weapon toward them. Major Hannah fired the first shot and dropped the guard beside his post.
3. Enemy soldiers of battalion-sized force resting in roadside ditches during a forced march to reinforce enemy units near St. Marie-du-Mont and behind Utah Beach.
4. German officers assembled in roadway preparing plan of attack. Artillery pieces in tow were pulled up just behind them.
   (Map was prepared with assistance of Prof. H. W. Hannah.)

lousy marksmanship and our unexpected move caused him to execute Plan 'How Able.'[4] Upon reaching Pouppeville, we found that General Maxwell Taylor and Colonel Gerald Higgins and elements of the Division Headquarters had already been there and done a real fine job of clearing out the Krauts, so we headed back to the Battalion. En route, we ran across another trooper who had his entire lower jaw shot away and he wanted a drink. I told him I wouldn't know where to put the water and he nodded, but I'm sure he didn't know how badly he had been wounded. I sent one of the men with him to take care of him and see that he found a medic, which he did, and no doubt this man is still alive."

Minton described the combat indoctrination of one of his platoon sergeants: "Hedgerow fighting was something else—good and bad. Tough for offense and good for defense. Movement up, over and around, and through the gate was really tough. I recall an incident involving my platoon sergeant, Staff Sergeant Ernest King. He spotted a Kraut on the opposite side of a hedgerow—threw a grenade and it came back pronto. He grabbed it—threw it back—it came back again. By this time he was about to die of fright, but as he made his last desperate toss he noticed he hadn't pulled the pin, so he pulled it—gave it about a 200 count and flipped it—WHAM!—no more Kraut, but a real smart sergeant by this time!"

Dropped from the same plane was PFC Donald Patton, who landed at the edge of St. Marie-du-Mont. He bumped heads with a sergeant near a stone wall and both men clicked off safeties before they got across to each other with their crickets. Patton said, "A short time later four of us were moving down the road together when we encountered a machine gun. Hitting the ditch we returned machine-gun fire and cusswords. Only a few Germans challenged us en route into St. Marie-du-Mont. Marty Martin, Bob Flory, and I buried all our gear except our weapons and moved in among the buildings. The town was in complete confusion and it was nearly impossible to tell which were friends and which were enemies. We reported back to our group which had grown to about a hundred. This was before daybreak. The beach pounding by the Navy and Air Force gave us time to become organized. We moved toward resistance near Vierville."

Though 1st Battalion troopers were scarce in the initial assembly, two-thirds of the planes had dropped their men close on the drop zone. Because of the heavy concentration of enemy troops about their fields, it was well into D-Day before the men were able to move into the vicinity of Culoville and Colonel Sink's headquarters.

Among the remaining one-third of 1st Battalion planes were those dropped east beyond the Douve River and those to the north in the vicinity of Ravenoville. Troopers from these planes had to battle their way to join their units.

A mortar cart, stuck in the doorway of the middle aircraft of a three-plane V, caused a delay in the jump for PFC Herb Clark of Baker Company and a member of Lieutenant Minton's 3rd Platoon. By the time the cart was freed and dropped clear, the three planes were across the Douve River and south of Brevands six miles from the Drop Zone "C" area. Clark said, "Five of us actually got together and used hit-and-run tactics for three days." French people came to the assistance of Clark and his group and provided food and shelter for them along with information on a large group of enemy soldiers who had a position only a few hundred yards away.[5]

Seven miles north of Drop Zone "C," the occupants of several Able Company planes came to ground. Some were totally lost and confused, while others discovered they had landed near Ravenoville.

The members of PFC Charles F. Knight's group were totally lost. He related, "No one knew where we were. I didn't know during the first hour or so. It was soon daylight. We tried to find our company but didn't have any idea where to look. Brininstool, Jones, Ponds, and Gaddy were all together in my group. We wandered around trying to get in contact with someone. We saw some Germans and fired at them and then hid. We were outnumbered and were just trying to harass them.

"Sometime in the morning we came on a group of troopers who had been hurt. We tried to help them by sharing our bandages. Jones was a medic and he did what he could. Together, we tried to determine our position. We saw a large column of Germans out in front of us. As we were debating whether to shoot at them or hide, we were surrounded by a group of 20 or 30 of them calling for us to surrender. We did. They searched and questioned us wanting to know where we had landed and how many we were. We didn't give away any military secrets. When we were searched, Brininstool had a large can with no label on it. The Germans questioned him about it. It was a canned chicken his mother had sent him. We did not want the Germans to eat it, so we told them it was explosives. They made us bury it. We would have liked to have marked that grave. The Germans asked us if we wanted to go to the rear or stay up front with them. All the wounded and Medic Jones went back to the rear. After hearing what happened to prisoners, it has been on my mind about Jones. I wonder if they made it. All the able-bodied stayed. We talked it over and decided we would have a better chance to escape with them than if we ended up in a wire cage.

"They were marching to the coast and didn't believe this was a large-scale invasion. Some planes came over and they shot at them with rifles. The planes turned and strafed our column, killing some of them."[6]

Sergeant Ted Vetland was forced to land with a heavy leg bag still attached to his foot because the mechanism used for jettisoning it had failed to function. He hit the ground quickly from a low height. Vetland remembered, "Surprisingly, I hit the ground in such a way that I wasn't injured and didn't suffer any ill effects. I unharnessed my equipment and headed for a hedgerow and started meeting others from A Company, but none from my stick. We landed up near Ravenoville.

"Met John and Joe Powers, Joe Hopkins, Devon Grahek, Joe Liccardo, and Liddell, all from A Company. We were to capture one of the two lower causeways. Seven or eight of us assembled near Ravenoville and headed for our original drop zone near Hiesville. We met a small German convoy heading toward the beaches and stopped it by firing at the first two trucks. In the fight that followed, Joe Liccardo was wounded, Devon Grahek was badly wounded, and I was hit in the leg.

We took one prisoner but we were outnumbered and re-treated to a ditch near by. Liddell had been a former medic so he took care of the wounded. Joe Liccardo appeared to have only a wound in the leg, but he died despite morphine and all efforts to save him. All D-Day we sent out scouts to find friendly forces, but they found only Germans. We moved to a safer place in the hedgerows for the night."[7]

Aboard the Able Company Headquarters plane had been T/5 Amos E. West, a radioman. He said, "We missed our drop zone by seven miles and I didn't find anyone other than Lieutenant Alden Brooks and Dale Atwood, along with about twenty other men. We tried to take a gun emplacement, but failed. I took a prisoner about 0700 on D-Day morning. He was the first one captured by our group."

Able Company machine gunner Sherwood Trotter had been knocked down by an enemy soldier who fired at him while he struggled with his parachute harness in the middle of a village square. He had quickly unharnessed his equip-ment and hurried out of the town and into the fields looking for others. Without a weapon save his hand grenades, he hoped to find firepower with reinforcements. Trotter re-called, "I finally got a cricket reply. It was 'Baby' Smith from my own plane. He was our bazooka man. Unfortunately, he had a bazooka but no ammo, and his carbine barrel was bent by the landing, so it was useless. We kept on going and even-tually numbered 10 to 12 men. All of the time we were headed in the general direction of what sounded like a real battle. About daylight we got into a small skirmish with our first Krauts. They were behind one hedgerow and we were across the field behind another. Within a short time, they broke off the engagement and disappeared. We relaxed and the next thing we knew, there were two G.I.'s standing on top of the hedgerow looking down at us. Everyone of us had fallen asleep and slept for about two hours. We then resumed our travel, finally arriving at St. Marie-du-Mont where we participated in the battle of the church tower."

As the day ended for 1st Battalion, many of its troopers were busy protecting the regimental command post. Others had moved south from St. Marie-du-Mont, following the retreating Germans toward Vierville. The men dug in and waited for tomorrow's attack. Those who were far-flung continued their slow movement back to their own units. Lieutenant Colonel Turner had only a few more hours to command his battalion. In the morning he would lose his life when he raised his head out of the turret of the lead tank in an attack toward St. Come-du-Mont.

Strayer's stray battalion

While General Taylor and Lieutenant Colonel Ewell achieved the Causeway 1 objective and Lieutenant Colonel Turner was sent by Sink to cover it also, it must be remembered that 2nd Battalion, under the leadership of Lieutenant Colonel Robert L. Strayer, was actually given the assignment of seizing Causeways 1 and 2. In the flak-punctuated flight across the Cotentin Peninsula, the serial had separated into two groups. The lead elements had flown into the Drop Zone "A" area where the pilots flashed the green light over Captain Frank Lillyman's 502nd and 377th Pathfinder team aids near St. Germain-de-Varreville. The second half of the serial dropped its men over and around Ste. Mère Eglise, about five road miles from the Hiesville Drop Zone "C" area.

Near St. Germain-de-Varreville, Colonel Strayer had been jarred hard on his landing and had spent considerable time separating his men from members of Lieutenant Colonel Pat Cassidy's battalion. Though dropped into two distinct areas, Strayer's men had the most rapid and complete assembly of any of the 101st regimental groups. Battalion Headquarters Company and Dog Company were in large part in this Drop Zone "A" area, as two battalion staff officers collected 170 men from those two units within the first hour. To this were added fourteen from Easy and Fox Companies. Colonel Strayer joined this force at 0330 with fifteen more 506th men and about twenty men from the 82nd Division.

After verifying his position with a Frenchman and a 502nd trooper as being in the vicinity of St. Germain-de-Varreville, Strayer ordered his battalion to move south just before daybreak. The advance was slow. The 200-man force was delayed by artillery fire as well as sniper resistance. At midday they were still bogged down near Causeway 4. Strayer was not in radio contact with his regimental commander, Colonel Sink, or Division Headquarters, and did not know that one of his assignments, Exit 1, was in the hands of other 101st troopers.

Part of Dog Company was detached from the force and it skirted the enemy battery at Le Grand-Chemin. This battery was being engaged that morning by troops under Easy Company's executive officer, Lt. Richard Winters. Dog Company of 2nd Battalion reached its D-Day assignments, Causeway 2, at 1330 and went into position immediately. There was very little resistance from the enemy. Much fighting had occurred in its vicinity earlier in the day.

T/5 Bill Maslowski had parachuted with Colonel Strayer as his radio operator. He had landed in a flooded area and crawled out of the water while enemy machine guns fired over his head. His SCR-300 radio was ruined by its immersion in the water and his weapon would not fire. Picking up an enemy rifle and joining up with four men from as many units, Maslowski fell into a long column moving south. He related, "We came to a town after the four of us had joined the larger body of troops and were firing at enemy snipers in the church bell tower with a bazooka. We made contact with our company there."

Another battalion radioman, T/5 Gordon E. "Wren" King, worked for the battalion intelligence officer, Lieutenant Lewis Nixon. Also on board the same plane had been Major Oliver Horton, the executive officer for the battalion. King said, "Our group collected about 150 men. We started feeling our way slowly down toward St. Marie-du-Mont. When our half of the battalion was organized, Nixon got our location as eight or nine miles from the planned DZ near St. Marie-du-Mont by questioning a local French farmer. The other half of the battalion had a hot firefight in which several of our men were killed. I saw a B-26 bomber get hit and go down in smoke toward the beach. At about H-Hour, B-26's were bombing in groups of six. Later in the day, we arrived near Division Headquarters.

I got my long radio antenna shot at, because it stuck up above the hedgerows."

Another soldier who had landed in the flooded area between two causeways was Sergeant Louis Truax from Dog Company. He had spent much time bobbing to avoid machine-gun fire directed over the surface of the flooded area. He managed to get on dry land after wading about 300 yards. A short time later he met one of his buddies, Ruel Weaver, near a hedgerow. Truax said, "We moved off to the west on what was left of a road. About every 150 yards was a deep hole, perhaps 80 feet wide and 40 feet deep. They must have been made by our bombers or German mines. As the sky was turning gray we met three men from the 82nd Division. We heard a small engine approaching so we knew it must be a Kraut. We took cover and waited. A German soldier appeared riding a motorcycle. Two or three of us opened fire and killed him and the motorcycle careened into a hedgerow.

"Then came a terrific artillery barrage. It was our own Navy big guns firing from out in the Channel. It was our first experience with heavy artillery fire and very disheartening. I believe it lasted for almost an hour. All we could do was lie in our German-dug foxholes and hope for the best.

"We found a larger road going south. By this time we had guessed that we must have landed somewhere near the beach east of St. Martin-de-Varreville. It must have been around 1300 when we met Lieutenant Joe F. MacMillan and part of our company near Audoville-la-Hubert.[8] From them I learned that the rest of our load landed near Ste. Mère Eglise. They had spent most of the night fighting in the town. We passed through St. Marie-du-Mont. We met stubborn resistance in Vierville."[9]

The second half of the 2nd Battalion serial jumped in the vicinity of Ste. Mère Eglise. Made up of members of a few Dog Company planes, most of Easy and Fox Companies, the men had a long march to get to their D-Day assignments. There seemed to be three alternatives to them: (1) move almost directly east by way of the Foucarville road and then to swing down the main road past St. Martin-de-Varreville and past Audoville-la-Hubert and to the causeways at Houdienville and Pouppeville; (2) move southeast to Les Forges, and then swing directly east on the direct route to St. Marie-du-Mont, and (3) stay and fight in Ste. Mère Eglise beside the troopers of the 82nd Airborne Division.

Several small groups used the route directly to the east. Lieutenant Dick Winters of Easy Company joined forces with 3rd Battalion Commander Lieutenant Colonel Robert Cole of the 502nd Regiment. Winters believed in the old adage of "safety in numbers," and so tagged along with the larger group. Moving along some distance behind was another group of thirty or so men led by another Easy Company officer, Lieutenant Harry "Limey" Welsh. Winters' group included men from each of the three line companies of 2nd Battalion.

Private Art "Jumbo" DiMarzio had participated in the ambush of the enemy convoy with Colonel Coles's force earlier. He was with two members of his Dog Company platoon, one being his leader, Lieutenant Ron Spiers, who had once served as a British commando. DiMarzio described their specific D-Day assignment: "Our particular mission was to take a manor house guarding a crossroads and to hold it for the beach forces coming in later. We arrived late and found the job had been done by others. We started looking for other Dog Company men."

Sergeant Robert "Rook" Rader, from Easy Company, landed only a hundred yards from Ste. Mère Eglise. He had lost all of his equipment and his only weapon was a sharpened jump knife. As trained, he backtracked his stick of men and found ten or twelve fellows and moved out toward the objective. He said, "I found 'Burr' Smith, the only one I can recall by name, and at one time our group had over a hundred men heading for the beach. The mission developed as one not covered in the marshaling area, some gun emplacements facing the beach, Lieutenant Welsh was in charge of my platoon but we didn't find him until later."

T/4 Robert "Burr" Smith landed in an apple orchard and immediately vomited. Feeling a little better he heard a motorcycle close by with some one calling "Hauptmann! Hauptmann!" Smith said, "One of my assignments was to blow communications cables in a certain manhole, but I never did reach that vicinity. We gathered a small group of stragglers and moved toward the designated drop zone. Bob Rader was one of them. Found Frank Perconte injured on the jump. We engaged in a minor firefight with 'White Russians.' Disengaged and continued to press toward Vierville. At dawn we joined the company, just before the raid on the 88's in which I did not participate."

"Our mission was to secure Pouppeville on the causeway," remembered T/4 Nick J. Cortese, a radioman from Fox Company. "The company mission was accomplished by General Taylor and a handful of men. On D-Day itself, I was with a group of 35 men under the command of Lieutenant Winters of E Company. This group consisted of men of all units of the 506th and some from the 82nd. This group captured a supply convoy of three trucks and two carriers with tracks like a tank and bicycle handlebars for steering. This convoy was carrying the payroll for Germans stationed at the guns on the beach."

Private Mike Ranney of Easy Company said, "Encountered sporadic firing during the night as our group headed generally for the beach area. By dawn, we were approaching the beach, in fact we stumbled into an area that was being heavily bombarded.

"We did not accomplish our specific task, which was related to a battery of four 105mm guns firing toward the beach. We ended up going after another battery of guns later in the morning, as we neared St. Marie-du-Mont. We heard guns firing to the road and kind of piled into the woods to investigate. We got within range and opened up on the gun crew—who dived into trenches built for this purpose. Guarnere and Lieutenant Winters led this action. I must confess I moved up somewhat cautiously, but did get into action in the late stages. Here I saw my first German prisoners, taken in the trench, and was surprised that they were afraid of being shot."

Staff Sergeant Carwood Lipton climbed out over the gate of a walled-in backyard he had landed in at Ste. Mère Eglise. He proceeded cautiously because the street was lighted by a fire. He said, "I found the chute of my number 2 man, Jim

Alley, as I worked my way out of town. Our assignment was to clear the causeway from St. Marie-du-Mont to the beach and knock out enemy installations in the vicinity. Others accomplished the mission, but we helped knock out a battery of 88's firing toward the beach. Until daylight, we cleared roads and captured prisoners. By daylight there were 13 of us from Easy Company under Lt. Richard Winters, and we were part of about 75 to 100 of 2nd Battalion of the 506th moving along the road toward St. Marie-du-Mont. We came upon the battery of enemy guns firing toward the beach and Easy Company was given the mission of knocking it out. We knocked out the guns and several of our group were decorated. Lieutenant Winters received the Distinguished Service Cross for his leadership. I was one of the thirteen who made the attack, along with Lieutenant Compton, Bill Guarnere, and Wynn—I remember that I had to bandage Wynn's butt!"

"Liebgatt," continued Lipton, "set up a base of fire with his machine gun and Mike Ranney pulled a flank attack with me. When we got around the flank, we couldn't see a thing because of the brush and high weeds so I climbed a tree. I was looking right into the Kraut positions around the guns and fired several clips of .30-caliber carbine ammo into them. They didn't see me and started pulling out and then, just like in the movies, I saw Compton and Guarnere running in and throwing grenades with almost every step. The Krauts pulled back a couple hundred yards to a tree line and then they saw me. I thought for sure they had me as they were clipping branches off and bullets were cracking all around me. That's the fastest I ever came out of a tree and when I got to about a dozen feet off the ground, I just dropped the rest of the distance. This action occurred at about 10:00–11:00 A.M. on D-Day. Our company was given the assignment, of that I am sure, because we were the unit of 2nd Battalion that had been given an extended assault training course before Normandy."

Lieutenant Richard Winters had been tagging along with Colonel Robert Cole's 3rd Battalion force. The groups parted company when they reached the vicinity of the upper causeways, the 502nd men going on to their objectives while the 506th men headed south. Winters wrote,[10] "About day-break, we were close to the beach and going through some machine-gun fire and also an occasional shell burst from our own navy offshore. About 0600, we bumped into Captain Jerre Gross of Dog Company with about forty men so we joined forces and headed south for our objectives. In a few minutes we bumped into the battalion staff and about forty men, so the battalion once more was a fighting unit.

"We hadn't gone far when we came across some dead Jerries and I was still looking for a weapon when I found an M-1 under the seat of a German wagon. So I was happy once again. A little further along, I had a revolver, belt, canteen, gas mask, and lots of ammunition, so I was feeling ready to fight—especially after I bummed some food from one of the boys.

"E Company now consisted of two light machine guns, one bazooka (without ammunition), one 60mm mortar, nine riflemen, and two officers. We were running across a lot of dead Boche as we moved down the road for our objective, but very little fire. Suddenly some heavy stuff opened up on the head of the column as they moved into a small town called Le Grand-Chemin. The column stopped, we sat down content to rest. In about ten minutes, Lieutenant George Lavenson (Battalion S-4) came walking down the line and said, 'Winters, they want you and your company up front.' So off we went. Up front I found Captain Hester, Lieutenant Nixon, and Kelley in a group talking it over. Seemed like Kelley had taken his company up to a position when he could see the 88's, but couldn't do anything about stopping their fire. Captain Hester showed me where a machine gun was and about where an 88mm was situated. That was all I knew.

"First thing I did was have everybody drop all equipment except ammunition and grenades for that's all we'd need, if things went good or bad. Then I placed one of my two machine guns in a position where he could give us a little covering fire as we went more or less into position. Next, I divided the group into two units. One went with Lieutenant Compton, the other with myself. He took one hedge, I another. When we reached the hedge that led up to our position, we stopped. Here I placed another machine gunner facing on the 88 that was pointing straight at us, with instructions not to fire unless he saw a definite target, so he wouldn't give his position away for he was without cover from the gun. Then we worked up to Lieutenant Compton's hedgerow. Here I spotted a Jerry helmet and squeezed off two shots—later found a pool of blood at this position—while the rest of us gave him covering fire. I fired occasionally to fill in spots when there was a lull in the covering fire due to putting in new clips. They took too long getting up and we spent more ammunition than we should have, but in return we received no enemy fire. Just as Compton was ready to throw his grenades I started up with the rest of the assault team so that we were all jumping into the position together as the grenades went off. At the same time we were throwing more grenades to the next position, and in return receiving small-arms fire and grenades. One man, Wynn, of West Virginia, was hit in the butt and fell down in the trench hollering, 'I'm sorry Lieutenant, I goofed off, I goofed off, I'm sorry,' over and over again. At the same time a Jerry potato masher sailed into the middle of us. We all spread out as much as we could, but Corporal Joe Toye of Reading, Pennsylvania, just flopped down and was unlucky enough to have the grenade fall between his legs as he lay facedown. It went off as I was yelling at him, 'Move, for Christ's sake! Move!' He just bounced up and down from the concussion and then bounced up unhurt and ready to go. A couple of us had tossed some grenades at Jerry at the same time, so we followed up our volley with a rush, not even stopping to look at Wynn. Private Gerald J. Loraine and Sergeant Bill Guarnere were with me as we pounded in on them. They both had tommy guns and I had an M-1 as we came into position. Three Jerries left the 88 that we had found working our way up and started running. It took only a yell to the other two and we opened up on our corresponding man for we were strung out, one, two, three and so was Jerry. Loraine hit his man with the first burst. I squeezed off a shot that took my man through the head. Guarnere missed his man, who turned and started back for the gun, but he'd only taken about two steps when I put one in his back that knocked him down, then Guarnere settled down and pumped him full of lead with his tommy gun. This fellow kept yelling 'Help, help' for about five minutes.

"We had just finished off these three when out stepped a fourth about 100 yards away. I spotted him first and had the presence of mind to lie down and make it a good shot. All this must have taken about 15 to 20 seconds since we rushed the position. My next thought was 'Jesus Christ, somebody will cut loose in a minute from further up the trench.' I flopped down and by lying prone I could look through the connecting trench to the next position, and sure enough there were two of them setting up a machine gun, getting ready to fire. I got the first shot in however, and hit the gunner in the hip. The second caught the other boy in the shoulder. By that time the rest of the group were in the position, so I put Toye and Compton covering up toward the next position and three to go over and look over the 88 and three to cover to our front. Then retraced my steps, looked Wynn over, who was still sorry he goofed off, saw that he wasn't too bad and told him to work his way out and back himself, for I couldn't spare anybody to help him. He took off.

"Just as I came back, Compton, who had been fooling around with a grenade let out a yell, 'Look out!' We all hit for cover but there was no cover, for you couldn't get out of the trench, and right in the middle of it was a grenade set to go off, which it did, but for some damn reason nobody got hurt. Then a Jerry, scared to death, came running down the trench with his hands over his head, so he was our first prisoner. We had a lot of trouble getting him out though, and finally one of the boys hit him with some brass knuckles and he lay there moaning for about a half hour until I went over, kicked him in the pants, and let him know that it was high time he got out, and he did as we wanted. No sooner had this happened than I spotted three Jerries for some damn reason walking toward our position along the hedge in a very informal manner. I got two others up there and we set our range for about 200 yards and let them come to about 225; somebody must have yelled at them for they stopped and seemed to listen. That's when I gave 'ready, aim' and just then this guy Loraine cut loose with a tommy gun, which wasn't worth a damn over 50 to 75 yards. One of us wounded one of them, but after that it was pure hell for they had machine guns on us all the time just cutting the top of the trench.

"It was time we took the second gun, I thought, so I left three behind and we charged the next position with grenades and lots of yelling and firing. I don't think anybody hurt anybody that time, but we did pick up those two I'd wounded when they tried to put a machine gun up.

"At this time ammunition was low as hell. I needed more men, for we were stretched out too much for our own good and those damn machine gunners never came on up after us as I'd instructed. So I went back for some. After about half an hour the machine guns finally got there, so I put them in place and decided to take the next gun. Two men from another company had come up also.

"On the attack, one of these boys, T/5 John D. Hall, was killed. We took the position and four prisoners and then again had to hold up. I sent four prisoners I had to the back and at the same time asked for more ammunition and men. Finally I spotted Captain Hester coming up, went to meet him and he gave me three blocks of TNT and an incendiary thermite grenade. I had these placed in the three guns we had already taken. Also he told me Lieutenant Spiers was bringing five men up.

"So while waiting I went about gathering documents and stuffing them in a bag. I found one good map showing all 88 positions and machine-gun positions on the peninsula. I sent these back and directed the destruction of the radio equipment, range finders, etc.

"Finally Spiers arrived and led an attack on the final gun, which we took, destroyed, and then withdrew for the machine-gun fire we were receiving from the house and other positions was pretty rough. First the machine guns pulled out then the riflemen. I was last, and as I was leaving I took a final look down the trench and here was this one wounded Jerry we were leaving behind trying to put this machine gun on us again, so I drilled him clean through the head—as I found out later—and then pulled out.

"On the way I found Mr. Andrew F. Hill, a Fox Company warrant officer, dead, as he had been killed trying to work his way up to us. In all we had four dead, six wounded, and accounted for fifteen dead and twelve captured.[11] The enemy force numbered about fifty.

"When we came out I put the machine guns firing on the position as well as a 60mm mortar as a sort of harassing fire.

"The Battalion sent for some tanks to help clean this job up and then left for the objective. About that time, Lieutenant Welsh and Lieutenant Roush came down the road with about thirty more men. I organized them into two groups and had them stand by. Lieutenant Lewis Nixon led the 4th Division tanks up from the beach, and I led the tanks into the 88 positions to clean them out."

Moving along with a second group of 2nd Battalion soldiers on the direct east-west route was Lieutenant Harry "Limey" Welsh, who had assembled 35 men near the outskirts of Ste. Mère Eglise. Many were from other units. He related, "Our assignment was going to a crossroads to take out machine guns in trenches and an 88 gun position, which was in an orchard not far from the beach. We were to proceed down the causeway and secure a bridge, check a village, and check the roadway for mines, and then move inland. We didn't complete this mission, but we did make it from Ste. Mère Eglise to the causeways by 0500 A.M. We removed a gun position at a roadblock, cleaned out a field of Germans, and blew up a wagon train of supplies on the way. We made our way through the night to get to the causeway to complete our mission. We met up with Lieutenant Winters at about 0900 A.M. We tried to cover his actions in taking an 88mm gun position. We lined up our forces at the head of the causeway. Moved inland against St. Marie-du-Mont. Got into a helluva fight there."

"I remember very well dragging my lame leg down that road that night and the look on all of our faces at the first sign of dawn to see this road littered with dead from both sides. You could just see exactly how they had died," remembered Private Edward. J. Mitchell. He had jumped near Ste. Mère Eglise, close behind Ray Taylor, as his assistant ma-

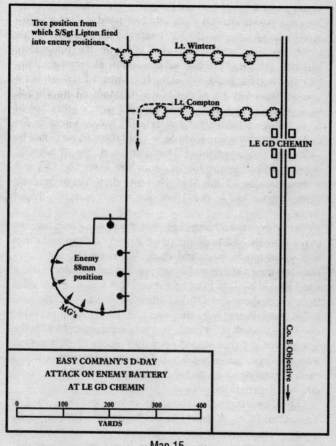

Tree position from
which S/Sgt Lipton fired
into enemy positions

Lt. Winters

Lt. Compton

LE GD CHEMIN

Enemy
88mm
position

MG's

Co. E Objective →

EASY COMPANY'S D-DAY
ATTACK ON ENEMY BATTERY
AT LE GD CHEMIN

0   100   200   300   400

YARDS

Map 15

(*Prepared from sketch which accompanied Lt. Winter's D-Day story.
Lipton's position has been added.*)

chine gunner. The opening shock of the chute had torn his heavy leg bag from his foot and injured his right leg. After landing in a tree, he had cut his risers with what he felt was the "sharpest knife that went into Normandy." He had tumbled to the ground, which didn't improve the situation for his game leg. His helmet had torn loose on the jump also. Mitchell related, "We had several minor skirmishes along this road and bagged a considerable number of Krauts, but it was on the outskirts of St. Marie-du-Mont where all hell broke loose. They started pounding us with a cross fire of 88's and we all dove for cover fast. Captain Gross and I ended up in a well-dug foxhole, where I thought we would be safe from almost anything. That didn't last long, though, as he sent me across the road to draw fire from two 88's that were camouflaged in a field. He sent other men to outflank them, but we had to draw their fire so our men could spot them.

"Both guns were dropping shells on us at one time so every time the shells dropped, we would raise up and fire a clip of ammo at them and duck. We were OK until they changed their pattern and I was just raising up once when a shell landed right in front of me and that was it. There were three of us there and I didn't know the other two. One was killed outright and the other one had his chest ripped wide open and I doubt if he made it. I was knocked cold with the left side of my face ripped open and pieces of shrapnel all over my face, neck, and head. The first I remember was a medic standing over me and asking if I thought I could smoke a cigarette."

Other small groups chose to move southeast to Les Forges, and then eastward to St. Marie-du-Mont in an attempt to reach their D-Day objectives.

The plane Fox Company commander, Captain Thomas P. Mulvey, was flying in caught fire shortly after the red light flashed on. He landed about one-half mile southeast of Ste. Mère Eglise on a little dirt road and machine-gun chatter seemed to come from all directions. Having suffered a leg injury, he crawled into a ditch and waited. At 0645 A.M., he was joined by Lieutenant Tuck, Tex Taylor, and Russ Schwenk, and some others. Mulvey said, "In the early morning we determined where we were. I sent the majority off in the direction of the beach toward Pouppeville. I kept three and we went to Ste. Mère Eglise. Joined up with Colonel Krause of the 505th of the 82nd Division. Unable to walk too well. Went off on a patrol or two. Group was under heavy cannon fire on D-Day night. It was touch-and-go most of that night and the next day. (Got a jeep ride to the 101st on D plus 2 and joined 37 members of my company. The balance was still unaccounted for and continued to trickle in over the next few days.)"

Sergeant Russ A. Schwenk landed near Ste. Mère Eglise. He recalled, "I met Roy Zerbe, from the 3rd Platoon. In a period of one and a half hours, I as commanding sergeant, assembled approximately 42 men and moved toward our objective on Causeway 1 at Pouppeville. After an eleven mile journey including detours and other incidents, we arrived at the objective Pouppeville, approximately at 11:00 A.M. General Taylor had the situation there in hand so myself and others joined our 2nd Battalion. We had avoided all action to move to the objective bypassing small and large firefights en route."

Private Roy "Dutch" Zerbe jumped from a plane in which the tail was burning fiercely. He landed near Ste. Mère Eglise. According to Zerbe, "We were to take the town of Pouppeville and drive toward Utah Beach and meet the 4th Division. We did partially complete our mission one day late. There were minor brushes with the Germans. We were trying hard to get to Pouppeville."

Corporal Richard W. Gleason of Dog Company heard the church bells of Ste. Mère Eglise as he floated to earth south of the village. He found the road leading to Ste. Mère Eglise. Gleason stated, "I checked my map as to our assembly area. It all appeared to be right so I set off down the road to the left in relation to our drop line. My cricket was in operation but I heard no answers. At the intersection I turned to the right and shortly met up with a few fellows from other parts of the division. In the next hour or so, our group grew till we had little better than two squads in strength and arrived at a French farmyard. There we holed up till daylight.

"While in this farmyard, we took stock of our situation. There was one officer in the whole group and several non-coms. At 0600 A.M., we were able to watch the bombardment of the beaches from our position. While watching I saw one of the B-26 bombers take a direct hit and break up into two balls of fire. We proceeded to move out shortly after and as we started one of the sergeants got hit in the neck. Apparently we had landed between Ste. Mère Eglise and Les Forges and to the east because we encountered the swampy area in that sector, near Boutteville in mid-morning. Somewhere along there we approached a large château and one of the boys caught an 88 shell in the chest and it about tore him apart. As we approached the road north of Houdienville, our forces were gradually depleted as different ones dropped off to go their separate ways to join their units. About 1500 P.M. I met up with my first visible enemy, dead in the ditch on the right, a little above the junction at Exit 2.

"Shortly after we met up with the lead elements of the 4th Infantry Division. Finally about 1700, I rejoined my company at Pouppeville. Along the way I tried to make radio contact but to no avail. I had time to grab a bite to eat before the company started to move out toward St. Marie-du-Mont at 1715. We were held up for a while till a sniper was dislodged from the church steeple in 'du-Mont.' We went on through town, and down the west side of the road toward Vierville. There were a lot of Horsa and CG-4A gliders scattered around the countryside south of St. Marie-du-Mont. We bedded down for the night just north of Vierville—it was very quiet."

Corporal Ray E. Taylor had already dispatched an enemy motorcycle and a command car when he finally got together with Sergeant Ed Martin. Both lay in the ditch beside Taylor's assembled machine gun, waiting and wondering what to do next. He related, "Just then more planes came over at treetop level and they started jumping men. The Germans started to fire at them and we could see their positions so we decided to try to knock them out. We found some boys from other companies and some from Dog Company who were hit and some hurt from the jump. We spent some time giving overhead fire for the 82nd and chasing a lot of Krauts out of barns and farmhouses. We freed two boys from my company who had been captured. We had a helluva fight near St. Marie-du-Mont later in the day."

Moving along the alleys and over backyard walls, other troopers found themselves completely lost. Ste. Mère Eglise was an unfamiliar name to the men. They were far from their drop zones and off the jump maps they carried. Many of them became involved in fighting near the fringes of the town and remained to fight where they had landed.

PFC James Alley landed behind the town hall in Ste. Mère Eglise. He said, "I found Paul Rogers and Earl McClung. We joined up with E Company of the 505th Regiment of the 82nd Division and helped take and hold the town. We were with them for ten or eleven days along with other 101st men—24 of them I think. Seems to me they had us out front all the time. We moved all over—can't say where, as they never told us much—just up front, 101st men!"

PFC Paul Rogers worked his way out of a large tree near Ste. Mère Eglise. He said, "I started over to where the main body was jumping. Ran through hedgerows and got all scratched up. Met up with Jim Alley and Earl McClung. We joined elements of the 82nd Division and helped capture Ste. Mère Eglise. Made patrols and 'got acquainted with the enemy.' I got a weapon before too many minutes had elapsed. I had lost everything when my English leg bag containing all equipment broke loose on the jump."

Private Earl McClung landed on the roof of a small building in Ste. Mère Eglise and bounced over the side into a backyard. A leg bag with which he had jumped was beside him, but it was empty. Everything had burst out through the bottom. As he struggled with his harness a Frenchwoman came out of the house and was trying to offer him a glass of milk. He said, "All I could think of was getting loose and away from that woman before some enemy soldiers spotted me. In my anxiety I cut the straps of my musette bag, also rendering it useless. I ran across an orchard and all I could hear was crickets. Found a road—a German machine gun opened up toward me from down the road and I took off across another field. I found another fellow named Payne. We wandered around and found five or six fellows from the 505th Regiment of the 82nd Division and finally ended up in Ste. Mère Eglise. Found some of the men from my outfit and joined them. Payne and I shot snipers out of high trees and finally Payne was shot in the foot."

Summary

Snipers continued their pesky activity into the night around Colonel Sink's 506th Regimental Headquarters. 1st and 2nd Battalion troops were dug in for the night in the vicinity of Culoville and Vierville.

The mission for 1st and 2nd Battalions had been completed. Causeways 1 and 2 had been cleared and were carrying the bulk of the heavy vehicular traffic moving inland and through the 101st Division positions. Enemy artillery positions had been destroyed at Le Grand-Chemin and Holdy.

Vierville's enemy strength had increased with the arrival of the German battalion which Sink and Hannah had encountered on their reconnaissance trip in search of Lieutenant Colonel Wolverton's 3rd Battalion. No inkling of 3rd Battalion's success or failure at the wooden bridges had reached Sink's command post.

Because his force was situated in the middle and near General Taylor's position, Sink was given the assignment to attack through Vierville and on toward St. Come-du-Mont on the morning of D plus 1. His men were resting. There would be heavy fighting on the morrow for the capture of Vierville, and the relief of Angoville and Addeville.

CHAPTER 14

Hold Those Bridges!

3rd Battalion of the 560th, commanded by Lieutenant Colonel Robert Wolverton, had been given the assignment of capturing the two wooden bridges across the Douve River to the northeast of Carentan. The troopers were also to seize the high ground overlooking the bridge positions on the east bank near Brevands. This was to be a meeting point for the Allied forces advancing from Utah and Omaha Beaches.

"Colonel Wolverton was in the door and grumbling as he knew we were not on our drop zone. It was a shock to see how light it was, with the enemy flares illuminating the countryside," said Staff Sergeant William Pauli, message center chief for the 3rd Battalion as he recalled the approach to the landing area.

All the occupants of his plane were destined to be killed or captured because the men dropped a half mile southwest of Drop Zone "D" in fields heavily fortified by German troops, who had been preparing a defense line in the area. Colonel Wolverton, battalion commander, was killed on the drop.

Distracted from concentrating on his landing because of the streams of tracers streaking upward, Sergeant Pauli recalled his drop: "I felt like a sitting duck. I let my chute oscillate to make a more difficult target. I swung onto the ground with great shock and pain. I found I could not move my legs and had great pain in my lower trunk. Finally got out of my chute and tried to orient myself. It sounded like a millpond with all those (mechanical) crickets. One of my runners was the first man I saw. Rinehart was a young replacement we got in England. I told him to take it easy until things quieted down, but he took off running and was cut down by a machine gun at the first hedgerow. A medic came by a short time later but could not help me, as I had no open wound. Colonel Wolverton was killed on the way down. Jack Harrison died of stomach wounds as a prisoner. I'd say half of the men were killed and the rest were captured.

"As daylight arrived, I covered myself with my chute, hoping to be picked up by our troops. I awoke when I felt my chute being pulled off me. I looked up to see two Germans, who stripped me of my watch, cigs, billfold, etc. They picked me up and took me to St. Come-du-Mont. Feeling low in spirits, I was surprised to see so many comrades-in-arms that were there ahead of me. Having only a field aid station, the Germans laid me in a barn with other 101st men. Captain Morgan (who had jumped with us) was there in the aid station doing what good he could for us."[1]

Aboard the same plane had been Corporal Ray Calandrella of Battalion Headquarters, who said, "I was in Colonel Wolverton's plane. He was killed, along with several others. I did not see him after the jump. On the ground I found myself alone in a large field. During the night, six or seven of us got together, and survived several small firefights. After daybreak, two more troopers joined us and that night, about 10 P.M., June 6th, we were ambushed, sustaining a loss of four men."[2]

Ambushes were numerous in the hedgerows. Enemy soldiers were active through the night and early morning hours. Medical aidman, T/5 John Gibson, went into combat with the 81mm mortar platoon, of Battalion Headquarters. He said, "Seven men assembled and moved cautiously across fields following ditches when possible. Approximately one company of German infantry waited across a dirt road in high weeds until we were close and then all hell broke loose. Ronzani and Abbey were point men and were killed by automatic weapons fire—both were hit numerous times in the chest area. Charles H. Lee escaped and fired back into the group. Shortly after, the four of us were captured. Lee was killed a few minutes later. His body was found by others in that area."

PFC George Rosie, who had tumbled through a wooden

fence as he landed on the edge of a road, corroborated Gibson's recollections. Rosie had some difficulty getting free because the lines were caught in the fence. He found Francis Ronzani, Charles H. Lee, Leo Krebbs, and Rowcliff. Rosie related, "We never did find out just where we were. About eight of us got together, ran into a White Russian outfit and after about two hours, three were killed and the rest of us captured."

Supply Sergeant Zolman Rosenfield, who had held two bundles containing rubber rafts during the entire flight across the Channel and over the peninsula, was fired on all the way down. "I landed all alone in a small field and heard shouting, firing, and men running," he remembered. "Before I did anything else, I loaded my pistol and tommy gun, then cut the straps to get out quicker. Got into the hedgerow and looked at my compass. Was supposed to go west to the assembly area—learned later that I had dropped west of the drop zone. As jumpmaster, I was to throw out two equipment bundles containing rubber rafts, and was supposed to get them to the wooden bridges. I met up with Lieutenant Howard Little of G Company, Ray Calandrella, and Sam Plyler, all 506th men, and four parachute engineers. Corporal Warren Nelson was my armorer. Anyway, some of the fellows came across Nelson all alone with our equipment bundles. They wanted him to join them, but he said, 'I'll stay and wait for Rosie.' He was killed there.

"As for my small group, somehow we found we were going in the wrong direction. Tried to get back, had several skirmishes, personally shot and killed four Germans from close range, right before dawn. They were walking on a raised road we had to cross. Hid out all day. Cossacks almost rode through bushes we were in. After dark, started back again and ran into an ambush."

The rubber rafts were not delivered to the bridge area.

Drop Zone "D" had been heavily ringed with enemy positions. Upon landing, the pathfinders found enemy fire as they sought to get their landing aids into position. As lead elements of the main body of troopers approached these particular fields from the west in their low-flying troop carrier planes, the Germans lighted a house which had been doused with kerosine. The holocaust illuminated the entire area.

Fortunately, the green light was flashed too soon in most of these planes and the "lucky" parachutists bailed out short of the flaming death trap that had been prepared for them. A few sticks rode on into the "proper" area and bailed out correctly. On the ground, a small group of pathfinders watched helplessly as the silently dropping men were picked off by machine-gun and rifle fire as they entered the circle of light.

From the fringes of the area where he had come to earth, Captain Charles Shettle, a battalion staff officer, witnessed the tragic episode. With the light from the giant bonfire, he was able to study his compass to determine the direction of his battalion assembly area. Avoiding the roads, he cut across fields and walked directly to the proper location, where he found himself very much alone. From there he moved northwest to the small settlement of Angoville-au-Plain. On the way, two officers and thirteen enlisted men joined forces with him. A brief council was held. Should they wait for more men or should they head for the bridges? Some wanted to wait. The captain had the rank and thought they should go. It sounded like an order—so they went.

Reversing direction before they reached Angoville, the group marched in the direction of the bridges. Along the way they picked up two more officers and sixteen enlisted men. The bridges were reached at 0430 A.M. As the group studied the situation trying to agree on the best approach with such a limited number of men, five more officers and fifteen enlisted men arrived on the scene.

A crossing of one bridge had to be made to establish a bridgehead on the eastern side. Captain Shettle called for volunteers. Two men stepped forward. One, PFC Donald Zahn, was directed to take a light machine gun to a low spot to the left of the bridge on the eastern end. He raced across the bridge in a low crouching run as enemy machine-gun bullets buzzed angrily past his ears. He dived into the shallow ditch beside the roadway untouched. Shettle then sent the second man, PFC George Montilio, with the ammunition. The pair quickly set up the gun and opened up, one feeding the gun while the other fired, thereby forcing the enemy gunners to keep their heads down. With this arrangement, two five-man patrols managed to make their way unscathed across the bridge to set up a skirmish line on either side of the machine gun. First light of day was just breaking and it was thought wiser to send the next group across by means of the girders on the underside of the bridge. This was accomplished by each man moving hand over hand as one would on an overhead ladder. With the machine gun firing short bursts as covering fire, the patrols were able to snake forward on their stomachs until they were in grenade distance. This combined force managed to destroy three machine-gun nests during the morning.

Feeling pressure on their front, the Germans continued to move in more reinforcements and the firing intensified. As the ammunition supply dwindled for the Americans, the advance elements were ordered to pull back to their own side of the bridge. The remainder of Captain Shettle's force now provided covering fire for this group as they retreated to the sheltered side of the bridge.

The importance of gaining a foothold on the east bank of the Douve River was stressed by the fact that many demolitions experts were assigned to the mission. Two sections of these men were assigned by 506th Regiment Headquarters. Five planeloads of airborne engineers from the 326th Engineer Battalion also had been briefed for this mission. PFC Keith Carpenter, a demolition man from 506th Regimental Headquarters, related, "I landed in an area that was flooded with a depth of two and a half feet of water. I started across the flooded area, moving toward the southeast. Shortly after this, I picked up Mike Marquez. He had dropped the trigger assembly to his rifle in the water and couldn't find it. Right after this, we picked up one other man. Quite a while later we ran into Jake McNiece and several others. We started out for the bridges. After daylight we hit the road near the farm where we later set up the aid station. We turned right at the farm and started for the footbridge. About halfway across the field, Clarence Ware was hit in the shoulder. When we arrived at the base of the footbridge there were three men dug in at that spot. We moved to the left and started to dig in, and the mortars started. It seemed to me they hit us with mortars three or four times that day. Across the bridge the Krauts were on high ground with a small wooded area at the peak of a hill. Just at dusk, two others and myself went back to pick up Ware, but he had already been moved back to the aid station. That night we watched both directions but it was a quiet night."

"I landed in a field within a short distance of St. Come-du-Mont," recalled PFC John Agnew, another 506th Regimental demolitions man. "I had chosen a Springfield bolt-action rifle which could not be broken down like the M-1. When I landed, it hit the ground muzzle first, and the shock dislocated my left shoulder. I got beside a hedgerow and all the German troops were running up and down the road directly behind it. I moved toward the edge of another field and met a man from a mortar section of one of the line companies. He was so scared and made so much noise I threatened to shoot him.

"Our mission was to reach the bridges and place our explosives and prevent enemy troops and armor from advancing across to counterattack our men. Neither one of our officers (Lieutenants Williams and Mellen) were with us.

"I then met Mike Marquez and some other men. We proceeded toward our mission. On the way, we met an officer and some men. We wanted to head toward the bridges and he let us proceed on our own. I then met Jake McNiece and Clarence Ware, and we put a charge on the power lines and blew them up. We proceeded toward the bridges. Ware got hit as we had to cross open fields without any cover. The rest of us got to the bridges and found we were isolated. I got permission from Captain Charles Shettle to blow a ditch across the road embankment so we could get through to our men on the other side of the roadway. Mike Marquez helped me. We laid our charges out across the roadbed and blew a ditch so we could get through without exposing ourselves. It worked. We were dug in along the bank. Enemy fire from across the river in a tree line and high weeds killed several of our men. The enemy was well concealed with a background behind him. We were lower and had no foliage to break up our silhouettes."

A third demolitions man was PFC John G. Kutz from Charley Company of the 326th Airborne Engineer Battalion. His jump was several miles from the objective. He said, "I landed in a flooded area. Crossed a road just behind three Germans moving a small artillery piece. I gathered my equipment and rested on the road bank for some time.

"Several men from my stick arrived a short time later. Sergeant Jim O'Laughlin, myself, and about four men from the 506th Regiment moved toward the bridges. On the way we blew some power lines down and quickly received fire from a wooded area. We took up the fight which lasted about fifteen minutes. During this delay, we were joined by three or four more men and the Germans decided to leave. We finished blowing the power lines. Then we came to a manhole—after taking the lid off, we saw underground wires so we blew them too. We moved on to the bridge, and we were fired on several times from wooded areas as we walked on the road. We kept walking and would fire a few rounds back at them and they seemed to disappear. I arrived at the bridge with about 50 to 60 pounds of C-2 (Compound 2) explosives like TNT. I had jumped with this, and also a box of eight Number 12 blasting caps, a roll of primer cord, a roll of safety cord, and some fuse lighters. These were the explosives we used to prepare the bridge for demolition.

"However, when I first got to the bridge, Captain Shettle had sent patrols across the bridge to seek out enemy activities. He also sent out a patrol for ammunition, weapons, first aid supplies, and food bundles. I was one of the members on this patrol. It was led by a fellow whom I knew only as 'No-No.' We found a field with supply drops. We started opening the bundles when a loud 'crack' sound passed close by. There was fire coming at us from a hedgerow. We returned the fire and 'No-No' made his way to the hedgerow but they were gone. We loaded up our equipment and started back. We had to cross a flooded area. When about in the middle, we drew fire again. 'No-No' and two other fellows took up the fight and moved toward the source of the firing, which was an old house. We got across and joined the firefight. 'No-No's' group made its way to the house and outran three Germans and the boys got them. Then we continued on to the bridge. We took up positions for firing across the river."

George Company

The rubber rafts pushed out of a plane by Staff Sergeant Zolman Rosenfield had been part of the special equipment by which George Company men had planned to assault the east bank of the Douve at the wooden bridges. The rafts were lost. Adversity continued to plague the men. Captain Harold Van Antwerp, the commanding officer of George Company, was killed on the jump as his stick landed in the swamp on the outskirts of Carentan. The men fought in small groups—some with Colonel Ballard[3] and his 2nd Battalion force of 501st soldiers, others performed well with Colonel Johnson at the La Barquette Locks, and some managed to move into the 3rd Battalion area with Captain Charles Shettle, where they served with distinction.

PFC Stanley B. Clever landed in water under heavy small-arms fire. His leg pack failed to release and he had to go underwater to get at the harness. Clever made his way cautiously through shallow water and up on high ground where he contacted several other men from his company and the battalion. He related, "I contacted Oakie Hildebrand and the two of us proceeded along the edge of the flooded area until we got together with several other 3rd Battalion men under G Company's Lieutenant Barling. We moved toward our objective. Had several small firefights and a lot of confusion. We arrived at the bridges about daybreak with approximately sixteen men. Can't recall when Captain Shettle took command—he could have been on the objective when we arrived. We dug in to secure the bridges and exchanged shots with the Germans across the river. H Company made a crossing but was forced to return. Bill Forrester and I went on patrol to find ammo—Bill got his canteen shot full of holes."

"I jumped from the plane at 400 feet and the pilot actually slowed down for the jump," recalled Sergeant John A. Westeris. "I found my jumpmaster, Lieutenant Jim Morton, who had sustained a broken leg, and several other men from my company. Sergeant Scofield and I helped Lieutenant Morton walk toward the objective. He insisted we drop him, so we could get there on time. We came to a group of men who were waiting for a lieutenant. We left Lieutenant Morton with them. Four of us started for our objective; saw the mass bombing of the beach. We stopped at a farmhouse for information and an old farmer pointed the way to the wooden bridges. There were about twenty men there. We pooled our ammo. We had one 60mm mortar with five rounds. We held the flank until relieved. I fired those five rounds at Germans leaving the bridge area."

"When we invaded Normandy, that wild unreal, bloody night last June, we were badly scattered," wrote Captain Jim Morton.[4] "The air corps had failed us miserably, and this, plus the fact the area was infested with German patrols and machine-gun nests, made chaos of our plans to reorganize. I broke my foot on a rock, but scrambled from my parachute harness and set out to find friendly troops. After coming upon Germans in three directions I tried another heading and was challenged by a voice from the bushes. It was Lieutenant John Kiley. We eluded an enemy patrol and proceeded to a road junction, where we were challenged. It was Joe.

"He had gathered a small band of paratroopers and was endeavoring to orient himself on a map. Chambliss, Meason, Bolte, Christianson, Barling, and Santasierro joined us. Luckily I had carried an aerial photo of the sector. We quickly located our exact whereabouts and struck for the objective. I couldn't keep pace with the force because of my injured foot, which worsened hourly. A mortar barrage scattered the column. I found myself alone and was soon unable to walk. Harold Van Antwerp had been killed in his parachute. Thus Joe took command of G Company."

PFC Jim "Pee-Wee" Martin survived a mortar barrage en route to the bridges. He remembered, "As I was making final adjustments on my equipment, a mortar shell plopped down about 15 feet away and threw me flat on my face. It didn't take me long to clear out of there. About a quarter mile away I saw someone sneaking along and challenged him, receiving the proper countersign. I approached him and found it was my buddy, Spiller. We kept on toward the objective, running into guys along the way.

"Some planes came over and the sky was filled with fire. Suddenly there was a brilliant ball of flame traveling in a half circle. It nosed into a dive to the ground, landing about 600 yards from us. It exploded on contact, flames billowing 100 feet into the air. It made a roaring fire which could be heard and seen long after we had gone by.

"After that plane cracked up, we continued on to our objective. We crossed a big dike about 800 yards from it, and started across the open field beyond. We hadn't gone far when two heavy machine guns opened up and we hit the dirt. About thirty seconds later the 88's and mortars opened up with devastating effect. One of the sergeants and I started to crawl out of the field of fire until he suddenly stopped and pointed out the muzzle flashes of an 88 which was in an open trench position.

"We each put a clip of ammo into it and were very promptly singled out and fired on, but the machine gun only kicked up dirt so they started shelling us. I didn't hear the first one come. It was just a terrific bang which made my ears ring. They fired five at us before we got under cover. Nine of us started to backtrack and go around the flank and we ran smack into a light machine gun. Everyone then opened up and the enemy soldiers left with their wounded. On at least five occasions there were machine-gun teams which tried to get behind us, without success. Finally we got to our objective, which was a bridge in front of a hill held by several hundred Germans. Sixty-nine of us troopers held that position for three days until we were relieved."

Martin added a poignant story about his platoon leader, who managed to reach the wooden bridges with the first groups. "Lieutenant T. M. Chambliss was the officer in charge of our group for this mission. He wasn't near me on the jump. Lieutenant Chambliss was an army brat—West Point—and the most idealistic person I ever knew. He was my platoon officer, very G.I., very strict, but fair. He never drank or ran around and all the other officers must have been a little envious because they pumped the men for any lapses which they might use to needle him. There were none. Since he was so 'West Point' about everything, I conceived the idea of asking, 'Are we Army or West Point?' All the guys in the 2nd Platoon liked the idea so I stenciled 'West Point' over the breast pocket of all of our combat jumpsuits. We all showed up in formation expecting an uproar, but the lieutenant gave no indication, then or in the days which followed, that he even noticed. This of course was a letdown, but we went into Normandy this way. The lieutenant got to the bridge before most of us. During the fighting in the exposed area near the bridge, he suddenly stood up and was shot twice through the mouth. I'm ashamed to tell you what happened next, but I must. As he lay dying, he asked if anyone was there from the 2nd Platoon, and when told there were none, he told the H Company sergeant who was cradling his head that he'd like to know why we put 'West Point' on our jackets. He wondered if we were mocking his background. I cried tears of shock and frustration and shame as his body was carried past my position. I keep wondering how he could have failed to perceive the great pride and affection we felt for him."

"I lost my leg bag when the chute popped open," recalled PFC C. A. Spiller, who had undergone the same artillery barrage as Martin. "I went hunting for a gun of any kind for myself, and for other members of my group. I found an equipment bag with a machine gun in it. Jim Martin was the first one I found after the D-Day jump. As we were walking to our objective I was very disgusted and began to sing 'Mare-Zi-Doats.' Later, after I was wounded, Martin kidded me that it was no wonder the Germans hit me. He said that he was about to do it himself!

"We were to take a bridge across the river. It was to be mined so that it could be blown up if we were unable to hold it. Lieutenant Chambliss was in charge of our platoon. My actions were very little. As we neared the bridge, the Germans opened fire. I was in a ditch with other fellows. The Germans zeroed in on our position with artillery. The first shot hit long, the second was short, and the third hit within eight feet of me. The man ahead of me was killed and I got hit in the

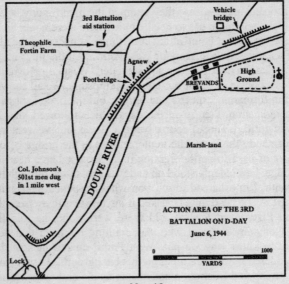

Map labels:

3rd Battalion aid station

Vehicle bridge

Theophile Fortin Farm

Agnew

Footbridge

BREVANDS

High Ground

DOUVE RIVER

Marsh-land

Col. Johnson's 501st men dug in 1 mile west

Lock

ACTION AREA OF THE 3RD BATTALION ON D-DAY

June 6, 1944

0   1000

YARDS

Map 16

The predawn mission of 3rd Battalion was to seize the two wooden bridges approximately two miles northeast of Carentan and to capture the high ground held by the enemy on the east bank near the small hamlet of Brevands. The enemy had excellent concealment on the east bank. Unlike the exposed west bank, a hedgerow ran parallel to the east bank of the river. This was topped by large trees and in addition, tall marsh grass and hedges grew down to the water's edge. In daylight, from his vantage point on the high ground, the enemy had unlimited observation for several thousand yards beyond the river. West of the river, the land was flat, broken only by raised roadways. Beyond the farms, the land was marshy and crisscrossed with canals.

The paratroopers were able to cross this exposed ground before daylight and they dug into the bank of the dike-like riverbank at the approaches to the bridges. Later in the day, John Agnew used explosives to make a trench across the raised roadway leading to the footbridge. This provided concealment for the men as they crawled along it to contact each other on either side of the roadway.

side. I then went into the first aid station and was taken back to England some time later."

Private James E. Montgomery crawled to the shelter of a hedgerow and tried to stand up. His legs wouldn't support his weight. He had sprained both ankles. He decided to hide in a nearby hedgerow, but the machine guns firing nearby had an unfamiliar sound. Assuming they were German, he decided to crawl away from them. He located Larry Kepler, who was the only member of his stick encountered that night. Montgomery said, "Larry Kepler and I left our hedgerow on the jump field and joined other men who were moving 'somewhere.' About daybreak, we were with a sizeable group on the banks of a canal. Then I saw Chaplain Tilden S. McGee of our regiment and Lieutenant Linton Barling of G Company. Chaplain McGee announced that he believed he knew where the bridges were and they left accompanied by no more than a dozen men. I attempted to follow, but because my ankles pained me so much, I quickly fell behind. I continued in the direction the group had taken. I was quite alone and lost. I occasionally met other small groups who didn't seem any better oriented than myself. After what seemed like hours (it couldn't have been later than 10:00 A.M.) I was exhausted and my ankles ached; I actually lay down under a tree and went to sleep. I can't account for this, except that I must have been in a state of shock. Nevertheless, I soon awoke to find one of the men from G Company bending over me to see if I was alive. I arose and staggered on. Miraculously, I found a farmhouse where Chaplain McGee and some medics had set up an aid station near the position at the bridges. I stopped long enough to get my ankles taped and then moved on to the bridges and joined the few men from my company who were there."

Staff Sergeant Merville Grimes had tumbled out of the plane as the last man of a nineteen-man stick and had landed on marshy land in the outskirts of Carentan. He related, "I was the last man out of Captain Harold Van Antwerp's stick. I landed in a swamp and spent the rest of the night collecting a small group of men and had to spend the day in the swamp. We finally reached our objective on the evening of D-Day."

At least one George Company soldier crossed the locks, which were the objective of the 501st Regiment. Sergeant Harvey Jewett lost his leg bag on the opening shock and slipped his chute to avoid the 20mm tracers coming up toward him. When he got to the ground, he later said, "I found myself with two grenades and a trench knife plus a clip of tommy gun ammo—but no weapon to fire because it had been tucked in my leg pack. I didn't find any members of my stick. I crossed the La Barquette Locks, met more men at the site and we headed for the bridges."

Plane Number 15 which had carried Sergeant Jewett into Normandy did not return to its base in England. It was shot down. However, George Company had been relatively fortunate in that most of its planes had dropped the men along the fringes of the drop zone, and for this reason they were able to move toward the bridges with relatively little delay.

How Company

Three planes carrying How Company personnel flashed the green light to the men over the area which the Germans had prepared as an ambush. Two others continued on for approximately thirteen miles in the direction of Omaha Beach, where the men were dropped. Yet, the company was well represented in the first forces to reach the downstream area. How Company also lost its commander, Captain Robert Harwick, who was quickly taken prisoner. PFC Owen R. Perry described the action this way: "Almost immediately after landing, I was under fire from automatic weapons from nearby hedgerows and flanked by an Austrian (German soldier) who spoke excellent English. After capture, I was allowed to help another H Company man to an aid station. He had a leg injury from the jump. We joined other prisoners near the aid station, including my captain, Robert Harwick. We were held near the drop zone throughout the day and moved on foot toward the southeast after dark. Allied shelling injured several of our men during the early evening. Later I was informed that Captain Harwick slipped away in the darkness. I prayed for his success."[5]

Communications Sergeant Gordon Yates jumped from the plane in which Lieutenant Meason had served as jumpmaster. The pilot had evidently found the way to the DZ in a roundabout way. "We were flying north to south when the green light flashed on and Lieutenant Meason went out and I was right behind him. He lit in his proper place, but I lit on the south side of the Douve River. 18 men were to have landed on the DZ. I lit 1800 yards south and each of the 16 men were scattered from there to Carentan. The last man hit the Carentan church steeple.

"I lit alone away from everyone. By crawling along the hedgerows and using the crickets, six of us had collected toward our objective. Some time after dawn we ran into seven more including 1st Sergeant Gordon Bolles. We were pinned down by fire from a group of houses. We didn't reach our objective on D-Day."

Supply Sergeant Fred Bahlau joined Lieutenant Meason in the approach to the bridges. He said, "After getting out of my chute I got my weapon ready. I must have been a little nervous because I fired a burst into the ground with my own tommy gun and thought sure as hell I was shot at. I'm sure that with all the shooting, barn burnings, etc., it wasn't noticed by the enemy.

"It was just after this that I bumped into a fellow from my company named Dworsky after exchanging cricket snaps. He and I approached a road approximately a quarter mile away where we picked up a force of about thirty men. I was ranking noncom so took charge heading toward the bridge, which was our objective to hold. On the way I picked up Jose Hernandez, a Mexican boy who had lost his M-1 which had torn loose on the drop, so I loaned him my .45 Colt pistol. (This of course was non-issue and bartered from the Air Corps at a London base.) I was leading the group for about a mile when I bumped into Lieutenant Meason from H Company and he took charge. From here we approached the bridge and held same."

"I was hit by small-arms fire as I landed in a swamp," said PFC Lawrence Davidson. "I fell in a canal ditch and a 501st man came along and pulled me out. After he left me, Gordon

Laudick from my company came along and helped me to an aid station. There were so many hurt worse than myself that I picked up a gun and went on. I found Colonel Johnson and his group from the 501st and fought with them for three days."

In his summary of the Normandy engagement, Lieutenant Richard P. Meason reported his personnel losses, the majority of whom were lost on D-Day. He wrote: "I jumped in Normandy with a total of my company and attached troops of 208 enlisted men and 11 officers. I took back to England 69 enlisted men and 4 officers. During the Normandy engagement I received my first Purple Heart."

Item Company

I Company was another unit that suffered the "misfortune" of dropping on or in close proximity to its assigned area, Drop Zone "D." This was noted by a report from Lieutenant James F. Nye, who said, "We lost one plane due to enemy fire and another dropped its stick in the Channel. Our pathfinders, to which my 2nd Platoon contributed a squad for security personnel, plus my assistant platoon leader, Lieutenant John Windish, jumped on top of waiting German paratroopers and were killed or captured. I had the rest of the platoon on the drop zone. I assembled with the rest of 3rd Battalion and with the few officers we had, we sent out patrols to determine our location and then proceeded to our objective. Our 60mm mortar was the battalion's sole artillery. Our company commander, Captain John McKnight, was captured and our executive officer, Lieutenant John Kiley, assumed command."

Two of the men who landed at the eastern end of DZ "D" and managed to work their way down to the southeast through marshy land crisscrossed with irrigation canals were Corporal Ted "Zeep" Dziepak and T/5 Elmer Gilbertson. "I landed in a canal just a few hundred yards southeast of Vierville," said Corporal Dziepak. "The canopy fell on the bank and the breeze pulled me out and into a swamp. I had to collapse my chute in the swamp. I watched other jumpers come in with searchlight beams focused on the open doorways. The men were under heavy fire from the ground. We were to take some pillboxes and gun emplacements near the bridges. We succeeded in taking an antiaircraft gun emplacement after our Lieutenant James D. Holstun was killed by 20mm or .50-caliber machine-gun fire. He had collected about twelve men before we attacked the position.

"While on the way to regroup with more men, we came upon another gun emplacement from which we received fire. We dove for roadside ditches which were in line for an enemy machine gunner. Somebody yelled, 'Get back on the road and lie down!' We saw the enemy position after Jerry threw up some flares. We got back into the swamp to get at the gun with a flanking movement. We heard the explosion of a grenade. It knocked out the enemy gunner. Then more enemy fire came at us from another position, so we pulled back into the swamp until daybreak. At that time we discovered that there were only three of us together. We waded a canal and flooded area to join more men in the distance, being all the while under constant fire from snipers and machine gunners."

"I had to step over a gaping hole in the floor near the doorway," said Corporal "Shorty" Gilbertson. "The plane on our left was burning and troopers were piling out. I landed alone in the center of a small field. A machine gun cut loose from the corner and rifle fire came from another direction but the fire was high. I got loose from my harness, took a compass bearing and headed in the direction that I believed would take me to the bridges. I bumped into Lieutenant Nye during the early morning. I had a comparatively uneventful trip to the bridges. I had to go through the area of the enemy machine-gun position in order to follow the compass bearing. I met a rather large group of men, who were unfamiliar to me, and stayed with them for a while. Then I left them as their direction started to vary from the one I wanted. Eventually I got to the area of the bridges. I met Jim Millican under a tree in a wide open field. He pointed out a shallow ditch I should follow in getting to the exposed bridge positions. A few moments later Jim was killed by a tree burst after I had moved off. One trooper ahead of me was wounded in the trip through the ditch. I patched him up with his first aid pack and proceeded to the bridge, which was nearest to an old house."

Two other troopers, Sergeant Harry Watson and T/5 Gene Kristie, did not reach the wooden bridges. Sergeant Watson, who was in charge of intelligence in his company, had landed in water in a flooded area less than a mile north of the bridges. He said, "I was shot in the head immediately upon landing but I managed to crawl to high ground in the vicinity."

T/5 Gene Kristie reported, "I was the last man in the last I Company plane when we got the green light to jump. I landed in water and had a difficult time getting out of my equipment because it was so wet. We spent all night trying to form a group to get to our objective. During the day we were captured along with our captain, John McKnight. Most of the men around us seemed to be members of the 502nd Regiment."

Another man whose arrival at the bridges was delayed for a day was PFC William P. Galbraith, a machine gunner in Lieutenant Jim Nye's platoon, but aboard another aircraft. He landed just south of St. Come-du-Mont along with his first sergeant Paul Garrison. He was to find himself holding the locks with Colonel Johnson's regiment instead of fighting at the wooden bridges with his own 3rd Battalion comrades. As Galbraith explained it, "I didn't see anyone near me get hit. There were no signals, lights, or bugle to assemble. I cut Sergeant Garrison free of his harness as he had broken an ankle. We tried to keep up with some 501st men we met but the sergeant couldn't keep up so we were more or less left alone. We found an equipment bundle and I managed to re-supply myself with ammo for my machine gun; damned near got shot for my trouble as the enemy had the bundle covered. We were forced to stay in a hedgerow until daylight as some of the boys from the 501st got caught out in the open in the light of a flare and were machine-gunned. When day broke we saw some of our troops just south of us about six hundred yards across a field. Sergeant Garrison had me go across the field to make contact with the distant group. I was forced to leave one box of machine-gun ammo on the way when a Kraut took target practice on me. I started out with two boxes and all the maps that Garrison had, as he was afraid he would be captured before I got back to him.

"After crossing the field I made contact with part of the 501st, and met Marion Hove from my company. He had joined their group. I informed them of Sergeant Garrison's position. Hove and I went back for Garrison. When we got back, he was crossing the field by hobbling on his broken ankle. He said he wasn't going to stay over there by himself. We took him to the 501st medics. Then Hove and I joined the 501st in the fighting at the locks. I told them I was a machine gunner and that Hove was my assistant. I wanted someone I knew around me. Anyway they gave me and Hove a machine gun and we stayed with them until D plus 1, when the P-51's bombed our bridges."

During the early morning operations at the bridge, Captain Shettle had received word by way of a patrol that Colonel Johnson had control of the locks which were a mile and a half west of his bridge position. Having gone to seek aid from that source, Shettle had found that Johnson intended to keep his 250-man force intact at the locks. Shettle did manage to get off a message by Lieutenant Farrell's radio hookup to the fleet standing offshore. The message was to be relayed to General Taylor asking for supplies and reinforcements, but it was never delivered to Division Headquarters.

The fact that he was able to send a message on the radio had given Shettle a lift because he certainly hadn't received any other encouragement on the visit to the locks. However during the early evening, 40 men arrived who had been dropped east of Carentan. With them were two bundles, one loaded with rifle ammunition, the other with K-rations. As darkness approached, several of the engineers and demolitions men who had been assigned to the mission wired the bridges for destruction in case the Germans began a strong counterattack. As D-Day came to an end for this group, they lay in their positions waiting for the enemy to make his move.[6]

In summarizing the actions of the 3rd Battalion, Dr.

Bernard J. Ryan, assistant surgeon for the battalion, wrote, "Of our battalion, Lieutenant Colonel Robert Wolverton and his executive officer, Major George Grant, had been killed on the jump, as had Captain Van Antwerp, commander of G Company. The three other company commanders, Captain Reed of Battalion Headquarters Company, Captain Harwick from H Company, and Captain McKnight of I Company had been captured. Captain Harwick escaped and became the battalion commander later. Captain Shettle, the S-3, was the senior officer of the battalion to arrive at the objective and took command there.

"All the companies' first sergeants had been killed or captured. Of the men of the 3rd Battalion, only 117 men of about 800 reached the objective. Our objective, the bridges across the Douve River, were later knocked out by American planes, but the Germans were unable to use them to bring up troops toward Utah Beach."

CHAPTER 15

The Glider Lifts

The original plan of the 101st Airborne Division was to send in, at daybreak of D-Day, by gliders, an entire infantry regiment, the Division Headquarters, field artillery, a communications company, and more medics. These would supplement the paratroopers to be dropped earlier. The gliders were to be towed by C-47 planes.

On hand to provide the transportation for these personnel and material were two different types of gliders, the American-built Waco CG-4A and the British-developed Horsa glider.

The Waco CG-4A, the American-built glider, had a tubular steel framework covered with canvas. It was smaller than the Horsa, more maneuverable, and could land on smaller fields. The payload was limited to 3,750 pounds. It could carry thirteen combat-equipped soldiers plus a crew of two, or it might carry a jeep or a quarter-ton trailer with a crew of three. Another type of load was a 57mm antitank gun with its handlers. On some missions the load could be increased by one glider trooper if one of them was qualified to serve as the copilot.

Equipment was moved into the glider through a hinged nose section, which served as the pilot's compartment. The hinged nose was raised and a jeep was backed in. Soldiers entered the craft through a side door. The tubular steel framework provided considerable safety during a crash landing.

The British-built Horsa was a much larger, all-plywood glider with a payload of 6,700 pounds. It provided space for a jeep with an attached howitzer, or a jeep with a trailer full of supplies, or a group of 32 airborne soldiers. The equipment was loaded through a large side door. To allow for quick unloading upon landing, the tail section was blown off by the use of primer cord explosives that jettisoned the back third of the craft. An ax applied to some bolts served the same purpose if necessary. Portable ramps carried in the glider were then used to move the vehicles to the ground.

The Horsa glider could land with a steeper glider due to the huge wing flaps. The glide speeds of the Horsa and Waco were similar. One danger, in a crash, was the fact that the Horsa splintered badly. The glider pilots of the Troop Carrier Command of the American 9th Air Force were not as familiar in flying them and preferred the smaller Waco glider.

Just prior to D-Day, the invasion planners received information from the G-2 Department of the Allied High Command that anti-glider traps and obstacles were being installed by the enemy. Some of these were known as "Rommel's Asparagus." These were sharply pointed poles stuck upright into the ground and interspersed on potential airborne landing fields. Barbed wire with attached mines was strung from pole to pole. Another obstacle was a deep ditch dug across any field suitable for airborne landings. Both obstacles were designed to cause crash landings. The French underground also reported the movement of crack antiaircraft units from the Russian front into the area around St. Come-du-Mont.

Authorities at Allied headquarters decided to revise the plans so that the gliders would arrive during the predawn hours to give greater safety from anticipated ground fire. The serial was further limited to artillerymen with antitank guns, some medical people with a portable field hospital, and some key radio communication equipment. One glider was to transport a small bulldozer to be used in clearing hedgerows to increase the size of the glider-landing fields and for making landing strips for light observation aircraft.

Another serial, or lift was to arrive before nightfall of D-Day with similar personnel and equipment. A third group, including the 327th Glider Infantry Regiment, was to be moved to the seaborne marshaling areas. They were to arrive at Utah Beach behind the 4th Infantry Division.

The revised plans involving the predawn flight were vigorously opposed by the Troop Carrier Command and the airborne divisions. The officers who were physically involved in the operation felt that one-half of the total force would be lost in crashes resulting from landing without adequate light upon small fields. That the fields had been prepared with traps was enough hazard even in daytime.

One of those who had been vocal in his displeasure at the changes was Colonel Mike Murphy of the A-3 Section of the Troop Carrier Command. He was in charge of the training program of the glider pilots. He wrote,[1] "My first orders were to train American pilots on the Horsa glider. In accordance with my instructions, we were to fly into Normandy at first light. I spent night and day traveling to the various bases demonstrating the ability of the British gliders on correct method of flight and approach and training men to land at first light.

"Approximately one week before the lift, we received orders to change to the American Waco gliders and that we would have to land in total darkness. Three days before the lift, I was called to a meeting of the high-ranking officers involved in the fracas. This included Generals Montgomery, Mallory, Vandenberg, Williams, and other Troop Carrier generals. I explained at this meeting that we could expect a minimum of 50 percent casualties if the operation was run at night and Montgomery mentioned that we would have to suffer it; that plans could not be changed at this time. We then scheduled the gliders to land in Normandy at 0400, thus giving the paratroopers two hours to evacuate the fields in which we were to land. Also, we were assured by the Air Force that the area would be neutralized, and that there would be very little enemy action during our landing."

As a minor concession to the pilots and glider troops, the planners offered the exclusive use of the safer, metal-framed Waco CG-4A glider for the night flight.

This caused a hasty revision in the load plans and forced drastic changes and reductions. The Waco had a payload of slightly more than half of the Horsa. Unit commanders had to prepare their loads on a priority basis—which equipment did they need first in France. Then only those priority items and personnel were assigned to the predawn mission. The first glider lift was known as the *Chicago Mission* and was limited to 52 gliders carrying 148 airborne soldiers with their equipment. Forty-four of these gliders carried sixteen guns and personnel of the 81st Airborne Antitank and Anti-aircraft Battalion. The 57mm guns (six pounders) were to be used in support of the parachute regiments against armored counterattacks. Two gliders carried engineers with a small bulldozer.

Two gliders contained vital signal equipment. One of these contained a special SCR-499 radio mounted in a quarter-ton trailer. It was handled by a three-man crew. The second signal glider contained a radio-equipped jeep with a two-man team. It was to tow the radio trailer from the landing zone to Division Headquarters at Hiesville. Three gliders assigned to the division medical company carried a portable field hospital. The chief of the first glider echelon was Brigadier General Donald F. Pratt, the assistant division commander of the 101st. He rode in the lead glider which was piloted by Lieutenant Colonel Mike Murphy, top glider pilot in the European Theater of War. A jeep driven by the general's aide, Lieutenant John L. May, was included in the load.

A second serial of 32 Horsa gliders was scheduled to land at 2100 on the evening of D-Day. It carried 165 airborne reinforcements for the antitank force, division medics, division headquarters personnel, and signal company men and equipment. The vehicles included more jeeps and some motorcycles for the airborne dispatch riders. Six more antitank guns and their crews from the 327th Glider Infantry Regiment and 19 tons of miscellaneous equipment filled out the load. The evening lift was given the code name *Keokuk Mission*. Both serials were assigned to use Landing Zone "E" near Hiesville.

The Chicago Mission

The gliders for the Chicago Mission were lined up on the runways on the afternoon of June 5th with all equipment firmly lashed in place. Captain Charles Van Gorder described the scene: "The gliders were lined up on each side of the runway for what appeared to be at least a mile. They were sitting so the first plane would pull its glider from a line on the left, the second from the right, and so on. Colonel Mike Murphy and General Pratt were in Glider number 1 and I was in Glider 2 in the lineup, which was the order in which we went into France."

The last-minute preparations of the glidermen before they marched out to their silent crafts were similar to that of the paratroopers. Captain Van Gorder stated, "Before we started, we put powdered charcoal over our hands, face, and neck to blend in with the darkness. We were also given a luminous button to pin under the lapel of our jump jackets and a popping cricket, which most of the boys taped to their rifle stocks. We went to our gliders as preassigned about 12 midnight on the night of June 5th. We were each given a Dramamine tablet to prevent airsickness. This was the first time I had seen this drug as it was new."

While it was clear and bright over the drop zones, the glider takeoffs took place during rain squalls. Lieutenant William G. Padrick recalled the airfield that night: "As we walked out to the glider it was dark and overcast and a storm was coming. While waiting in the glider, we had a brisk shower during which time my memories turned back to a statement made during a last speech to the men that we would take no prisoners on the first day. I wondered if the Germans would have a similar policy with captured airborne troops."

PFC George S. Schulist rode in the same glider with Lieutenant Padrick as his jeep driver. He said, "It rained the night we took off, and it rained on and off during the early part of the flight." The glider carrying General Pratt began its takeoff at 0119 from its base at Aldermaston, England. The remaining gliders were quickly hooked to their tow craft and the entire lift was quickly airborne and assembled into flights of four as they made a final sweep over the airfield.

In an unusual incident, one of the 52 gliders quickly returned to earth. Private Edward Hajduk was on board. He said, "I was in the glider carrying the jeep that was to tow the

SCR-499 radio trailer from the landing zone to the command post. Our glider broke loose from its tow craft shortly after takeoff. The pilot brought it down safely in a large field approximately four miles from the airbase. In a few minutes we were racing back to the airfield.

"There we were questioned individually by a military police officer to determine whether or not the release had been deliberate or accidental. A short time later, our group was cleared and we rushed to the takeoff area where another glider was quickly readied for our use. The jeep was loaded into this glider. Ground crew personnel quickly hooked it to a tow plane. Without further incident, we arrived over the landing zone in Normandy at approximately 0600, two hours later than scheduled."

T/5 Bill Lees, one of the operators for the high-powered radio set, recalled that his craft had a darned smooth takeoff. "The three of us started smoking right away and I think there were at least two cigarettes going all the way to the French coast. We tried talking but it was too noisy. Passing over the Channel, I could see boats below which I knew would be at the beachhead the next day."

The gliders in the Chicago Mission followed the plan as the earlier troop carrier planes. Colonel Murphy said, "The lift was flown across the water at 2,000 feet to 1,500 feet passing between the Guernsey and Jersey islands. We hit the west coast of the Peninsula around 2,000 feet and lowered to around 600 feet."

Captain Van Gorder was impressed with the view as he looked back toward the rear of the column. "That was a very impressive scene. When we were in a curve, one could see the blue formation lights on the top of the planes' wings, stretched back through the sky like a graceful ribbon for miles."

Van Gorder continued his story: "For this Normandy trip with the assault wave, we had a pilot and copilot and each man had a flak suit. My glider carried myself and four or five enlisted men, all seated around a lashed-down jeep trailer containing sterile supplies for 75 operations." The rain clouds disappeared. The sky became almost cloudless over the Channel, and the planes and gliders cast ghostly shadows upon the water.

T/3 Johnny Walker, T/4 Marion Byrd, and T/5 Bill Lees, the radiomen in charge of the surviving radio set, were unaware that the other crew had suffered a premature release over English soil. Their radio trailer was firmly lashed behind the pilot's compartment. The airborne soldiers sat behind the trailer with Byrd and Walker occupying seats on the right side while Lees sat directly in front of the door on a little hinged seat.

As they flew on, Lees reflected, "My thoughts went back to the preparation for the ride, and I recalled how Lieutenant James Moore, the officer in charge of the Signal Company glider echelon, had fussed nervously over us all afternoon and into the night. Lieutenant Moore's own group was not leaving for another twelve hours, but he had been seeing each of his boys off with the parting remark, 'I'll be praying for you guys.' It left us with a warm glow."

The radio team chief, T/3 Johnny Walker remembered, "I flashed my light on periodically to check the lashings. It was much too noisy for talk. We sat in silence with only the red glow of cigarettes indicating each one's presence. Below us, in the moonlight, we could see the long silvery wakes of the ships, in convoy, headed for the invasion beaches further to the east."

As the coast of France appeared below them, the pilots of the tow planes brought their ships to a lower altitude. It remained quiet for a few minutes. Flak began to thump around the tows and gliders. Small-arms fire snapped through the tail section of the radio glider. Walker added, "The glider swerved madly from side to side as the pilot tried what little evasive action he could at the end of his tow rope."

Colonel Murphy at the wheel of the number 1 glider recalled, "It was a beautiful and peaceful night and then about halfway across the twenty-two miles of Cherbourg Peninsula, we encountered heavy ground fire from there to the landing zone. Colonel W. B. Whiteacre and General Beech were flying the lead tow plane and we were on schedule at all checkpoints. I did not experience antiaircraft fire; however, the corridor was completely lit up by tracer bullets, forming all kinds of patterns. I recall talking by telephone to the tow airplane, which had not seen the first tracers. The pilot asked me where they were coming from and if we were hit. It appeared they were aiming at the exhaust flames, but we had a number of strikes in our machine."

Relating his account of the flight over the peninsula, Captain Van Gorder stated, "We were to go in over the west side of the Cotentin Peninsula, opposite from the Omaha and Utah Beaches because, as was explained to us, this side had been given concentrated bombing for the past few days and nights by the Allied planes and was completely bombed-out. Everything was quiet until we passed over the coastline. This suddenly lit up like a gasoline bonfire all along the coast for miles. We were flying at an altitude of 600 feet to be above the small-arms fire and below the ack-ack range. We held our course in the face of all this explosive activity, which I thought showed great bravery on the part of the pilots and copilots, and went in over the coast, deep into the peninsula's base, then turned toward the beaches on the opposite side.

"At one time, a German 88mm gun fired almost straight up at us, just missing, but the blast sent our glider high into the air. Fortunately, we were pulled back in line by the tow rope. All along the way to our landing zone we received sporadic small-arms fire."

T/5 Bill Lees[2] wrote, "All too soon, we hit the coast of France. It looked dark, quiet, and peaceful from the air, but only for a while. About two miles inland, all hell broke loose. At first, it wasn't close but then we were in the middle of it. Tracers ripped through the tail of the glider and flak burst so close that the glider bounced from side to side. We were in the hotbox for about ten minutes. How we ever got through the barrage, I'll never figure out."

"As we flew over land, I could see fire flash from the guns on the ground," remembered PFC George Schulist. "The flak was so heavy that to me it looked like the Fourth of July from the sky. I saw one C-47 get hit by flak and crash to the ground."

An artilleryman, Sergeant John Weaver, related, "We met some flak. It looked like everything under us was on fire—probably the Air Corps had paid them a visit."

Lieutenant Padrick from the same unit remarked, "We began to receive antiaircraft fire—beautiful, yet frightening, orange balls of fire coming up through the air and arching off in a curve. Always the fire was directed at the tow ship ahead, with its exhausts belching bright blue flames. The antiaircraft fire, though directed at the tow planes, was also in front of us, so we had to pass through it—with no parachutes. Our only comfort was to try and get further into our helmets.

"As we established a route, the Germans marked this with orange flares. Everything had been done to save our eyes, and all of a sudden we were blinded by clusters of bright orange lights."

The tow craft picked up the beams emitted by the Eureka set up on Landing Zone "E" shortly after they arrived over the coast. This area was located on the western edge of Drop Zone "C" near Hiesville.

Colonel Murphy described the area. "We had computed the average field to be 800 feet in length, and the longest landing run was 1,200 feet. Also, during the briefing, myself and others had studied reconnaissance photos and determined the height of the trees, and all pilots knew they could expect forty to sixty foot trees bordering the landing area."

The lift of gliders managed to stay in formation of flights of four, in right echelon, even in the area of intense flak and small-arms fire. Colonel Murphy added, "This permitted a left 90-degree turn by missions and they would be in landing pattern. Because so many gliders were in preflight at the same time, in practically the same zone, we designed a landing pattern for each machine to avoid midair collisions. Each glider pilot was to use the pattern regardless, which for the most part they did; thus resulting in landing the machines from all cardinal points of the compass. We were unfortunate in that there was a twenty-seven mile an hour tailwind blowing on our landing pattern and many machines ended in the fencerows. Some missions, including mine, had a

270-degree pattern to our landing area. A lot of the glider pilots had a 90-degree and 180-degree pattern. This was necessary to keep gliders separated in free flight after cutoff. I think that every third aircraft did land in a separate field."

As they approached the landing zone at an elevation of 400 feet, the pilots could see the green lights of the T flashing before them. The serial split into columns of two to avoid congestion. In their turns, most of the pilots lost sight of the ground signals and released over the smaller fields outside the boundaries of Landing Zone "E." The T had been set up by Lieutenant Lawrence G. Hensley's pathfinders. Captain Lillyman, the commanding officer for the D-Day pathfinder groups, remembered, "The lights were set up and working well until the second glider in on that field smashed into the string of lights as it slid over the grass. The remaining gliders had to land by moonlight."

Colonel Murphy brought his glider in near Hiesville on the proper field. He said, "My wheels were locked and sliding on the dew-covered grass for approximately eight hundred feet, when normally we could stop in two hundred to three hundred feet. My machine, in addition to carrying a jeep, had all the command radio equipment and was about one thousand pounds overloaded. If it weren't for maintaining air discipline, we could more easily have landed in the other direction and could have stopped midway on the field.

"In my machine also was Lieutenant Lee May, General Pratt's aide. I recall whispering back to whoever could listen that we were within a few feet of a German tank column. At this time, I was projected through the trees, my body shoved out the left side of the glider and I was looking at those machines, wondering when they were going to come to life. For some reason for which I will never be able to explain, they moved on. I counted five. One tank couldn't get started and it was later rendered useless by one of the paratroopers."

Captain Van Gorder described his landing as follows: "Finally, our twelve-hundred foot landing field came into view, pictured just as we had learned in the briefings. After turning loose from our C-47 tow ship, we made a landing in an area that seemed perfect. It would have been perfect had it not

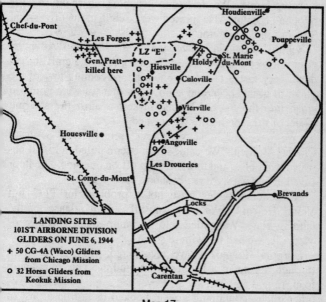

Map 17

LANDING SITES
101ST AIRBORNE DIVISION
GLIDERS ON JUNE 6, 1944
+ 50 CG-4A (Waco) Gliders
  from Chicago Mission
o 32 Horsa Gliders from
  Keokuk Mission

Houdienville
Chef-du-Pont
Les Forges
Pouppeville
LZ "E"
Gen. Pratt
killed here
Hiesville
Holdy
St. Marie
du-Mont
Culoville
Houesville
Vierville
Angoville
Les Droueries
St. Come-du-Mont
Brevands
Locks
Carentan

been for the grass being wet with dew. With the brakes on, we slid about a thousand feet into a hedgerow. A tree, approximately one and a half feet in diameter, stopped us suddenly. The glider struck the tree center between the pilot and copilot."

Seated in their firmly lashed-down jeep, Lieutenant Padrick and driver George Schulist provided recollections of their landing. Padrick recollected, "We missed the landing zone by several miles. We crashed in an apple orchard injuring the pilot and copilot. Also injured were Schulist, my driver, and Sitz, our radio operator."

Schulist provided his version of the landing: "After the pilot released the tow rope from the glider, the craft started down very fast. I could see the treetops coming toward the glider at great speed and soon I saw that we were going to crash into the trees. I braced myself against the steering wheel of the jeep before we crashed."

"We were cut loose very low," remembered Sergeant Charles Marden. "We came down over a poled field, hit between two poles, and tore the wing off on one side. The floor caved in and we were really shook up."

Airborne obstacles were not a problem for PFC Jim Viano. He said, "We were way off on our release for the landing zone. We glided into a swamp south and east of Vierville. We had to swim to shore."

Corporal Eugene Howe recollected, "My glider went through a gate in a hedgerow in landing. The companion load tripped and cartwheeled over the same hedgerow. Another glider, containing a jeep, hooked its tail on a post in landing and Corporal Jim Pate received fatal injuries."

It took expert handling to land such temperamental craft. T/3 Johnny Walker related his pilot's maneuvering: "Our glider brushed a treetop and slipped sharply into a small field. I held my breath and waited for the impending crash. Instead the pilot got it leveled out and touched down in a field softened by the heavy rains of the past several days. As the pilot applied the brakes, the tail section rose sharply threatening to flip over. Gradually it settled down as the glider came to a halt."

The field markers had been wiped out by one of the early gliders. The partly obscured moon was now sinking down in the western sky. It became increasingly difficult for the pilots to recognize the fields in the landing zone. Only six of them dropped into the confines of the zone. Another fifteen landed within half a mile, while another ten landed in a closely packed group west of Les Forges. The others were scattered east and southeast of the proper zone. One tow plane strayed from formation and released its glider five miles south of Carentan. Enemy fire brought down one plane and its glider approximately eight miles west of the landing zone.

After the shock had worn off from the crash landings, the men began to think about getting into areas more safe than the confines of the wrecked gliders. Colonel Murphy had been thrown partially outside of his glider. He said, "Lieutenant LeMay had a submachine gun and stood guard while I unscrewed myself out of the mass of tubing. When I lowered myself to the ground, hanging to the glider nose, I was unable to stand up and fell in the side ditch. I finally got back into the field and asked LeMay to check on the passengers and he said they were seriously injured, if not worse. I remember asking him to check their pulses and he said he tried but was so nervous he couldn't get any results. I believe he was in the midst of trying to help me over to the machine when Captain Van Gorder arrived."

Captain Van Gorder, whose glider had struck a tree, found much medical work awaiting him as he scouted the wreckage of several gliders. He said, "I stepped out the side door to evaluate our situation. About that time another glider whistled across the field and slid into our tail section, headfirst. This was very unusual. I went back to see what happened and while walking around our craft, a frightened herd of cattle came stampeding by. There were two fortunate happenings that night: (1) Our field was one of the few that the Germans hadn't fortified with anti-glider poles and (2) Our glider stopped in an area shaded from the moonlight by the large tree we had struck.

"I went up to the hedgerow and looked over into a road. The earthen bank was about five and a half feet high, and I could see over it well enough to identify three small German tanks, stopped in the road, with Germans sitting on the sides of the tanks, with their rifles across their laps trying to see into the field where we had landed. I was so close to them that I thought they saw me and would at least throw a potato masher over the hedge. I scampered down the hedgerow bank and they drove away.

"I walked down the hedgerow about fifty to one hundred feet, where another glider had done the same thing as ours. I talked to the pilot who had by then extracted himself from the wreckage. He was Colonel Mike Murphy, who had suffered a fractured femur. He said he would be OK until I could check the inside of the distorted glider and see how General Pratt and the copilot had fared. By then a lieutenant, the general's aide, had rounded up some paratroopers and guarded the glider while I took off my gear in order to get in through the wreckage. There I found the general sitting in the front seat of the jeep with his head bent forward on his chest and no pulse felt anywhere. I assumed that when the glider struck the hedgerow, he had been instantly killed by his helmet coming forward and snapping his neck. The copilot registered no pulse either. He had taken the brunt of the force in his position.

"We got Colonel Murphy squared away somehow and comfortable when just before dawn I saw a figure coming across the other side of the field. This turned out to be Major Albert J. Crandal, who had landed elsewhere and worked his way to our location."

Colonel Murphy added, "I remember Major Crandal and myself looking at a picture and marking it as to our exact location and suggesting the route to the château which the medics had apparently picked out prior to the lift. One of the medical officers sent two corpsmen to secure it. There was some conversation about my leg and a promise to send someone back to pick me up. I refused sedatives at the time because I wanted to remain alert. During the early part of the day, I was loaned an M-1 (my weapon was bent in a bow shape) and managed to scoot up and down the side ditch doing a little shooting whenever it would help."

Captain Van Gorder added, "Soon after dawn, when we had gathered up several wounded from adjacent areas, Major Crandal found some men with a jeep and set out in search of the Château Colombières where he began setting up our hospital and then returned to pick up the wounded and myself."

All members in the glider in which Lieutenant Padrick had landed were knocked out as a result of the crash. Padrick recalled, "On coming to, I kicked out the escape panel and stepped out to tumble end over end as we were wedged in the crotch of a tree.

"I removed the ninety-pound flak jacket and with cotton in my mouth from fright, tried to reconnoiter the area. All the while as I crawled and crouched, something was riding up around my neck and choking me half to death. After having gone several hundred yards on all fours and been shot at, I returned to the glider to find that I still had on my phosphorescent Mae West life preserver, which made me an outstanding target for a great distance."

Shortly after Lieutenant Padrick went off on his reconnaissance, PFC Schulist regained consciousness. He likewise stepped out of the escape door and pitched headfirst onto the ground. He said, "I was stunned because it was farther than I had anticipated. I got up from the ground and heard someone walking and talking. I used my cricket and clicked, I received a response. In the shadows, I could barely make out some paratroopers. They said they were from the 566th Regiment."

Schulist returned to his glider to assess the physical condition of the other men. He said, "The pilot had a broken leg and the copilot had a busted kneecap. My face was banged up. My nose was bleeding as were my upper and lower lips and my lower teeth were loosened. This had occurred after I hit my head against the steering wheel. (We were riding in the jeep). My chinstrap had broken from the helmet and the steel shell had landed on the hood of the jeep.

"I called Sitz to help me lift the pilot up and we placed him on the hood of the jeep to help ease his pain. His leg was broken by a sheared off tree stump that broke through the floor of the glider."

Lieutenant Padrick corroborated this account: "All the others now having revived, we administered to the pilot and copilot and the three of us (Schulist, Sitz, and I) took off as we had a mission. As an officer, my mission that night was to protect General Pratt, and at daylight, to assault with the glider forces, the village of Hiesville. However, as we did not land on the designated landing zone, and as I was lost and unable to find the DZ, I found a stick of 82nd Airborne men and joined them to form a roadblock and wait for daylight."

Another crash landing was described by Sergeant Marden: "The floor had caved in and so we had to take our antitank gun out of the side of the glider. One of our pilots was injured. We tried to regroup after removing the gun and helping the wounded. I recall removing Corporal Jim Pate from his glider. He was beyond help with a head injury."

Sergeant John Weaver had landed in what appeared to be a small lake. He said, "I had lost my helmet on the landing but soon found it. All was quiet at 0405 A.M. by my PX watch. We assembled by using our crickets. We lay in a hedgerow until daylight. We later spotted a medical jeep and followed it to our assembly area after helping to burn some gliders. Our mission was to use our antitank guns on all enemy tanks passing our lines."

The glider which carried the heavy radio trailer met no obstacles on its landing. Bill Lees related, "We got out of the glider—me first—and when I hit the dirt, there was nothing but cow manure. But that was the least of my worries. There was machine-gun and rifle fire down at the end of the field and it got pretty rough for a while. I saw two more gliders land. Later, a short distance away, I saw the glider in which General Pratt lost his life. His pilot, Colonel Murphy, was lying in a ditch—alive, but injured. We stayed in a ditch until about 1000 A.M. when it was fairly safe to move around. A jeep towed us to the CP."

"With the glider pilots aiding us, we quickly unlashed the trailer," said radio team chief Johnny Walker. "The nose was unlatched and raised and the trailer was jockeyed from within. Next we maneuvered it into the shelter of a hedgerow.

All of us took cover in the ditch beside the hedge. We waited for our jeep to arrive from its landing spot. (Little did we know it was still in England.)

"Time passed. Firing continued in the area until daylight and suddenly slackened and finally ceased. Our group was getting anxious. I directed Sergeant Byrd to go down the hedgerow in one direction looking for a jeep while I went another way. Lees and the glider pilots stayed on guard duty to protect the valuable radio equipment.

"About 0900, Byrd hailed a jeep that was being driven from one of the fields by a lieutenant of one of the parachute regiments. He asked the officer if he would tow our radio trailer to the Division CP and this he consented to do very quickly. Byrd directed the officer to the hidden trailer. I was just returning empty-handed from the other direction. The trailer was quickly hooked on and the entire group loaded into the trailer and onto the jeep. With no more incidents along the way, our radio team arrived in Hiesville before 1000 A.M. The officer in charge directed the trailer into a nearby field where it was covered with camouflage netting. The gasoline-powered generator was carried farther down the hedgerow. Foxholes were hastily dug in the shelter of the hedgerow bank. We were ready for business."

In the meantime, Colonel Thomas Sherburne, Captain Cecil Wilson, and PFC Julian Necikowski from Division Artillery, had arrived at the fields shortly after the landings had been completed. With a small group of ten infantry paratroopers, they had proceeded from the division headquarters assembly area (to the south of St. Marie-du-Mont) to aid in directing the glider troops and equipment to the command post at Hiesville. Because everyone had been confused about the location of the assembly point, Colonel Sherburne had waited until first light revealed the church spire at St. Marie-du-Mont. He learned his correct position.

Sherburne's recollection of the event is as follows: "In the D-Day planning, the division staff had directed me to move out from the command post with a company of paratroopers to provide cover and direction for the glider arrivals. Because of the scattered jumps, the force had been limited to ten men. Along the route of march to the landing zone, we picked up a large number of 82nd and 101st paratroopers. Our group was shot at several times resulting in the wounding of two men.

"We had failed to arrive at the field before the first gliders landed. However, the pathfinders had been on hand to light the field and guide the craft with their radio beacon and as our group arrived, these men were already beginning to depart for other assigned tasks. Some of them were busy collecting supply bundles in the surrounding fields.

"We located General Pratt's glider and noted that General Pratt and the copilot were beyond aid. Colonel Murphy was located in a ditch and was given additional first aid. The general's aide was not present. He had gone in search of help. The occupants of the last gliders were still unloading at the fields under fire from a German machine gun, which was set up in a tree platform covering several of the larger fields. This gun fired at anyone who moved on the fields.

"From positions of concealment in the hedgerows, we yelled directions to the glidermen and steered them away from the machine gun. Small-arms fire was snapping about the area and mortar shells were thumping into the fields as the glider reinforcements found their way to our group using the cover of the hedgerows."

During the morning, this group collected 115 glider troops, 3 jeeps, 6 antitank guns, and 35 prisoners and proceeded toward Hiesville. The infantrymen sought out and dispersed the snipers who persisted along the route. Sherburne's crew reached Hiesville at noon and proceeded to set up the command post prior to the arrival of General Taylor and his staff later in the day.

Lieutenant Padrick, whose responsibility had been to provide security for General Pratt, arrived at the designated landing zone in the afternoon. He related, "I found only six gliders there, where we should have had twenty-six, and only one of them was undamaged.

"My mission was a failure before it began. General Pratt was dead. The efforts to protect him had killed him. The bottom of the glider had been armor-plated with steel plates and he sat on a parachute pack. The steel plates increased the glider's weight and added to its landing roll. The parachute elevated him. The general was a short man, but sitting on a parachute pack, he was just high enough for his head to strike a cross member in the glider, and this broke his neck when his glider crashed into trees at the end of the field. Until late that afternoon, we remained in the area tending the wounded and posting guards," Padrick concluded.

PFC Schulist had arrived at the landing zone with Lieutenant Padrick. He related, "The lieutenant told me that I should go to the 506th command post because they wanted a jeep driver. When I reported there, I was told to drive down the road and pick up General Taylor. When I reached his area, I found him walking toward the CP with two MP's. I told him that I had been sent by the 506th men to pick him up. He said he preferred to walk."

A few hundred yards to the north of the command post, the division medics were busy with their field hospital. They had selected the Château Colombières as the most suitable site for their work. The men had arrived from the glider fields with their trailers filled with operating equipment. These were rigged quickly. The surgeons were ready to perform the first operations by noon.

After setting up the radio, the signalmen visited with the members of the Lecaudey family whose home had so suddenly become the center of activity for the 101st Airborne Division. The rough looking Americans with blackened faces were a welcome sight. Sergeant Walker remembered, "Wine was brought from the cellar and our combined group drank toasts to both of our countries, though neither group really understood the language of the other. Byrd and I returned to the radio to make further preparations for the arrival of the headquarters' personnel. Colonel Sherburne had passed on the word to our people that the headquarters paratroopers had planned to participate in the attack on one of the causeways near the beach."

The radio set was placed in operating condition. Shortly after 1400, communications were established. Kangaroo Forward was in contact with Kangaroo Rear (Kangaroo was the code name for the 101st Airborne Division). Since no command personnel had been present earlier to authorize messages, radio traffic was not transmitted for several hours.

General Taylor and his headquarters group arrived at Hiesville at approximately 1700 hours. The division commander appeared pleased with the arrangements which had been made to establish a closely knit headquarters area. A short time later, Captain Bill Breen (Signal Company) had been briefed by Sergeant Walker as to the presence of the two radio sets, which had arrived via glider. (Ed Hajduk and his driver had driven without incident from the glider field earlier.)

Captain Breen notified the division commander that a glider-borne radio was in contact with base camp in England. General Taylor directed a staff officer to draft the first message. The jeep-installed radio was directed to establish contact with 7th Corps Headquarters on its command ship off Utah Beach.

Shortly after 1730, Corporal Lees, who was on duty at the time, began transmitting the first radio message from the continent to England. The message was then decoded at division base camp and relayed by telephone to General Eisenhower at his field headquarters in southern England. [A photostat copy of the message appears on page 327.]

The Keokuk Mission

The second lift of gliders departed from Aldermaston, England, at 1830 P.M. with 32 Horsa gliders towed by C-47's. As has been previously related, the Horsa gliders had not been used on the first lift. Aboard were more antitank gunners with their weapons, a large contingent of division headquarters people including members from the G-departments (G-1, G-2, G-3, and G-4), and more military policemen. Also included were the "Headquarters Commandos," who were the officers' orderlies, cooks, cleanup crews, and guards. A large group of signal company men including wiremen, message center members (code clerks, dispatch riders, and runners), and most of the radio platoon were

THESE SPACES FOR MESSAGE CENTER ONLY

| WE FILED | MSG CEN NO | HOW SENT |

MESSAGE (SUBMIT TO MESSAGE CENTER IN DUPLICATE)   CLASSIFICATION

DATE 6 JUNE 44

BNCROO REAR

IM LL AS FOLLOWS ALL 10
BJECTIVES TAKEN CB COMMUNI-
CATIONS LA CH AD AO FC BA NIC
KK THROUGH ON WF EXITS AO HL
LE AND CL BL EJ HL LC AND
XC LP CN BADLY MIXED THROUGH
DRING EJ REQUEST FM ON CL FC
LE IK LL 1730   (1912:)

OFFICIAL DESIGNATION OF SENDER   TIME SIGNED

AUTHORIZED TO BE
SENT IN CLEAR   SIGNATURE OF OFFICER   SIGNATURE AND GRADE OF WRITER

This photostat is a copy of a message provided for this account by former T/3 Johnny J. Walker of the 101st Airborne Signal Company, team chief of the SCR-499 radio team set up in Hiesville. He said, "We realized the importance of this first message so we made an extra copy of it at the time so I'd have something to remember the occasion."

included. For equipment, they brought along radio jeeps, trailers filled with reels of field wire, switchboards, radio batteries, and motorcycles for the dispatch riders. Another group of medics was also in this serial with stores of plasma, litters, dressings, and surgical equipment. Six gliders contained jeeps with attached .37mm antitank guns and their five-man crews. Thirty men and one officer had been selected from the 327th Glider Infantry Regiment to provide antitank support for the three parachute regiments. Two guns were destined for each of them.

Reports had reached the men before departure that the invasion was progressing well. T/5 Bill Finn remembered, "All during the day, there was much excitement watching the many flights of bombers going and coming on their shuttle bombing runs. One or two of them, as I recall, had to make emergency landings at our field. Then came D-Day afternoon and our turn. As we were standing beside our Horsa glider waiting to load, I remember asking Lieutenant James Moore, who went in with our serial, what word if any had come from the invasion and how things were going. His answer was that everything was just fine, and going great. I'll admit this was a little reassuring."

Master Sergeant John McCarthy was one of the few soldiers to fly into France without spending time in a marshaling area. He recalled, "As a member of G-1 (Personnel Department), my group had been taking reports coming in from the beachhead areas. Two hours before flight departure time, I had been driven to the field. I had a meal in one of the mess tents, and then reported to my glider which was number '4' in the serial.

"Our glider contained a jeep and an attached trailer filled with equipment. The jeep was for Colonel Gerald Higgins, the division chief of staff, who had parachuted in with the division headquarters group. The jeep was driven by T/5 Leo Plotke. The only other person aboard besides the two man crew was an officer from CIC who had arrived in England only two days before. Needless to say, he was overwhelmed with all the rapidly moving events of the past few days."

The takeoff was uneventful though the tow planes had to strain harder to get the heavier gliders off the ground. The planes formed into four-plane columns once more. The skies were relatively clear. The lift passed the IP (Initial Point) at Portland Bill on time. For this serial, the plan called for a different approach to the landing zone. The planes and gliders approached from the east, passing directly over Utah Beach on their way inland.

"On the trip over, one of our men became violently airsick," said PFC Jack Kessel, a radioman from Signal Company. "His urge to lie down in the crowded glider led him to crawl under the jeep. Somehow, the cords on the Mae West life jacket hooked onto the housing of the jeep causing the carbon-dioxide capsule to inflate it. The poor soldier was pinned firmly to the floor by the inflated preserver pressing against the underside of the jeep. The soldier let out some yelps to let the others know of his predicament. Lieutenant James Moore moved forward and punctured the preserver with his combat knife. By the time the soldier crawled forth, the glider was preparing to land."

Only one of the men mentioned looking out at the invasion craft as the gliders flew over the beach. Sergeant John McCarthy was impressed with the magnitude of the invasion fleet. He recalled, "As far as the eye could see, there were ships of all descriptions. Though I had spent months typing landing tables for personnel and equipment, I didn't realize the invasion was to be such a mammoth one."

The landing aids were ready for them. The pathfinders had returned to the field earlier from the command post to direct the evening flight. Captain Frank Lillyman described the aids used to bring this lift in to the landing zone: "For the daytime landing of gliders, my crew and a few others we assembled, did the marking. We used panels for the T, a Eureka set, and green smoke. The panels were placed in a 'T' shape with the Eureka at the north end of the field and the smoke almost in the middle with me."

Enemy soldiers were still a threat to the landings. Small groups had infiltrated the hedgerows about the division command post. Large groups of the enemy were in and about Turqueville, two miles to the north, and in the vicinity of Vierville, and St. Come-du-Mont to the south. These enemy soldiers waited until the gliders were released from their tow craft, and then began peppering them with small arms fire as they descended. Only a small number of the gliders managed to reach the large fields in the DZ. The rest lost altitude rapidly and the pilots had to prepare for landings on fields unsuited for these larger machines. Crackups in trees, ditches, and hedgerows were the rule, rather than the exception.

One of those having a successful landing was Sergeant McCarthy. He related, "Our pilot did a superb job as he dropped onto the soft field. The tricycle landing gear prevented it from nosing over and the glider came to rest twenty yards from a hedgerow."

Finn had one of the typical crash landings. He recollected, "As we got nearer to our landing area, we could clearly see below the anti-airborne obstacles set into the ground just waiting to gouge into us. As the pilot cut loose and began to bank in and drop, we remembered another thing was there—the hedgerows. We were coming in pretty fast and I remember thinking to myself and maybe even loudly, 'Come on, boy, get those flaps down!' We landed at a high rate of speed and missed the stakes and wires but not the hedgerow. As we crashed through, the landing gear tore off and we began skidding on the belly, This was not the best thing for a plywood glider and soon the floor began to disintegrate. The thing came to a stop—but not before my musette bag and ammo pouches had disappeared."

Private Charles Laden, a radioman with Signal Company had this recollection: "Our flight approached Normandy over Utah Beach and passed a few miles inland and cut loose. As we came in for the landing, Pilot Cohen yelled, 'Look out!' The glider flew through a hedgerow, breaking in two. Equipment was tangled in treetops and in the hedgerows. It included motorcycles and key radio equipment. I was thrown out of the glider.

"The odor of gunpowder was very strong. The air was still and not much small-arms fire could be heard. I saw men of the 101st roaming the fields individually seeking out enemy snipers."

Three members of a five-man antitank team from the 327th Glider Regiment (Martin Levak, Arno Whitbread, and Charles Wiszowaty) rode in on the same glider. In charge of the team was Corporal Levak, who stated, "We were riding in Horsa glider LJ-796. British pilots H. W. Staples and C. E. Brooks were at the controls. Our landing was perfect and was made in a small field. We had to use an axe to get the glider apart. We had a heckuva time getting our jeep and gun out. We picked up some paratroopers and an officer and acted mostly as riflemen that last part of D-Day. We went to the 502nd command post where we set up our gun at a road junction. The glider pilots were with us. We didn't get any sleep that first night."

PFC Charles S. "Whiz" Wiszowaty had been given the assignment of chopping a hole in the roof for escape purposes if the glider crashed in the Channel. He didn't have to unfasten the axe which was strapped to the floor of the glider. He remembered, "As we passed over the beach and the combat area, the copilot turned and yelled back to us, 'Brace yourselves forward, we're going in!' The landing was a little rough and bumpy. We landed somewhere near Hiesville. We all came out safe and a little shaky. To get out of the Horsa glider with a jeep and .37mm gun, we had to cut away some bolts near the tail end of the glider. We then pulled the tail section loose, put out skids, and jockeyed the gun and jeep out along these portable ramps. You never saw a faster movement, just to get away from the open field. Shortly after that, a parachute officer and five men met us. We were oriented as to location and sent off to the command post of the 502nd Regiment."

"I remember that one of the wheels broke off the glider just before it skidded to a halt," said PFC Arno Whitbread of the same glider group. "There had been some small-arms fire directed at us as the pilot cut loose and headed for the landing zone.

"We had some difficulty getting the antitank gun out of the glider as a couple of the men hit the ground while we were under small-arms fire. They would not get up to help us move the gun from the glider."

The enemy had moved in on the glider fields. Captain Frank Lillyman and his pathfinders went to the rescue of the occupants of a glider that landed in an area a short distance from their position. He said, "I took my squad to locate an isolated glider a short distance away. When we arrived, Germans were shooting at the glider and its occupants with machine guns and mortars. We engaged the enemy and one of them got me in the arm with a machine pistol (burp gun). As I fell, I got a mortar splinter in the face."

Sergeant McCarthy's glider number 4 had come to rest safely in a soft field only twenty yards from a hedgerow. He observed, "Glider number 3, which was just in front of ours, slammed into an earthen bank and collapsed in a pile of splinters. The copilot was killed as were several MP's and headquarters people. I raced over to give aid and was immediately fired upon from a hedgerow corner. I assumed a prone position quickly. Uninjured glidermen from the wrecked craft were removing those who had survived the crash.

"I managed to snake forward to the wrecked glider where I located an old friend, Sergeant John Paris. He was one of the badly injured who had been pulled from within the wrecked glider. We had entered service together from Chicago and both of us had been with the 101st Division since it was activated at Camp Claiborne, Louisiana, in 1942. Unfortunately, Paris died a few minutes later from his injuries.

"The equipment remained in our glider because the enemy gunners fired at us each time we approached the rear of the glider to blow the tail section off. Our soldiers crawled off the field on their bellies. No friendly troops appeared on the field to assist us. We finally waited in the cover of the hedgerows for darkness to cover our movements."

The Signal Company glider carrying Bill Finn and other members of the Wire Platoon and their equipment had skidded to a halt on its belly after passing through a hedgerow. The badly shaken Finn said, "We got out of the glider and were almost immediately fired upon from the other side of the hedges. The jeep and trailer loaded with supplies were still in the glider. Just across the hedges from our machine, two or three craft from Division Headquarters Company had landed and were, like us, under fire. Within a few minutes, a couple of these men came running through the hedgerow telling us that several of their men had been killed or wounded from the German fire. One of our men had been wounded. Danny Miller had been shot through one side of the face and I had a near miss as a bullet ripped into my rifle stock. About then, one of the Headquarters Company men who had come through the hedge was hit in the head and killed by much closer fire as the enemy moved along the hedgerow. We were in a field with no more cover than a front yard and couldn't get out, so we waved a white flag. I don't think we were far from the Division CP."

With darkness approaching, Sergeant McCarthy was in the hedgerow with the CIC officer, Plotke, and the pilot of the wrecked glider. He said, "Somehow this glider pilot had miraculously survived a crash in which his compartment was completely demolished. He did have difficulty moving about due to a broken heel. He was given a shot of morphine to ease the pain. The CIC man, whose briefings had been rushed and sketchy, directed me to take charge of the small group.

"I knew we were less than a mile from Hiesville and the command post. I reasoned that it would be safer to travel on foot in enemy infested territory than to chance a jeep ride with such a small group of men. Near the hedge was a hard-surfaced road leading toward Hiesville. We started out in the darkness, moving cautiously along the deep ditch beside the road. Our group stopped occasionally to listen and then moved forward.

"We stopped once more when a burst of small-arms fire was heard in front of us. On the road, several hundred yards to our front, voices were heard. Orders were being given and acknowledged in German. Then the sound of marching feet with the click-clicking of hobnailed boots could be heard approaching in the direction of our small group in the ditch. Our foursome went flat on their stomachs hardly daring to breathe as the enemy platoon marched by.

"I got my group moving again a short time later. Shots and shouts were heard from the direction of the glider fields. Unarmed medics and headquarters men were being rounded up by the enemy. I kept moving my group along the ditch. We came to the entrance of a farmyard.

"I said, 'I think we'd better find a place to hide for the night. We'll never make it in the dark. Stay put while I take a look around.' I crawled ahead into the barnyard and searched about in the gloom. A shadowy hedgerow loomed near the barn. Beside it I noted a shallow ditch. I went back for the rest of my party. They followed me to the ditch where they promptly stretched out. I remained awake. The others quickly fell asleep and started a chorus of loud snoring, which was quieted momentarily by a nudge or a kick. A nearby horse stamped and snorted throughout the night as if it were answering the snoring soldiers."

The gliders carrying the Signal Company soldiers had fared about as well as the headquarters gliders. Several made safe landings but one piled into a tree and was badly smashed. Several signalmen were killed while six were injured.

Lieutenant James Moore, in charge of the forty-one-man communications echelon, gathered his men from several gliders. They unloaded equipment under small-arms fire and started toward the command post taking the injured with them. Along the route they were again fired upon by the enemy who used burp guns, machine guns, and rockets from the shelter of the hedgerows. Sergeant Bill Harrison, who had been injured in the glider crash, received serious wounds as he lay exposed to the enemy fire on a litter stretched across the hood of the jeep. This vehicle and two motorcycles were destroyed. During the engagement, the men successfully routed the enemy and arrived at the division command post without further incidents.

The radio equipment brought in by the group proved extremely valuable the next day when spare sets had to be sent to the parachute regiments which had lost their radios in the initial drop and had been without contact with division headquarters through most of D-Day. The radios provided General Taylor with an opportunity to coordinate the movements of his attacking forces.

The wire platoon brought in trailers loaded with communications wire with which to connect the various regimental and battalion headquarters by field telephone with the 101st Airborne Division Headquarters at Hiesville.

Though the gliders had smashed into hedgerows and trees and fatal landings had occurred, casualties were not as heavy as had been anticipated. Of the 148 men who rode in during the predawn lift, five men were killed, seventeen injured, and seven were missing or captured. During the evening flight, about a third of the 165 men were lost with fourteen killed, thirty injured or wounded, and ten missing or captured. Much vital medical, hospital, and communication equipment for the forward airborne positions had been brought in by the gliders at considerable human sacrifice.

Had the Germans completed their anti-airborne preparations, the outcome for these men would have been even more hazardous. Fortunately for the glider troopers, the timetable for the preparations had been upset.

Major General Gerald J. Higgins, who served as colonel and chief of staff of the 101st Airborne Division on D-Day, related, "One captured German officer, who had been in charge of the planting of poles in the fields, told us that the Germans calculated the earliest date the Allies could make the drop and the invasion proper would be the 21st of June. Accordingly, they had their sights set on finishing the job by the 15th of June, with the real pressure to be put on in the last ten days. In fact, in order to keep the mines, which were attached to the barbed wire strung from pole to pole, from being detonated by grazing cows, the mines were not to be activated until the 18th of June. After that, the French were to keep their cattle out of those fields under penalty of their cows being shot. As you know, this never came to pass as the invasion took place some two weeks earlier than their calculations."

CHAPTER 16

Angels of Mercy

The cry, "Medic!" was heard frequently in the midst of battle. To answer this desperate call, there was an aidman assigned to each platoon. A medical staff of two officers with M.D. training and a group of sixteen technicians was assigned to each battalion. Invariably, regardless of his rank, the aidman was known as "Doc." Also, affectionately, he was called, "The Pill Roller."

Many of the survivors of D-Day owe their lives to these daring men, who ignored exploding mortar shells, tracers, and the boom of the deadly 88's to go to the aid of distressed comrades in the hedgerows and drop zones. Their jumps were particularly dangerous because, in the hours of darkness, the enemy could not distinguish them from combatants. "Doc" went into combat without a weapon to protect himself. His greatest fear was getting a bayonet in the belly before he had an opportunity to get clear of his parachute. At least one of the aidmen was riddled as he hung in a tree, struggling to get free of his harness.

"Angels of Mercy" is the term assigned to these dedicated men by PFC Tom Mulligan, who received medical attention while in critical condition. He said, "I was dropped far from our designated drop zone (near Valognes) and got together with three others about 0300 in the morning. One of the members went out to do some scouting and never came back.

"Around daybreak the remaining two enlisted men with Lieutenant James G. Pearson ran into a squad of Germans. We had a brief fire fight in which Lieutenant Pearson took several hits in the head. I received gun shot wounds in the face and stomach. The lieutenant and I spent the whole day lying in the field under guard by the Germans. Lieutenant Pearson lived for thirteen days. I stayed with him till he died.

"In the PW enclosure was our battalion surgeon, Captain Felix Adams. He dropped into the backyard of a German division command post and was quickly captured. 'Doc' Adams was performing all of his medical duties on all the casualties. I cannot say enough for him. Before he reamed a slug from me, he told me to get loaded but good because he didn't have the necessary medical supplies to deaden the pain. Then he removed the bullet. He was truly an 'Angel of Mercy.'"

Parachuting Padres

Included among the noncombatants and serving side-by-side with the medics were the chaplains or "parachuting padres," who, besides looking after the spiritual lives of the men, were also trained in first aid. These men were armed only with communion or Mass kits in addition to their first aid equipment.

Among these devoted "padres" was Father Francis L. Sampson, who helped tend the wounded first at the Fortin Farm near the wooden bridges and later at the aid station at Addeville. In describing his D-Day experiences, Chaplain Sampson wrote: "I lit in the middle of a stream over my head and grabbed my knife to cut my bags from me (my Mass kit, doctor's kit, etc.), but I could scarcely move to free myself. The canopy of my chute stayed open, and the strong wind blew me downstream about a hundred yards into shallow water. I lay there a few minutes exhausted and as securely pinned down by equipment as if I had been in a straitjacket. None of our men was near. It took about ten minutes to get out of my chute (it seemed an hour, for judging from the fire, I thought that we had landed in the middle of a target range). I crawled back to the edge of the stream near the spot where I landed, and started diving for my Mass equipment. By pure luck, I recovered it after the fifth or sixth dive.

"Luckily, I spotted my assistant not very far away, still struggling to get out of his chute. We got together and made for the nearest hedgerow that would offer cover. We no sooner got there than a plane on fire came straight at us. It crashed about a hundred yards in front of us and threw flaming pieces over our heads. We prayed for the men who were still in the plane and then watched and prayed for the men in two other planes that crashed about a mile away. My assistant had lost his weapon in the stream, so we welcomed two of our men who came crawling along the hedgerow."

Father Sampson continued his account: "Our little group discussed what we ought to do and then started toward the place where we judged our troops might assemble. We moved slowly under concealment of the hedgerows and were glad to see a half-dozen paratroopers running down along the ditch by the road. They were not of our regiment, but told us where we might find the 501st, or a part of it. We went in the direction they pointed until we came under heavy enemy rifle fire. We ducked into a nearby farmhouse, where we found about twenty-five troopers, all wounded or injured from their jump. It was just a three-room house, and the French farmer, his wife, and little girl were being of what help they could to the wounded. Chaplain McGee, a splendid Protestant chaplain from the 506th Parachute Regiment, was giving first aid as best he could. He had run out of sulfa drugs and since my assistant and I had quite a bit of medical supplies, he was very happy to see us. We worked with the men for the better part of the day. Chaplain McGee was a former aid man in the enlisted ranks during peace time before he went away to study for the ministry, so he directed our first aid work with the wounded.

"About four in the afternoon a wounded soldier came in and told us that he and his buddy had been shot a hundred yards or so from the house. His buddy still lay where he fell. Chaplain McGee and I went to find him. He was already dead. We dragged him back, rolled him in a blanket, and put him in the shed. Then a mortar shell hit the back door of the house just as the French woman and her little girl were bringing in water from the well. Both were killed. As I knelt to anoint them, the farmer threw himself on their bodies and broke into agonizing sobs. When I put my hand on his shoulder, he jumped up, his hands and face smeared with the blood of his loved ones, and went yelling down the road shaking his fists in the direction of the Germans.

"Some of our patients were getting worse, and Chaplain McGee said that they had to have a doctor. I decided to try to find our regimental aid station. My assistant stayed to offer what help he could to Chaplain McGee. After going about a half mile, I found a patrol of men. They told me where they thought the aid station might be. Since the area was under fire, I avoided the road and went by way of the swamp. The deep swamp was filthy and cold but afforded good cover. Addeville was the village the soldiers had told me to go to. With dusk closing in, I arrived there to find Major Allen in charge of about two hundred men scattered throughout the village. They were having a real fight with a German unit a few hundred yards up the road. I went first to the aid station to tell Doc Carrel about Chaplain McGee's predicament.

" 'Kingston,' he said to the assistant surgeon, 'you take Cleary and follow the Father's directions to that group of wounded.'

"I then went to speak to Major Allen. He was on the SCR-300 radio talking to Colonel Johnson. Allen motioned for me to stand by. Johnson was, as usual, talking loud enough even over the radio to be heard by everyone around. 'We're going on down to the locks,' he said. 'You'll have to withdraw from your own position and come with us.'

" 'I can't,' said Allen. 'We'd be overrun. And how long will you last at the locks if we don't hold off here?'

" 'ALLEN,' he yelled, 'DON'T TALK TO ME LIKE THAT! DO AS I SAY!' Allen looked at me and winked, laughing noiselessly. 'Think it over, sir,' he replied. Johnson's reply was one long string of oaths. Allen laughed quietly again and said, 'Yes, sir. Right away, sir.'

"Allen then turned to me. 'Father, we're pulling out in about an hour. Tell Doc Carrel that the walking wounded and the aidmen and you and he will go with us. When we move, we've got to go quickly, because the Krauts will close in on this place fast. I'd like to stay and hold, for it's a good high position, but we don't have enough men to do it.' What he was trying to say was that the non-walking wounded would have to be left behind. It was one of those decisions officers hate to make, but for the safety of the whole unit are sometimes forced to make. Allen was back on the radio calling in heavy support fire from the light cruiser eight miles away at sea. 'Give me six more rounds on the same coordinates as the last.'

"Doc Carrel looked at me when I told him what Allen had said. 'This is a bad time to leave them,' he said. 'Neither side is taking many prisoners now, and the Germans will consider them a liability.'

" 'I don't think they will do anything to them. Their record as far as the wounded is concerned is pretty good,' I said. 'At any rate, I'm staying with them.'

" 'Well . . . ,' Doc Carrel, a real friend, started to say something, then just shrugged his shoulders He looked around the big room and pointed out the most serious cases to me. 'That man in the corner won't live—hand grenade went off in his pocket. His leg is gone, and he's ground up inside. Fenton on the bed should pull through if you can get a full unit of plasma in him. He has a big hole in his back, but no vital organs touched. There are two broken legs among this group— they have splints on. The man with the head wound . . . I don't know how serious it is, but for the time being he can't see. Just change the dressing now and then. Do what you can for the others; they should pull through. There are fourteen non-walking wounded in these two rooms and the shed. Incidentally, there's a psycho in the shed. Better keep him away from the others.'

"Doc then called the aidmen together. 'One of you is going to stay here with these men and the chaplain.' He had a number of straws in his hand. 'Here, draw one. The short straw stays.' A man by the name of Fisher drew the short one.

"As soon as the last of our forces had left, I made a white flag from a sheet and hung it out the door. Darkness came quickly, and I expected the Germans to come within an hour. Fisher gave the man with the grenade wounds another unit of plasma while I changed the dressing of the man with the head wound. With the walking wounded gone we had more room in the main part of the house, so I moved all but two men in the main room. Every fifteen minutes I would go out and wave the white flag because I was afraid the Germans, suspecting a trap, would fire hand grenades and mortars into the house before approaching it.

"All night long this went on. The boy with the grenade wound died in my arms about four A.M. clutching the crucifix I had taken down from the wall. It was a peaceful and holy death. All the boys joined in prayers for him. The medic Fisher and myself again changed all the bandages of the men. As I was cooking some hot chocolate, I looked out and saw Germans set up a machine gun in the front yard. I grabbed the white flag and went out. A German jumped at me and stuck a Schmizzer grease gun in my stomach.

"I could see by the badges on their breast that these soldiers were Hitler's Fallschirmjagers (paratroopers). I tried to tell them that the house was full of wounded men, but two of them pushed me toward the road and prodded me with their weapons. When we had gone about a quarter of a mile, they stopped. One of them pushed me across the road ditch and against the hedgerow. He stepped back, and both soldiers pulled the bolts of their weapons. I said a quick act of contrition. (It later dawned on me that whenever I was in any great danger, instead of the act of contrition, which I intended and tried to say, I always said the grace before meals . . . Bless us, O Lord, for these and all Thy gifts, which of Thy bounty we are to receive through Christ Our Lord).

"Just then there were some shots fired a few feet over our heads. It was a German noncom firing to attract the attention of the men I was with. He came running down the road and stopped when he reached us. He was a fine-looking, tough soldier of about twenty-five. He spoke to my two captors and told me in broken English to come with him. I told him I was a Catholic priest and showed him my credentials. To my real amazement he snapped to attention, saluted, made a slight bow, and showed me a religious medal pinned inside his uniform. (A great many German soldiers wear medals or religious badges and carry rosaries and prayer books.) The noncom took me a little farther down the road to a German officer who, in turn, called an intelligence man who spoke English. I explained that I was a chaplain and knew nothing of military value. I requested to be allowed to stay with my wounded men. The officer permitted this, and my noncom friend took me back. The Fallschirmjagers had ransacked the house of what food they could find, picked up a few hand grenades that our men had left in the yard, and filled their canteens with wine from the barrel in the shed.

"The Catholic German noncom, in a very friendly way, told me to stay with my 'comrades' (I was so glad of the universality of the Church). He said that a German doctor would come in a day or so. I had to show him the wounds of all the men and practically every square inch of the house-drawers, cupboards, attic, etc., to be sure we weren't hiding any weapons. Then he left. But the Fallschirmjagers dug in about the grounds and in the adjoining fields."[1]

Chaplain John S. Maloney, who served with the 506th Parachute Infantry Regiment on D-Day, experienced anxiety as he got out of his chute. "It was due to nervousness and the desire not to attract the wrong kind of attention," said the good Father as he expressed his fears. "I just hated to be bayoneted, having parachuted without a weapon for self-defense."

Father Maloney hurried from field to field where skirmishes occurred, ministering to the wounded of both sides. In a modest understatement, Father Maloney summed up his day: "I was kept busy going here and there—trying to find the aid stations—being directed to the wounded by their buddies."[2]

"I landed like a ton of bricks," remembered Protestant Chaplain Raymond S. "Chappie" Hall, who was also secretly referred to as "Jumping Jesus" by the men of the 502nd Parachute Infantry Regiment. "Chappie" Hall had almost been shot because he didn't have a cricket and he did not know the password. His many duties in the marshaling area had kept him from attending any of the briefing sessions.

"I found a few men during the night," Hall said. "Then a glider crashed in an orchard. I ran to it and the pilot and copilot's legs were broken in several places. Snipers opened fire and our men took off except for myself. I stayed under the jeep in the glider and managed to give both men hypo shots. Then I got out to cut a branch for a splint. The other men finally came back.

"I found my way to the division medical setup and stayed there working on wounded—first aid, smokes, water, prayers, etc. Spent the remainder of D-Day and all the next night there because of the terrific casualties. Had no sleep for two nights."

Several hundred casualties had been gathered at the Division Hospital at Hiesville, and medical officers, aidmen, and chaplains worked overtime to meet their most pressing needs.

Frustrated

For some medics, D-Day brought frustration and hopelessness due to injury, danger of capture, or a misplaced drop. PFC Robert C. Barger, personal medic to General Taylor, described his misfortunes: "My drop was a fast one. When I came out of the plane my chute opened and upon looking up to check it, I saw tracers going through. I started to slip and in my scared moments, climbed clear to the canopy, causing it to stream. I dropped rapidly and sustained a broken pelvic bone, cracked my hip, broke my right arm, cracked some ribs and dislocated my right shoulder. That was my D-Day action—all goofed up. Two men found me and moved me over by a hedgerow and left me covered with my chute. I lay there until noon of June 8, when I was found by a patrol looking for snipers."

Acutely uncomfortable and in constant danger of death or capture, Captain Bernard J. Ryan, assistant surgeon for the 506th's 3rd Battalion, spent D-Day in the flooded area near St. Come-du-Mont. His service to others was delayed several days due to his own desperate struggle for survival.

"I landed in a swamp (flooded area) between St. Come-du-Mont and Carentan." Captain Ryan recalled. "The place where I landed was about knee-deep in water. After freeing myself I took about two steps and was up to my neck in water. I soon met up with a couple of enlisted men, one of whom was a sergeant from my battalion.

"A plane had crashed and was burning on higher ground toward St. Come-du-Mont. We could see some figures around it, thought they were probably Americans and started through the water which in most places was knee-deep. The deep places into which I had initially foundered were ditches around the fields. We approached the burning plane through the water and when we were about 200 feet from it, the people around it (they turned out to be Germans) opened up with machine-gun fire on us. We scattered, I lying on my back and swimming backward away from the fire which was right over us. I lost the other men and never saw them again. I learned later that the sergeant was killed that night when he engaged another German group with his revolver.

"I tried to get out of the swampy area all night but was met with fire whenever I approached dry land. My last approach was the high roadway between St. Come-du-Mont and Carentan. At that time it began to become daylight and I took refuge in some low brush in the swamp just a few yards from the St. Come-du-Mont to Carentan road. In order to conceal myself, I had to sit up to my neck in water all day, D-Day, while German vehicles ran back and forth along the road above me.

"Naval shells started coming in from our ships in the Channel, apparently trying to knock the road out. Every time one of them hit in the swamp near me it would throw up tremendous quantities of wet earth which would land all about. I thought I was going to be crushed by one of these tremendous clods of wet soil.

"I froze all day but night finally came about 11 P.M. and I set out again. Water was up to my neck intermittently, but I finally got on some soggy ground where I found a parachute and crawled under it for the rest of the night. The next morning I could see Germans running around on the field in the direction of Addeville. I was quite close to them, but stayed under the chute all day and none ventured into the swampy area."[3]

Staff Sergeant Robert J. Reynolds, medic for the 1st Battalion of the 501st, was dropped south of Carentan, where, unarmed and frustrated, he spent over a week trying to join his unit.

Reynolds said, "Upon landing I found only Corporal Abbie Webber, another medic who was either second or third in the stick, and a battalion radioman named Elliott. Our plane had belly bundles as well as those in the door and we found all the bundles because we landed near them. I believe at least one of the bundle lights was working and I turned it off and we broke down the door bundles, which were medical and consisted of two mountain packboards, each containing two chest packs supposedly filled with medical supplies. Webber and I each loaded up with a mountain pack. We probably waited for 20 to 30 minutes for others to assemble on the bundles. There were isolated small-arms shots in the vicinity and we also heard a small motorcycle to the west of us—on the whole though, it was very quiet. We did observe the tracers and searchlights and in particular recall one plane, we thought to be a C-47, circling higher and higher trying to evade the searchlight beams, only to be finally hit and plunge to the ground. This activity was far away and to the northeast of where we were. We also saw one planeload of parachutists drop quite a ways south of our own location. During our time at the bundles we waited for any kind of assembly signal—our 1st Battalion had a hunting horn that was to be blown. Thought once or twice that we heard it in the distance, but I expect it was our imaginations.[4]

"Finally we decided to strike out to the northeast in the general direction of all the fireworks (ack-ack). Our backpacks were heavy and we went slowly, stopping frequently to check the slightest noise. We went probably a mile, more or less, without a sign of anyone. It was eerie to say the least. Never, on any practice jumps or maneuvers had we ever failed to meet anyone before. We were lost but didn't know it.

"By the third or fourth time we stopped, we were exhausted—more, I expect by the nervous strain than by the physical exercise. Anyhow, we all went to sleep and awoke at early dawn which I would guess about 0430. Neither Webber or I (as medics) were armed and Elliott, the radioman, had a folding stock carbine and a busted radio. One of the back packs held only cigarettes—and none of us smoked!"[5]

Captured

There were medical officers captured on D-Day who carried on their work, tending the wounded and jump-injured inside enemy facilities. It will be recalled that the 377th Parachute Field Artillery had experienced a very poor drop, with its personnel dumped in the vicinity of Valognes and Monte-bourg and almost as far north as Cherbourg. Both of the 377th surgeons, Captain Felix Adams and Captain Ernest Gruenberg, fell into the hands of the enemy.

Captain Felix M. Adams had received a glancing blow on the side of his helmet from a piece of shrapnel and had been knocked unconscious. Upon regaining consciousness, he learned that he had come down on the roof of a building of a German command post somewhere in the vicinity of Valognes. A group of about fifteen German soldiers clustered about him, wondering what to do with their first captive. After one of the enemy soldiers cut him free of his harness, he was helped to his feet and discovered difficulty in walking because of a knee injury suffered on the landing. He was immediately taken into a barbed wire enclosure about ten yards from where he had landed.

Adams wrote, "As soon as I was taken into the barbed wire enclosure, the Germans took my medical kit, plus my camera and two canteens of bonded bourbon. About an hour later, American wounded started coming in. One of my aidmen, Francis Capizzi, also came in. I later found that none of the others in my stick came out alive, or were not captured, except Lieutenant William Shrader. All were killed or taken prisoner shortly after landing. My buddy, Dapper Neilson, was killed a short distance from the barbed wire enclosure. I managed to recruit a detail to bury him in a churchyard in Montebourg shortly after daybreak of D-Day. From external appearances he was killed either during or shortly after landing.

"About 1000 A.M., my medical kit was returned, and I

was able to give a little first aid. Shortly after this, Captain Lawrence Corley and an unidentified enlisted man came into the enclosure carrying a ladder on which they were carrying Lt. Jim Pearson, who had been shot in the head.[6] He died later at the Luftwaffe Hospital in Cherbourg. Larry Corley, a good friend of mine, was not wounded and hence was taken to another compound and remained a prisoner throughout the war.

"I told the enemy soldiers I was a doctor and they later introduced me to a German doctor who allowed me to work on my own, although for head and abdominal wounds there was nothing I could do. The Germans were very generous in supplying me with drugs such as morphine, and sulfanilimide—although my only type of anesthetic was morphine plus large quantities of cognac."[7]

The 3rd Battalion of the 506th Regiment was particularly proud of its surgeon, Captain Stanley E. Morgan, whose work has been cited with the following commendation: "Captain Stanley E. Morgan was captured shortly after his landing in the village of St. Come-du-Mont. He had the misfortune to sprain an ankle on the jump. After a short interrogation, he was conducted to a German 'Krankenstube' situated in St. Come-du-Mont, where he courageously and fearlessly rendered first aid and definitive surgical care to the huge number of American and German casualties who were brought in. Here with the assistance of a German medical officer and enlisted personnel, together with Sergeant Mainard D. Clifton, he worked constantly for three days in grave danger both from revengeful Germans and from our own artillery fire. The town was under siege by our own troops and finally was captured on the afternoon of June 8, 1944, releasing Captain Morgan and Sergeant Clifton.

"Captain Morgan, by his heroic conduct and utter disregard of danger, was an inspiration to the many wounded American paratroopers who were huddled together under his care. He managed by both his diplomatic and forceful manner to direct the evacuation of our seriously wounded by the Germans, securing a lion's share of the limited facilities available, and at the same time salvaging and keeping with him our less injured until the triumphal entry of our own troops. The wounded were all loud in their praise of him, and Germans captured in later stages of the campaign remembered him vividly."[8]

Also captured on D-Day were 501st surgeons Captain Robert Blatherwick and Lieutenant Tom Johnson of 1st Battalion who were misdropped southeast of Carentan. As Blatherwick recalled it, "My assignment was to establish a battalion aid station and organize evacuation routes. All of us were hoping to assemble with our units as planned, but were aware that we had not landed at the designated DZ. The eight men who got together with us were not all from my plane and none of them were from my detachment.

"We were captured during the forenoon of D-Day and taken to a church where other prisoners had been assembled by the Germans. I would estimate the total group to be about 30 men. Among them was Lieutenant Thomas U. Johnson, who was my assistant surgeon. A battalion staff officer, Major Phillip Gage, Jr., was there seriously wounded. We did what we could for him. Shortly after, we joined a larger group and we were moved farther east and Lieutenant Johnson and I were separated from the other prisoners. We were held at a German unit headquarters within hearing range of the guns at Utah Beach."

Aid Station at Mesières

The flooded areas behind the beaches were death traps for many men. PFC John H. Wilson, a medic attached to 1st Battalion Headquarters of the 502nd Regiment, survived his watery landing to set up an aid station at Mesières, near WXYZ, the enemy artillerymen's barrack complex.

Wilson remembered, "I landed in a flooded area. It surprised me and I was so damned scared I almost drowned. The area was covered by machine-gun fire. We were about five miles from our DZ. The shroud lines were wrapped around me and I couldn't remove the reserve or main chute. Someone finally waded out to me and helped me out. I remember him saying, 'Let's get the hell out of here! The Krauts are shooting at us!' I could hear water splashing and Germans talking. Someone finally threw a hand grenade at them. I could hear a death rattle plainly. We waded to a causeway where it sounded like a thousand crickets were assembled. A captain was getting our position from a map. There were about thirty men there. The officer directed me to a man with a broken leg. I put splints on it. Mortar shells began to drop and the captain moved us out. I believe it was Captain Hancock.

"I lost everything on the jump but one medical kit with a fifth of booze. This was for treating men in shock. I gave one drink to the man with the broken leg. There was one other man with our group with a broken leg. He was from the 82nd Division. I tried to hide him for pickup in daylight. He threatened to shoot me if I left him. A couple infantrymen carried him.

"Our battalion aid station was in a farmhouse near headquarters. No doctor was there on the first day. Had bad casualties all day. Sergeant Eugene Forbes, Ward, and myself were the only medics to reach Battalion Aid the first day.

"On the evening of the first day, a C-47 on a resupply mission crashed near us. I helped check the crew over and only one of them was hurt. We gave them each a drink of cognac that we found in our farmhouse. The worst casualty of the day was Lieutenant Brandenberger. His arm was nearly off at the shoulder with no room to stop bleeding. We finally packed it and we did evacuate him. I have often wondered if he lived."[9]

In No-Man's-Land

There was a wide area of farmland intentionally flooded by the Germans stretching from Vierville to the Douve River. It was crisscrossed with canals and causeways that often led to isolated farmhouses sitting as if on islands in the marsh. A few of the farmhouses became medical aid stations in this "no-man's-land."

T/5 Ray Barton was assigned as a medic to 2nd Battalion

of the 501st. As a medic he was the last to jump from his plane. He said, "I landed in a large drainage canal in about four feet of water. My wristwatch stopped when I hit the water—about 0145 in the morning.

"The canals had some barbed wire strung along the edges—trip wires about 18 inches high. The land was very flat and swampy and crisscrossed with small drainage canals.

"On D-Day I attached myself with a large group of 82nd men. I stayed with them for several days and set up an aid station in a home. Had lots of wounded prisoners. The group I was with attacked several enemy ack-ack units that were shooting at the gliders as they came in. Our linemen did rather well, as the Germans were quite busy looking up in the sky."

Private Albert D. Hutto, a medic from the 1st Battalion of the 501st, also floundered in this marshy area. He said, "I found myself with five other privates or PFC's. Without anyone to take command, and without maps, we decided to dig in for the night in what appeared to be a cluster of trees in the half-light, several hundred yards away. The other area in all directions faded into darkness. Our first obstacle was a wide creek. One man swam across with a jump rope, and with a man at each end, we started pulling ourselves across. It was over our heads in the center. Four had crossed and I was about to start when a noise in the rear brought the two of us to the ground. I was sure it was Germans, but tried my cricket. After a few tense moments another cricket answered mine. I got up and met Lieutenant Hugo Sims of the 2nd Battalion of our regiment. I told him there were six of us, all privates, and that we were headed to dig in for the night. He was headed for the regimental objective. He had a dozen or so men with him and we quickly added six more.

"We had to use the rope over the creek since that was the way Sims was headed. We were probably halfway between Vierville and the Douve River, and somewhere southeast of Vierville. As we continued on we joined up with two other groups containing two or three jump-injured troopers. We had been moving along slowly and not too far from the original landing spot when we came to a farmhouse on the edge of the flat marshy area we had been crossing. One of the jump-injured was unable to continue, so after a brief confab, it was decided that I and a couple of other medics should set up an aid station at the house for the injured. This was where I would remain for the next three days.

"The house was sitting like an island in the low-lying area, except on one side where the road led by the house. We had an unobstructed view of several hundred yards in three directions, especially to the east and south, and the road and trees from the 4th direction did not offer much cover to anyone approaching.

"People came and went. The French family moved down the road to a nearby house. As the day went on these people arrived on the scene: Captain Louis Axelrod, Staff Sergeant Lee Edwards, Chaplain Kenneth Engle, PFC Robin Pledger, Engle's assistant, and Private Carl D. Ancell, all noncombatants from our regiment. Two young linemen from the 2nd or 3rd Battalion wandered in. One of them had injured his eye. I remember fixing an eye patch for him, and the two of them rode off on the farmer's horse, with the farmer's consent. The horse came back in less than an hour. Later that day, one of them returned to report they had been ambushed, and he was not sure what had happened to the other man. (When we moved out three days later, we found his body beside the roadside, with eye patch still in place.)

"D-Day was the same day that Captain Axelrod and Chaplain Engle were ambushed nearby while riding in a wagon. I do not remember if they had started from the house or another point, but they ended up at the aid station, pretty shaken by their experience. It was probably the afternoon of the 6th that a line of people were seen passing across the area to the east of the house. We had perhaps a half dozen linemen then, some injured, but not too badly. One feigned injury. It was difficult to tell if the people in the field were soldiers or civilians, but someone finally decided they were German soldiers. It was a lucky guess, for Sergeant Edwards and I were observing from a second-floor window and we couldn't be sure. Since this was the first kill for everyone there, each had his first reaction. The people would fall or hit the ground as they tried to continue on under the distant fire. Sometimes we would see them rise to run a little further. No one could be sure whether the long-range fire was doing any good. Later a group of American paratroopers came in across the field and reported there was a wounded German soldier. Sergeant Lee Edwards and I took our single litter and got him. He turned out to be a young German, about 19 years old, named Hans. He was shot in the abdomen. Getting him back to the house was not too easy, since we had to wade several creeks to our waists. He spoke 'school English' and all of us made friends with him before he died on the morning of the day we left for Vierville."[10]

T/5 Wayne Walton, a medic for the 2nd Battalion of the 501st Regiment, attended wounded Americans and Germans on a spot of high ground in the midst of the marsh, somewhere south of Hutto's aid station. He jumped with Captain Louis Axelrod, the assistant surgeon, but was not to see him for several days. Walton said, "I landed in a flooded area. There were three other medics with me (Sgt. Robert Shell, George Atchinson, and Richard May). At the first light of day, the Germans opened up on the four of us with machine-gun fire. We rolled in a canal and swam to a field with hedgerows and trees along it. We were taken by a German patrol along with several wounded men. We were liberated a short time later by a mixed patrol of 101st men. While we were being liberated by the Americans, there was a very active firefight. One German was shot about a foot away from me. I hit the dirt as fast as he did.

"I was ordered by the officer in charge of the patrol to stay with the wounded and they would send me help to get us. (It was three days before help arrived and several men died before we could get them out.)

"After the 101st patrol left us with the wounded, we gathered up all German guns, grenades, and ammo and dumped them in a canal. We were giving morphine shots, plasma, sewing up chest wounds, etc.—very busy trying to make those with broken bones comfortable.

"The day ended for me taking care of wounded Americans and Germans in 'no-man's-land' somewhere along a flooded area. A member of a German patrol put a gun to my chest that evening. One of the Germans wounded spoke to him and they left."

A Red Cross in the field

T/5 Howard Rogge was an aidman on the staff of Major Douglas Davidson, regimental surgeon for the 502nd. Landing in a small wood lot near Ste. Mère Eglise, he found his way to Lieutenant Colonel Cole's battalion and was shortly setting up an aid station in a field near a crossroad.

Rogge related, "I joined Colonel Robert Cole from 3rd Battalion. We captured some Russians and their supply wagons. I set up an aid station near a corner where the action had occurred and there were casualties from both sides which I took care of."

Near St. Martin-de-Varreville, an aid station was set up in a field by Captain Hugh Caumartin, surgeon of 2nd Battalion of the 506th. He had dropped in the 502nd drop zone several miles from his own objective at the two lower causeways. Despite wounds sustained on his drop, Captain Caumartin hobbled about the field on a splinted leg, administering to the casualties from the many sharp engagements of that area.

Caumartin described his experiences: "I was hit twice on the drop, once in the nose—and I worried about what my wife would think when I returned without a nose. Before I could worry further, I was hit in one leg. I hit the ground hard—there was no support in that leg. The enemy was firing on the field in which I dropped. Machine guns were sending streams of tracers in cross fire only a few feet over my head. I lay there trying to survey the situation. Others were dropping into the same field and the surrounding area. They were being hit and hurt. A young trooper named Martinez from New Orleans came crawling up. He had been hit and needed assistance. I was in considerable pain, so I gave myself a syrette of morphine. We crawled off the field to a defilade near a hedgerow.

"I treated and bandaged Martinez, who had been hit in the

head. It was a superficial wound which had creased his skull. My leg was bleeding so we put a tourniquet on it and later a splint. Martinez was ambulatory so I sent him out to bring in the jump-injured and the wounded. He would bring them in, some were bad, some were superficial and I did what I could for them. We collected a sizable group.

"I followed the rules of the Geneva Convention throughout. I figured our chances would be better. I had the men cache all weapons in the hedgerows. We set out our lightly wounded men as scout observers. Our aid station remained in the field. Our Red Cross flag was placed in view near the men.

"We remained in the field for two days. On the second day, a German patrol came by. There was no firing. They had noted the flag and the officer in command spoke excellent English. He asked, 'Who is in charge here?' The men pointed me out. I explained that all the weapons had been cached and all of my people were injured and wounded. He asked if we needed anything. I said I was in need of medical supplies. He didn't have any to spare, but did say he would inform the local farmers to bring us food and wine. As I spoke French fluently, we had already made such arrangements with the people and had been supplied with both.

"The German officer chatted with me for some time. I learned he had worked in New Orleans for two years before the war and yearned to get back there again. After informing us our troops would reach us the next day, he began to move off. He stopped for a moment and called back, 'War is hell!' Then he marched off with his men. Soldiers of the 4th Infantry Division reached us the next day."

Church sanctuaries

Nearly a quarter century after the fierce action of D-Day swirled about it, the small Norman church at Angoville-au-Plain still retains the permanent bloodstains on its unvarnished, ancient pews.[11] It was used as an aid station on that day and its pews served as resting places for the casualties of both sides.

Private Kenneth Moore, of 2nd Battalion of the 501st, tended the wounded there. He related, "Private Robert Wright and I were the only medics to assemble with the 2nd Battalion at Angoville-au-Plain and Les Droueries. During the day we assembled 75 casualties in a church. We collected the men in light two-wheeled farm carts. In the church little was said. The men had been hit and kept some of their weapons and I was afraid one of our people would kill the Germans and then we would have been cooked.

"At dusk on D-Day, we were told our troops could not hold the church. We both stayed with the wounded and shortly after that, the Germans came into the church. An officer asked if we would care for their wounded also till we could be evacuated. We agreed and the German officer left. During the night the churchyard was a battleground. Two of our men died during the night.

"At dawn an American tank appeared outside the church and fired through the windows with machine guns. We displayed panels and contacted the troops. They were 506th people and armor from the beach."

A church near St. Come-du-Mont also served as a medical sanctuary. Medic Bill Kidder, an aidman from 3rd Battalion of the 506th, related his experiences there: "I crawled to the intersection of a hedgerow, where I found one of our fellows hanging in his chute from the hedgerow with a broken arm. I had just finished getting him out of his chute when a German mortar round came in wounding me and killing him. I then continued down the row, where I joined up with some of the others and made our way toward St. Come-du-Mont.

"There were no medical officers with the mixed group that gathered together. On the morning of the 6th, I set up an aid station in a church near St. Come-du-Mont. There were two of us medics in the group—Frank Fabian and myself. The two of us took care of all the casualties bringing them into the shelter of the church. The Germans overran the town on the 8th and Fabian took the walking wounded and got them away from the town. I stayed with those who couldn't walk. Regardless of the church being plainly marked with the Red Cross, we were hit day and night with mortars and machine-gun fire. We held them off until the next day when our troops returned. We had over 80 wounded men in the church by the time the 'beach forces' reached us and arranged for medical evacuation. During the waiting period, our medical supplies were used to aid local residents as well, which included an elderly man and a small girl of about six years of age with a severe head wound. Her father was so grateful for the help given his daughter that he offered what must have been his prize possession, his gold pocket watch—which, of course, I didn't accept. I've often wondered if the child lived—the wound was quite severe."

Addeville—Lock aid stations

Though churches, open fields, and roadsides served as aid stations, the most common were the French farmhouses. Such a one, with a barn attached, became the Addeville headquarters for Major Francis E. Carrel, regimental surgeon for the 501st. This busy station was described by Father Sampson earlier in this chapter. When Colonel Johnson ordered Major Richard Allen to abandon the defense of Addeville and bring his troops down to the locks as reinforcements, it became necessary for Major Carrel and the walking wounded to move also. Father Sampson chose to stay behind at Addeville to look after the severely wounded.

It had been an exhausting day as well as one fraught with personal dangers for Major Carrel, who remembered, "D-Day ended for me with a sniper bullet in the knee, a mortar fragment in the cheek—otherwise real tired. Of course, the action did not stop—only slowed down some. Shelling of a town to our near west was pretty noisy."

Corporal Robert E. Schill was a medic serving with Major Carrel. He had jumped with 3rd Platoon of Charley Company. He said, "Everything was a mess. I hooked up with some men near a canal and was taking care of some wounded in a small farmhouse. Later on, Father Sampson, the Catholic chaplain, came along and took charge. I stayed there for most of the first day and then moved on to the locks with Major Carrel."

PFC Blas Valdon of Baker Company served as medic in a bombed-out house near the locks. He had landed in a swamp some distance southeast of St. Come-du-Mont and had joined another B Company man, an engineer, and a trooper from the 506th Regiment. "About 0300 we made contact with more men," said Baker. "At one point, I remember a trooper carrying a .30-caliber machine gun and he was weighted down with so much equipment I offered to help him. He agreed. I took some belts of ammo and several hand grenades and carried these for him. There were about ten of us in the group. We heard voices on the other side of the hedgerow. When one of the guys checked, they turned out to be a company of lost Germans. We lay against the hedgerow almost holding our breaths until they passed. Had they caught me with that ammo and grenades, I would not be here today because I never thought to remove my Red Cross brassard when I volunteered to help the machine gunner. Later, we found a few more men of which Colonel Johnson happened to be the ranking officer. Colonel Johnson had difficulty in finding his officers. Communications were very poor.

"The day ended for me in a bombed-out house administering first aid to several wounded troopers from the locks fight and victims of 88 shellings."

Culoville aid station

Major Louis P. Kent, regimental surgeon of the 506th, aided by Captain Logan B. Hull, assistant regimental surgeon, and Captain Willis P. McKee of the 326th Airborne Medical Company administered to the wounded. These included a little French boy who was operated on for a bullet wound.

Captain McKee jumped with ten of his aid men of the 326th Airborne Medical Company. He related, "We dropped on DZ 'C' with the headquarters of the 506th Regiment. Our mission was to remain at the drop zone and take care of the DZ casualties, thus allowing the regimental and battalion doctors to go with the troops on their missions. We had previously selected a nearby farmhouse for an aid station. Fortunately, we landed just where we expected. I got out of my harness and crawled to a hedgerow. With the aid of the cricket, all ten of the enlisted men were assembled in 15 to 20 minutes. We found a gate and road which we identified and knew exactly where we were—approximately two hundred yards from the preselected farmhouse.

"Since we were afraid there might be German troops in the house, we decided to wait until daylight to move in. We collected about fifteen casualties, mostly jump injuries, and arranged them along a hedgerow and cared for them until morning.

"We then moved into the farmhouse. A young French couple and two small children occupied it. We took over all except the kitchen and one bedroom. At that time we had no very serious casualties.

"The Frenchman of our farmhouse had a donkey and a two-wheeled cart, which we pressed into service for collecting casualties. We were well supplied by the belly loads dropped from our plane, all of which we recovered. We amassed quite a number of casualties and were able to give them good first-echelon care."

PFC Stanley J. "Stub" Shrodo was one of the medics who jumped with Captain McKee. He recalled, "I jumped on D-Day in the number 3 plane of the 506th Regiment with Captain Maloney, Colonel Robert Sink, Captain McKee, and a number of our medics. On the spot I landed was a growth of nettleweed. It didn't itch because I was too scared. I helped my buddy Jack Revier out of his chute. We headed for the shelter of a hedgerow. After securing our field, we had to gather our equipment chutes and set up a collecting station for the drop injured. My particular assignment was to report to the 506th Aid Station and get its position and then go to the 326th Medical Company with the information so the wounded could be evacuated readily and the number of casualties determined.

"At daybreak, an officer took charge and got organized. Captain McKee set up the aid station and I went with the 506th, then reported back to McKee. My next job was to locate the 326th Medical Company and report the position of the 506th Aid Stations. I managed to find them."

T/5 Paul Miller, chief medical technician for the 506th, described the early morning collection of jump-injured. He said, "I was jarred on the landing and twisted both knees and ankles but managed to keep going. I found out later that I hadn't landed far from Colonel Sink. My chute had dropped over me and it appeared difficult in the dark to find my way out from under it. The shroud lines were all tangled up around me. Once free, I crawled toward a fencerow and into a German private who was shot by some unknown person. I was in the hands of the enemy three times in one hour the night of the jump and was released either by our own troops or by the enemy to take care of the wounded. I ran across a pathfinder, who had a broken leg, treated it and kept going. He was from Harrisburg.

"My job was to treat all wounded and when the headquarters section was secure, we were to set up an aid station. I was chief surgical technician. I finally attached myself to a small group and met Colonel Sink and set up a collecting point for wounded and jump-injured. I treated them as best I could in the darkness and helped to keep the area secure."

Captain Logan B. Hull, assistant surgeon of the 506th, reflected upon all the confusion and summarized the medical service at Culoville. "I jumped with regimental headquarters as assistant surgeon in the vicinity of St. Marie-du-Mont. I was to establish the regimental aid station and help Major Louis Kent coordinate it with the regimental headquarters and 3rd Battalion aid stations. By noon, we had accumulated enough aid personnel to form an aid station for treatment of wounded, both ours and German. Three of our officers were lost, two with injuries while the third was captured, so we were shorthanded.

"Confusion was everywhere. There was no good system for evacuation of wounded until the beachhead was secured and the station hospital functioned. Personnel were mixed up and misplaced generally. Our regimental aid station had to serve as a treatment and holding center for wounded from all units because of the breakdown in evacuation. Many wounded could not be treated adequately in our small aid station which, at best, was designed for first aid only. Front lines were nonexistent in the early days of the Normandy campaign."

The little walled-in hamlet of Holdy, with its cluster of five buildings, was in the midst of some of the bloodiest and most hideous action of D-Day. Already before four in the morning, Captain George L. Lage, surgeon for the 2nd Battalion of the 502nd, had selected one of the buildings for an aid station. Here were brought jump-injured and the casualties from the action in the capture of the powerful battery of German 105mm guns nearby.[12]

Captain George L. Lage, a medical man trained for surgery, found himself very early on D-Day morning as the senior officer in charge of thirty troopers. He assumed tactical responsibility temporarily as well as tending to jump-injured and wounded in spite of ankle injuries he himself had sustained in the drop. He wrote of his numerous activities:

"I was the senior officer present and was expected to do something. I outlined a plan of an advance guard, the main body, and the rear guard. I had four injured men, mostly sprains (no bullet wounds yet), so I said I'd bring up the rear with the injured. We started up the line, but the injured, including myself, were so slow that we lost the rest of them after 150 yards. Another lieutenant with a sprained knee joined us just as we started off. At a road junction we found other paratroopers had set up a position with a couple of machine guns and several rifles. They had run into enemy opposition so we stopped to take stock of the situation.

"Being a medical officer, I'm not supposed to know anything about military tactics, but being in a spot, I put the little knowledge I had absorbed by association into practice. We set up our machine guns in a better position and sent two patrols to find out what was in front of us.

"I had the injured lieutenant take over the tactical situation. He knew a lot more about it than I. I set up a temporary aid station by the side of the road and fixed up the sprained ankles and knees so that these boys could go with us.

"Bullets began whistling over our heads. It was German fire. Soon we heard our answering fire. One man came back from the patrol and told of a group of five buildings a quarter mile down the road from which the Germans had been driven out. We left a machine gun and three men to guard this road junction. The rest of us moved cautiously into the village.

"We cut telephone and electric lines first to disrupt communications. The fireplaces of two houses had live coals in them. The next morning we learned that the French people who lived there had been having a party. When we began dropping, the Germans had made every one leave for protection.

"I inspected the first building for booby traps, then set up an aid station in it. I had one aidman with me. The house was blacked out with shutters. I had some candles and flashlights with me and very soon was ready to take care of cases. By 0400 A.M., two other medical officers and four aidmen had arrived with a large load of supplies. As soon as a man showed up with a weapon at our post, we sent him to help man the defensive line about the building. Two of the boys knocked out a machine-gun nest, but were badly wounded in the legs by another one across the road. We went after them, brought them back, and gave them plasma and treatment.

"Near 0400 A.M., gliders began to come in. Two of them crash-landed near us. Part of our boys went out to cover the landing and protect the glidermen from machine-gun and rifle fire. Some of the newcomers were injured, and brought in for treatment. The others formed into groups and joined their outfits. About this time we learned we were six miles from our objective, but only one mile from the Division command post.

"About an hour later, all hell broke loose and bullets hit the house and all around it. A force of Germans had started a counter-offensive. Everything we had—a few tommy guns, rifles, and three machine guns—were opened up on the attackers. They lost ten men to our one. One of the boys grabbed a machine gun and went up to an attic window firing it from the hip. This new position gave us the advantage. The Germans moved back with our boys at their heels. We killed about a hundred of them and took thirty prisoners. Of these, twenty were wounded so our medical force had a busy time until they were patched up.

"Some of the boys on patrol came across a wrecked glider containing a jeep that had been abandoned, so they pried it out picking up a trailer someplace, and came riding in like kings. This was all very serious business, but everyone was having the time of his life. Their confidence was building up every minute. I don't think anybody could beat these fellows now.

"The boys gave me the jeep to use as an ambulance. I found a driver, and we set out to find a place to move our patients. The road between our place and the division command post had been cleared except for occasional snipers.

"I made some red crosses with red parachutes on a white one so we thought we were safe in driving off. I guess it was because the snipers missed me as we drove along. We would tear down a stretch of road until we came to a curve, then go very cautiously. When we were sure there weren't any enemy—off we'd tear again.

"When we arrived at the command post they had started to set up a hospital. Supplies and personnel had arrived by glider. We turned about and started for our outpost to start evacuation. On the first trip back I found four of the eight resupply bundles I had dropped the night before. From that time on we had lots of medical supplies.

"Our force then began spreading out in a circle sweeping everything in front of us. As we made contact with units on either side, we kept strengthening our position. Patrols went after snipers all afternoon. Three boys brought in fifteen prisoners who had been hiding a half mile away. The troopers had smug grins, but the Germans were scared with no fight left.

"The afternoon was quiet except for the patrols. I got a couple hours sleep and something to eat. I could hardly walk because my ankles were so sore and swollen. I was afraid to take my boots off because I knew I would never get them back on again. We had been so busy I hadn't had time to do anything about them and now it was too late. The other medical officers tried to evacuate me, but I wouldn't go. Now that I was here, I wanted to stay and see the rest of the action. I could work in the aid station and knew I was needed.

"About dusk more gliders came in. Mortar shells started dropping close to us, and it was pretty hot, but we stuck it out. After things were quiet, we slept in shifts, each of us got about two hours' rest.

"Many other things happened from the time we landed, but I prefer to forget them. These were some of the atrocities that the Germans committed on our paratroopers. Many were shot as they were coming down, as was to be expected, but some of the cruel, cold-blooded things that some of the Germans did made us all see red.

"From that time on, we decided if they wanted to fight dirty we could too. We took very few prisoners compared to the number we could have, just for that reason. This war business is ghastly at best, but it can be terribly horrible."[13]

Captain Bert Clement, surgeon for 1st Battalion of the 506th Regiment, suffered two fractured vertebrae and a slipped disk on his drop. He, too, was involved in aid work in the Holdy area, just west of St. Marie-du-Mont.

Clement related, "My sergeant came back from the line where he had jumped, and we went back a few hundred yards and tried to get our bundle. There was a little confusion with the enemy up there, so we left it for the time being and went back later and got it. At that time, several men from our drop stick had arrived and we started down a little road toward St. Marie-du-Mont. We stopped at a crossroad where there were a bunch of houses and there was a lot of shooting around there. We joined some other fellows and spent the rest of the night taking care of wounded and injured.

"We had sporadic mortar fire off and on during the day and early evening where we were located. As it got light, some of the German mortar positions were popping at us. We got one using an upstairs window where the fellows set up with machine guns trying to do something with them.[14] Of course, that ended that episode right there.

"Later, back at our temporary aid section, we were watching the C-47's fly in the big Horsa gliders. One of the C-47's, with the tip of one wing turned up about four feet, came over very low and cut the Horsa glider off just above the tall trees. Of course, the only way the glider could go was down and he hit the tree which put him in a dive, and he came in on a fast glide as he hit the ground. Several of us went over there. I never saw a gorier mess in my life, before or since. The glider hit at about a 60 degree angle and everyone and everything in it was tangled up in a mess. People, pieces of people, guns, ammunition, seats, and things like that. It was certainly a gory mess. We got them cleaned out and a few of them were alive, or almost alive. We did what we could for them, but there was not any place to take them at that time. So we fixed some shelter for them, and left them with glider fellows who arrived at that time to take charge of them."

Fortin Farm

Down by the Douve River, where the action involved the wooden bridges, an aid station had been set up in the Fortin farmhouse by medical technicians Staff Sergeant Talfourd T. Wynne and Corporal Thomas E. Call, who had survived machine-gun firing and mortar shelling to reach this objective. Assisted by Chaplain Tilden McGee and Father Francis Sampson, the medics labored without the guidance of a surgeon. Father Sampson, it will be recalled, set off for Addeville, where Major Carrel released Captain Kingston to head for the Fortin Farm aid station.

In the meantime, Captain Nick Sorenson, surgeon of the 2nd Battalion of the 501st, had arrived at the Fortin Farm. He said, "I assembled to the rear (line of flight) and we retrieved a large para-bundle of medical supplies. We went through about a mile and a half of unsecured territory to a French farmhouse where some 18 to 20 wounded troopers had been gathered. Administered medication and 'IV albumin.' Had several critical cases, but all survived. The French farmwife and her young daughter had been killed by enemy mortar fire in the garden back of the house. We made a large red cross out of white and red bedding and placed it on the rooftop."

PFC Hank Rossetti of the 2nd Battalion, 501st Medical

Detachment, had also reached the Fortin Farm. He said, "We were to set up a battalion aid station. I spent the whole night in and out of canals. We finally reached a farmhouse. We were shelled in the morning. A young girl who lived there ran out of the house. Her mother followed, snatched her up, and both were killed by an almost direct hit. We buried them almost where they died."

At Ste. Mère Eglise

Much military action, involving mostly the 82nd Airborne Division, occurred in Ste. Mère Eglise. Many 101st men also landed in and around the town and joined the 82nd in attacking enemy positions.

Captain William G. Best, surgeon for 1st Battalion of the 502nd Regiment of the 101st, set up an aid station in one of the homes. Among his D-Day experiences was the delivery of a baby to a young French housewife during the evening. Captain Best related, "The baby I delivered was in the house we used as our aid station. This occurred about 9 or 10 P.M. on D-Day when the father of the baby ran in waving his arms. Sergeant Ernest Labadie, one of our medics, spoke some French so I was informed that the man's wife was in the late stages of labor and needed help. I helped to deliver a male baby who was named Jean Yves Bertot. I did not see or hear from the Bertot family until two or three years ago, when I wrote to the mayor of Ste. Mère Eglise and shortly thereafter I received a letter from the baby I had delivered, who was now 20 years old."

PFC Clarence "Bucky" Merrill, medic for Dog Company of the 506th Regiment, was forced to jump over Ste. Mère Eglise when his plane was hit. He said, "I worked my way up a ditch until I found the road into Ste. Mère Eglise, which was only about five hundred yards away. I found a few other men from my company. My first task was a sad one. My jumpmaster was our company executive officer, Lieutenant Walter J. Gunther. He landed in a tree in the churchyard at Ste. Mère Eglise. The Germans from their vantage point in the church steeple had shot him in his perch. I cut him down

and buried him. I was very busy in Ste. Mère Eglise working on wounded men of the 82nd Division until D + 3. I
worked on wounded around the clock as the Germans counterattacked several times to recapture the town. Much of the
town was leveled and we had many KIA's' and wounded."

Château Colombières

The division hospital was established at Château Colombières, a large country house at Hiesville, a few hundred
yards north of General Taylor's division command post. The
owners of the château moved their personal belongings out
and reserved one room for themselves.

To provide personnel for the division hospital, the 326th
Airborne Medical Company arrived in four echelons. The
first group had parachuted in during the early hours with the
various regiments to supplement regimental medics in car-
ing for the jump injured in the drop zones. They were to con-
verge on the division hospital. The second group was a
three-glider contingent which arrived at 0400 A.M. with operating equipment loaded in quarter-ton trailers firmly lashed
in the gliders. With them was Captain Charles Van Gorder,
one of eight volunteers of the 3rd Auxiliary Surgical Group.
A third group, under the leadership of Major William
Barfield, arrived by way of Utah Beach at noon of D-Day.
The fourth group arrived with the evening glider lift.

Captain Charles Van Gorder's glider had crash-landed
against a hedgerow bank near Hiesville. He had gone to a
nearby glider where he found its injured pilot, Colonel Mike
Murphy, working his way out of the wreckage. Inside he had
discovered the dead copilot and Brigadier General Don F.
Pratt, the assistant commander of the 101st Airborne Division, who had also been killed.

While treating Colonel Murphy, the medical officer noticed
a figure coming across the field. It was his own commanding
officer, Major A. J. Crandal, the chief surgeon of the 3rd
Auxiliary Surgical Team, who had also dropped in the vicinity. Soon after dawn, the major found some men with a jeep

and set out in search of the Château Colombières, which had been preselected as the site of the division hospital.

Van Gorder related, "Major Crandal began setting up our hospital and then returned to pick up the wounded and myself. We had the hospital in the château in operation by 0900 on June 6. This was the first Allied hospital to be in operation in Normandy.

"We set up our operating rooms on the second floor of the château where Major Crandal, Captain Rodda and myself; with Captain Willis McKee and Captain Roy Moore and some other medical officers from the 326th Airborne Medical Company, carried out the surgical procedures. The room I worked in had six operating tables made of a litter on medical supply chests standing on ends (one at the head and one at the foot). I remember that we wore our helmets while we operated because frequently bullets would come in the windows, striking the walls of the room. Captain Dworkin of our team supervised the anesthesia by organizing the dentists of the medical company and some of the medical officers using mostly intravenous sodium pentathol, although we brought in some anesthetic machines, which Captain Dworkin used on specific cases.

"Our operative cases were picked from the wounded in the yard by some of the medical officers who did the triage. That is, picking the wounded whom they thought we might save by operation and treatment. It was necessary to look over all the wounded and send us only those who had a chance to be saved by an operation. Some of the cases were hopeless and would only take our time from those who could be saved.

"By nightfall the yard was full of American and German wounded—about three hundred in all. The army gave us 92 quarts of whiskey issued to the medical company for use during the invasion. I could not understand why for a day or two."[15]

Captain William J. Waldmann was the surgeon for 3rd Battalion of the 501st. He managed to find his way to Division Headquarters and Château Colombières, where he assisted the other medics. He said, "After wandering around alone for an hour or so, keeping away from the Germans, I met a soldier from the 506th. After daylight we found two more soldiers of the 501st. Shortly after, we found the 506th Regimental Headquarters and from there I went to Division Headquarters at Hiesville. I assisted the 326th Medics with the wounded until midnight or thereabouts, and then went to my battalion."

The seaborne echelon of the 326th Airborne Medical Company came ashore at Utah Beach about noon on D-Day. They moved as quickly as possible to Château Colombières to provide much needed reinforcement for Major Crandal's staff.

Staff Sergeant Edward Miller of the 326th described the landing and the trip to the château: "The Krauts put out the welcome mat. Fortunately, they didn't hit our craft, though a few others were hit. I recall having a vantage point in the landing craft and calling out the distances to those huddled below.

"The landing was routine (they said). We waded in waist-deep water. My buddy, Irving Miller, awkward by nature, promptly fell on his face as he started ashore.

"Our group consisted of two officers and thirteen enlisted men, commanded by Captain Jake Pearl. Because none of the other groups were in the area where we landed (near Causeway 3), the officers went inland, leaving me to follow with the enlisted men if they did not return in an hour. Two of the men promptly crawled in shell holes and went to sleep. Honest! The rest of us watched as the Krauts shelled the landing area. They hit one craft-marker balloon after another. Eventually the officers returned with directions for locating the company. We hitched rides atop jeep-drawn trailers. The medical company had set up in a château. We went to work immediately and that continued until the place was blasted on June 9."

Sergeant John E. Woodrich, another medic of the 326th, stated, "We went in over the beach. One landing craft was blown out of the water as we approached the beach, and Major Barfield, who was a 'gung ho' character, yelled 'Charge!' as we jumped off and the next sound we heard was 'glub-glub' as the water was over his head.

"When we started up the causeway a couple of Germans came out of a pillbox and tried to surrender to us medics, and you never saw so many medics scramble for cover because we had no weapons and had no idea how many Germans were still in the pillbox.

"Our mission was to set up the company and treat the wounded for the division. We were too busy treating casualties to notice what went on around us. I was in surgery and I recall going up to the second floor of the hospital and as I climbed the stairs, casualties were stacked up on the stairs all the way up. There was blood everywhere. I got sick at the sight, but after a breath of air, I went back up and was too busy to get sick anymore."

T/5 W. Paul Nabours, Jr., was a member of Staff Sergeant Ed Miller's medical group. He related, "There were thirteen of us from the 326th Airborne Medical Company who were put on board a landing craft with some infantry of another division. We were very disappointed in having trained almost eighteen months for glider landing and then having to go by ship.

"We went in on Exit 3. The sand was very nice up to the seawall. We waited in shell or bomb craters for mines to be checked out.

"As we were going up a hill the ditches on both sides of the road were filled with dead Germans. We were held up at St. Marie-du-Mont by a sniper in a church steeple that overlooked the road we had to use. We were picked up in jeeps from our company and taken to the château, where the 326th Airborne Medics were operating. The division surgeon and his staff were with us. We worked through the night on casualties from glider landings, parachute drops, as well as battle casualties. Most of us didn't sleep for two or three days because we were so busy. I had been bored with medic training, but when real work was assigned, it really meant something to me. It was a good feeling to help those who needed it so badly."

On June 9, the Germans bombed the hospital, killing eleven and wounding fifteen. Six of the dead were medical personnel. Fortunately most of the wounded had already been evacuated to England.

Aid station at the seawall

Captain Edward A. Flanigan, surgeon for the 81st Antitank Battalion, had been prepared to accompany his battalion into Normandy on the predawn glider lift. However, a few days before D-Day, due to a shortage of gliders, his group was assigned to the seaborne echelon.

"We were let out in the water up to our armpits and scrambled ashore to the seawall," remembered Flanigan. "I don't know how far we were from Hiesville. I took care of some wounded on the beach and evacuated them to the amphibious engineers. I spent D-Day treating and evacuating men on the beach until dark, then I set up an aid station at the seawall."

Summary

This epic of the medics as "angels of mercy" on D-Day is but a part of their tale. There were many other aid stations set up throughout Normandy where the valiant effort of the medics salvaged innumerable broken limbs and life where death was imminent. No tribute can begin to do justice to their heroism.

CHAPTER 17

At Day's End

Of the 6,670 paratroopers of the Screaming Eagle Division who set out across the English Channel, all but seventy jumped into Normandy in the early hours of D-Day. Only 1,100—or approximately one-sixth of the total dropped—were assembled into organized fighting groups by H-Hour, 0630, the time of the beach landings. This number swelled to about 2,500 by evening. Many had fought individually before locating other friendly soldiers. Makeshift groups did a remarkable job of accomplishing missions that had been assigned to battalion and regiment-sized units.

Reports of parachute landings over a widely scattered area from Caen on the east, to the Brittany Peninsula on the west, Cherbourg on the north, and St. Lo on the south, continued to upset the Germans. Reports of the landings on the invasion beaches were considered to be diversionary tactics. It was difficult for reinforcements to be rushed to all the reported parachute and glider landing areas. There were just too many of these landings reported. Accounts of landings involving men from a few lost planes often resulted in exaggerated numbers being reported.

If the airborne commanders were upset because of the scattered drops and poor assemblies, the enemy had more difficulty. The Germans had scattered their forces over the countryside in platoon strength (40 to 50 men). Communications were by telephone and motorcycle messengers.

The Americans, singly and in small groups, raised havoc with all wire communications as lines connecting these platoon-sized enemy units were cut and recut. When the field phones went out, the enemy dispatch riders went forth—never to be seen or heard from again. The grenade in the hand of a paratrooper proved a deadly weapon.

German platoon commanders lost all contact with neighboring units. No orders arrived. In this fashion, the small enemy forces fought, surrendered, or died as they were being engaged by American paratroopers who didn't know where they were, but knew what they were doing. The enemy in turn knew where they were, but didn't know what was happening. Some were overawed by the power displayed as hundreds of planes passed overhead at relatively low altitudes with red and green wing lights displayed. From these they had witnessed the dropping of countless parachutists. Their commanders had warned them paratroopers did not take prisoners. Because of this misconception, many German soldiers fought on hopelessly until they were finally slain or badly wounded.

Objectives assigned to the 101st Airborne Division were not all taken by the end of D-Day. The bridges west of Carentan were still held in strength by Germans who realized the importance of them for their own plans. American forces in sufficient strength could not be mustered for the task of capturing them. Two units of the 501st Regiment (one commanded by Colonel Johnson at the locks, and the other led by Lieutenant Colonel Ballard) were both completely engaged with enemy units and could not march on the bridges. They had to rely on defensive tactics—namely sitting in foxholes waiting for the enemy to make thrusts. The division commander, General Taylor, knew nothing of their whereabouts. No radio contact had been established with them. The third group under Lieutenant Colonel Ewell was still under the control of General Taylor as his reserve unit and cover for division headquarters. The capture of the bridges would take the combined efforts of several regiments over the next few days.

The 502nd Regiment had completed the task of clearing the causeways. The 4th Infantry Division had spearheaded a force of 20,000 men who came over Utah Beach on D-Day. This division experienced little of the pressure found at Omaha Beach. The enemy was occupied with forces both in front and behind him with no communications to his rear headquarters.

With the coastal artillery battery completely destroyed by Air Force bombing, and its artillerymen routed by Staff Sergeant Harrison Summers and his crew at WXYZ, and no obstacles to impede their march inland along the three lower causeways, the two spearheading regiments (8th and 12th Infantry Regiments of the 4th Infantry Division) suffered only 197 casualties. Of this number, 60 were lost when their landing craft hit a mine.

At the close of D-Day, the men of the 502nd were in holding positions, aiding the 4th Division in keeping the northern flank protected against enemy counterattacks.

Colonel Sink's 506th Regiment was concentrated mainly in the center of the division perimeter near Culoville and Vierville. Lieutenant Colonel Strayer and his 2nd Battalion had completed the long march from the wrong drop zone to their objective at Causeway 2, and then had moved to the area of regimental headquarters at Culoville. As the day came to its end, the regimental commander, Colonel Sink, still had no knowledge of the 3rd Battalion, nor did he know that its temporary commander, Captain Charles Shettle, continued to hold the wooden bridges northeast of Carentan. However, Shettle had lost his bridgehead. The 506th Regiment, nevertheless, was in position to be used by General Taylor for tomorrow's attack toward St. Come-du-Mont and the Carentan highway bridges.

The two glider serials had brought in valuable equipment to be used in the fight on D plus 1. Less than forty percent of the equipment bundles dropped with the paratroopers had been recovered. Valuable communications equipment, mortars, and 75mm pack howitzers had been lost and their absence stymied D-Day attack plans. The equipment brought in by the gliders, however, was almost all recovered in useable condition even from the badly wrecked crafts. The antitank guns would increase the firepower of the infantry units when they ran up against enemy armor tomorrow. The glider-borne communications equipment enabled the division to contact the outside world. Radios lost to the regiments would be replaced tomorrow and the attacks could be coordinated from a central command post.

Other elements of the 101st that had been left behind in England came in by ship across the Channel throughout the long hours of D-Day. The largest group was the 3,179-man 327th Glider Infantry Regiment merged with the 1st Battalion of the 401st Glider Infantry Regiment. Original plans for these airborne soldiers to arrive by glider had been scrapped. As they disembarked, some went into bivouac near Utah Beach and others assembled on D plus 1 near St. Marie-du-Mont, ready to assist in the drive to clear the peninsula.

Arriving on D-Day and successive days were other reinforcements, including the 321st Glider Field Artillery Battalion aboard the *John S. Mosby* and the ill-fated *Susan B. Anthony,* which hit a mine and sank with its cargo of guns and engineer equipment. The artillerymen aboard her were rescued by other craft, as were the 326th Airborne Engineers also aboard.

The complications of the giant landing separated men and guns of the 907th Glider Field Artillery Battalion. The men arrived on D-Day and their guns on the 9th.

Three batteries of the 81st Antiaircraft and Antitank Battalion landed on Utah Beach fifteen minutes after H-Hour and set up their weapons on the beach. They provided .50-caliber machine guns to cover the seaborne landings against strafing attacks by the German Air Force. At least two enemy planes were knocked from the sky by this unit.

Baptism by fire

Perhaps D-Day doesn't stand out as the most exciting day in the lives of the surviving 101st Airborne soldiers, but it was their baptism by fire. First impressions are lasting impressions. Lessons were quickly learned. It didn't take the men long to distinguish between the ripping sounds of enemy guns and the staccato of American weapons; between the unsynchronized drumming of enemy bombers and the steady droning of Allied planes.

Command personnel learned who would be the tried-and-true leaders. Platoon officers discovered that combat brought out the best qualities of their men, and privates and corporals rapidly climbed in the ranks.

Weeks and months of bitter fighting were in store for the young Eagles. Savage fighting would result on the approaches to Carentan (Purple Heart Lane) and in the town itself before a juncture could be forced with the Allied troops marching westward from Omaha Beach.

There would be larger airborne operations planned in the future, such as the assault on Holland and the jump across the Rhine. However, never again would the Allies attempt a large-scale night landing from the sky. The operation had eased the way for the seaborne troops, but the airborne soldiers had paid a heavy price for that success.

CHAPTER 18

The French Were Waiting

Conditions in occupied Normandy were relatively stable for two years after the German army of occupation moved in. During the middle of April of 1944, changes were noted. The mayors of the towns were directed by area commanders to provide special details of townspeople and neighboring farmers for a project designed to "protect" them from airborne invasion from England.

To hinder the landing of Allied gliders, the "impressed" workers, under the armed supervision of engineer units, cut young trees from the neighboring hedgerows, stripped them of their branches, and placed them in holes three feet deep in the larger fields. The poles were spaced 65 feet apart and barbed wire was strung from post to post. Mines were to be connected to them later. The project went on slowly. A few poles appeared each day in the neighboring fields.

At the same time as the above orders were issued, there were directives that all radio sets had to be turned in at the town halls. People in the Cotentin (Cherbourg peninsula) were no longer permitted to listen to broadcasts of the BBC from England. Penalties were threatened if this order was unheeded.

In May, the marshes the Germans had flooded were losing water though the German engineers attempted to keep them at a high level. Pesky mosquitoes appeared in huge swarms in the evenings from these large spawning grounds.

Near the base of the peninsula, in the vicinity of Beuzeville-la-Bastille and Bauptois, small bridges were bombed late in May. Leaflets floated down from the sky giving general directions to the people. They also contained pictures of the uniforms worn by British and American paratroopers along with the shapes of jeeps and Allied tanks that could be expected in France at any time.

During the evening of May 29th, Allied aircraft appeared over the coastal towns of Foucarville and St. Martin-de-Varreville. The family of Mayor Alexandre Renaud, of Ste. Mère Eglise, watched from upstairs windows as the spectacle began. Mayor Renaud wrote: "Hundreds of flares fell to earth. They disappeared behind the line of trees and it seemed to us that a new dawn was breaking over the sea.[1]

"Soon more flares appeared and remained floating in the sky. Against the dull roar of the big engines we heard the whine, then the explosions of the sticks of bombs. The windows rattled in Ste. Mère Eglise. It was like daylight, a garish blue daylight without shadows of half tints." The bombers were out to destroy the coastal battery at St. Martin-de-Varreville.

German troop movements increased with a steady streaming of men and equipment up the Cotentin peninsula. Enemy forces of Asiatic origin (Russian, Georgian, and Mongol) appeared in ever-increasing numbers. These troops were commanded by German officers and noncommissioned leaders. Units moved into small towns, set up fortifications, and just as mysteriously moved out in the night. The German troops stationed in the area were certain a landing would take place somewhere in Normandy.

As D-Day approached, the people watched as fighter-bombers dived toward railroad and highway bridges west and south of Ste. Mère Eglise, leaving columns of heavy black smoke to drift away with the wind. Little did the populace know that the Allies were attempting to sever the Cotentin peninsula from the main part of France, in order to prevent the movement of German armor and reinforcements when the invasion began.

The bombings continued into the nights. "During the early nights of June, the inhabitants awakened to the sounds of war," wrote Mayor Renaud. "Constantly at night the window-panes and the shop windows would shake. We would learn in the morning that a farm had been destroyed and its inhabitants torn limb from limb. And yet, life goes on as before. The bombs appear to fall more or less at random, without any general plan. 'They are just clumsy and made a mistake, we say.' "

The impressed workers were prodded into completing the trenches being dug around Ste. Mère Eglise. These revetments wormed their way in and out of the orchards while the placing of "Rommel's Candles," as they were called by the French, continued in the fields but not energetically.

Monsieur Andre Mace, a resident of Ste. Mère Eglise, had not turned in his radio (to the authorities) and spent many hours listening to reports coming out of England. He remembered, "I had received an order from the mayor, and been appointed chief of my block or sector in digging the ditches. We sensed that the landing was approaching."

In the little town of Appeville, six kilometers southwest of Ste. Mère Eglise lived Henri Jouaux, Jr. With his father, he operated a large dairy farm. He said, "Along with other farmers in our neighborhood, we were forced to place anti-glider poles in the large fields. The enemy soldiers were patient with us even though we made the work drag. On June 5th, the enemy soldiers did not come to get us to do the work. We sensed that they were afraid that the invasion was very near."

Other Normans also remembered that the Germans did not come for them on the 5th. Monsieur LeBlond served as the director of the Public School for Boys in Ste. Mère Eglise. As a member of the detail preparing the poles in the fields near the town, he enjoyed the respite. He said, "In the afternoon of the 5th, I went to see the effects of an important Allied bombardment on a fortified German position at St. Martin-de-Varreville, approximately six kilometers from our town. The batteries were completely destroyed."

"I was fishing in the Fierre Village on the banks of the Merderet River, in the section where Generals Ridgeway and Gavin of the 82nd Division were to land," recalled Henri LeJouard, newspaperman in St. Mère Eglise. Earlier he had planted poles in the fields and cut trenches around the villages and prepared fortifications.

Alphonse Voydie, mayor of Graignes, a town some distance to the southeast of Carentan stated, "I was busy in the administration of my affairs in order to escape as much as possible the annoyances of the Germans." The annoyances he referred to included the planting of poles in the marshes.

In Ste. Mère Eglise the day was relatively calm. The German antiaircraft battery stationed in town was in the town square most of the day and busy servicing the guns and equipment. Mayor Renaud noted the first small change in the late afternoon. "At about six P.M., two small Allied fighter planes came down from an overcast sky. They cruised very low over the church spire, then circled the village. The Germans fired. They disappeared into the clouds. At eight o'clock in the sky from which the clouds had cleared, we saw them again, describing wide circles around us. The night promises to be very beautiful."

The last light of day hadn't disappeared on the westward horizon yet. Mayor Renaud added, "It has not come completely, when the humming of the big planes begins again. The engines are so numerous that it is impossible to make out the directions of the squadrons. Shots are fired from the steeple, from the fields, and from the trenches.

"Over the coast, the sky is again flare-lit. We climb once more to the third floor and the same light meets our eyes as the week before, but a little farther away toward St. Marcouf; the same aurora glows, the same explosions shaking the house like a giant battering ram.

"We had just lain down on our beds when we heard a violent pounding on the front door. I got up. People were coming to tell me a villa on the other side of the square at the entrance of La Haule Park was being gutted by fire. The fire brigade was vainly striving to gain control of the flames. We made a chain as far as the cattle-market pump. Men ran along with their canvas buckets and threw the contents into a large tub. Through the bushes great shadows could be seen moving about. The wind blew the flames sidewise, and bits of burning paper and hay were spinning toward a loft twenty yards away filled with straw and wood.

"In the air, heavy bombers were passing in great waves from west to east. The machine guns were cross firing above our heads, and hundreds of big luminous flies whistled, yelled, and whined, occasionally coming up with a smack against the walls of the burning house. The antiaircraft men in field dress, with their weapons loaded, watched us. The distant explosions of heavy bombs shook the earth.

"Suddenly the fire alarm sounded, sad and lugubrious, a succession of short notes. At this precise moment a wave of big transport planes with all lights on, came over at treetop level; another followed immediately, then still more. And something like enormous confetti came out of their bellies and dropped rapidly to earth."

Parachutists!

Alexander Renaud added, "The pumping stopped and all eyes turned upward. The flak crews opened fire.

"All around us, the airborne soldiers dropped heavily to the ground. By the light of the fire, we could clearly see the men at the end of their lines, maneuvering their parachutes. One of them, less skillful perhaps, landed in the midst of the flames. Sparks flew up, and the fire became fiercer. Another suddenly wriggled like a worm. His hands shot up and gripped the risers; his legs contracted violently. The big parachute dropped in the meadow.

"In an old tree all covered with ivy there hung a great white veil, and at the end of it was a man moving. Clinging to the branches, slowly like a reptile, he was making his way down. Then he tried to unfasten his belt. The flak gunners saw him. At a few yards range, the machine guns spat out their sinister rattle. The unfortunate man's hands fell, and the body swayed and hung limply at the end of the lines.

"Before us, a few hundred yards off, near the sawmill, a big transport plane crashed to earth, and soon a second fire was raging. The alarm was still clanging. We were now full in the firing zone from the steeple, and bullets were smacking into the ground not far from us.

"The night was warm and the moon sliced the scene into wide strips of light. Meanwhile, at the pump, a paratrooper suddenly emerged from the shadows to the middle of a group of our people. He covered us with his tommy gun, but seeing that we were French, he did not fire. A German sentinel who was hiding behind a tree gave a great shout and fled at his best speed. The paratrooper tried to ask a few questions, but as nobody in the group spoke English, he crossed the road and was lost in the night.

"Above the fire, the great planes continued gliding over and dropped their human cargoes on the farther side of the cemetery. Soon, the antiaircraft gunners, realizing the importance of what was happening, ordered us to go indoors immediately. On the square, a German soldier passed us. 'Tommy parachutists all kaput!' he told us, and was careful to show us the body of a man lying near his parachute.

"I could not resist the temptation to go into the garden, from which the view extends over the countryside. From the house there was only a courtyard to go through, then the sea road. I crept down the little lane running alongside a river that had been widened and deepened here to serve as a public washing place. Flattened against the bank, which ran down from the garden and above the washing place, I could gaze on the fairy-tale spectacle. The moon, very near the horizon, shed a bright light on the expanse of water and left me in the shade. The machines were still passing overhead at the full speed of their engines. The sky was continuously crisscrossed with the fugitive lights of tracer bullets, and sometimes these lights would seem to disappear into the huge fuselages.

"In the east, the big elms of the manor fields stood out like shadow pictures against the red background of a fire. Without a stop the confetti continued to fall to earth. The dull blows of the big bombs were still shaking the earth. As I wondered about the parachutists coming from the planes and the thoughts that were going through their minds, a transport plane appeared over the houses just east of my hiding place. To right and left the parachutes unfolded, and two of them came to rest in my garden. A moment or two later, shadowy forms appeared on the enclosing wall. A third parachute, the last to leave the C-47, was gliding toward me. In a flash I saw the paratrooper wriggling at the ends of his lines a few yards above my head. With a resounding splash, the man sank into the river. The parachute caught in a small apple tree hung across the path. Loaded as he was with emergency rations and munitions, and entangled in his lines, the poor fellow was going down without a cry, without a murmur. Thanks to the parachute I had no difficulty hauling him to the bank.

"The soldier had no helmet. Half fainting, he was coughing and spluttering trying to get rid of the water that filled his eyes and mouth. Then he looked at me, and I read astonishment in his face. 'Tommy?' I asked him.

"Probably not understanding, he answered, 'Yes.' 'Don't be afraid,' I added in English.

"At that he looked at me again and—I don't know why—felt my hat, then my coat. 'I am French,' I told him laughing, 'and a friend.'

"He must have thought he was a prisoner, and now as he began to grasp the situation, he quickly got rid of his bonds. Like a gentleman, he introduced himself, 'My name is . . .' Despite all my efforts I cannot remember his name. 'May I help you?' I asked.

" 'Thanks, I must go,' he replied in a calm voice, which was a strange contrast to his earlier agitation. He pointed to a fresh wave of planes that had just come over the line of trees standing like powerful sentinels at the end of the meadow, indifferent to the majesty of the scene.

"In the wake of these great night birds, other paratroopers, like the seeds of the maple tree, were silently descending; and soon the domes of bright-colored silk, silvery in the moonlight, rested on the meadow grass.

"His orders must certainly have been to join his group and every wasteful minute might be fatal to himself and to his companions. Dripping with water, without a rifle, he stepped over his parachute. I piloted him a few paces away to where some steps led up to the bank. He was reeling like a drunkard, and yet before disappearing, he turned around toward me and said, 'My parachute is for you. Good-bye.'

"I answered with a friendly wave. The shadow disappeared and then reappeared at the bottom of the garden, climbed the wall and faded away forever."

Newspaperman Henri LeJouard remembered the early action: "I went to look at a fire in La Haule Park where I met several German soldiers in full uniform. As I was watching the fire I was standing beside a German. The Americans began to drop from the airplanes as they passed overhead. The German soldiers took off. My first American dropped into the little wings which bordered the square of our church. Afterwards the paratroopers fell on all sides. This resulted in the townspeople fleeing for shelter, as did many of the Germans."

Two women living in the small hamlet of Mesières remembered those first hours when the parachutists were dropping. Unknown to them, their small village was designated as the WXYZ objective for the 502nd Parachute Infantry Regiment. Many of the buildings housed the German troops whose responsibility was the battery of large coastal guns situated in the St. Martin-de-Varreville area about a thousand yards to the east.

Madame Louis Caillemer lives in the same house she occupied on D-Day near the eastern edge of Mesières. Her house served as the billet for one of those enemy soldiers. She recalled, "The major in charge of the German artillery troops moved into my home on May 28 because of the heavy and continuous bombing attacks on the guns and fortifications." She pointed to the stairway. "He had a room upstairs."

She continued, "I remember that his telephone rang frantically after 2200 P.M.,[2] and I heard the hurried and excited conversation. After this the major made several quick calls to his men. I could hear the soldiers assembling on the road. Shortly afterward, they rushed off to their posts. The major left quickly and it was the last I saw of him.

"I looked out of my back door a short time later and saw numerous parachutists dropping in the fields immediately behind my house. I heard the strange sounding clicking noises for many hours. About 0200 A.M. a loud pounding was heard at the door. I went to answer. Confronting me was a bayonet-armed soldier with a blackened face. He asked for Germans and searched the downstairs rooms. With a bayonet in my back, I preceded the soldier upstairs, where he continued his search. Satisfied no enemy troops were in the house, he left."

At the western edge of Mesières lived Madame Leopold Groult. "I saw some of the men jumping in the bright moonlight," she remembered, "and I heard the crickets near the house. I became very frightened when I heard a loud crash first on the roof and again beside the door. It was caused by the fall of a steel helmet from a soldier who was struggling to get free of his parachute in the tall tree beside our house." However, no strange soldiers came to her door as she cowered in the darkened home.

Little did Jean Lecaudey, a twenty-one-year-old farmer in Hiesville, dream when he saw his first parachutist float down into a neighbor's garden, that his home would become a beehive of military activity in the days to come. The Lecaudey farm had been previously selected as the site of the 101st Airborne Division Command Post. On the evening of June 5th, he had been visiting with his family at the home of a nearby neighbor. They had hurried home to be indoors before curfew. Recalling the parachute jumps, Lecaudey related, "It was about 10:30, solar time when I saw my first parachutist descend in the garden of a neighbor while many others floated down in the vicinity.[3] I called to the one in the garden. He advanced toward me showing a long dagger. I made him understand I was French. He asked where the German artillery battery at Holdy was located."

Monsieur and Madame Ferdinand Fortin still live in their old and weathered thatch-covered house about two hundred yards north of the La Barquette Locks.[4] Fortin had been frightened just like the others when he encountered his first paratrooper. He said, "An American parachutist armed with a long knife and hand grenades appeared at our door at 0300 asking for directions, and the location of enemy outposts."

"The constant sound of the clickers and their answers in and about our farm" were the biggest impression left on Madame Marie Therese James. As a seventeen-year-old, she lived in the same house she now occupies in Culoville, only a few hundred yards northeast of the buildings that once served as the 506th Regimental Headquarters. She added,

"Because of the noise and activity and shelling of the aircraft passing overhead, our family ran outside to the safety of some trenches that had been dug for us. In the darkness as we sat huddled together. We heard the low murmurings of American soldiers in the nearby shadows. In an adjoining hog sty, the pigs became nervous from all the noise and set up a loud chorus of squealing and grunting. A paratrooper threw a grenade into the pen where it exploded. Fortunately, none of the animals were killed. One of the pigs had to be killed a short time later due to lameness. Our family members were busy picking grenade fragments from the cooked pork for several weeks during the meals."

Another Culoville resident, René LeCarpentier, described the predawn experience of one of his friends, who raised fine race horses in the area. LeCarpentier recalled, "My friend was awakened by the aerial bombardment in the vicinity. He observed a paratrooper as he landed in the small yard where he kept his horses. The animals set up a terrific racket as they raced and snorted about the confine. My friend was terribly afraid. He hid under the staircase. A short time later, the squeaky door of the house opened slowly and the hidden farmer could hear the slow measured steps of the soldier as he conducted a cautious search of the rooms. A short time later my friend heard a 'thump' and this was quickly followed by loud snoring. The parachutist had discovered the man's bed and was fast asleep in a matter of seconds."

Daybreak

Many people who had observed the Allied paratroopers floating down from the sky or had been disturbed by a knock at the door had assumed them to be English or "Tommies."

Mayor Renaud wrote: "Bit by bit, the night began to split up; the milky dawn showed a few outlines, the outlines became better defined and we were dumbfounded to see the square occupied not by Germans or Tommies, but by Americans!

"We recognized first of all their big rounded helmets, which we had all seen reproduced in German magazines.

Some were sleeping or smoking, lying under the trees. Others, rifle in hand, lined up behind the wall and the little communal building, known as the public weighing place, and were covering the hostile church.

"Their fierce and somewhat untended look reminded us of movie gangsters. The helmets were covered with a net of khaki cord; the faces of most of them were grimed with soot, like the heroes of detective stories. Their getup, to us who were accustomed to the German discipline and correctness, seemed absolutely careless. Just plain brown boots to halfway up the calf, belts of machine-gun cartridges hung round their shoulders and waists. They were armed not only with tommy guns but with enormous revolvers which stuck out over their hips. Their figures were entirely without line; the ample wind-jacket, all folds and of a vague color between gray, green, and khaki, opened in front to form a vast pocket in which were heaped munitions and rations. They also had a pocket for field dressing and trouser pockets. On the sides and behind, pockets up the legs. Further, strapped to the right calf, was the long sheath of a dagger. That was how the soldiers of America appeared to us for the first time in the dawn of the 6th of June, 1944."

M. LeBlond described his early morning encounter with the paratroopers: "During the morning of the 6th, at about 0500, a group of five or six parachutists gathered together on the road near the garden gate of the school. I went towards them and explained to them that a glider, carrier of a cannon and munitions had landed about 0200 in the field next to the school.[5] They followed me and disengaged the cannon, which was put into position at the western edge of the road leading out of Ste. Mère Eglise."

Paul Renaud, the eldest son of the late Mayor Alexandre Renaud and aged thirteen at the time, recalled, "I opened the shutters of my bedroom window in the morning (0700) and looked out on the scene below. There were some American paratroopers sitting on the park benches. Others were asleep on the ground. One man was trying to coax a girl to come down from her upstairs window by offering her candy and gum. I got some gum that morning. It was the first in four years."

Monsieur Alphonse Mauger lives in St. Come-du-Mont. He remembered that the wartime mayor, Gustave Laurence, had done much to aid the first Americans. "Mayor Laurence had picked up a wounded man, Judels by name, from a field near the town and carried him to the mayor's home, where he administered first aid and hid him. Our town remained in enemy hands until the 8th of June."

Mauger related another story to point out the bravery of their mayor: "A paratrooper came crashing down on the roof of one of our two-storied houses near the church. His chute was draped over one side of the roof while the trooper hung limply over the other side feigning death in view of the enemy soldiers who moved about in the square below. An enemy officer ordered our people to climb a ladder to cut the parachutist's lines so his body could drop to the cobblestoned surface below. The French people, and especially Mayor Laurence, refused to perform the brutal deed. Mayor Laurence climbed the ladder and cut the back-injured parachutist free and lowered him gently to the waiting Germans. He was carried into the aid station behind the church.

Action during the day

Mme. Leopold Groult witnessed some of D-Day's heaviest action, that of the siege of WXYZ, the barracks complex at Mesières. As the hail of bullets and bazooka rockets was directed toward the last and largest of the German barracks, Mme. Groult led her family out of her home situated just across the roadway. She said, "We went out of the back door and ran to the ditches along which we crawled south to get away from all the shooting."

In a small farmhouse about six hundred yards west of the site of the two wooden bridges that had been the objectives of the 506th Regiment's 3rd Battalion lives M. Theophile Fortin, cousin to Ferdinand Fortin, of La Barquette Locks. Fortin remembered that his home was used as a medical aid station for several days. He sadly recalled that his wife

Suzette and daughter Georgette had been killed on D-Day, victims of enemy shelling. The child had run out into the yard and the mother had followed in a vain attempt to save her.[6]

The widow Louis Regnault lives on a substantial farm just to the north of Sainteny, which is located about ten kilometers south of Carentan. During the early days of the fighting, shortly after D-Day, Frenchman Jean Capitem, an underground worker and former French marine, had informed the people in the vicinity that he needed food for a group of about twenty-five paratroopers he had hidden at Raffauville Manor about a mile to the north. Among these were Privates Chester Brooks and Richard Frame of the 501st Regiment's 1st Battalion Headquarters, and Corporal Harry Plisevich of H Company of the 501st. Madame Regnault said, "We provided them with ample food. I gave directions to Ste. Mère Eglise to a group of them."

Describing the heavy fighting which took place in and around Ste. Mère Eglise on D-Day, Monsieur LeBlond, the former director of the Public School of Boys, said, "A German counterattack with armored vehicles was coming south from the direction of Montebourg. It was stopped by paratroopers and glidermen before the entrance of Ste. Mère Eglise. Another attack along the road from Beuseville-au-Plain (to the northeast of Ste. Mère Eglise) had the same end."

Newspaperman Henri LeJouard also recalled the heavy fighting: "At Ste. Mère Eglise, on the Carentan Street (Highway N-13), the Germans tried to retake the town by coming from the village of Fauville. In this street, many were killed on the 6th of June."

Robert Mauger, farmer, had spent the day of the 5th in the fields thinning turnips with his father. The members of his family were not too disturbed with the dropping of the parachutists because they had noted men dropping about eight days earlier and assumed that this event, like the previous one, was part of the German army maneuvers. He recalled, "On the morning of June 6, at 0100 A.M., there were ten parachutists near our farm. We asked them where they had landed—Did you land at Foucarville? No, they had dropped at St. Marie-du-Mont. Later in the morning an officer and about fifty men were assembled at our farm at 0500 A.M.[7]

"At the end of our road, the parachutists made many explosions on trucks containing German ammunition and many German soldiers were killed. As a result of the fires and explosions, some of the buildings near the trucks burst into flames."[8]

M. Henri Jouaux, Jr.'s farm in Appeville is situated about six miles directly west of the Drop Zone "C" area near Hiesville. Many of the 501st Regiment's 3rd Battalion and Division Headquarters personnel had dropped in the vicinity. Jouaux related, "On the night of the 5th of June we were unable to sleep. The airplanes were making so much noise and we were not surprised to see the parachutists descend. The first American I recall was walking in a wheat field at 0500 A.M."

While driving through the area, Jouaux pointed out a hilltop that had provided good observation to the east near Houtteville. He said, "This is where some American parachutists destroyed two enemy tanks. Only one American was killed."[9]

Jouaux, with the help of his 70-year-old father, spent several days searching for lost and injured American parachutists in the surrounding fields. These were taken to a secluded farm building near Appeville, where they were provided with food, wine, and blankets. The men were then taken in groups of five by farm cart to the north end of a narrow peninsula, where the Jouauxs had concealed a flat-bottomed skiff. They loaded the soldiers in the boat and poled them to the north side of the Douve River under the cover of darkness, where they were able to contact friendly troops.

On a later trip, while carrying wounded and injured soldiers to the boat, the group was ambushed by two German soldiers. The aged father was shot in the back and killed while the son escaped through the hedgerow. That group of paratroopers was captured. However, the younger Jouaux continued to assist the remaining troopers concealed in the grain house.[10]

In the southeast of Carentan, in the town of Graignes,

Alphonse Voydie, who has served as its mayor since 1943 observed, "I saw a large number of airplanes which flew over us. Getting up very early the next morning, I went into the field in back of my home and discovered American parachutists there. I was informed that additional parachutists had gathered at the village. I left to make contact with them and we organized their defense and provided them with food. They had landed in the flooded marshes at Graignes by mistake. We continued to provide food and shelter for them. The parachutists were attacked by the Germans on Sunday, June 12, around ten o'clock. They resisted all day and did not succumb until the night was over. The large numbers of Germans and the lack of ammunition was too much. About 40 of them were killed and about 130 of their comrades hid themselves in the homes of the inhabitants, who succeeded in getting part of them to a boat with which they were carried to Carentan, already occupied by American troops. Others, like Frank Juliano, were hidden in attics where they waited for the liberation of Graignes, which occurred on July 13, 1944."

The mixed group of 82nd and 101st paratroopers also included some glidermen and their pilots. They set up a perimeter defense about Graignes and sent out patrols to carry on sabotage missions, blowing bridges and ambushing patrols. Unfortunately, a member of a three-motorcycle enemy patrol managed to escape. The next day, enemy units attacked the town with mortars and artillery. The Americans suffered heavy casualties and were forced to flee during the night. Some were carried by boat to the American positions farther to the north. Others hid in the homes and in the woods. In revenge the Germans killed the two village priests while the mayor escaped by hiding.

One of the men who risked his life carrying the Americans toward Carentan by boat was Albert Maugey, who recalled, "We hid the parachutists under piles of hay in our boats and poled them down to Carentan past the enemy outposts."

In remembrance of the 6th of June of 1944, Madame

Simone Renaud, widow of Alexandre, the esteemed mayor
of Ste. Mère Eglise, wrote the following:[11]

TO THE 82ND AND 101ST AIRBORNE
DIVISIONS OF AMERICA

You have jumped down in a Summer night
>On the soil of France,
Airborne! You, first, have set up the flowers of hope
>To bloom again.
In shackled Normandy where the black crossed planes
>Watched in the sky.
And the first one, you have written at a stroke
>This page of History
Which future men will read unbelieving!
>Such a grand page
That it will be told to the little ones
>After the old way of the legends.

Once upon a time, winged angels
>Came diving down from the moon-lighted sky
To drive away the devils
>Enslaving our poor country.

By night, from the black marsh, the flames of fires and tracer
>bullets
>Sprang to them
Who soared above, full of scorn, with wide-spread parachutes
>Till dawn peeped. . .

Then, all of a sudden, they glided down
>On our roofs, our towers,
Laying their blue, white, green, gold, speckled silk veils
>just like large wings!

And when, cool and laughing, they would say
>"Everything is O.K."

A wave of hope surged again in our anxious hearts
    During the fierce fight.

O Friends, one day, later on, laden with memories
    Proud of your victory,
To this Norman countryside you will wish to return
    Where your glory was born.

And Sainte-Mère-Eglise, chosen among all other places
    For the first fighting to start,
Like a tender mother to her children
    Will stretch her arms to you and say:

Be praised, honored, you, Airborne, who have been so grand
    In the epic days.
With your sooty faces and white silk parachutes
    You have swept the clouds.

And with your gleaming wings you have driven away,
    In a mighty swoop,
O sky sweepers,
    The barbarian foe!

Notes

Chapter 1

1. While the events were still fresh in his mind, Lieutenant Richard Winters wrote a vivid and extensive account of his experiences in diary form while recuperating from a wound at an aid station just behind the MLR (main line of resistance) on June 22, 1944. Excerpts appear throughout the text.
2. Laudick lost his life during the fighting and Davidson visited his buddy's widow when he got home. A romance blossomed and the widow became his bride.
3. These comments are from a letter Martin sent home on July 15, 1944.
4. From a diary excerpt by Lieutenant Richard Winters in France on June 22, 1944, he added, "Now at D plus 16 that's a standing joke and has been for the past fourteen days."
5. General Taylor received his second star (major general) on about D plus 5.
6. From the scrapbook of former S/Sgt Jerry McCullough of H Company of the 3rd Battalion of the 506th Regiment.
7. Colonel Wolverton lost his life on the Drop Zone only a few hours after the above scene.
8. From a letter Koskimaki wrote to his parents on July 15, 1944.
9. From Pee-Wee Martin's first letter to his parents on July 15, 1944.

Chapter 2

1. Barton actually landed one and a half miles north of the spot at which the team was to assemble.
2. Information provided by Colonel Frank Lillyman, who served as chief pathfinder for the Normandy operation.
3. Information provided by Mike Ranney, who was a close friend of Harris. "Salty" lost his life on June 11, 1944, in the attack on Carentan.

4. Information provided by Colonel Lillyman.
5. This episode is more fully described in the chapter "Hold Those Bridges!"
6. Newcomb ended his report with, "The Germans finally discovered the three of us approximately ten hours later. They had enough weapons to overpower us. I had an M-1, one fellow had a .45-caliber pistol, and the third had a carbine. Larson, I learned after the war, was only ten feet away from us. He stayed hidden for three or four days, but our three-man group became POW's."

Chapter 3

1. "Stick of jumpers" refers to the number of men who jump as a group from a plane.
2. Captain Francis J. Liberatori, the company commander who was badly wounded later in Normandy.
3. Excerpt from a letter written by Jim Martin on July 25, 1944.
4. The Navy shot down many of the troop carrier planes with the loss of many lives at that time.
5. Schuyler M. Jackson. "Daddy, what was D-Day?" *Parade,* The Sunday Picture Magazine. New York. June 7, 1959, pp. 2–4.
6. From a letter by Frank Styler to his parents on June 21, 1944.
7. From a letter Koskimaki wrote to his parents on July 15, 1944.
8. Excerpt from diary of Lieutenant Winters written at an aid station on June 22,1944.
9. An excerpt from PFC Guerdon Walthall's first letter home after the invasion.

Chapter 4

1. Fires were caused by Allied bombing raids in the flight corridor.
2. The static line was a heavily reinforced canvas strap about fifteen long. It enabled a trooper to fall clear of the plane before it pulled the parachute from its pack. Free-fall jumps from these low heights—and with such heavy loads of equipment—would have been extremely hazardous.
3. Purifoy added, "I saw the pilot the next day and all the crew members got out safely with us."
4. In checking with the men of the stick later, Truax discovered that the first one landed near Ste. Mère Eglise, while he landed just behind the beach—a distance of approximately four miles between the first and last man.

5. This was undoubtedly the Headquarters plane for Easy Company of the 506th Regiment, which was blown to bits with all its occupants.

6. Doctor George Lage's letter appeared in the *Portland Oregonian* on January 14, 1945.

7. Schweiter added, "I landed almost perfectly in the vicinity of or on the prescribed DZ, but didn't know it at the time."

8. The second unnamed writer added, "They later held an inquiry into why the pilot failed to drop us, but I never did find out anything more about it."

9. In his visits to the various marshaling areas, General Taylor had urged all of his men to yell out, "Bill Lee" in honor of our former division commander. In March, General William C. Lee had suffered a heart attack and had to leave his division as it was making its final preparations for the big invasion. He had planned the airborne phase.

Chapter 5

1. An excerpt from Winter's diary for June 22, 1944.

2. Koskimaki was one of many men who recorded their experiences in letters a few weeks after D-Day, when writing home became permissible.

3. An excerpt from Walthall's first letter to his parents from a hospital in England, where he lay recuperating from wounds.

4. An excerpt from Styler's first letter to his parents on June 21, 1944.

Chapter 6

1. PFC William H. Smith, number "4" in the stick, died from his injuries on the evening of D-Day.

2. Reuben, Robert E., "Number Six O.K.I," *Liberty.* XXI. No. 35, pp. 19–20. *Liberty* Magazine Inc., New York.

3. Reuben, op. cit., 20.

Chapter 7

1. WIA: Wounded in Action.

2. Taken from Walthall's first letter to his parents from Normandy.

3. From a paper, "As I Remember the Invasion of France, D-Day," written on August 11, 1944, for Colonel Gerald Higgins.

4. Schweiter was captured and held prisoner for about a day when U.S. troops advancing from Utah Beach caused the Germans to

withdraw, leaving their prisoners behind. Schweiter joined Division Headquarters at Hiesville.

Chapter 8

1. Chute didn't open fully,
2. The raised highway causeway between Carentan and St. Come-du-Mont.
3. See "Flight Across," page 43.
4. Captain Blatherwick was also listening for Wilson's horn!
5. Browning Automatic Rifles.
6. T.O. : Table of Organization.
7. See comments of Lieutenant Heber Minton on page 223 for a similar report.

Chapter 9

1. See Map 2 on page 32.
2. The experiences of Father Sampson and his wounded charges appear elsewhere in this account in the chapter called "Angels of Mercy."
3. The bodies of the three officers were picked up by Lieutenant Sumpter Blackmon and a burial detail a few days later.
4. Major Phillip Gage, Jr. was executive officer for 1st Battalion.
5. Sergeant Beall had been with Captain Robert H. Phillips and his Charley Company stick.
6. Chapel at St. Georges-du-Bohon.
7. See chapter, "Angels of Mercy," page 337.
8. Corporal Harry Plisevich and his stick members from How Company.
9. Brooks and Frame, along with Corporal Harry Plisevich, of H Company of the 501st, were concealed in the woods north of Sainteny. French underground leader, Jean Capiten, looked after their immediate needs and eventually got them back to the American lines a week later.
10. There were no native crickets in France that made this particular clicking sound.
11. During the fighting for Graignes, Captain Loyal Bogart lost his life when enemy reinforcements arrived to attack the mixed group of 82nd and 101st men defending the town.
12. Phillips and his mixed group were kept busy for a week outwitting the enemy. This included shooting up enemy convoys, ambushing motorcycle messengers, and destroying enemy equipment on numerous occasions. They finally made contact

with the 101st Division at Carentan a week later. Only one man was lost, Lieutenant Edwin B. Hutchinson, of Baker Company, who lost his life on the last day behind enemy lines just before the group made contact with the American forces near Carentan.

13. See chapter entitled, "Angels of Mercy," page 337, for Moore's account.

14. See Young's comments on pages 67–68.

15. Captain Francis Liberatori.

16. The enemy troops that had driven the 326th Engineers from Angoville were probably the same troops that blocked the northeast movement of the Dog Company patrol.

Chapter 10

1. Divarty stands for Division Artillery.

2. Captain Leo H. Schweiter's plane.

3. Reuben, ibid.

4. T/5 Edwin Hohl received the posthumous decoration of the Silver Star for his action.

5. According to Major Francis E. Carrel, surgeon for the 501st Parachute Infantry Regiment, "This was a short-range bullet used in close quarters where there would be danger to friendly forces if they were long range."

6. Captain Vernon Kraeger lost his life in the fighting in Holland on the second airborne mission.

7. Corporal Virgil Danforth was promoted to sergeant a few hours later and two days later became platoon sergeant. He was awarded the Distinguished Service Cross for his part in the D-Day fighting.

8. Reuben, ibid.

9. Radio operators from other units had been having similar difficulties with communications equipment. See pages 165–166 for comments on communications personnel of the 506th Regiment.

10. Blau added, "On the third day I started picking up bits of conversation between units on my SCR-300 radio and on the next day we got back to our own outfit."

11. SCR-300 radio weighed 37 pounds; the antenna case just 2 or 3 pounds!

12. This group got back to Division Headquarters on June 10.

13. Ashbrook was only a short distance away from Holdy, where the badly mutilated bodies of ten captured paratroopers were found. They had been tortured before being put to death.

14. Karabinos' material was taken from a summary report he wrote for the Division chief of staff, Colonel Gerald Higgins, of his group's actions on July 1, 1944. He had recommended that the individuals involved be awarded the Combat Infantry Badge.

15. See PFC James Evans' account on page 110.

16. Urbank had landed in a well populated cow pasture, and where there were cows, there were 'puddles.' He had crawled through them to get out of range of the enemy gunners.

17. Sherburne's account appears in the chapter called "The Glider Lifts."

Chapter 11

1. *Parade Magazine, Chicago Sun-Times,* June 7, 1959. "Daddy, what was D-Day?" Schuyler W. Jackson, pp. 2–4.

2. Jackson, ibid.

3. The CP location Captain Phillips is referring to is the one near St. Martin-de-Varreville, to which Colonel Moseley would have gone.

4. The aid station at Hiesville was the Château Columbiéres.

5. The action at WXYZ has been reconstructed with the aid of Harrison Stimmers, Elmer Brandenberger, and Roy Nickrent.

6. Brandenberger also added the following: "I later found that my left arm had been almost completely severed from my body, hanging on by only a small portion of inside skin. As a matter of fact, Cassidy had considered cutting it the rest of the way in order to get a compress over the stub to stop the bleeding. It is still a useful part of my body twenty-two years later, thanks to the skill of certain members of the Army Medical Corps."

7. See Map 9 on page 198.

8. Harrison Summers was awarded the Distinguished Service Cross. Unfortunately, Burt and Camien were not similarly recognized.

9. Captain Fitzgerald survived this action only to die in an auto accident in Germany at the end of the war.

10. See Corporal Mike Gromack's description.

11. See Corporal Kermit Latta's comments on pages 236–237.

12. The Germans had blocked the drainage ditches to the sea leaving inundated areas of a mile or two behind the beaches traversable only by causeway or chest-deep wading.

13. Former White Russians who had been impressed into the German army.

14. Smit and the two enlisted men spent the night shivering in wet

clothes under two pines not far from the pond. Next morning, they found two unoccupied enemy squad tents nearby, both well stocked with food and water. The author found the pond and pines while on a research trip in Normandy in July 1967. Smit said the area as shown in the pictures taken by the author had changed little from what he remembered.

15. Appears on French maps as Hameau-Fornel.

16. Bernard McKearney—from a letter written to his mother late in the Normandy campaign.

17. Captain Lage's account appears in the chapter "Angels of Mercy."

18. This village was Holdy.

19. Regimental communications Sergeant Elden F. Hermann verified this when he reported, "About daylight, we came across Major Vaughn, our regimental supply officer, and Lieutenant Bone, our regimental demolitions officer. They were both dead and so were a few Germans and horses on the road."

20. Lieutenant Robert G. Pick, "Paratroopers of Purple Heart Lane," *Saturday Evening Post,* Philadelphia (September 9, 1944), pp. 22 and 91.

21. According to Dalton Gregory, this group was surrounded for several days. He said, "On the second day the navy started shelling the area and we sent up orange smoke to identify ourselves. That second night we were attacked again with grenades, and we beat them back killing a few Jerries. The third day, French people bought us ammo and food that planes had dropped on D-Day and gave us the information that the Jerries were at a crossroads about a quarter mile from us and dug in. Seaborne troops landed in our sector and pushed in 500 yards and dug in. We sent a patrol out to them asking for help and they refused us, stating they had orders to land and dig in. Again that night we beat off another attack. On the fourth morning the seaborne troops started to push and they arrived in our position in good shape, knocked out the Germans at the crossroad, and found a tunnel from that position to our strong point from where the grenade attacks were coming. They gave us a truck and driver and took us to Vierville."

22. This has since been verified.

23. Records show that Dobbyn was awarded the Silver Star decoration for his part in the D-Day fighting.

Chapter 12

1. See Map 12 on page 239 for the drop patterns of the 377th Battalion.

2. Mulligan praised his officer: "Lieutenant Pearson lived for 13 days. I stayed with him till he died. He actually saved my life during our brief skirmish. If anybody deserved a medal, this officer did."

3. Van Duzer added, "After being treated for my wounds, I went to work as an aid to the very much overworked medical officer. There were some 200 wounded American prisoners of war in the camp, and Captain Adams and other aidmen worked as much as 48 hours at a time, operating, setting broken bones, and otherwise treating the men for their various injuries."

4. Kolesar ended his story by saying, "Our group dwindled to four men when we finally reached our lines. Those fourteen days were a nightmare—stealing chickens for food, drinking water out of ponds from which we had to first chase the cattle, sleeping in hedgerows, and praying to find our way back. We slept mostly days and traveled at night. Still we could not avoid the machine-gun nests. Each encounter took two or three more buddies. Then one night we lost a few because one man in line fell asleep. All those captured were later released. We arrived at Division Headquarters on D plus 14 after being picked up by 4th Infantry Division troops."

5. See comments by PFC John Steinfeld on page 201.

6. Latta added, "the hero of my experience was an airborne medical officer, Captain Felix Adams, from Vinita, Oklahoma, who jumped unarmed into battle and was a prisoner when he hit the ground. He ministered to 180 wounded G.I.'s in a convent in Valognes, France. During the time he took care of us, the city was leveled by bombs and shell fire. I am sure he saved many lives. Thanks to his care, my arm, which had a bullet hole through the elbow, was healing nicely when we were liberated on the 28th of June. A description of Felix Adams' actions appears in the chapter entitled "Angels of Mercy," on page 337.

7. This group eventually joined forces with another under the command of Major Louis H. Cotton, the executive officer for the battalion. They reached friendly lines five days after their drop into Normandy, losing four men on the way.

8. Charles Knight directed Tinley to post a guard. Tinley chose to stand the watch himself, however, and neglected to tell others where he was positioned.

9. When Sergeant Tinley was captured by the Germans, he was shipped toward Paris. Because a number of prisoners had been escaping, the Germans informed the sergeant that he was responsible for the remaining prisoners in his car. The next time one escaped, the sergeant would be taken out and shot for permitting him to escape. Tinley decided that it was about time for him to take off—which he did. He was able to stay with a family near Paris. When the Allies liberated Paris, he returned to his unit.

10. This battery came through the Normandy conflict with relatively few casualties. Bloor noted, "Battery A had ten casualties to bring their 94-man unit to 84 for duty upon return to England in July."

11. Surbaugh added, "On D plus 1, a total of 130 German soldiers from the shore installations surrendered to us. A battalion of the 22nd Infantry Regiment of the 4th Infantry Division relieved us of the prisoners and we stayed with this force until June 10th."

12. Gammon continued, "On D plus 1, we moved back into Ste. Mère Eglise. We made contact with our Sergeant Nick Pickard with three men on D plus 4. On D plus 5 we made it back to our battery, and reported to Captain Robinson. We had eleven men, which was more than one-fourth of what the battery had left."

13. It may have been Le Ham.

14. This group of soldiers moved out of the woods when they saw some Americans studying maps in a neighboring field on D plus 5 and were provided with transportation to return to their units.

15. Also called Rommel's Asparagus or Rommel's Candles.

16. This was Captain William Brubaker.

17. Culpepper added, "During the next two days, we set up a perimeter defense at the crossroads and held out until advance units of the 4th Infantry Division reached the area. By that time, we numbered about 35 paratroopers and had 80 German prisoners to turn over to the advancing troops."

18. Culpepper stated, "My battery loaded out in England with 90 men and officers. When we returned a little over a month later, I was the only officer and had 30 men left in my command. We loaded six 37mm guns for the drop from separate planes. So far as I know they were dropped safely, but I never saw one of the guns on the ground, and I had no report as to their effectiveness."

19. The men never reached their intended position. They were trapped near Valognes.
20. Culp added, "We were put on a train out of Cherbourg and traveled by rail as far as possible, then started to walk. On the evening of June 10, 1944, we were strafed by a flight of four P-47's. There were 200 men in the PW column and 122 were killed or wounded by the strafing. Sent to a Trappist monastery made into a German hospital. We were freed by the 9th Infantry Division on June 30th and sent back to England."

Chapter 13

1. See chapter 10, "So Few Led by So Many," on page 153.
2. Narrative reconstructed from data received from H. W. Hannah, University of Illinois.
3. See Lieutenant Bernard McKearney's report on pages 221–222.
4. Retreat from his position.
5. From the three-plane group, a total of 13 men got together and were able to unite with Rangers spearheading the 5th Corps advance for a union with the 101st Airborne near Carentan on D+7. Two of the men from Clark's stick were lost when they attacked an artillery weapon on the second or third day.
6. These men remained prisoners for two days before they managed to escape and returned to their units.
7. Vetland added, "The next day, the 4th Infantry Division arrived. They were using paratroopers as scouts. Grahek and I were taken to England and the others later rejoined Company A."
8. Colonel Strayer had sent Lieutenant MacMillan with part of Dog Company south toward Causeway 2 while the rest of his column was held up by artillery fire farther north.
9. Early on D-Day, the town of Vierville contained few German troops, but the enemy soldiers encountered by Colonel Sink and Major Hank Hannah on their reconnaissance trip occupied defensive positions in and around town.
10. An excerpt from a diary entry by Richard Winters on June 22, 1944, at an aid station where he was being treated for wounds.
11. Lieutenant Winters forgot to mention the four 88's!

Chapter 14

1. Troops of the 101st Division captured the town of St. Come-du-Mont on June 8. Those prisoners able to walk were evacuated to the south, while the seriously wounded or injured, like

Pauli, were left behind. He was evacuated to England and returned to the Division in time for the Holland invasion.

2. Calandrella added, "On the afternoon of the 7th, the other three were killed, and I had just given first aid to one of them, and baptized him before he died, when I was captured by nine or ten German paratroopers. For eighty-three days I was a prisoner. On August 29, a fellow from another division and I completed our escape at Chalons-sur-Marne, after the Germans had moved the rest of about 600 prisoners into Germany."

3. See comments of Mike Nassif on page 147–148.

4. From a copy of a letter written on March 8, 1945, by Captain James Morton, executive officer of 3rd Battalion Headquarters Company of the 506th Parachute Infantry Regiment at a hospital in Staunton, Virginia, where he was recuperating from wounds. It was written to Mrs. J. B. Doughty, Jr., wife of his close friend, Lt. Joe Doughty, who had also been wounded in action. Copy sent to Mrs. Richard P. Meason, widow of the former H Company executive officer who was active at the bridges on D-Day.

5. Captain Harwick managed to find his way back to 3rd Battalion two days later and was promoted to battalion commander. He was the only company commander to appear after the jump.

6. This small force eventually grew to 150 men. They remained without communication until D plus 2, at which time word about their well-being reached Colonel Bob Sink at Culoville. The bridges were bombed out on D plus 1 by Air Force fighter bombers, though Chaplain McGee tried to wave them off with orange identification panels. When no word of their capture had reached Allied Headquarters, their destruction by the Air Force had been ordered.

Chapter 15

1. From a letter by Colonel Murphy to Dr. Charles Van Gorder, a medical officer who was a participant in the same lift into Normandy.

2. From a letter written in July 1944 by Bill Lees to his fiancée.

Chapter 16

1. The small village of Addeville and the aid station were hit numerous times by heavy shells from the Allied fleet off the Utah Beaches. The German troops suffered heavy casualties during the night. The next morning American troops arrived to rescue

the wounded and Chaplain Sampson and his medic Fisher. The material quoted above is from Father Francis L. Sampson's book, *Look Out Below!* (Catholic University Press, Washington, 1958), pp. 59–64.

2. Chaplain John S. Maloney was decorated with the Distinguished Service Cross for his D-Day actions.

3. Captain Ryan remained under that chute until Friday morning (D+3), when reinforcements from the beach cleaned out the Germans near him. During his stay with the Germans (only 100 yards away), Ryan had some K-rations and two canteens, one with water and the other filled with bourbon. He remembered, "The one with the whiskey tasted terrible out of the canteen."

4. See comments of Richard Frame on page 107.

5. Reynolds, Webber, and Elliott spent eight days prowling about the swamp approximately seven kilometers south of Carentan, where the action finally caught up with them.

6. See comment of Tom Mulligan on pages 337–338.

7. Captain Adams was liberated when the American forces reached Cherbourg and was returned to England for a stint in the hospital before he returned to the 377th Parachute Artillery Battalion in time to make the airborne invasion of Holland on September 17, 1944.

8. Taken from the Medical History of the Normandy Campaign, for the 3rd Battalion Medical Section, 506th Parachute Infantry, August 2, 1944.

9. Lieutenant Elmer Brandenberger survived to tell his WXYZ story in the 502nd chapter on pages 191, 193, and 194.

10. The aid station was overrun by Germans and the defenders were worried about their fate. Several German soldiers went inside and apparently Hans had put in a good word for them about their treatment of him because the enemy left the medics there to look after their own wounded and Hans. Only the surviving line company men were marched off by the German paratroop unit that had overrun them.

11. The author visited this church in July 1967, and was shown the blood on the pews.

12. See Holdy action in Chapter 13, "The 506th Regiment," and Bernard McKearney's report in Chapter 11, "Five-O-Deuce."

13. From letters Captain George L. Lage sent to his wife after descriptions of the fighting were permitted. Printed in the *Portland Oregonian,* January 14, 1945.

14. See Captain George Lage's report for similarity.

15. Van Corder added, "We started operating at noon of D-Day. By the 7th or 8th, after operating constantly without rest, I began to see why the whiskey was issued. By taking a nip now and then, day and night, we were able to keep our strength and carry on with the surgery.

"On the night of June 9, I was so exhausted during an operation that I fell asleep in the middle of surgery and my head slumped forward into an open abdomen. A short time later, Major Crandal finished the operation and suggested I get some sleep. On the way to my tent, I met a sergeant on the stairway who offered me some hot chocolate he was making. I thanked him but refused and continued on to my tent near the hedgerow. Before falling asleep, I decided to take the noncom up on his offer and returned to the landing of the building. At that time, while drinking my chocolate, I heard a low-flying plane approach. It dropped two bombs that did much damage to the hospital and would have killed me had I been in my tent."

Chapter 18

1. Material on Mayor Renaud is quoted from his account, *Ste. Mère Eglise: First American Bridgehead in France.* Odile Pathé, France, 1944, with permission of his widow, Mme. Simone Renaud.

2. The Allied invasion forces were operating on Double Summer Time, which was two hours ahead of that kept in the Norman villages. 2200 hours would have been midnight Allied invasion time.

3. 12:30 A.M. Allied invasion time.

4. Ferdinand Fortin is cousin to Theophile Fortin, who lives near the wooden bridge at Brevands.

5. Probably a 6-pounder or .57 mm gun with which glider artillerymen were equipped at this time.

6. Fortin married his wife's sister and had a new family.

7. This was Lieutenant Bernard Bucior and men from Charley Company of the 502nd Regiment, who used that particular farm as his headquarters.

8. These trucks were set afire by men of Charley Company, and possibly by Lieutenant Morton Smit and Private Harold Boone.

9. These were the two tanks destroyed by the group commanded by Major Paul Danahy and LTC Raymond Millener. Private Robert Hayes was a member of the group. All three were members of Division Headquarters.

10. During the summer of 1976, I received a letter from James D. Bashline (H/501) in which he related having been helped by Frenchmen in the vicinity of Appeville. He had been accompanied by Private Richard U. Rock.

11. Renaud, Simone, *Les Pommiers Ont Refleuri,* 1951. Paris: Editions De La Revue Moderne. pp. 12–14.

Contributors

Capt. Adams, Felix M.,
  Med/377
PFC Agnew, John, HQ/506
PFC Aiken, McIntyre, G/501
PFC Albers, Edward, I/506
2 Lt. Allen, James, 2/502
PFC Alley, James, E/506
Sgt. Amburgey, Eugene,
  HQ/501
Pvt. Angelini, Rinaldo, B/502
PFC. Armbruster, Byron,
  B/326/Eng
T/5 Armstrong, John R., C/501
Pvt. Arnold, Richard, B/501
Sgt. Asay, Charles V., A/502
Sgt. Ashbrook, William P., Div.
  HQ

Cpl. Backensto, Francis, A/81
S/Sgt. Bacon, John, H/501
Pvt. Badenhop, Herman F.,
  D/377
S/Sgt. Bahlau, Fred, H/506
T/5 Baker, Howard, A/502
T/5 Baker, Leland, B/502
Pvt. Baldwin, Kenneth,
  HQ/501
T/4 Banyas, Andal, B/502
S/Sgt. Banker, Otis, 326/Med
PFC Barger, Robert C.,
  326/Med

1 Lt. Barham, Allan C., B/502
PFC Barnes, Robert F., A/502
1 Lt. Barnes, Henry, 326/Med
PFC. Barrickman, John, 2/506
T/5 Barton, Raymond,
  Med/501
Pvt. Barton, William H.,
  PF/377
Cpl. Bateman, Foster M.,
  Sv/506
S/Sgt. Beam, Jerry N., 1/506
Pvt. Begault, David, C/377
S/Sgt. Benecke, Edward, A/377
Capt. Best, William G.,
  Med/502
T/4 Beyrle Joseph R., I/506
1 Lt. Blackmon, Sumpter,
  A/501
PFC. Blain, Joseph A., H/502
Capt. Blatherwick, Robert,
  Med/501
T/5 Blau, Vincent F., HQ/501
1/Sgt. Bloor, Howard K.,
  A/377
T/5 Bogus, Leo, 1/502
2 Lt. Borrelli, Anthony, A/506
T/5 Braddock, Glen, PF/502
PFC. Brannon, William C.,
  D/506
1 Lt. Brandenberger, Elmer,
  B/502

Sgt. Brandt, John, I/502

2 Lt. Brierre, Eugene D. 101/MP

PFC. Brooks, Chester, 1/501

Capt. Brubaker, William, HQ/377

Pvt. Burgess, Robert, B/501

Pvt. Burgett, Donald R., A/506

1 Lt. Burns, Robert G., I/502

Sgt. Bruff, Thomas, Div. HQ

Cpl. Cadden, James J., C/506

PFC. Cahoon, Robert, C/502

S/Sgt. Calabrese, Nicholas, Div HQ

PFC. Calandrella, Ray E., 3/506

Cpl. Cardwell, Leonard, HQ/506

1 Lt. Carlsen, Charles E., Sv/501

PFC. Carlson, Laverne, HQ/501

PFC. Carpenter, Frank, C/501

PFC. Carpenter, Keith, HQ/501

Maj. Carrel, Francis E., HQ/501

Lt. Col. Cassidy, Patrick, 1/502

Sgt. Castona, Donald, G/501

Capt. Caumartin, Hugh, Med/506

PFC. Cavanaugh, Eugene T., G/501

T/5. Chapman, Charles D., 101/Sig

Cpl. Chapman, Francis W., C/377

Pvt. Chapman, Robert R., B/501

Cpl. Cheney, William W., HQ/506

Cpl. Chiccoine, Jules, HQ/506

Pvt. Clark, Herbert, B/506

Pvt. Clarke, Allen V., F/502

Capt. Clement, W. B., Med/506

Pvt. Clever, Stanley, G/506

PFC. Cione, Louis W., 2/506

PFC. Cisiak, Robert, C/501

S/Sgt. Cook, F. Bruce, HQ/501

Cpl. Copas, Marshall, D/377

T/4. Cortese, Nicholas, F/506

PFC. Cousins, Frederick, Div. Arty

1/Sgt. Cox, James C., C/326 Eng

Lt. Col. Cox, X. B., HQ/81

PFC. Coyne, Thomas J., F/501

T/5. Craney, Joseph, 2/502

Pvt. Croat, Carl J., 326/Med

T/4. Crowder, William, HQ/377

T/5. Culp, Loren S., D/377

Capt. Culpepper, Fred, D/377

PFC. Currie, Archie, 326/Med

Pvt. Curry, Harold F., A/502

Cpl. Danforth, Virgil, G/501

Pvt. Dansereau, George, H/501

Pvt. Darcy, Robert G., H/502

PFC. Davidson, Lawrence H., H/506

PFC. Davis, Walter E., G/501

T/4. Dawson, Ronald, D/377

PFC. Dekle, Zelmah Q., Med/501

PFC. DeMay, William, HQ/377

S/Sgt. Denovchik, Nicholas, A/501

PFC. DeSalvadore, Donald, B/502

T/4. Detrick, James O., PF/377

PFC. Dewitt, Frank J., 1/506

Pvt. D'Angiolini, Anthony, B/501

PFC. Lacy, John C., 2/501

Cpl. Ladd, Richard M., HQ/502

PFC. Laden, Charles, 101 Sig

2 Lt. Lake, Robert, C/502

PFC. LaMagdeleine, Leslie, D/506

Pvt. Lamb, Waylen, HQ/501

Cpl. Lambert, Ernest, B/501

Pvt. Lambert, Kenneth, 1/501

PFC. Landry, Malcolm B., HQ/506

T/5. Lappegaard, Ray, 3/501

Pvt. Larkin, Bernard, G/502

Cpl. Larson, Thorwald K., PF/501

Pvt. Lashen, Gerald, A/81

Cpl. Latta, Kermit R., Div Arty

PFC. Layser, Ned, D/501

T/5. Lees, William J., 101 Sig

Maj. Legere, Lawrence J., Div HQ

Cpl. Levak, Martin, HQ/327

Cpl. Liapes, Gus, 1/506

PFC. Liebman, Ben, HQ/506

Pvt. Lillibridge, Robert W., D/501

Capt. Lillyman, Frank L., PF/502

Sgt. Lindsay, Patrick, A/501

S/Sgt. Lipton Carwood C., E/506

T/5. Lisk, Richard R., PF/502

PFC. Looney, Frank, E/81

Pvt. Loyen, Larry, B/506

Sgt. Ludwig, Joseph, H/502

PFC. Lukasavage, Walter, I/506

Capt. Lunin, Arthur, Med/501

Pvt. Lysiak, Michael A., 101 Sig

T/5. MacDowell, Clifford, PF/502

PFC. Mace, John P., 326 Med

Sgt. Macri, Patrick, 101 Sig

PFC. Maggio, Charles, G/506

1 Lt. Malek, Leo E., F/501

1/Sgt. Malley, Charles, PF/506

Capt. Maloney, John S., HQ/506

PFC. Maione, Angelo, F/327

Sgt. Marden, Charles, A/81

Pvt. Marohn, Robert, C/502

Cpl. Marohn, John, E/501

Sgt. Marshall, Clifton, A/377

PFC. Martin, James H., G/506

T/4. Maslowski, William, 2/506

PFC. Mathiason, Clair L., G/506

1 Lt. Matthews, Robert, A/377

PFC. Mawhinney, Robert, B/502

Gen. McAuliffe, Anthony C., Div HQ

M/Sgt. McCarthy, John, Div HQ

Pvt. McClung, Earl V., E/506

S/Sgt. McCullough, Gerald, H/506

PFC. McFaul, Nelson, A/506

Pvt. McGowan, Richard F. I/501

Pvt. McIntosh, Ben, B/502

Pvt. McKay, Albert J., C/377

1 Lt. McKearney, Bernard, E/502

Sgt. McKearney, James B,. 3/501

Pvt. McKinney, Woodie, E/501

Capt. McKee, Willis P., 326 Med

PFC. McNiece, Jake, HQ/506

1 Lt. Meason, Richard P., H/506
PFC. Mentone, Dominick, I/501
T/5. Merlano, Louis P., A/502
PFC. Merrill, Clarence, Med/506
PFC. Michel, William, A/501
Pvt. Michels, Edward, Med/501
Sgt. Miller, Edward, 326 Med
Sgt. Miller, Michael G., F/502
PFC. Miller, Owen E., Med/501
T/5. Miller, Paul R., Med/501
Capt. Miller, Walter L., HQ/327
Sgt. Millman, Jack E., HQ/327
1 Lt. Minton, Heber L., B/506
PFC. Mishler, John, PF/501
S/Sgt. Mitchell, Charles A., B/506
Pvt. Mitchell, Edward J., D/506
T/5. Mole, Harry T., 2/501
PFC. Momcilovic, Barney, 1/501
PFC. Montgomery, James E., G/506
PFC. Moore, Kenneth, Med/501
Cpl. Morganelli, Paul, A/326 Eng.
1 Lt. Morton, James G., 3/506
T/5. Mullen, William R., D/502
Pvt. Mulligan, Thomas, C/377
Capt. Mulvey, Thomas P., F/506
Lt. Col. Murphy, Michael, 9AF TCC
T/4. Murphy, Thomas P., 3/501
PFC. Murphy, Walter T., C/377

Sgt. Nabours, J. Paul, 326 Med.
PFC. Nadeau, James, F/501
Pvt. Nassif, Michael, G/506
PFC. Necikowski, Julian, Div Arty
T/5. Neils, Edward H., 101 Sig
Sgt. Nelson, Ed, D/502
Pvt. Nevison, Charles L., E/501
Pvt. Newcomb, Leonard J., PF/501
S/Sgt. Nicholas, John, Med/501
PFC. Nicholas, Lemuel L., D/502
PFC. Nichols, Forrest J., B/502
Pvt. Nickrent, Roy, 1/502
T/5. Nolley, Harold, Med/501
Cpl. Nye, Donald E., HQ/502
1 Lt. Nye, James F., I/506

Col. Oldfield, Barney, USAF
Sgt. Oliver, Kenneth, Med/501
Sgt. O'Neill, Charles, F/501
PFC. Orlowsky, Fred, G/501

PFC. Paczulla, Robert A., HQ/502
1 Lt. Padrick, William G., B/81
Cpl. Palys, Frank, HQ/506
1 Lt. Pangerl, Joseph, HQ/502
Sgt. Passanisi, Robert, HQ/377
T/4. Pastorius, Thomas, HQ/502
Sgt. Patheiger, Fred, HQ/502
PFC. Patton, Donald, B/506
S/Sgt. Pauli, William L., 3/506
Pvt. Pawlitz, Bernard, C/377
Sgt. Pentz, Chester, B/502
PFC. Perry, Owen R., H/506
Sgt. Peterson, Robert, Med/506

Sgt. Phalen, Charles S., 326 Med

Capt. Phillips, Ivan, HQ/502

Capt. Phillips, Robert H., C/501

PFC. Philp, Alexander, E/501

1 Lt. Pick, Robert G., HQ/502

PFC. Plemons, James R., D/502

Cpl. Plisevich, Harry, H/501

Pvt. Pribbenow, William, E/502

T/5. Pritchard, Hugh E., D/506

T/4. Procknow, George, 101 Sig

PFC. Purifoy, James D., 2/501

PFC. Racette, Harry, HQ/501

Sgt. Rader, Robert, E/506

Cpl. Randell, Charles, B/506

Pvt. Ranney, Michael, E/506

Cpl. Reese, Lavon P., E/506

Cpl. Reinbold, Sidney, D/502

Reuben, Robert, Reuters

Cpl. Revord, Harold, 3/502

S/Sgt. Reynolds, Robert, Med/501

T/5. Rinehard, Earl, Div Arty

Sgt. Robare, Carl H., D/502

PFC. Rocca, Francis A., PF/502

T/5. Roe, Fred, Sv/506

PFC. Rogers, Paul C., E/506

T/5. Rogge, Howard B., Med/502

S/Sgt. Romano, Phillip, 101 MP

Capt. Rosemond, St. Julien, HQ/377

S/Sgt. Rosenfield, Zolman, G/506

PFC. Rosie, George, 3/506

Sgt. Ross, John E., 326 Med

PFC. Rossetti, Hank, Med/501

Sgt. Rousseau, Hector, Med/501

T/4. Rowles, Richard G., E/501

PFC. Rubino, Tony D., H/506

PFC. Ruedy, Warren, G/501

PFC. Runge, Leo F., HQ/501

T/5. Ryals, Robert, 3/501

Capt. Ryan, Bernard J., Med/506

PFC. Sacchetti, Louis, 1/502

Pvt. Sacco, Thomas, D/506

Cpl. Salley, Robert, HQ/326/Eng

PFC. Sample, John R., PF/377

Capt. Sampson, Francis L., HQ/501

Cpl. Santini, Peter J., 2/502

Pvt. Schaffer, Jack, F/501

Cpl. Schill, Robert E., Med/501

PFC. Schulist, George, B/81

Capt. Schweiter, Leo H., Div HQ

Sgt. Schwenk, Russell A., F/506

T/5. Schwerin, William F., 3/501

1 Lt. Sefton, George, 2/501

PFC. Sepcich, Leopaul, A/377

T/4. Seney, John, 2/502

Sgt. Shaw, Charles N., H/506

PFC. Shear, Walter C., I/501

S/Sgt. Sheldon, Leo, 101 Sig

S/Sgt. Shenk, Jay B., C/502

1 Lt. Shepard, Corey R., 3/502

Col. Sherburne, Thomas, Div Arty

Cpl. Shively, Gordon, 101 Sig

Cpl. Shoutis, Harold, A/501

1 Lt. Shrader, William E., HQ/377

PFC. Shrodo, Stanley J., 326 Med

PFC. Shuman, William L., B/377

S/Sgt. Shurter, Robert A., D/506

Capt. Simmons, Cecil, H/502

Pvt. Slizewski, Edward, G/506

1 Lt. Smit, Morton, C/502

S/Sgt. Smith, O. G., A/501

Pvt. Smith, Ralph R., F/501

Pvt. Smith, Raymond, PF/502

Sgt. Smith, Robert B., E/506

Cpl. Smith, Robert W., A/501

Capt. Sorenson, Clarence, Med/501

PFC. Spiller, C. A., G/506

PFC. Spitler, Harry, Div Arty

Lt. Col. Sommerfield, Arthur, Div HQ

1/Sgt. Sprecker, Kenneth, H/502

Col. Stanley, F. A., HQ/326/Eng

Pvt. Steele, Earle C., H/502

S/Sgt. Steen, William, A/81

PFC. Steinfeld, John, C/502

Pvt. Stiles, Howard, PF/502

PFC. Storeby, C. E., C/326/Eng

Cpl. Straight, Gaylord C., 1/502

PFC. Straith, Donald, A/506

Pvt. Sturgess, William K., 101 Sig

PFC. Styler, Frank, HQ/501

S/Sgt. Summers, Harrison, B/502

Sgt. Surbaugh, Fred, A/377

1 Lt. Swanson, Wallace A., A/502

M/Sgt. Taylor, David M., HQ/502

Gen. Taylor, Maxwell D., Div HQ

Cpl. Taylor, Ray E., D/506

PFC. Tessoff, Peter, I/501

PFC. Theaker, Clarence, Div Arty

PFC. Thomas, John E., C/501

Cpl. Thompson, Harold, HQ/501

Cpl. Thomas, Norwood, Div Arty

1 Lt. Thornton, Jack F., 3/501

S/Sgt. Tinley, Clyde, HQ/377

PFC. Trotter, Sherwood C., A/506

Sgt. Truax, Louis E., D/506

PFC. Tryblowski, Frank, HQ/377

Pvt. Turk, Walter M., G/501

Sgt. Urbank, John, G/501

Cpl. Utz, Vincent, HQ/506

1/Sgt. Vacho, Paul S., 2/506

Cpl. Vaclav, Frank, C/506

PFC. Valdon, Blas, Med/501

Sgt. Van Duzer, Franklin, HQ/377

Capt. Van Gorder, Charles, 326 Med

PFC. Vargas, Greg, B/377

Sgt. Vetland, Ted, A/506

Pvt. Viano, James, A/81

Pvt. Vivo, Michael, A/81

Capt. Waldmann, William, Med/501

T/3. Walker, Johnny J., 101 Sig

Cpl. Walton, Wayne, Med/501

PFC. Walthall, Guerdon, G/506

Acknowledgments

Though a large part of the work on this book is from the contributions of former members of the 101st Airborne Division, the account would never have reached fulfillment without the assistance of the following people and institutions:

Staff Sergeant Glenn Koons, the noncommissioned officer in charge of the Pratt Museum at Fort Campbell, Kentucky, for the use of materials from the 101st Airborne Division D-Day collection.

Walter L. Miller, Jr., former Secretary-Treasurer of the 101st Airborne Division Association, and a former 101st communications officer, for the use of pictures from the Association files and current addresses of former Screaming Eagles.

General Services Administration, National Personnel Records Center, for unit rosters of the 101st Airborne Division.

William J. Nigh of the World War II Division of the National Archives, for materials pertaining to the 101st Airborne Division Signal Company.

Public Information Division, Office of Chief of Information, Department of the Army, for many of the photographs appearing in this account.

Brigadier General Robert L. Schulz, U. S. Army (Ret), former aide to General Dwight D. Eisenhower, for information concerning D-Day communications to higher headquarters.

Bud Wacker, city editor of the *Buffalo Evening News,* Buffalo, New York, for his assistance in locating the next-of-kin of Edwin S. Hohl.

Evelyn R. Schwartz, sister of deceased war correspondent Robert E. Reuben, for the use of pictures and materials from her brother's collection.

Mrs. William E. Shrader, for the use of the wartime maps of her late husband and her editing and encouragement in the preparation of this account.

Madame Simone Renaud, widow of the wartime mayor of Ste. Mère Eglise, who made the arrangements for my Normandy visit. It was her knowledge of the fighting areas that led me to meet many of the French survivors of the D-Day fighting in Normandy.

Messrs. Daniel Dupont and *Maurice Renaud,* for the chauffeur service and work as interpreters on my trip to Normandy.

M. Henri Jouaux, Jr., for his guided tour of the area near his home in Appeville, where many men of my unit participated in D-Day actions.

The wonderful librarians and archivists at the Main Library of the City of Detroit, for their assistance in locating current addresses of more than 2,000 former Screaming Eagles.

Sheila Page, for her suggestions for compiling this account.

Stella Stone and *Joyce Swartout,* for their assistance in typing the original manuscript.

Theodore P. Savas, of El Dorado Hills, California, for re-typesetting this work, thereby making the new 2002 Casemate edition possible.

David Farnsworth, of Casemate Publishing, for bringing this book back into print, and providing it with a wide distribution.

Special thanks to my wife, *Eva,* for the encouragement she gave me to get this book written before the years had dimmed all memory of the incidents that took place on that memorable day, and for her many hours of checking and correcting materials for historical content and composition. Her custodial care of wartime letters and diary has proved invaluable.

Major General Patrick Cassidy, for the copy of Cassidy's Battalion, which provided the background for the actions of that unit.

Catholic University Press, for permission to quote liberally from Father Francis L. Sampson's account, *Look Out Below!*

Bibliography

Airborne Operations in World War II. ETO. USAF Historical Studies: No.
97. USAF Historical Division, Research Studies Institute, Maxwell
Air Force Base, Alabama, 1956.

Carrell, Paul. *Invasion—They're Coming.* Translated from German by
E. Osers. New York: Dutton, 1962.

Carnes, Cecil. "Paratroopers in Purple Heart Lane," *Saturday Evening Post.*
September 9, 1944: pp. 22, 91–93. Curtis Publishing: Philadelphia.

Collins, Mary Alice. (Transcription) *Mary Alice Collins Programme, Interview with Harry Plisevich.* London, July 28, 1944.

Currahee—Scrapbook Sergeant of the 506th Parachute Infantry Regiment.
506th Parachute Infantry Regiment. Germany, 1945.

Howarth, David. *D-Day.* New York: Pyramid Books, 1960.

Jackson, Schuyler W. "Daddy, what was D-Day?" *Parade.* June 7, 1959,
pp. 2-4. Parade Publications, Inc., New York.

Malone, Ted. (Transcription) *Westinghouse Presents "Top of the Evening,"
Interview with Sergeant Franklin K. Van Duzer,* London, July 28,
1944.

Marshall, Col. S. L. A. *Cassidy's Battalion,* Battalion and Small Unit Study
Number 9. Historical Section, European Theater of Operations,
1944.

———. *Night Drop.* Boston: Little, Brown and Company, 1962.

Rapport, Leonard and Northwood, Arthur J. *Rendezvous with Destiny: A
History of the 101st Airborne Division.* Washington: Infantry Jour-
nal Press, 1948.

Renaud, Alexandre. *Sainte Mère Eglise, First American Bridgehead in
France.* Odile Pathé, France, 1964.

Reuben, Robert E. "Number Six O.K.!" *Liberty,* XXI, No. 35, pp. 19-20.
Liberty Magazine, Inc., New York.

Ryan, Cornelius. *The Longest Day.* New York: Simon and Schuster, 1959.

Sampson, Chaplain Francis L. *Look Out Below!* Washington: Catholic University Press, 1958.

Utah Beach to Cherbourg. American Forces in Action Series, Historical Division, Department of the Army.

If you've enjoyed this, the first of
George E. Koskimaki's 101st Airborne trilogy,
you won't want to miss the next in the series

HELL'S HIGHWAY:

A Chronicle of the 101st Airborne

in the Holland Campaign

Please read on for an exciting
sneak preview . . .

Responding to the red smoke signal, men of the 1st Battalion of the 506th Parachute Infantry Regiment headed for the wooded area at the southern edge of the drop zone. Colonel Robert F. Sink moved to the location immediately and began to send the men off in groups of fifteen to twenty with an officer. Three bridges were the objectives with the main highway bridge as the key target. The two secondary spans, about 1,400 yards on either side of the highway bridge, were also to be seized. Company "A" was to go for the main bridge. The smaller bridge to the west was to be taken by "C" Company. "B" was in reserve. One of the 2nd Battalion units was to head for the 3rd span, east of the main highway.

A few minutes after the first groups headed out on their missions, a Dutchman approached First Lieutenant Norman Dike, the assistant S-2 for the regiment and informed him that the two auxiliary bridges had been blown by the Germans several days earlier.

A log for Company "A" of the 506th Regiment was provided by First Lieutenant William C. Kennedy which provided a description of the rapid assembly by members of the company and the key assignment which had been given to them:

> Thirty-five minutes after the jump, the company commander, Captain Melvin O. Davis, and two officers, Lieutenants George Couch and George Retan, together with about 65 other men of the company moved from the assembly area toward the company objective. Company 'A' had been given the principle mission of taking the main bridge across the Wilhelmina Canal, just south of Son. Sergeants

(Burley) Sizemore, (Don) Barlowe and (Roy) Stringfellow were part of the group that moved to the bridge.

Almost half of 1st Platoon was late in arriving at the assembly area as they were dropped some distance from the rest of the 506th Regiment. A member of that group was Corporal Charles Shoemaker who related: "Most of the men were from 1st Platoon which was being led by Second Lieutenant James Diel. We didn't reach the unit before it left on its mission toward the Wilhelmina Canal bridge at Son."

Platoon leader First Lieutenant David Galarneau had been tangled with an equipment bundle on his landing and sustained a multiple ankle fracture. As 2nd Platoon leader, he did manage to hobble off the drop zone and by late afternoon reached the hospital in Son. His assistant platoon leader, Second Lieutenant George Retan, had gone along with Captain David and the first elements of "A" Company. He was destined to become the first KIA for "A" Company.

"I was first scout," said Sgt. Don Brininstool. "Captain Davis was just a short distance away. About the first sixty men from "A" Company headed for the bridge. I was on the left flank followed by Liddell, Borchers, Impink and Carter."

Brininstool added, "A new replacement ran up to me and said, 'If this is combat, it's not half bad!' I told him he hadn't seen anything yet. 'Just wait awhile!' About this time I heard the first shot and this young trooper must have been one of the first casualties after leaving the drop zone."

Sgt. Joseph P. Powers remembered the name of his plane as "Round Trip Ticket," which he felt was a good omen. The return part of that trip would see him back in England in a few days. He wrote: "After the assembly, Captain Davis led us down a road toward Son with 2nd Platoon in the lead. We finally came to a halt in the backyard of what I was later told was a monastery or school for boys about to enter the priesthood."

The "A" Company log provides a rather complete picture of the action as the group neared Son and the bridge area:

About 400 yards southeast of the assembly point about half a squad of enemy riflemen fired on the force. However, this resistance was overcome in about five minutes and Captain Davis and his company pressed on about 800 yards from the first point of enemy contact and to the south. PFC Herbert Erickson, who was scouting to the front sighted two enemy riflemen who withdrew behind a barn when fired on. At this point the group was about 200 yards from the bridge and the objective. The 2nd Platoon was leading the attack. A German 88 gun opened up, firing into the trees and above the heads of our troops. Sergeant Joe Powers of 2nd Platoon was hit by shrapnel at this time and was believed to be the first casualty.

Captain Davis urged the company forward. The enemy fire from the 88 gun increased in intensity and was joined by enemy mortars. In about fifteen minutes five men were killed and eight wounded. Among those killed was Lieutenant George Retan. The wounded included Lieutenant George Couch and First Sergeant Burley Sizemore. Sergeant Don Barlowe ordered the company to withdraw about 25 yards to a rear position in a ditch that afforded comparative cover. This was about two hours from H-hour or jump time. Immediately thereafter, Major LaPrade appeared and took command of the situation.

PFC Nelson A. McFaul was in the midst of the action. He wrote: "Everyone assembled at the south end of the drop zone and were proceeding down a country lane toward Son. We entered a wooded area just north of a sanitarium and came under fire. It appeared to be artillery and mortar fire with explosions everywhere. The men ahead had stopped and were using the trees for protection. Sergeant Don Barlow and I tried to get them moving and to get behind the sanitarium for better protection against the artillery fire."

"We immediately came under some intense artillery and machine gun fire having been spotted entering our positions," said Sergeant Powers. "We had not been able to use the brick building of the monastery as cover so Captain Davis ordered us to move forward in the direction of the bridge which was our objective. Upon rising to move forward, I was flattened by an explosion and took a hunk of shrapnel in my right elbow, shattering it. I had lost my weapon so I crawled back in the direction we had come from meeting other members of the company who were moving up and they directed me to a medical officer who proceeded to treat me."

Nearby was PFC Nelson McFaul. He said, "I stopped to nudge someone when I was hit in the leg by a tree burst. I moved back out of the tree line and came upon Dick Harms, who had been wounded in the right shoulder. It didn't appear critical. I dressed it and sent a medic back to check him. At the time I was working on Harms, I heard First Sergeant Burley Sizemore yell at someone to get out here and put a tourniquet on his leg before he bled to death."

As the artillery, mortar and machine gun fire commenced from the enemy positions, machine gunner Don Brininstool reacted. "We ran to get our machine gun in place. All hell broke loose. Liddell and Borchers placed our gun in position and I took over the gun with Liddell on my left and Borchers on my right with the remainder of the first wave still further right. A shell exploded near the gun. I thought half my face was blown off. I felt my face which was bleeding from the nose and both ears and covered with sand, but still in one piece. I checked with Liddell. He was hit around the elbow and Borchers was hit in the groin. After giving first aid and telling them to stay very still so we would not get another shell, I checked to see what other damage had been done.

"The Germans must have been watching us from the church tower. Captain Davis was hit along with most of the first wave. The Germans had blown the bridges to the right and left of Son earlier. After finding a couple more troopers still walking, we headed for the main bridge."

As they caught up with the advance elements of Company "A", Corporal Charles Shoemaker and the 1st Platoon contingent came upon the battered group. They moved past Sergeant Don Barlow and the survivors of the air bursts and mortar barrages near the sanitarium. Captain Davis had been wounded, and Second Lieutenant George Retan had been killed. Shoemaker and his group moved on toward the bridge which was number "1" priority. He wrote: "We got down to the canal and there was an 88 gun position that had been knocked out. A couple of our people were there. A very young German soldier was lying at the bottom of the gun pit. His belly had been opened from side to side. Another one was standing there wringing his hands. He told one of our people who spoke German that they had grown up together in the same village and were very close. Neither one of them was over sixteen years of age. He begged one of our men to put his friend out of his misery. Of course, nobody would do that. Then he begged somebody to give him a gun so he could do it. Nobody offered him a gun. I don't know what happened from there on, as we kept moving."

With Company "A" as the point of the attack toward the Wilhelmina Canal bridge, Company "B" was following, ready to move in as support for the spearhead force. PFC John Garrigan wrote: "I do remember we were held up for a few minutes behind 'A' Company and we didn't know the reason at the time. While waiting, a medic came by and noticed my hand was all bloody—how, I don't know—but he decided to fix it with a bandage. By the time he was done, we were told to move out and that is when I saw 'A' company as we went through them, all in bad shape. Captain Davis of 'A' Company was there, badly wounded.

"We hit the edge of the tree line and took off across the wide open field heading for the bridge, our objective. Duane Zentz and I headed for the center of the field where a German artillery piece was located. With the field buzzing with bullets, we finally made it to the gun emplacement and jumped in. The next move was for a little house on the edge of the canal. The soldiers crossing this field didn't have much of a chance. I saw so many of our boys going down. Zentz and I made the house which did have enemy, who were running away from us as we turned the corner of a fence line. There was Joe Gendreau, a clean shot in the head. I felt a great loss at that moment but headed for the canal bridge just as it was blown up—another great disappointment."

Private Robert W. Wiatt, a replacement for "C" Company for the Holland operation remembered, "The mission of 'C' Company was to take a bridge west of the main bridge at Son. I joined a group of other 'Charley' Company men only to learn the bridge we were to take had already been destroyed. We then headed through some woods toward Son and the canal. We passed an 88mm gun that had been taken out by the Air Force. It was here that I saw the first dead person in my life."

As the action in the woods near the sanitarium wound down, Sergeant Joe Powers, first "A" Company man to be wounded when the enemy fired tree bursts into the positions, describes what ensued shortly afterwards as he was treated for his wound by a medical officer. "He ripped my sleeve open, checked the wound and gave me a shot of morphine. He bandaged my arm and offered a drink from his canteen. I had a canteen of water and told him so but he said, 'Drink this anyway!' I did and it was some of the best Scotch whiskey I had ever tasted. I thanked him and he tied my arm in a vertical position to a small bush and told me to lie there until I was picked up.

"From out of nowhere the Dutch civilians started appearing—men, women and children, oblivious of the danger to themselves. They piled cookies, cakes and other foods on my stomach as I lay there, coaxing me to eat and trying to make me comfortable. Between the morphine and the Scotch whiskey I wasn't feeling too badly about then."

After the 1st Battalion had been sent on its way in a flanking movement of the Wilhelmina bridge position, Colonel Robert F. Sink learned from the Dutch resistance forces that the two smaller parallel bridges had been blown several days earlier. This added further impetus to the necessity to capture the main bridge before the same fate befell it.

As 2nd and 3rd Battalions and Regimental Headquarters personnel completed their assembly, some of the men had been confused by the smoke signals of the 502nd on DZ "B" and were late in reporting. The arrival of the glider echelons in the same fields a short time after the paratroopers had landed caused further delay.

PFC John Vlachos noted: "Men and women were running out on our drop zone picking up parachutes while we were still under fire. I crawled to the edge of the field where the woods began. There was a German ambulance well marked with Red Crosses that had been strafed by our fighter planes and set afire. I opened the door and saw two German medics and a nurse. They were burned and charred."

On Colonel Sink's order, 2nd Battalion moved out, down the main road to Son. He followed it; after him came the platoon of "Charley" Company engineers, Regimental Headquarters Company and the men of 3rd Battalion.

Marching down the road, Colonel Sink remembered several enemy tanks near Wolfswinkel which he had seen from his plane. He sent a patrol to investigate. Before the patrol could get there American fighters came over head, saw the tanks, attacked, and knocked them out. Here was another demonstration of the air superiority that had made a daylight jump possible. The feelings of the men, already favorable toward the Air Force on account of the almost perfect jump, warmed even more.

T/5 Gordon E. King jumped with Captain Charles Shettle as his radioman. He wrote: "We hadn't been on the ground long when Sink's jeep came in and I rode with him into Son because his operator had not shown up yet."

King added: "We noted Mustangs strafing the highway even before we jumped and saw smoke where they had been operating as we headed for the highway and turned south toward the canal and Eindhoven. Sink couldn't wait to see if the bridge was still OK and headed south with 'yours truly' hanging on for dear life to the folded windshield while carrying my SCR-300 on my back and riding on the hood."

"Out in front of everybody was Sergeant Allen L. Westphal leading the entire regiment," recalled Sergeant Hugh Pritchard. "We were moving swiftly through the main street of Son. I was on the sidewalk on the left taking a little cover while Westphal was in the middle of the street at doubletime and yelling, 'Come on you guys!' Suddenly a burst of German machine gun fire raked the street with one slug getting Westphal through the calf of the leg. He quickly crawled over to me and said, 'You know, that was stupid of me, wasn't it?' "

In the town of Son, a strategically placed 88mm gun covering the road opened fire. The advance elements went down. As a member of the leading platoon from Company "D", Sergeant Louis Truax wrote: "I was running down the street toward the Son bridge. I was on the right side and Sergeant Willis Phillips was on the left. We were going house to house. There was still food on the tables the Germans had left there. Phillips was killed by small-arms fire from the Krauts still in the buildings or by a mortar shell."

As leader of the "anti-tank" section of 2nd Battalion, Sergeant Jack MacLean recalled when his group was called forward. "A pair of 88 guns were firing directly down the street and impeding our advance. We had the first of many such commands to follow with 'Bazookas up front!' Private Glen Lindsey, highly skilled with his work with the weapon, moved forward into position, fired one round at the 88 nearest our group, disabling it and killing one of the Germans."

Six others fled the gun position heading toward the bridge. A "D" Company machine gunner finished off those men as they retreated.

The nearest 88 had held up "D" Company. About that time, Colonel Sink came upon the scene. Private Paul Z. Martinez was there. He said, "Colonel Sink came up and asked, 'What's the hold up?' At the same time a couple guys were helping Allen Westphal after he was wounded. Captain 'Mac' (Joe MacMillan) kept yelling at us to get across the canal."

Three troopers were within a hundred yards of the bridge when it was blown up by the enemy.

Sergeant Hugh Pritchard added to his account: "We were about 200 feet from the bridge when the Germans blew it. We jumped back under the cover of buildings while huge chunks of wood and other debris rained down all around us. I had no idea I was that close to the bridge, and I am sure that if Westphal had not been shot, creating a temporary delay, we (he, I, and others) would have been on that bridge when it went up."

Sergeant Jack MacLean continued his story: "I gave Lindsey some cover fire and headed for the bridge. Then it blew right in my face. I was dazed. I turned and headed for the embankment and saw Westphal facing south and placing fire across the canal. As I fired at enemy running out of a building I turned and saw troopers coming along the bank. They were not from 2nd Battalion so I headed back to my own people. I found Lindsey had been wounded and a medic had fixed his arm. Ray Taylor and Jeff Rice of 'D' Company were occupying the building just northwest of the canal."

One of the troopers moving toward the bridge along the canal bank from the west was Sergeant Philip Carney, who served as radio operator for 1st Battalion commander, LTC James LaPrade and was close on the heels of his commander as they approached the bridge. Within fifty yards of the bridge, the Germans who had demolitions in place, blew up the bridge. Sergeant Carney wrote: "We were so close that I got splinters in my face from the flying debris when we reached the bridge under fire from the other side."

Elements of 1st Battalion and the three rifle companies of 2nd Battalion had fought their way to within a hundred yards of the bridge. Colonel Sink was near by as was General Taylor, who had accompanied the troops of 1st Battalion. The first men from 1st Battalion had appeared just prior to the bridge being blown.

Moments after the explosion, LTC Jim LaPrade, along with Lieutenant Milford F. Weller and Sergeant Donald Dunning came running up near the destroyed span, followed by Sergeant Philip Carney and his assistant, Corporal Ogden Stutler. Carney added to his story: "Colonel LaPrade yelled at me, 'Sergeant, get those radios across to the other side.' LaPrade jumped into the canal and swam across to the other side. I looked around and found a piece of debris—a wooden plank. I placed the two radios on the plank, peeled off my combat jacket, my steel helmet and my M-1 rifle. I balanced them on the plank. I had Ogden Stutler with me and I told him to strip off some of his equipment so he could swim easier. Pushing off into the water with one hand holding on to the radios and the other hand holding on to the rest of my gear, kicking my feet for locomotion I started across the canal. Stutler had neglected to strip off some of his gear and as a result, halfway across the canal he yelled to me, 'I'm sinking, I'm sinking!'

"At that moment I had to decide what to save—him? the radios? or my equipment? I grabbed Corporal Stutler by the back of his combat jacket with one hand and with the other held on to the two radios, and watched my steel helmet, combat jacket, and my M-1 rifle sink out of sight. Still kicking my feet, I was able to get them all across to the south side of the canal and Colonel LaPrade was able to use the radios."

Lieutenant Milford Weller and Sergeant Donald Dunning followed Colonel Jim LaPrade in swimming across the canal. Other 1st Battalion men obtained a small rowboat and several squads were ferried to the south bank. Together with the group that swam across, they dispersed the enemy firing from the nearby houses.

To provide for "blown bridge" situations the 3rd Platoon of "C" Company of the 326th Engineer Battalion had jumped with the regiment. Though they didn't locate the bundles they had dropped from the planes, all three sticks had come down in a closely bunched group. With platoon leader, First Lieutenant Harold E. Young, they followed the 2nd Battalion toward Son and the bridge. Lieutenant Young wrote: "Within 20 minutes or so I heard an explosion up ahead. Instinctively, I knew that the bridge across the 80-foot wide Wilhelmina Canal had been blown. Within three minutes word was passed back down the line 'Engineers up front!' From two years of training and the Normandy experience my platoon was well trained. We jogged along and went directly to the bridge which had been blown by the retreating German soldiers with a previously planted explosive.

"There was a circular concrete pier with about 20 feet of open water on each side. The infantry was jumping in and swimming from the north bank to the pier and from the pier to the south bank. We had no engineering equipment and we had to get a footbridge across to move the entire 506th Regiment across. We had trained for many kinds of improvisations but not this. The bridge was adjacent to the village of Son. I sent men to find hammers, nails, boards, planks, etc. Somebody located two boats which we placed midway from the shore to the pier. Then we made a rickety bridge that worked provided my men helped steady the infantry as they moved across. Before midnight the entire regiment had crossed. Some of my men located bigger and better planks and, in the middle of the night, replaced the rickety bridge with a fairly substantial one."

As the crossing of the make-shift bridge by over two thousand troops went on for several hours, men had to hunt down the remaining snipers in the area. PFC John Garrigan added to his story. "We set up positions on the bank of the canal until the bridge was passable and then we went on again. The enemy was still running. Finally it was time to hold up for the night."

Private Robert Wiatt remembered: "We were under some fire at the time. We moved between some houses south of the canal with very little trouble and halted for the night in a ditch south of Son."

After the troops had crossed over the makeshift bridge, the men were posted toward Eindhoven on either side of the road. T/5 Charles McCallister had this recollection: "That night I drew the first shift at guard and when my turn was up, I believe a light rain was falling. I elected to sleep in a chicken coop, rather than the slit trench I had dug. By that time, nothing could have disturbed my sleep and the next morning I found myself covered with chicken mites, which gave me a lot of discomfort as I remember very well."

Earlier timetables had called for the 506th to take Eindhoven by 2000 hours on the 17th. A civilian report stated that a German regiment had just moved into town. General Taylor, in his conferences with British generals, had pointed out that it might not be possible to secure all the objectives on D-Day and suggested that Eindhoven might not be taken the first day. While talking with Colonel Sink at the bridge site, Taylor agreed that an overnight wait was advisable.

The "A" Company log provides the situation of the unit once the bridge objective was reached.

About 1900 hours, First Lieutenant Bill Muir, who had assumed command, moved the company, less the 1st Platoon, to a bivouac area about a mile south of Son. Patrols were sent out from this point east and west of Son.

The 1st Platoon with Second Lieutenant James Diel commanding, was left on the south bank of the Wilhelmina Canal to defend the bridge from again falling into enemy hands and to prevent its further destruction. The night was uneventful.

According to PFC James H. Martin of "G" Company, his platoon was also detailed to remain on the north side of the canal. Their first night job was to guard Division Headquarters.

When the 506th Regiment launched its attack toward Eindhoven, the engineers had already begun work on an idea presented to platoon leader Harold E. Young. He wrote: "Early the next morning, a number of my men suggested that we build a raft to move jeeps back and forth. I was undecided. I went to see our battalion C.O. (LTC Hugh Moseley). When I got to General Taylor's headquarters, I heard him telling Moseley most emphatically that he wanted jeeps across that canal by noon. When Moseley came out I told him what the men had suggested. 'Go ahead and do it!' he said. I dogtrotted back to the canal. My enterprising men were already locating metal barrels to which they only had to make wooden bungs. How many barrels to hold a jeep? Somehow we decided on 16. These were assembled and held together in a wooden box with a flat top of boards to hold a jeep. We had some rope and tied it to each end to move the raft back and forth. The raft would hold one jeep and one man had to be on the raft to keep it from tilting too much. It worked and we took many men alone or jeeps across. The infantry had commandeered a panel body truck and they brought wounded to the south bank where they were put on the raft and taken to the north side. I sent my men looking for materials and in the afternoon they built a bigger and more substantial raft so we had two of them moving continuously.

"In a parachute outfit the men were always teasing the officers. Sergeant Andrew Shlapak, the platoon sergeant, was on the south side. Just about the same time a truck load of wounded pulled up and General Taylor came up. Both wanted to move to the other side. Sergeant Shlapak yelled out, 'Shall

I take the wounded or the General first?' Taylor was busy reading some reports. I yelled back, 'Take the wounded first!' and Taylor simply stepped back, not giving any thought to what was going on.

"It was a hot, sunny day and pulling the raft back and forth was tiring. We moved civilians across when the raft was free. Shortly before noon a gray-haired farmer came to the south side with two handsome work horses. He spoke Flemish and we couldn't understand him. We decided he wanted his horses on the north side so we took them over. But he didn't go away. He kept talking to us. Finally we took him and his horses back to the south side. In the middle of the night it occurred to me, finally, that he wanted us to use one horse on each side to pull the rope to relieve the tired men who were pulling.

"One of the glider engineer platoons came to relieve us the next morning. We demonstrated how to use both rafts with particular attention to the first one which was so rickety but had never failed us. As we left, we watched them put a jeep on the first raft and move it across to the south side. Just as it got to the south side, the jeep went overboard."